Media Divides

Media Divides

Communication Rights and the Right to Communicate in Canada

...... Marc Raboy and Jeremy Shtern

with William J. McIver, Laura J. Murray,
Seán Ó Siochrú, and Leslie Regan Shade

UBCPress · Vancouver · Toronto

20 19 18 17 16 15 14 13 12 11 10   5 4 3 2 1

Printed in Canada on acid-free paper

Library and Archives Canada Cataloguing in Publication

Raboy, Marc, 1948-
    Media divides : communication rights and the right to communicate in Canada / Marc Raboy and Jeremy Shtern ; with William J. McIver ... [et al.].

Includes bibliographical references and index.
ISBN 978-0-7748-1774-5 (bound); ISBN 978-0-7748-1775-2 (pbk.)

    1. Communication policy – Canada. 2. Mass media policy – Canada.
3. Telecommunication policy – Canada. 4. Freedom of expression – Canada.
5. Privacy, Right of – Canada. 6. Copyright – Canada. 7. Mass media – Law and legislation – Canada. 8. Civil rights – Canada. I. Shtern, Jeremy, 1976-
II. McIver, William J., 1963- III. Title.

| P95.82.C3R32 2010 | 302.230971 | C2009-907044-8 |

e-book: 978-0-7748-1776-9 (pdf); 978-0-7748-5930-1 (epub)

Canadä

UBC Press gratefully acknowledges the financial support for our publishing program of the Government of Canada (through the Canada Book Fund), the Canada Council for the Arts, and the British Columbia Arts Council.

This book has been published with the help of a grant from the Canadian Federation for the Humanities and Social Sciences, through the Aid to Scholarly Publications Programme, using funds provided by the Social Sciences and Humanities Research Council of Canada.

Printed and bound in Canada by Friesens
Set in Giovanni and Scala Sans by Artegraphica Design Co. Ltd.
Copy editor: Francis Chow
Proofreader: Stacy Belden
Indexer: Heather Ebbs

UBC Press
The University of British Columbia
2029 West Mall
Vancouver, BC V6T 1Z2
www.ubcpress.ca

Contents

List of Illustrations / vii

Preface / ix

Acknowledgments / xi

Abbreviations / xiii

**Part 1: Communication Rights and the Right to Communicate –
The State of the Art**

Introduction / 3
MARC RABOY AND JEREMY SHTERN

1 Histories, Contexts, and Controversies / 26
MARC RABOY AND JEREMY SHTERN

2 Implementing Communication Rights / 41
SEÁN Ó SIOCHRÚ

Part 2: Communication Rights in Canada – An Assessment

3 The Horizontal View / 63
MARC RABOY AND JEREMY SHTERN

4 Media / 91
MARC RABOY

5 Access / 120
LESLIE REGAN SHADE

6 Internet / 145
WILLIAM J. MCIVER JR.

7 Privacy / 175
LESLIE REGAN SHADE

8 Copyright / 196
LAURA J. MURRAY

Part 3: Policy Recommendations and Alternative Frameworks

9 Fixing Communication Rights in Canada / 219
MARC RABOY AND JEREMY SHTERN

10 Toward a Canadian Right to Communicate / 249
MARC RABOY AND JEREMY SHTERN

APPENDIX 1: Relationships in Transition CFP 2005 –
Communication Rights and the Right to Communicate / 267
THE LAW COMMISSION OF CANADA AND THE SOCIAL SCIENCES AND HUMANITIES
RESEARCH COUNCIL OF CANADA

APPENDIX 2: The Communication Rights Assessment Framework and
Toolkit (CRAFT) / 270
COMMUNICATION RIGHTS IN THE INFORMATION SOCIETY (CRIS) CAMPAIGN

APPENDIX 3: Strategic *Charter* Litigation and the Right to
Communicate in Canada / 285
SIMON GRANT

Notes / 294

Works Cited / 329

About the Authors / 369

Index / 371

... Illustrations

Figures

1 The social cycle of communication / 13

2 The Access Rainbow model / 138

3 Sending packets over interconnected networks / 150

4 Potentials for non-neutral network behaviour / 160

5 Categories of VoIP service / 169

Table

1 Access Rainbow summary / 139

... Preface

In November 2005, the Social Sciences and Humanities Research Council of Canada (SSHRC) and the Law Commission of Canada (LCC) launched a timely call for proposals on the theme of "Communication Rights and the Right to Communicate."[1]

We received a grant from the LCC and SSHRC to conduct research and analysis around this question and to draft a report for the LCC based on our findings. For scholars with an interest in doing critical research that contains the potential to affect real-world structures and experiences, this was in many respects an ideal partnership. As a team of academic specialists on various elements of Canadian communication policy, our role would be to provide an empirical assessment of the state of communication rights in Canada. The LCC, meanwhile, as an arm's-length government agency, could draw on its mandate to advise the minister of justice. Under the *Law Commission of Canada Act*, the minister of justice is, in turn, required to respond officially on behalf of the government in a timely fashion to any report received from the LCC.[2] This meant that our research into and analysis of the state of communication rights and the right to communicate in Canada could be undertaken with the ultimate view of taking action to improve it and a not entirely naïve expectation that they just might do so.

Shortly after, however, the LCC's funding was withdrawn as part of a $2 billion reduction in government spending by the recently elected Harper government's effort to "ensure all programs are effective and efficient, are focused on results ... and aligned with the government's priorities."[3] Although this did not affect our grant and only increased our resolve to meaningfully investigate these issues, the LCC was forced to immediately cease and desist. This meant that we were pushed to reconsider not only where and in what format we would seek to disseminate this research but also whether our work could still hope to contribute to the improvement of policy and practice around communication rights and the right to communicate in Canada.

We had always intended to work closely with the LCC to explore what our assessment and analysis of the state of communication rights and the right to communicate in Canada implied, and the LCC's evisceration meant that we now needed, in designing, conducting, and presenting our research, to focus more explicitly on how action could be taken to improve the state of communication rights and the right to communicate in Canada. Absent the partnership of the LCC, we had to assume the dual role of critical researchers and promoters of reform to the best of our abilities or face the unsatisfactory compromise that we had "done our part" in merely presenting our research. Our strength in this area lies not in any direct links to the government but in whatever weight might be attached to our credentials as academic specialists.

Research matters in policy making, and where and how it is published matters for the impact of such research. Our view is that we can gain the most influence for our argument by presenting it in a peer-reviewed academic publication such as this volume. In turn, we hope that this volume might give valuable leverage to others who may have more sway in the policy process than we do, who will be encouraged and enabled to run with the ball there.

Taking action to improve the realization of communication rights and the right to communicate in Canada does not involve only governments. In some respects, it already involves governments too much (often, as we will discuss, government is not only part of the solution but also part of the problem). More importantly, it involves people. It involves citizens and it involves expressions of citizenship. The problem is that it involves them all too infrequently. Of course, there are problems in the institutional framework in which communication occurs in Canada and in the actions that government takes. There are possible reforms that should be pursued in the effort to remedy these issues. At the same time, however, there is, as we point out in this book, a great distance between institutions and people in Canada where communication is concerned. Furthermore, people do not generally understand their communication rights and very rarely push hard enough to claim them. Activists, community groups, and nongovernmental and civil society organizations in Canada lack literacy and coordination with regard to media and communication issues and the capacity to present claims that can compete with those of government and industrial stakeholders. We hope this book will speak to these audiences.

Acknowledgments

This research was made possible by a grant from the Relationships in Transition program jointly administered by the Law Commission of Canada and the Social Sciences and Humanities Research Council of Canada. Additional funding was provided by a strategic research grant from the Beaverbrook Fund for Media@McGill. The publication of this research in book form was supported by the Aid to Scholarly Publications Programme (ASPP) and benefited immensely from the commitment and engagement of senior editors Emily Andrew and Randy Schmidt of UBC Press. Ann Macklem expertly, and gently, guided us through the editorial production process.

Our team first met to discuss and plan this project at Media@McGill in June 2006. We would like to thank Susana Vargas Cervantes for helping with the organization of those sessions. We were fortunate to be able to include Montreal-based communication activist Alain Ambrosi in those discussions, and would like to acknowledge his influence on this research and thank him for his participation and his unique insight into the topic. Matt Dupuis from the department of Art History and Communication Studies at McGill provided technical support for our online collaborative tools. Media@McGill Outreach Specialist Claire Roberge assisted indirectly in countless ways throughout the period during which we were writing this book.

A small army of research assistants contributed in various ways to our research. We acknowledge each of their contributions in the relevant sections, but thank Geneviève Bonin, Normand Landry, Evan Light, Aysha Mawani, Mary Milliken, Jennifer Parisi, Kirsty Robertson, and Gregory Taylor here as well.

We thank McGill University law professor Tina Piper for her insightful and constructive critical reading of an early draft of parts of this book that were presented at the McGill Arts/Law Colloquium series in January 2008. The questions and comments raised in response by scholars from both faculties participating in the colloquium were also helpful. Professor Piper later graciously agreed to read and comment on a more substantive draft of this book, for which we express a further debt of gratitude.

Participants in Marc Raboy's 2008 graduate seminar on Global Media Governance struggled with us over the question of what a Canadian right to communicate might look like and how to get there. Simon Grant, a McGill law student at the time and now a practising lawyer in Toronto, allowed us to include an adapted version of a paper written for that seminar as an appendix to this book.

Fortunately, given that the rough cut of the bibliography was around 100 pages long, one of us happens to be related to a librarian; Laura Shtern graciously helped us track down and organize our references.

We also thank the anonymous reviewers who evaluated the manuscript for UBC Press. Each of these critical readings helped us not only to address the weaknesses of the initial version of this manuscript but also to better understand and appreciate its strengths.

Abbreviations

ACLU	American Civil Liberties Union
ACTRA	Alliance of Canadian Cinema, Television and Radio Artists
AMARC	World Association of Community Radio Broadcasters
APC	Association for Progressive Communication
APTN	Aboriginal Peoples Television Network
ARC	Alliance canadienne des radiodiffuseurs communautaires du Canada
ARCQ	Association des radiodiffuseurs communautaires du Québec
ARPANET	Advanced Research Projects Agency Network
BBC	British Broadcasting Corporation
BDU	broadcast distribution undertaking
CAIP	Canadian Association of Internet Providers
CAIRS	Co-ordination of Access to Information Requests System
CAP	Community Access Program
CARFAC	Canadian Artists' Representation/Le Front des artistes canadiens
CAW	Canadian Auto Workers Union
CBC	Canadian Broadcasting Corporation
CBNC	Crossing Boundaries National Council
CBSC	Canadian Broadcast Standards Council
CCPA	Canadian Centre for Policy Alternatives
CCTV	closed circuit television
CDM	Campaign for Democratic Media
CIGF	Canadian Internet Governance Forum
CIPPIC	Canadian Internet Policy and Public Interest Clinic
CIUS	Canadian Internet Usage Survey
CMCC	Canadian Music Creators Coalition
COPPA	*Children's Online Privacy Protection Act* (US)
CR	communication rights

CRACIN	Canadian Research Alliance for Community Innovation and Networking
CRAFT	Communication Rights Assessment Framework and Toolkit
CRFC	Community Radio Fund of Canada
CRIS	Communication Rights in the Information Society
CRTC	Canadian Radio-television and Telecommunications Commission
CSIS	Canadian Security Intelligence Service
CTF	Canadian Television Fund
CTV	Canadian Television Network
DFAIT	Department of Foreign Affairs and International Trade
DMCA	*Digital Millennium Copyright Act* (US)
DNS	Domain Name System
DoC	Department of Communication
DOC	Documentary Organization of Canada
e2e	end-to-end
ECOSOC	Economic and Social Council (UN)
EPIC	Electronic Privacy Information Center
EU	European Union
FCC	Federal Communications Commission (US)
FGHRs	first-generation human rights
FINTRAC	Financial Transactions and Reports Analysis Centre of Canada
FISC	Foreign Intelligence Surveillance Court (US)
FLQ	Front de Libération du Québec
FOI	Freedom of Information
GAC	Governmental Advisory Committee (of ICANN)
GATS	*General Agreement on Trade in Services* (WTO)
HTTP	Hypertext Transfer Protocol
IBI	International Broadcast Institute (later IIC)
ICAMS	International Campaign Against Mass Surveillance
ICANN	Internet Corporation for Assigned Names and Numbers
ICCPR	*International Covenant on Civil and Political Rights* (UN)
ICESCR	*International Covenant on Economic, Social and Cultural Rights* (UN)
ICT	information and communication technology
IDRC	International Development Research Centre
IGF	Internet Governance Forum
IHAC	Information Highway Advisory Council
IIC	International Institute for Communications (previously IBI)
IMC	Independent Media Center

INS	Immigration and Naturalization Service (US)
IP	Internet Protocol
ISP	Internet service provider
IT4D	information technology for development
ITU	International Telecommunication Union
K-Net	Kuhkenah Network
KO	Keewaytinook Okimakanak
LCC	Law Commission of Canada
LEAF	Women's Legal Education and Action Fund
NAM	Non-Aligned Movement
NATO	North Atlantic Treaty Organization
NCRA	National Campus and Community Radio Association
NFB	National Film Board
NGO	nongovernmental organization
NIEO	New International Economic Order
NSA	National Security Agency (US)
NWICO	New World Information and Communication Order
OECD	Organisation for Economic Co-operation and Development
OIPCBC	Office of the Information and Privacy Commissioner of British Columbia
OPC	Office of the Privacy Commissioner of Canada
OTA	over-the-air
P2P	peer-to-peer
PANS	public access network services
PIPEDA	*Personal Information Protection and Electronic Documents Act*
POTS	plain old telephone service
PSTN	public switched telephone network
QoS	quality of service
R2C	right to communicate
RCMP	Royal Canadian Mounted Police
RDS	Réseau des Sports
RFID	radio frequency identification
RIA	rich Internet application
SCA	Speech Communication Association
SGHRs	second-generation human rights
SNS	social networking site
SOCAN	Society of Composers, Authors and Music Publishers of Canada
SSHRC	Social Sciences and Humanities Research Council of Canada

TCP/IP	Transmission Control Protocol/Internet Protocol
TPRP	Telecommunications Policy Review Panel
TSN	The Sports Network
UDHR	*Universal Declaration of Human Rights* (UN)
UNESCO	United Nations Educational, Scientific and Cultural Organization
UNGA	United Nations General Assembly
VoIP	Voice over Internet Protocol
W3C	World Wide Web Consortium
WACC	World Association for Christian Communication
WIPO	World Intellectual Property Organization
WSF	World Social Forum
WSIS	World Summit on the Information Society
WTO	World Trade Organization
XML	Extensible Markup Language

PART 1

Communication Rights and the Right to Communicate – The State of the Art

Introduction

Marc Raboy and Jeremy Shtern

Origins of an Idea

There is compelling tangential evidence about how deeply the critical threads of communication rights discourse run in Canadian thinking in, of all things, a 1949 book review of a volume devoted to chronicling the Canadian activities at the United Nations from the previous year. The book in question (Canada 1949, 109) describes a Canadian intervention in the freedom of information debates held at the UN Human Rights Commission in 1948 as follows: "The Canadian delegation held that free access to sources of information and freedom of expression are indispensable to the democratic process. Without a precise knowledge of the facts, the chief Canadian delegate argued, the people could not intelligently exercise their powers of discretion and control over their governments." On which the book review's author remarked: "This blithe statement ignores the growth of massive communication enterprises which have been known to wrap themselves righteously in the mantle of freedom of information in the very act of omitting or distorting information essential to a democratic population. The difficult question of ways and means to secure a responsible, as well as free press is overlooked" (Shea 1949, 439-40).[1]

The same essential point can still be made today to advocate for communication rights; it has, in fact, been reiterated and developed at points in between in reports and articles from activists and scholars, civil servants, and government departments.

Canada made an important contribution to the emerging global debate on communication rights and the right to communicate (CR/R2C)[2] in the 1970s, with the report of an official government-sponsored study group known as the Telecommission.

The Telecommission was launched in September 1969 as a comprehensive study mandated by the newly created federal Department of Communication

(DoC) to examine "the present state and future prospects of telecommunications in Canada" (Canada 1971, vii). Its stated purpose was "to gather as much information as possible, together with the widest cross-section of opinion," and produce a report of interest to governments, the telecommunications industry, private and public institutions, and the "public as a whole." More than forty different studies were organized under the coordination of a high-level directing committee,[3] and, in total, more than 8,000 pages of background material were produced. These extensive activities were the basis for the 1971 report *Instant World: A Report on Telecommunications in Canada.*

Instant World concluded that the establishment of a Canadian right to communicate was required in order to confront the social implications of the ever-increasing centrality of technologically mediated communication to Canadian society. The report justified its call for a right to communicate as an evidence-based conclusion that emerged bottom-up after "time and again, participants in the Telecommission studies called for recognition of a 'right to communicate' as a fundamental objective of Canadian society. The subject dominated the seminars and conferences, and was raised in many of the individual studies" (Canada 1971, 232). The report stated in no uncertain terms:

> The predominant theme underlying nearly all the discussions at the seminars was that the "right to communicate" should be regarded as a basic human right. In the impending age of total communications, the right to freedom of assembly and free speech may no longer suffice. Many people are unable to communicate; they do not receive the messages distributed by communications systems, they lack the know-how to use them, and above all, they are deprived of the opportunity to send messages through them. The basic decisions that govern the development of communication systems are political; therefore, if all Canadians are to be provided with the minimum services needed for the exercise of a right to communicate, political decisions and money will be required. (38)

The *Instant World* notion of the right to communicate stemmed from the belief that equitable communication is fundamental to democracy (especially 232), and the report made the case that "if it be accepted that there is a right to communicate, all Canadians are entitled to it" (229).

Published only two years after a seminal paper by a senior French cultural mandarin, Jean D'Arcy (1969), had first introduced the notion of the right to communicate to the international community (see Chapter 1),[4] *Instant World* is possibly the most substantial official document framing the concept of communication rights in Canada. Moreover, it played an influential and catalytic role in the development of the international R2C movement, not only providing the first real elaboration of what could be meant by the right to communicate but also setting a key precedent that policy makers and governments could and would take the notion and its legal and policy implications very seriously. It may not be a stretch to argue that the *Instant World* discussion of the right to communicate was a crucial step in the evolution of the idea from abstract concept to global policy issue and basis for an activist movement. In any case, evidence of the contention that *Instant World* is in fact "one of the most comprehensive and original sets of materials in the development of the right to communicate" (Richstad et al. 1977, 114-15) can be found by examining the bibliographies of most treatments of the issue.[5]

In addition to its historical significance, *Instant World* accurately anticipated how mass communication would change and evolve in the subsequent decades. Its predictions of how future technical and social developments would facilitate what it called an "impending age of total communications" have proven to be remarkably accurate. For example, *Instant World* foresaw the impact of what we refer to today as "technological convergence": "The conjoint technology of communications and computers," it said, "promises the development, probably before the end of the 20th century, of information systems that may to some extent replace paper and its storage" (Canada 1971, 230).

This prediction was based on the assumptions – since proven correct – that telecommunication networks would be increasingly used to provide remote access to computer memory, that computer processing speeds and memory capacities would increase rapidly over the coming years, and that small, low-cost freestanding computers (along the lines of what we now know as the PC) as well as smaller-sized multifunction high-speed devices (such as the iPod) would be cheaply fabricated and marketed to the general public, with the sum effect that "much heavier demands for *mobile communications*" (Canada 1971, 118, emphasis added) could be anticipated in the future. *Instant World* also predicted that this variety of compact, light, autonomous, mobile, and relatively cheap apparatuses would make radio and television content ubiquitous.

In addition, the report anticipated many of the phenomena characteristic of today's "new media":

- *Broadband services* were seen as a necessary response to the need to interconnect and to populate the range of new communication devices with content (118).
- *On-demand programming*, parallel with and as an alternative to scheduled services in broadcasting, was seen as the most logical application of broadband to broadcasting distribution systems (118).
- Regarding *electronic service delivery* (and what we now know as *e-mail*), *Instant World* argued that information systems "will partly replace or transform methods of administration, book-keeping and clerical services, postal operations, publishing, banking, transportation, modes of entertainment, and the means for their enjoyment" (230).

Instant World also foresaw the importance of the then nascent use of earth-orbiting *communication satellites* and, under the label of the "wired city" (230), the emergence of urban interconnection movements along the lines of the *municipal Wi-Fi public Internet connectivity projects* that have developed in Canadian cities such as Montreal, Toronto, and Fredericton in the early twenty-first century (see, for example, Powell and Shade 2006).

It was argued in *Instant World* that, if such a communication environment were to emerge, there could "be no doubt that unremitting effort and attention will be needed to eliminate or at least control the possible anti-social by-products of the technological revolution, while at the same time striving to put new opportunities to the best use. What is needed is a sustained effort to foresee the social and economic effects of the new technology, and to plan accordingly as far in advance as possible" (Canada 1971, 125).

Despite the international influence of the report, extensive and forceful evidentiary support for its conclusions, and the expressed enthusiasm for the idea of a Canadian right to communicate by high-level Ottawa insiders, the concept was virtually abandoned by the government of Canada. Certain programs that emerged around the same time – such as the Challenge for Change initiative of the National Film Board (NFB) and the community cable access requirement of the Canadian Radio-television and Telecommunications Commission (CRTC) – arguably gave some substance to the R2C in Canada in practice.[6] But, the term "right to communicate" itself fails to appear in any subsequent policy papers or reports and did not directly form the basis of any legislative action (McPhail and McPhail 1990; Birdsall et al. 2002; Hicks 2007).

Furthermore – and significantly – *Instant World* did not deal substantially with a range of what we now consider to be "conventional" media issues: corporate concentration of ownership, public funding, cultural diversity, and intellectual property rights. We now realize that the communication environment, especially technologically mediated communication, needs to be viewed holistically, as difficult as this often appears to be for policy makers.[7] And so, one of the greatest challenges of this book is to try to develop a conceptual understanding of CR and R2C that takes account of the various subfields in which communication rights play out and to see the idea of a right to communicate as encompassing all of them.

Despite falling back from the forefront of the domestic public policy agenda, Canadian interest in the right to communicate has not waned. As the "age of total communications" forecast by *Instant World* in 1971 has gradually shifted from "impending" to "emerging," the idea of a Canadian right to communicate has been sporadically revisited by activists and scholars working in a variety of disciplines, and individual Canadians have been particularly active in international debates on CR and R2C.[8] Official Canada, meanwhile, has been a generous contributor to international public discourse on a range of important CR issues, from freedom of expression to cultural diversity and information technology for development (IT4D).[9]

The experience of John Humphrey, considered by many to be Canada's most distinguished human rights activist, illustrates a great deal about how human rights, public policy, and government rhetoric tend to be linked in Canada. In the process, it underlines why we have designed this study so as to problematize these linkages.

Human Rights, Cultural Policy, and the Insufficient Rhetoric of "Brand Canada"

Researching her 2001 book, *A World Made New: Eleanor Roosevelt and the Universal Declaration of Human Rights,* Harvard law professor Mary Ann Glendon (2000, 250) was so taken by what she uncovered about the role of Canadian John P. Humphrey that she published a sidebar paper "to pay tribute to this 'forgotten framer' [who] helped to set conditions for a better future on our increasingly conflict-ridden, yet interdependent planet."

In his capacity as director of the fledgling United Nations Human Rights Division, Humphrey himself wrote the first draft of the *Universal Declaration of Human Rights (UDHR)* in 1947. In a letter to his sister, written three days into this task, Humphrey said, "I am now playing the role of Jefferson."[10] Glendon (2000, 250) summarizes Humphrey's seminal contribution to the making of the *UDHR* as "buttressing its aspiration toward universality by drawing on sources from many different legal cultures" and points out that "both during the drafting process and after the adoption of the Declaration, Humphrey and his staff provided essential continuity, backup, and staying power for the often-embattled U.N. Human Rights Commission." While Humphrey's name may be little known abroad, this is hardly the case in Canada.

Humphrey's role in the drafting of the *UDHR* is celebrated domestically, particularly by the government of Canada itself. For instance, under the heading of "Canada's International Human Rights Policy," visitors to the Department of Foreign Affairs and International Trade (DFAIT) website are informed that "Canada has been a consistently strong voice for the protection of human rights and the advancement of democratic values, from our central role in the drafting of the Universal Declaration of Human Rights in 1947-8 to our work at the United Nations today" (Canada n.d.).

If by "our role," the government of Canada is using the royal "our" in the sense of "any and all Canadians, including John Humphrey," then this can be considered an accurate statement. If by "our role," however, this statement refers to the role of the government of Canada – the same government of Canada that was, on 7 December 1948, one of only seven countries (Canada and the six-member Soviet Bloc) to abstain from the vote taken by a UN committee on whether the *UDHR* should be submitted for approval to the full UN General Assembly (UNGA) – then it is hard to argue that "central" has a positive connotation in describing "our role" here.[11]

According to Hobbins (2002), the relationship between Humphrey and the government of Canada actually deteriorated in the aftermath of the *UDHR* episode. For the remainder of his career, Humphrey would go on to occupy a variety of high-level posts concerned with the study and realization of human rights both internationally and domestically. In these roles, he was a frequent and vocal critic of the government of Canada's human rights record for nearly fifty years. The net effect was that "policy makers probably grew very tired of this criticism and ultimately found it simplest to ignore him" (1). The Jefferson of the *UDHR*, indeed.[12]

The process through which the government of Canada appropriated the legacy of John Humphrey, to the point where his role in the *UDHR* drafting process can be claimed by DFAIT as part of a collective accomplishment despite Canada's ambivalence over the course of that episode, illustrates a great deal about the relationship between rights discourse, government policy, and on-the-ground practice that we seek to problematize in this study. It is joined in this respect by numerous other examples.

In the midst of Louise Arbour's term as UN High Commissioner for Human Rights, the government of Canada's lack of concrete action in the area of human rights led Amnesty International to release a report entitled *Canada and the International Protection of Human Rights: An Erosion of Leadership?* (Amnesty International 2007). An admonition of the Canadian government from Arbour herself is cited in that report, yet, as was the case with Humphrey, Arbour's accomplishments circulate through Canada's foreign policy documents and the rhetoric that surrounds them is used to promote the notion that, by promoting "Canadian values," the government is intrinsically supporting human rights.

All of this can be attributed to an effort to associate human rights with "Brand Canada." Efforts to construct and promote a narrative in which something called "Canadian values" are intrinsically wedded to the realization of human rights and social justice concerns are generally associated with the Chrétien Liberal government of the 1990s.[13] Perhaps the strongest example of this was the inclusion of something called "Canadian Values and Culture" as one of the three pillars of Canada's foreign policy between 1995 and 2005. These Canadian values were said to include not only respect for human rights but also the importance of cultural affairs, including Canadian communication and cultural industries (see Canada 1995, section V; Canada 2003a). Canada puts a great deal of stock in its image as a champion of human rights, and there is no shortage of positive accounts surrounding the claim that no other country protects what we call communication rights to the extent that Canada does.

The challenge of this study is to hold Canada accountable to its own high standard by examining the links between rhetoric and action and to determine how the actions of our government reflect on the claims that it makes about its role in realizing communication rights. In assessing the realization of communication rights in Canada, however, we have tried to be sensitive not only to gross abuses of government power but also to the more subtle nuances around how public policies, the manner in which they are implemented, and the actions of various stakeholders affect the realization of communication rights. We also aim to situate the Canadian debate in a broader, global context.

Bringing an International Debate (Back) Home

Discussion of the links between rights and processes of communication burst onto the international scene at the highest level with the 2003-05 World Summit on the Information Society (WSIS) (Raboy and Landry 2005; Mueller, Kuerbis, and Pagé 2007). At the same time, media, communication, and human rights activists from around the world placed this concern on various national, regional, and global agendas through sustained lobbying efforts in arenas such as the WSIS and venues such as the World Social Forum (WSF). These activities crystallized in an international advocacy campaign for Communication Rights in the Information Society (CRIS), which in the early to mid-2000s became an increasingly important player in the burgeoning international social justice movement (Padovani 2005; Padovani and Nordenstreng 2005; see also Chapters 1 and 2 of this volume).

In parallel, the role of media and communication in the realization of human rights came under attack in Canada in a stunningly wide range of guises, from the Juliet O'Neill and Maher Arar cases to the reduction of public broadcasting services, the proposed deregulatory revisions to national telecommunication policy, and the controversies surrounding Internet network neutrality. Communication rights are also at stake in ongoing debates on radio spectrum ownership, the impact of media mergers on diversity, and the possible liberalization of foreign ownership regulations in broadcasting and telecommunication, among many other examples.[14]

As we have seen, Canada talks a good game around the right to communicate and is generally pointed to as an influential leader on the topic internationally, and individual Canadians are at the forefront of thinking and activism concerning this issue. Paradoxically, however, and despite Canada's record in international diplomacy, human rights, and innovative practices in the fields of media and information and communication technologies, substantive policy development regarding the right to communicate in Canada has been relatively weak. Thus, the initiative that led to this book not only was timely but also stepped into a relative vacuum.

The premise for the call by the Social Sciences and Humanities Research Council of Canada and the Law Commission of Canada was that "it is no longer clear that a legal framework based primarily on freedom of expression is adequate to the diverse purposes we might imagine for law in supporting democratic communication under contemporary conditions," and that, in response, we need to ask "what other principles and legal instruments might be necessary to supplement this right, and to make it real in the complex political, economic and social context of contemporary Canada." The call defined communication rights as "a broad range of other principles relevant to democratic communication" that buttress the universal human right to freedom of expression, and it described the right to communicate as "an umbrella-like" notion that "could encompass a range of principles that are not reducible to either freedom of expression or the related communication rights."

This book represents a preliminary effort to examine from various policy directions and disciplinary fields how this problematic plays out specifically in Canada. In an effort to avoid the fixation on the United States found in much Canadian communication policy analysis, we set Canadian communication rights debates mainly in the context of Canadian history, international organizations, and the emerging global media and communication policy environment. It is our view that a narrow and exclusive focus on "national" concerns is sometimes used to avoid the political and policy choices and responsibilities that Canadians and the Canadian government have to make in the area of communication governance.[15] We also think that it is useful to avoid preoccupation with the strong traditions that frame speech debates in the United States when reflecting on freedom of expression in Canada. Giving consideration to the US First Amendment notion of free speech – a degree of nominally absolute protection from government interference that is unique to the United States – is of little immediate relevance to the situation in Canada and inevitably leads to intractable debate with free speech fundamentalists that prevents consideration of other important communication rights issues. This book thus examines the system of policy and practice that interconnects a wide array of largely distinct communication policy issues and investigates whether Canada's legal framework for governing communication is adequate to the diverse purposes that we might imagine for law in supporting democratic communication. In turn, we consider what supplementary principles and legal instruments might be necessary to strengthen the links between human rights and processes of communication in the complex political, economic, and social context of contemporary Canada.

Canada is a signatory to numerous international agreements that are generally considered to constitute a universal human rights framework with respect to communication (see Chapter 1). Thus, universal communication rights are intrinsically also Canadian communication rights, and communication rights can be said to apply to Canadians insofar as they can be said to exist in general. But this is only the baseline. Universal communication rights are augmented, enforced, and sometimes contradicted in the domestic sphere by national legal frameworks and public policies and practices. Constitutional law concerning communication in Canada – as at the international level – has been largely limited to protection of the bedrock right to freedom of expression and specification of its legitimate limits. Communication law and policy, on the other hand, seeks to address a range of concerns with respect to national sovereignty, cultural diversity, social justice, and identity by prescribing measures that deal with issues such as media regulation, spectrum management, access to telecommunication services, and more. As we shall show, there is a disconnect between the constitutional protection of freedom of expression and the realization of all such measures in practice. In short, the state of communication rights in Canada is precarious, and part of this disconnect stems from what we observe to be a systemic failure of Canadian communication policy in overseeing a just distribution of our communication resources. Those Canadians who have direct access to the media and communication technologies, who enjoy copyright protection and the capacity to communicate effectively, benefit from a different quality of freedom of expression from those who do not.[16] These are just some of the "media divides" referred to in the title of this book.

The Social Cycle of Communication

This study is premised on the Law Commission of Canada's definition of communication as "the core of democratic public life. In forms ranging from dialogue between citizens on a local, national or international scale, or between citizens and governments, to the various practices associated with the production, circulation and consumption of information, communication is central to the operation and legitimacy of democracy. In addition to these functions, communication also enables the social relationships and cultural practices that have been identified as foundational to the vibrant and diverse public cultures upon which democracy rests" (see Appendix 1).

This approach draws from thinking that is well established within the mainstream of political philosophy and free speech scholarship.[17] It holds that the prospects for democracy in a large, modern society where notions of community can no longer plausibly remain based strictly on face-to-face interaction are intimately tied to the creation of spaces of communication wherein the entire public can engage in transparent, informed, and sustained democratic discussion. This view of communication is not universally influential, however. Raymond Williams (1976, 63) reminds us that "in controversy

FIGURE 1

The social cycle of communication

The contrast and complementarity
between freedom of expression and communication rights is illustrated
in the "social cycle of communication" (adapted from CRIS 2005a).

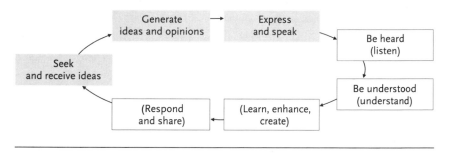

about communication systems and communication theory it is often useful to recall the unresolved range of the original noun of action, represented at its extremes by *transmit,* a one-way process, and *share* ... a common or mutual process." Communication can, in other words, mean dramatically different things to different people in different contexts.[18]

The Dutch scholar and human rights activist Cees Hamelink (2003, 155) argues that existing international human rights standards are largely based on a model of communication that, influenced by the mathematical theories of Shannon and Weaver (1949), posits communication as a linear, unidirectional process rather than as "a process of sharing, making common or creating a community." This distinction between communication as one-way transmission and communication as sharing forms the basis of what the CRIS campaign calls the "social cycle of communication" (see Figure 1). Figure 1 shows the communication process as a multifaceted cycle. The gray boxes represent the activities within this cycle that are encapsulated by the one-way transmission view of communication. When the white boxes are taken into account as well, we begin to approach a dialogic notion of communication as sharing.

Our assessment of communication rights in Canada uses the idea of the social cycle of communication by positioning it as a normative claim about the ideal role of communication in Canadian society. In other words, ensuring the realization of all of the functions encapsulated by the social cycle of communication is what we view as the normative purpose for Canadian law and policy in supporting democratic communication under contemporary conditions.

When we talk about rights in relation to communication, we refer indiscriminately to the rights promoted by international human rights agreements and those laid out in the domestic human rights framework (such as the *Canadian Charter of Rights and Freedoms*), as well as areas of law and public policy that articulate the claims that citizens can make on their governments and on each other, and the corresponding obligations of each. Chapter 1 does some of the work in particularizing this concept of "rights." The choice to situate this study in the language of rights is a conscious one and is not taken naïvely or unproblematically.

Through these discussions, and by framing our understanding of communication rights and the right to communicate around what we call the social cycle of communication, we use the language of rights as a way of capturing and accounting for the trade-offs and balances that must be struck in communication policy – between freedom of expression and privacy, for example.

The interrelated concepts of communication rights and the right to communicate emerge organically out of this set of normative assumptions. Together, these notions refer to a distinct approach to conceptualizing the law and policy framework that is required to ensure the realization in practice of the entire social cycle of communication and to produce clearly definable analytical categories for assessing it.

The idea of communication rights refers to all of the provisions that are required in order to ensure the realization of the social cycle. Freedom of expression covers certain key communicative functions (the ones in the gray boxes in Figure 1) but is not in itself a sufficiently comprehensive basis for the entire social cycle of communication. Communication rights, therefore, include other distinct *flanking* or enabling rights that are required to complete the right to freedom of expression to ensure that all people are able to seek and receive information, generate thoughts and opinions, have others hear, understand, learn from, and create on the basis of freely expressed ideas, and share with and respond to the ideas of others.[19]

Focusing on the realization that all of these are distinct, separate, and disparate rights is one approach to translating the concept of communication rights into the policy realm. An alternative would be to adopt a singular, encapsulating right to communicate. The status, history, and conceptual as well as juridical challenges of efforts to establish a universal right to communicate are discussed in Chapter 1.

Both notions – communication rights and the right to communicate – are based on the premise that the whole of the social cycle of communication is greater than the sum of its parts. The CRIS campaign makes the case that "while communication rights can be realized only through a set of enabling rights, securing them at the same time gives new and additional meaning to those enabling rights. The dividend comes through the empowerment of all as equals within the communication arena, and the potential for a virtuous cycle of communication. This generalized capacity for ongoing dialogue, in turn, leads to further communication, and to a cycle that ultimately deepens democracy, mutual understanding and respect" (CRIS 2005a, 25). This can be accomplished by securing all flanking or enabling communication rights at the same time, by establishing and securing the realization of a right to communicate that encapsulates them all – or by following a common approach that encompasses both. We reflect on how each option can apply to the Canadian context in Chapters 9 and 10.

Our approach in this book has been to both assess the ensemble of communication rights in Canada as a systemic issue (what we call the horizontal view) and to investigate, in greater depth on a thematic basis, the realization of specific sets of communication rights (what we call the vertical view).

The Horizontal View

The horizontal view of CRs and the R2C includes the following elements:

- in-depth interrogation of the conceptual and practical basis of the notions of CRs and the R2C as well as their applicability to the situation in Canada at present (this Introduction and Chapters 1 and 2)
- a cross-cutting and comprehensive audit of the realization of communication rights in contemporary Canada (Chapter 3)
- recommendations aimed not merely at the reform of individual policies or agencies but also at a broad reorientation of the system of communication in Canada and the legal and policy framework in which it operates (Chapters 9 and 10).

The task of assessing communication rights and the right to communicate in Canada involves an exercise in mapping and evaluating the various domestic laws and policies that impact communication rights and that are relevant to discussions of the right to communicate. Our take on the horizontal view on communication rights is primarily based on the application of a methodological instrument developed by the CRIS campaign, the Communication Rights Assessment Framework and Toolkit (CRAFT) (CRIS 2005a).

The CRAFT proposes a methodological approach to the evaluation of communication rights in a specific jurisdiction, using a matrix that was developed and tested on the ground against the policy and legal contexts in four countries (Brazil, Colombia, Kenya, and the Philippines) and one regional entity (the European Union).[20] It has its origins in a process somewhat similar to our own, in that the concept of "communication rights" in all of its diversity was first intuitively disassembled by the country teams working together, and subsequently reassembled to reflect the relationship between the constituent parts of the framework as well as the realities of different social, cultural, legal, and political contexts.[21] The framework was then applied in each of the participating entities.

In our case, between June 2006 and early 2008, a team of academic specialists on various elements of communication and media policy in Canada undertook a collaborative effort to respond to the questions posed by the CRAFT.[22] The responses generated drew on a number of sources, including research conducted by the members of our team for the "vertical view" chapters of this book. This was complemented by additional contributions based on previous studies and personal expertise that individual team members had accrued over years of involvement in teaching, research, and advocacy of communication policy in Canada.

A variety of methodological approaches ranging from interviews to documentary analysis are represented in the data used in our assessment. Despite the element of subjectivity inherent in this approach, the diversity of methods used by our team members provided an important measure of triangulation when it came time to tease out the commonalities indicated by the CRAFT framework.

We began by collecting as much data as we could around each of the CRAFT questions. While we did not answer questions that demanded areas of specialization that were not represented in our team, there were, in the end, few questions where this proved to be the case. Through a period of commentary and exchange within the team, we refined these responses to the individual questions. Over the course of this conversation, new issues emerged and certain responses were reframed or removed. We then synthesized these findings into a series of discussions of the state of the art in a handful of identifiable communication rights issues in Canada: freedom of expression; freedom of the press and media; access to information; diversity of media content and plurality of media sources; access to the means of communication; access to knowledge; right to equality before the law, one's honour and reputation, and to protection against unwarranted damage to them; right to privacy; minority cultural and linguistic rights; and the right to self-determination and to take part in government. Each of these issues was evaluated not in the broadest sense but in relation to media and communication. In other words, in order to avoid presenting our assessment in a cumbersome question-and-answer format that would include many redundant responses as well as unanswered questions, we, in effect, reassembled the CRAFT framework's list of questions into a more manageable list of readily definable communication rights.

Reflection on Method

One insightful reader of an early draft of parts of this book, McGill University legal scholar Tina Piper, asked whether it was fair to say that the CRAFT framework had a built-in methodological bias toward negative evaluations, in particular toward highlighting challenges to Canadian law and policy that had emerged as media controversies.[23] This is, in our view, probably true and certainly deserving of some reflection.

Piper had not in fact seen the CRAFT prior to asking this question; however, she rather accurately anticipated what it looks like. The CRAFT questions are generally posed to examine non-compliance. For instance, CRAFT question D1.3 asks: "Are there adequate measures to ensure that all linguistic communities have access to a minimum of society's knowledge available in appropriate language and form?" (CRIS 2005a, 74). Rather than focus on Canada's globally acknowledged status as champion of official bilingualism, we instead focus our assessment on underlining the fact that official bilingualism policy regarding the Canadian media is not always equal and systematic, on questioning the status of other minority languages, and on suggesting that linguistic duality in the Canadian media is promoted at the expense of a broader focus on securing the communication rights of an increasingly culturally diverse Canadian population.

One point that came up in our earliest discussions of the potential utility of applying the CRAFT framework to Canada was the idea that Canada would be a "hard case" for an assessment of communication rights. Although meant to have universal applicability, the CRAFT was developed primarily for use in assessing the realization of communication rights in developing countries with limited historical commitments to democratic governance and the enforcement of human rights. Could the framework be meaningfully applied to Canada? Canada is a country, after all, that revels in its worldwide image as a champion of international human rights and a model of intercultural dialogue. A place where protective cultural policies, universal public service, and non-market communication governance have historically been central to the concept of nationhood and to the agendas of governments. The sort of interrogation that the CRAFT framework would make of Colombia, for example, might contribute little to our understanding of communication rights in Canada. In the end, these reservations did not dissuade us from undertaking the CRAFT assessment of communication rights in Canada, but they do underline an important point to make in introducing our findings.

In assessing the realization of communication rights in Canada, the critical predisposition of questions posed by the CRAFT framework – in addition to enabling us to mine our thematic studies for overlapping themes that complement it – proved to be a sufficiently fine analytical tool. We acknowledge that our assessment tends to privilege flaws in the system and sometimes does not explicitly underscore areas where communication rights in Canada are adequately achieved. We think, however, that there is something of deeper value to the situation of communication rights in Canada in adopting a critical posture.

There is no way to sugarcoat this: our view of communication rights in Canada is a highly critical one. We think that the problems we will point to are cause for significant concern and require immediate action in order to redress certain issues and develop suitable alternatives regarding others. It is important to point out, however, that we can focus our critiques, and indeed our recommendations, at this level of activity around communication rights only because, as a precondition, the principles of human rights, democratic governance, and non-market roles for communication are formally well established in Canada. In being highly critical of the realization of communication rights in Canada, we will make the case that some principles are not leading to the realization of their stated desires in practice and that, in other areas, principles need to be rethought.

This study did not address, in any comparative sense, the position of Canada relative to other countries. Despite our critical assessment of the state of communication rights in Canada, it is still our impression that the realization of communication rights in Canada is, if not quite ideal, as strong as it is anywhere in the world. That is, it is not our intention to suggest that Canada is doing worse than Colombia or the Philippines, merely that Canada is doing worse than Canada seems to think it is doing and that Canada could and should do better than Canada does.

The Vertical View

The vertical approach to assessing communication rights in Canada involves a series of thematic studies that draw on a variety of methodologies to examine the links between communication rights and a selection of key specific public policy areas that we argue are central to shaping communication in Canada at present: media, access, Internet, privacy, and copyright.[24]

Each one is something of a hot-button issue area for communication rights in Canada. They all reflect on how emerging technologies and changing social trends such as multiculturalism and globalization are stretching the existing policy frameworks for Canada's communication system. Each thematic study examines a particular policy framework as well as the practices around it. Each suggests how single areas of information, communication, cultural, or human rights policy cannot be dealt with alone, and how the policy objectives in each of these areas can be met only when flanking rights – policy objectives in related areas – are also achieved. In each of these studies, our assessment points to specific issues and problems that are in need of urgent attention, and we make a series of policy recommendations designed to contribute to improving the status of communication rights (see Chapter 9).

Our vertical and horizontal views of CRs and the R2C in Canada are both parallel and intersecting. Each vertical chapter reflects in its own way on the realization of freedom of expression in Canada, on its status as a two-tiered freedom, and on the importance of viewing communication policy making as part of a social cycle of communication.

Overview: Part 1

In this introductory chapter, we argue that the prospects for democracy in Canada depend not only on the formally acknowledged right to freedom of expression but also on a "social cycle of communication" that includes protection for the rights to seek, to receive, to impart, to listen, to be heard, to understand, to learn, to create, to respond, and even to remain silent. Democracy also entails responsibility, constraints, and limitations where the exercise of the rights of one group or individual impacts on the rights of others.

Developed primarily with regard to global discussions around universal human rights, the notion of the right to communicate is politically controversial and conceptually fluid. It is not our intention to invoke this contested rights construct unproblematically. In Chapter 1, we examine the international history of CRs and the R2C and the associated political, philosophical, and juridical controversies.

In Chapter 2, Seán Ó Siochrú, the international spokesperson for the CRIS campaign, reflects on the challenges that have confronted the campaign in its efforts to engage non-specialist activists and capture public attention during the WSIS proceedings and since. Discussing CRs and the R2C in relation to human rights, social justice, and the communication for development perspective, Ó Siochrú suggests that CRs and the R2C can be valuable mobilizing tools when they are used to "frame" media and communication policy issues.

Overview: Part 2

Chapter 3 synthesizes our assessment of the realization, in practice, of communication rights in Canadian law and policy. We identify the policies and laws that are relevant to the realization of communication rights in Canada and highlight cases, controversies, and issues that empirically demonstrate the conceptual critiques of the principles at the core of debates surrounding CR and R2C, pointing readers toward the more in-depth discussions of relevant issues that are presented in the rest of Part 2.

In Chapters 4 through 8, we present a series of thematic studies that examine, with a narrower focus and in greater depth, certain issues where cross-cutting trends are particularly relevant and where the realization of communication rights in Canada is particularly problematic, to an extent that would seem to call into question the very orientation of communication policy making in Canada at present.

Through fundamental changes in the traditional media policy areas of regulation, predominance of public institutions, and support for Canadian content production, Canadian media are changing. Marc Raboy argues in Chapter 4 that these changes raise troubling questions for communication rights. In his discussion of communication rights and the Canadian media,

Raboy examines issues such as community broadcasting, concentration of media ownership, the lack of diversity of voices in the Canadian media, and the conceptual basis of regulation in the media sector.

Extending the discussion from traditional media, in Chapter 5 Leslie Regan Shade considers and contextualizes the evolving concepts and policies surrounding universal access to information and communication technologies (ICTs) in Canada. She provides a socio-technical model for defining access to ICTs, looks at debates surrounding digital divides from recent Canadian scholarship, and provides an overview of federal ICT programs and policies in Canada.

Questions of access aside, the Internet has been an enabler of many significant changes to social and technical aspects of communication. It has changed many norms, including the reach and cost of communication services. In Chapter 6, William J. McIver Jr. makes the case that the Internet is, as such, a necessary site for examining communication rights. His chapter looks at technologically grounded issues, including network traffic shaping, semantic Web and Web 2.0 technologies, and Voice over Internet Protocol (VoIP) telephony, and how they relate directly to social communication in Canada.

The type of communication facilitated by the Internet is not without its drawbacks, however. Nor can the existence of cyberspace be seen as somehow making communication immune to the realities of the world we live in. In her second thematic contribution to this volume, Leslie Regan Shade makes the case that the need for privacy rights has been significantly amplified by the development of intrusive technologies of surveillance in a post-9/11 political climate suffused with global security concerns. Chapter 7 addresses these issues and argues that the challenges of emergent material technologies coupled with political technologies of regulation and governance necessitate a reconsideration of a privacy rights platform for the twenty-first century.

Copyright law is a piece of the communication rights puzzle, as it can either foster or impede the development and dissemination of ideas and human expression. In this respect, it is an issue that cuts across concerns about communication rights with regard to media, access, Internet, and privacy. In Chapter 8, Laura J. Murray discusses how Canadian copyright law is a better tool for communication rights than its counterparts in many other countries but how, nonetheless, the rights of owners of copyrighted material are often emphasized to the detriment of the rights of users. In addition, her interviews with artists and creators in Canada point to a general lack of awareness of the relative advantages that Canadians have in the communication rights aspects of copyright.

These vertical chapters make no claim to uniformity. It is not our intention that they be symmetrical. Each author is a distinguished policy specialist in his or her domain, and there was no attempt to get them to speak in a common voice or fit all of the chapters into a common mould. They do complement each other in a series of important ways, however, all of which develop and reflect upon the central arguments about communication rights and the right to communicate that are then taken up in Part 3.

Overview: Part 3

Our assessment of the performance of existing institutional structures (public institutions, regulatory bodies, government programs, accountability mechanisms, and so on), the adequacy of the legal and regulatory frameworks governing these structures, and the nature and degree of public participation in the design and execution of communication policy in Canada underlines numerous instances in which inadequate or nonexistent provisions in other areas of Canadian law and policy are creating a chilling effect on freedom of expression. In Part 3, we argue that the role of law and policy in supporting communication rights in Canada is highly problematic at present.

Across the spectrum of Canadian law and policy related to communication rights such as access to information, freedom of the press, and the right to honour, dignity, and reputation (in relation to media and communication), we discuss gaps that exist between the principles declared in Canadian policy and communication rights as realized in practice on the ground, as well as law and policy-making activities in Canada that have failed to adapt to new developments and that lack coordinating principles and common objectives. We argue that communication law and policy in Canada have failed to adequately adapt to the shift to digital media, to respond to the emergence of the Internet, to protect human rights in the post-9/11 security environment, and to accommodate the pressures of copyright reform and a host of other current trends.

On the basis of this assessment, enriched by the detailed thematic or "vertical studies" presented in Part 2, we make the case in Part 3 that the Canadian communication system lacks coherence and that steps need to be taken to eliminate parallel and conflicting principles, monitor performance, and enforce existing rules, and that, overall, freedom of expression is experienced as a two-tiered freedom in Canada. Chapter 9 is therefore devoted to a discussion of possible policy remedies that are intended to improve the conditions observed in our assessment.

The sum effect, we argue, is a great distance separating the Canadian communication system from the everyday lived lives of most Canadians that reflects stark inequalities between the ability of different sectors of society to exercise their communication rights meaningfully. In addition, we question whether freedom of expression – a largely one-way process of information transmission – is sufficiently suitable as a defining legal principle for supporting the diverse roles that law and public policy could play in supporting democratic communication in contemporary society.

Before thinking about new policy in the effort to recapture communication rights, we argue that Canada should actually use the policies it already has. We recommend the further development of analysis and monitoring functions across the full range of Canadian communication policy making that would evaluate and ensure, on an ongoing basis, that existing Canadian policy objectives related to communication rights are being met, or that would at least report on how they are not. We propose greater coordination between government, nongovernmental organizations (NGOs) and civil society groups, and academic researchers.

The civil society sector has been a key driver in the push for the realization of communication rights internationally and in other countries. Dedicated funding for public interest advocacy of the type that is available to US civil society groups from private organizations such as the Ford Foundation, or to European NGOs in the form of direct government subsidies, simply does not exist in Canada on the same scale. Overall, we recommend that there be a serious process of reflection on the role of civil society groups within the Canadian communication policy framework and consideration of how the indispensable work they do could be better supported and accounted for by public authorities.

Generally speaking, communication policy in Canada has been intimately tied to cultural development and sovereignty, to the ongoing project of forging a national identity across Canada's linguistic, cultural, and regional divides, and, in turn, to protecting this fragile state of affairs from being subsumed in our monolithic neighbour to the south. Yet, in an increasingly globalized communication environment, we are left asking how sustainable is a media system oriented toward the protection of national sovereignty. Media policy making in a globalized and multicultural Canada requires a shift in focus from nation building to the promotion of diversity and the expression of multiple forms of citizenship.

Our study repeatedly underlines the need to bring the media closer to people. Supporting community media is one way to accomplish this; a renewed focus on local media is another. Neither, however, is adequately provided for in Canada at present, despite the grand claims made by official policy documents such as the federal *Broadcasting Act*.[25] In parallel, the Canadian media need to be further diversified in terms of their ownership, management structures, representation of minorities, and other areas. Bringing the media closer to people also involves ensuring that Canadians are empowered to use the media that they create, that reflect their lives and environments, and that their tax dollars fund. This means a greater policy orientation to open access that includes making publicly subsided cultural products accessible to everyone.

Finally, in Chapter 10, we argue that the establishment of a Canadian right to communicate could encapsulate all of these initiatives and reflect on how and where such a right could be established in Canadian law, what it might look like, and what the challenges and impediments to doing so are.

Critics of the establishment of a right to communicate have always been preoccupied with the question of what kind of human right the right to communicate should be: a "negative" right, like freedom of expression, that gives individuals protection from the state, or a "positive" right that ascribes a role of collective protection to the state. Supporters of the establishment of a right to communicate have never been able to agree on what they see as an acceptable response to this question. While this remains a current concern for supporters of the right to communicate and a standard rebuff by its critics (see, for example, Mueller et al. 2007), the literature on human rights has long accepted the view that the dichotomy between these two types of rights is a false one. The communication rights literature remains uniquely preoccupied with this dilemma, due largely to the fact that the intellectual basis of the movement consists primarily of media and communication scholars and activists rather than human rights specialists. As we shall see, the issue remains unresolved and an international debate on the question continues.

In 1971, *Instant World* presented the right to communicate as "the need to put a soul in the system" (Canada 1971, 39). Our assessment of communication rights and the right to communicate in Canada at present aims to see how far we have come toward that end. This involves looking beyond rhetoric and examining the capacity that Canadians have to make claims about the communication system that is so fundamental to the way we experience our everyday lives. For all that Canada does and tries to do in the area of communication rights, our assessment is that we are still a long way from having a system with this sort of soul.

1
Histories, Contexts, and Controversies

Marc Raboy and Jeremy Shtern

Communication rights and the right to communicate have been developed, elaborated, and applied primarily at the global level. Although Canadian actors have sporadically – and importantly – contributed to these discussions, our assessment of communication rights in Canada must be seen mainly as an exercise in applying an international framework to our national context. Thus, discussion of the international activity that has shaped communication rights is necessary in order to transparently and reflexively adapt it to the Canadian situation.

The foundation and core of the international regime of human rights is the 1948 *Universal Declaration of Human Rights (UDHR)* and its two separate treaty instruments: the *International Covenant on Civil and Political Rights (ICCPR)* and the *International Covenant on Economic, Social and Cultural Rights (ICESCR)*, each of which was ratified in 1966. Taken together, these documents constitute what is commonly referred to as the "International Bill of Rights" or the "International Bill of Human Rights."[1]

Parts of these documents reflect directly or indirectly on communication in society – the social cycle of communication (see Introduction) – and taken together, they can be said to constitute a set of acknowledged communication rights. At the same time, the treatment given to communication issues in the International Bill of Rights documents does not go far enough and fails to include most of the flanking rights that we referred to in the Introduction. The international movement to establish a singular right to communicate has been an ongoing attempt to pick up these pieces.

Early Political Controversy Surrounding the Right to Communicate
Efforts to enshrine the functions associated with the social cycle of communication within the universal human rights framework have always

proven controversial. Even the drafting of the *UDHR* was dominated by the fierce and highly partisan disagreement characteristic of the Cold War.

The initial planning of the *UDHR* called for an article on freedom of information. A UN General Assembly (UNGA) declaration from 14 December 1946 described freedom of information as "the touchstone of all the freedoms to which the United Nations is consecrated," and instructed the Economic and Social Council (ECOSOC) to arrange a conference whose purpose was to "formulate its views concerning the rights, obligations and practices" (Canada 1949, 108) relevant to these issues and make recommendations to the General Assembly about what related articles warranted inclusion in the *UDHR*. The rationale for this conference was that "understanding and cooperation among nations are impossible without an alert and sound public opinion" (108).

It was the perspective of journalists and publishers in shaping public opinion, however, and not the public's own role in forming and voicing this opinion within the mass communication environment, that was further privileged by the details of the UN Conference on Freedom of Information that was held at Geneva in March and April 1948. The same 1946 resolution calling for the arrangement of the conference explicitly instructed that "delegations to the conference shall include in each instance persons actually engaged or experienced in press, radio, motion pictures or other media" (Canada 1949, 108). What we would refer to today as "civil society" was effectively absent.

The UN Conference on Freedom of Information pointed to the fundamental right to freedom of information as nothing less than "essential in the cause of peace and for the achievement of political, economic and social progress" (Canada 1949). In addition, it forwarded forty-three resolutions to the UNGA for consideration, and three separate draft conventions were suggested: one sponsored by the United States on the international gathering and transmission of news; a French initiative giving states the right to obtain publicity to officially correct misinformation affecting their international relations; and a British draft convention delineating the basic elements of freedom of information and the obligation of states to establish non-official organizations to monitor the standards and professional conduct surrounding information dissemination and reception. A subcommittee on freedom of information worked on versions of the same ideas for the draft articles to be included in the *UDHR*.

Freedom of information as discussed in this context can be defined as "the freedom to seek out information and ideas, the freedom to express opinions and to spread information by different means and the freedom to receive information and ideas" (UNESCO n.d., 3). From the perspective of the newsgathering associations, this included a policy environment that would facilitate the right to send newsgatherers anywhere there is news; the right of newsgatherers to transmit their reports without censorship and at reasonable cost back to their home countries; and the ability to publish and sell the products of "worldwide news organizations" in all countries (Binder 1952). Freedom of *expression*, as an extension of freedom of opinion and as a necessary precondition to freedom of the press, was an important component of this view.

Driven by Western governments and news organizations, discourses regarding freedom of information thus blended concerns for the protection and expansion of information markets with concerns about the role of propaganda in the escalating ideological, economic, and political conflicts of the Cold War (see Whitton 1949). The ideological centrepiece of all of these initiatives was the US notion of a global "free flow of information," according to which "information may flow freely and unimpeded across national frontiers" (UNESCO n.d., 9).

The USSR and its allies countered with the idea of a balanced flow and exchange of information that condemned warmongering through propaganda but justified government authority over information and journalists. Although they were largely regarded as bit players in the debate at this point, a diverse group of smaller countries seemed to find common ground between the two extremes. Binder (1952) refers to a group of Latin American and Arab countries and labels these the "middle ground group." Here, and in pointing to the role of Sweden, which he characterized as a Western country with a government-run media that was particularly assertive about the need to expand the parameters of the polarized debate, Binder could easily have been describing the R2C debates that would take place within the UN Educational, Scientific and Cultural Organization (UNESCO) more than twenty-five years later.

Very quickly, however, the debate over freedom of information became polarized and intractable. The socialist countries blocked approval of the remaining draft articles as well as for a Convention on Freedom of Information that had been proposed by the United States and the United Kingdom. As a result of the rapidly escalating controversy, the UNGA decided in late

1948 to defer consideration of all items related to the debate except for article 19 (on freedom of expression) until after the adoption of the UDHR. In the end, only the article relating to freedom of expression was adopted by the UN Human Rights Commission for inclusion in the final draft of the *UDHR*. A Convention on Freedom of Information was drafted in early 1951 only to be sidelined when a vote at the ECOSOC taken in September that year decided "not to convene an international conference of plenipotentiaries for formulation and signature" (Binder 1952, 218). Between 1962 and 1980, an item regarding freedom of information appeared on the agendas of both the UNGA and the ECOSOC every year. Neither would ever lead to conclusive results (Kortteinen et al. 1999, 402).

Communication Rights as Part of the International Human Rights Regime

Notwithstanding the political intrigues that we have just described, a legal regime of international human rights was put in place after 1948 and has continued to develop over the past sixty years. The notion of communication rights is most straightforwardly introduced by examining the relationship between communication and this regime of universal human rights.

The notion of communication rights relates to the legal principles that people can use as a basis for making claims about how the media and communication systems in their societies should be structured. We can talk about communication in the language of human rights to the extent that international law addresses aspects of the processes of communication in society, both directly and by implication.

Information and communication issues are directly treated in the International Bill of Rights, which articulates the right to freedom of expression in article 19 of both the *UDHR* and the *ICCPR*. Article 19 of the *UDHR* states: "Everyone has the right to freedom of opinion and expression; this right includes freedom to hold opinions without interference and to seek, receive and impart information and ideas through any media and regardless of frontiers."[2]

In addition, other articles within the International Bill of Rights reflect some dimension of the process of communication in society, even if communication is not necessarily their primary focus. To speak of communication rights as legally binding human rights guaranteed in the International Bill of Rights is therefore to invoke the following:

- a right to freedom of expression and opinion
- a right to participate in one's own culture and use one's mother language, including ethnic, religious, or linguistic minorities
- a right to enjoy the benefits of scientific progress and its applications
- a right to information regarding governance and matters of public interest (access to information)
- a right to the protection of the moral and material interests of authorship
- a right to one's honour and reputation and to protection against unwarranted damage to them
- a right to privacy
- a right to peaceful assembly and association
- a right to self-determination and to take part in government
- a right to free primary education and progressive introduction of free secondary education.[3]

Although not always their primary intent, each of these rights includes a dimension that bears on the process of communication in society. These emerge more clearly as communication rights if we add the phrase "in relation to media and communication" to each right.

In articulating and providing legal personality to universal human rights, the *UDHR, ICCPR,* and *ICESCR* are supported and expanded on by a panoply of secondary agreements, legal instruments, and precedents dealing with the interpretation and application of specific rights (Drake and Jørgensen 2006, especially 16). Various studies and scholars have compiled extensive lists of the international instruments that comment on or in some way pertain to the relationship between human rights and the process of communication.[4]

These listings constitute what is in many respects an ad hoc and inefficient framework. Not all parties are willing to connect the numerous and disparate dots or even accept the interpretation that rights protections for processes of communication have reached beyond the bounds of article 19. "While communication rights can be realized only through a set of enabling rights," the Communication Rights in the Information Society (CRIS) campaign explains, "securing them at the same time gives new and additional meaning to those enabling rights" (CRIS 2005a, 25). With the goal of securing communication rights, there have been significant intellectual, activist, and political efforts to establish a singular *right to communicate* that could encompass a range of principles that are not reducible to either freedom of expression or the related communication rights listed above.

Enter the Right to Communicate

The movement to establish a right to communicate is largely based on the premise that freedom of expression does not comprehensively address the social cycle of communication in modern, technologically mediated societies. Proponents of the right to communicate posit that, while many communication rights do exist through secondary implications and liberal interpretations of existing human rights provisions, communication processes are so central to contemporary society that a comprehensive communication rights framework is required. During the past forty years, this idea has circulated in discussions about universal human rights in a range of international institutions.

The first explicit mention of a right to communicate is generally credited to Jean D'Arcy, a former senior official of French television and the director of radio and visual services in the United Nations Office of Public Information. As director of programming for the French public broadcaster in the 1950s, D'Arcy had been considered a courageous and visionary executive and was known for his vigorous defence of journalistic freedom.[5] In a 1969 paper written for the European Broadcasting Union, he argued: "The time will come when the Universal Declaration of Human Rights will have to encompass a more extensive right than man's right to information, first laid down 21 years ago in Article 19. This is the right of man to communicate. It is the angle from which the future development of communications will have to be considered if it is to be fully understood" (D'Arcy 1969).

Interestingly, D'Arcy's paper did not contain any further explanation of what he meant by the right to communicate. The notion itself would resonate, however, and has since been studied, expanded upon, and problematized by others, without any clear agreement about what the right to communicate might actually mean.

As we discussed in the Introduction, one of the earliest and most significant of these pioneering efforts was done within the Canadian government's then newly established Department of Communication (DoC). Its 1971 publication *Instant World* presented a baseline definition that "the rights to hear and be heard, to inform and to be informed, together may be regarded as the essential components of a right to communicate" (Canada 1971, 4). This Canadian report is widely considered a seminal document in the global development of communication rights discourse.

Other important hubs of activity relative to the right to communicate emerged in the early 1970s, including the work of the Speech Communication Association (SCA) and the East-West Communication Institute at the

University of Hawaii, largely through the coordination efforts of Professor L.S. Harms[6] as well as the International Broadcast Institute (IBI).[7]

The Swedish National Commission for UNESCO began working on the right to communicate as early as 1972. Communication governance in Sweden during much of the twentieth century was structured around two key policy principles: maintaining a free press and a highly interventionist role for government regulation in the public interest. As early as the freedom of information debates in the late 1940s, it had been clear to Sweden that this policy approach was increasingly untenable as global debates became polarized between the contradictory ideals of untrammelled censorship and complete laissez-faire communication markets.

The eighteenth session of the UNESCO General Conference, held in 1974, passed a resolution presented by Sweden that authorized the director-general of UNESCO to "study and define the right to communicate" and report back to UNESCO at the next General Conference in 1976 (UNESCO 1974). In response, UNESCO Director-General Amadou-Mahtar M'Bow convened an informal working group charged with defining the right to communicate and set about consulting with communications organizations around the world about their perspective on human rights and communication. L.S. Harms was a member of this working group and prepared the draft of its report. The final report was, as charged, submitted to the nineteenth General Conference of UNESCO in 1976, with the conclusion that "additional study and research on various aspects of the Right to Communicate" was required and should be included in UNESCO's program of activities (Richstad and Harms 1977, 126). Under the aegis of UNESCO, a group of experts on the right to communicate was established in 1978. The effort was abandoned before its goals could be realized, however, as UNESCO was constrained by both political controversies and conceptual and juridical debates over the links between the universal human rights framework and processes of communication.

The New World Information and Communication Order
Over the course of the UNESCO activities of the late 1970s and early 1980s, the idea of a right to communicate came to be inextricably linked to the Non-Aligned Movement (NAM) of UN countries launched in the early 1960s and largely composed of developing, postcolonial states. Having established – against the resistance of the more powerful states – the notion of a New

International Economic Order (NIEO) as a viable force in international politics by the early 1970s, the 1973 NAM summit declared that "the activities of imperialism are not confined solely to the political and economic fields, but also cover the cultural and social fields" (Padovani and Nordenstreng 2005). Spearheaded by the NAM, this line of thinking grew into the movement for a New World Information and Communication Order (NWICO) that would dominate the UNESCO agenda for the better part of the next decade and emerge as the most significant political battleground to date over the role of communication in struggles for human rights.

The argument in favour of a NWICO was based on the following contemporary realities of global communication:

- The "'free flow of information' doctrine," introduced in the 1940s and central to UNESCO activities since the 1960s, was being used to justify liberalization of global communication regulation and reinforce the dominance of Western media and news content.
- Concentration of media and communication industries was increasing and translating into ever-greater foreign ownership in smaller and poorer countries.
- The importance of Western-controlled technologies in media production and dissemination was increasing, making it difficult for others to keep up (CRIS 2005a).

In response, the NAM pushed the NWICO as a policy prescription based on the so-called Four D's:

- democratization (pluralism of sources of news and information)
- decolonization (self-reliance and independence from foreign structures)
- de-monopolization (of concentrated ownership in communication industries)
- development (Nordenstreng 1986; Padovani 2005).

The NWICO also found political support within the socialist bloc, the historical site of opposition to the free-flow principle.[8] As such, the NWICO was fervently opposed not only on economic but also on political and ideological grounds by the most powerful Western countries as well as the communication industries and institutions of the West. The residual political baggage and ill-will from the freedom of information debates of the 1940s would only exacerbate an already divisive issue.

In an effort to avoid a seemingly intractable direct confrontation between the West and the NAM and its supporters, the nineteenth General Conference of UNESCO in 1976 created an International Commission for the Study of Communication Problems, chaired by Nobel and Lenin Peace Prize laureate Sean MacBride.[9] What became known as the MacBride Commission centred on an extensive program of consultation and research. A number of the submissions that it received focused on the right to communicate, including texts submitted by D'Arcy and Harms. *Many Voices, One World*, the report of the MacBride Commission, was presented to the twenty-first General Conference of UNESCO in 1980 (see UNESCO 1980). It devoted an entire subsection to the right to communicate and its role in the democratization of communication. Recommendation number 54 of the MacBride Commission report reinforced this link, arguing that "communication needs in a democratic society should be met by the extension of specific rights such as the right to be informed, the right to inform, the right to privacy, the right to participate in public communication – all elements of a new concept, the right to communicate" (265).

The creation of the MacBride Commission succeeded in delaying the inevitable showdown between the NAM and the Western countries by four years, but *Many Voices, One World* did little to dissipate the tensions. Not limiting their displeasure to the MacBride Commission report itself, the opponents of the NWICO mounted a full frontal attack on the institutional credibility of UNESCO as the organization that had convened and then endorsed the findings of the MacBride Commission. Western governments, led by the United States and supported by the private media industry and its lobby groups (including, for example, the World Press Freedom Committee), accused UNESCO of attempting to impose government control of the media and even of trying to suppress freedom of expression (CRIS 2005a, 17). The United States pulled out of UNESCO in 1984, and the United Kingdom and Singapore followed suit soon after.[10] In 1987, M'Bow, who had been personally involved in the R2C discussions, was replaced as director-general of UNESCO.[11] By that time, new medium-term plans for the organization's activities would make only cursory mention of the NWICO, while the "free flow of information" had been reinstated as a central doctrine. The result was that, by the 1990s, the profile of the right to communicate as a political issue had diminished in the intergovernmental arena.[12]

Rebirth and Renewal: The Emergence of the CRIS Campaign

A victim of its association with the ill-fated NWICO debate, the right to communicate largely disappeared as a political issue between the mid-1980s and the early twenty-first century. For activists and scholars, however, it retained much of its provocative appeal as a construct able to invoke a whole series of issues about media, democracy, and international development. As discussed in greater analytical detail in Chapter 2, the themes raised by the NWICO continued to resonate in academic and communication activist circles (see Traber and Nordenstreng 1992), and throughout the 1990s more and more moves were made to coalesce these diverse actors and interests. The so-called MacBride Roundtables on Communication and numerous other conferences and meetings were soon augmented by loosely coordinated action in the form of initiatives such as the People's Communication Charter, the Cultural Environment Movement, and the Platform for the Democratization of Communication.[13] The focus of these efforts was not just the democratization of communication as a positive value in and of itself but also the fostering of a role for the media in the democratization of societies.[14]

Often unaware of each other's existence, nongovernmental organizations (NGOs) and activist groups were emerging globally around communication issues such as community and alternative radio, video and other media, free and open source software, and media gender bias. At the same time, relatively new information and communication technologies, most notably symbolized by the arrival and diffusion of the Internet, were being taken up by social protest movements in Latin America, the US, and East Asia, as well as networks of activists engaged with issues surrounding the environment, gender, and human rights (see Ambrosi 2001).

In addition, by the late 1990s, the Internet was central to the organization of a burgeoning transnational anti-globalization movement (see Deibert 2002). The challenge was how to refute the conventional view that the media are "value-free containers" of information, how to problematize media as a social issue, how to mobilize activism around the principle that the media can be contested spaces, and, in the process, how to create a new social movement around media and communication out of these disparate but vibrant groups (Raboy 2003, 112).

Many of these initiatives came together in 1999, to form a loose association of media activists called Voices 21. A statement by Voices 21 made the case that "all movements that work toward social change use media and communication networks," suggesting that it was therefore essential that all such groups focus on current trends in media and communication, such as increasing concentration of media ownership. Voices 21 proposed the formation of "an international alliance to address concerns and work jointly on matters around media and communication" (Voices 21 1999).

The UN's World Summit on the Information Society (WSIS) – in the early stages of organization at the time – represented an ideal venue for action. The summit's foundational documents indicated that it was to be a multistakeholder process, with a large place for civil society participation (see Raboy and Landry 2005). But when a letter to the summit organizers requesting a meeting to "clarify the opportunities for civil society involvement as well as generate ideas and possibilities about the [WSIS] process" went unanswered, the Platform for the Democratization of Communication convened its own meeting in London in November 2001.[15] At this meeting – called to push along civil society participation in the WSIS – the group was renamed the Platform for Communication Rights, and the CRIS campaign was launched.

In framing a social movement with designs on influencing intergovernmental policy making around right to communicate discourse, the CRIS campaign could hardly be accused of following the path of least resistance. To many in the intergovernmental policy-making community, the mere association of R2C with the NWICO history made it a total non-starter. In addition to the political controversy that we have already discussed, however, the juridical and conceptual foundations of the idea of the R2C were also contested, even among its supporters. While a case could be made that the Cold War politics and polarized ideological conflicts that had been so problematic to the history of the R2C were no longer cause for concern in intergovernmental negotiations by 2001, the invocation by the CRIS campaign of this historically loaded concept carried with it additional baggage, namely, that the conceptual and juridical debate about what exactly could be meant by the right to communicate had yet to be resolved.

Conceptual/Juridical Tensions

The most significant and potentially intractable conceptual debate around the right to communicate is the question of what kind of human right the right to communicate should be.

The most common categorization tool used to make normative distinctions between different human rights is the generational model. The eventual separation of the rights first outlined in the *UDHR* into the two distinct conventions, the *ICCPR* and the *ICESCR*, reflects a widespread acknowledgment

of the philosophical and juridical differences between what have become
known as first- and second-generation rights.

The *ICCPR* (including article 19) represents, to this line of thinking,
"first-generation human rights" (FGHRs) while the *ICESCR* specifies what
are seen as "second-generation human rights" (SGHRs). This distinction is
made on the basis of the *ICCPR* rights having, as a group, a shared historical
context, conceptual approach, and potential for enforcement that differ significantly from the history, conceptual approach, and enforcement strategy
common to the group of rights captured in the *ICESCR*.

Historically, ICCPR rights, including freedom of expression, were all
largely recognized in numerous national-level constitutions throughout the
eighteenth and nineteenth centuries. On the other hand, *ICESCR* rights represented, legally at least, relatively new constructs that entered rights discourses in the postwar era without the same degree of national-level precedent.

Conceptually, first-generation rights can be distinguished from second-
generation rights in at least two significant respects: the question of to whom
they are granted and the question of the juridical means by which their application is pursued. The *ICCPR* first-generation rights are seen as rights that
are provided to *individuals* through a *negative* approach, while the *ICESCR*
second-generation rights are viewed as *collective* and *positive* rights. According
to Drake and Jørgensen (2006, 14), FGHRs are "negative rights" in the sense
that "they proscribe state interference with individual freedoms," while SGHRs
are "positive rights" in that they "require states to create the conditions in
which individuals and collectives can enjoy a certain quality of life, or to
provide certain goods or services to that end."

With regard to their *enforcement*, while first-generation rights are seen as
a series of individual guarantees that are strictly and immediately enforceable,
many human rights experts argue that the realization of second-generation
rights is undermined by its contingency on state resources. Drake and Jørgensen (2006, 14) summarize this perspective as the view that "the CESCR,
though also a legally binding treaty ... is more aspirational and progressive
in nature, and the realization or violations of the rights it entails are open to
greater latitude in interpretation" (see also Roth 2004). In sum, it is argued
that the enforcement of second-generation rights "boils down to a promotional obligation which ... deliberately refrains from establishing true individual rights" (Tomuschat 2003, 39).

The major conceptual challenge associated with the right to communicate stems from the fact that, as an object for human rights discourse,

communication can be interpreted to fit rather neatly into either of these seemingly exclusive juridical frameworks.

The argument that the right to communicate should reflect the approach of first-generation human rights invokes the normative view that free individuals and not the state must remain the ultimate decision makers about what communication is permitted and between whom, even if the maintenance of individual rights comes at the expense of collective issues such as the protection of cultural identity (Kuhlen 2004). Thus, many press and media groups as well as freedom of speech and anti-censorship activists argue that any collective claims to communication rights would have undesirable political and/or ideological effects on the individual's capacity to communicate freely in society and might result in increased government control tantamount to censorship.

At the same time, however, it is argued that the dominance of mass media, the unequal access to means of communication, and the privileged position of profit-driven corporations in modern society necessitate a positive, collective approach that obliges states to ensure that rights frameworks protect the role of communication in society. In this view, the individual simply lacks the ability to communicate effectively in a technologically mediated context; thus, the state must bear responsibility for ensuring that communication processes support the needs of society. A strong case can therefore be made that communication, as an inherently social process and one that implicates groups as well as individuals, requires rights that would be affirmed by imposing obligations on governments to bear the burden of ensuring that people do have the means and ability to communicate.

This fluidity is acknowledged by even the strongest supporters of the right to communicate. For instance, in his 1982 report for UNESCO entitled *The Right to Communicate*, Desmond Fisher laments that "there is no doubt the whole argument over locus of the right to communicate is one of the most intractable sticking points in the debate. If it can be solved, the main stumbling-block will have been removed and the task of ... having it acknowledged in national and international legislation will have been greatly eased" (Fisher 1982, 27). Fisher, however, also highlights the great utility of the concept itself:

> The concept of the right to communicate offers the possibility of
> ending the impasse ... It expresses a more fundamental philosophical principle and has a wider application than previous formulations

of communications rights. It springs from the very nature of the human person as a communicating being and from the human need for communication, at the level of the individual and of society. It is universal. It emphasizes the process of communicating rather than the content of the message. It implies participation. It suggests an interactive transfer of information. And underlying the concept is an ethical or humanitarian suggestion of a responsibility to ensure a fairer global distribution of the resources necessary to make communication possible. (8)

Contemporary Discourses

As we have just seen, the challenges associated with framing intergovernmental activist efforts around the R2C have been both political and conceptual. The CRIS campaign employed discursive links to the right to communicate in full awareness of the political and conceptual baggage of the term. As one of this chapter's authors[16] has previously written: "The link made by CRIS between communication rights and civil society participation in the World Summit on the Information Society was not a casual one" (Raboy 2004b, 95). The campaign, however, also used the notion of communication rights to deploy the same core set of normative assumptions to avoid rehashing the unproductive aspects of the NWICO debates. The CRIS approach was thus ultimately informed by "the benefit of strategic hindsight" (CRIS 2005a, 18).

As we discussed in the Introduction, the strategy mobilized by the CRIS campaign as a response to these tensions focuses on securing existing rights related to communication, on framing freedom of expression as part of a social cycle that can be achieved only where other distinct flanking or enabling communication rights are also realized and, in parallel, on working toward the ideal of establishing a yet-to-be-defined right to communicate. The key distinction between previous outings of the R2C and the CRIS approach is that CRIS is interested not only in establishing a formal legal statement of the right to communicate but also in raising awareness concerning all links between discourses of human rights and the social cycle of communication: "The right to communicate can be used as an informal rallying cry for advocacy, appealing to a common sense understanding and the perceived needs and frustrations of people in the area of communication ... but, also can be used in a formal legal sense, in which a right to communicate should take its place alongside other fundamental human rights enshrined in international law" (CRIS 2005a, 20).[17]

By framing the right to communicate "as an informal rallying cry," the CRIS campaign succeeded in reviving the notion of the right to communicate in intergovernmental politics largely by embracing the notion's conceptual fluidity. In the process, the lack of precision that could be perceived as a vulnerability in the idea of a right to communicate was turned into an opportunity to develop the idea of communication rights. In the following chapter, Seán Ó Siochrú, the international spokesperson for the CRIS campaign, expands on this assessment of what communication rights mean and do in the contemporary context, explores the utility and legitimacy of the term as the basis for policy analysis and advocacy, and reflects on the development and use of the Communication Rights Assessment Framework and Toolkit.

2
Implementing Communication Rights

Seán Ó Siochrú

The right to communicate has come a long way since Jean D'Arcy first expressed the concept in 1969. During its four-decade journey, it has been subjected to intense scrutiny and analysis from a diversity of perspectives; it has faced and survived adversity, enriched by the experience in the end; and can now inhabit comfortably the span between a right to communicate, as a right enshrined in international law, and communication rights as an expression of social justice on the ground. But communication rights are still a long way from taking hold in a manner that makes a concrete difference to people's lives and must still be described as a work in progress. The question now is whether such rights have earned sufficient respect and gained sufficient impetus to push further forward; and if so, how such progress can be achieved.

Stages in the Communication Rights Debate

Four stages can be discerned in the evolution of the international debate on communication rights, in terms of participants, content, and arenas of interaction.

1969-75: Launching of the Concept. Jean D'Arcy's ideas resonated first among media practitioners. Wider discussions were initially taken up by the International Institute for Communications (IIC), a professional association,[1] and from there began to reach a wider circle of academics, lawyers, communicators, and government officials. At this stage, the priority was to develop the concept further, to explore it in legal terms, and to determine what it might mean in practice.

1975-86: Onto, and Exit, a Major Stage. Soon the right to communicate found itself debated on a much larger platform, as it became linked to the discussion of a New World Information and Communication Order (NWICO). This debate took place at the level of international organizations and states and soon focused on the United Nations Educational, Scientific and Cultural Organization (UNESCO). It significantly changed the content and dynamic of discussion about communication rights in several ways.

1986-99: Regrouping in Civil Society. With the collapse of debate at UNESCO into acrimony and recrimination, discussion on the right to communicate continued at a much lower key, in some respects not only retreating to its initial manifestation among journalists and media practitioners but also, very importantly, opening to new constituencies of nongovernmental organizations (NGOs) and civil society activists.

1999-2006: Re-engaging in New Arenas. During the 1990s, debate and activism among civil society participants grew in various guises, but as the end of the decade approached, there was a danger of losing momentum. At this point, the World Summit on the Information Society (WSIS) presented an opportunity to move onto another plane. Specifically, the WSIS offered both an opening to link together the numerous groups active in issues central to a right to communicate – although many of these groups may not have recognized them as such – and an opportunity to initiate debate at the intergovernmental level, this time driven by voices from civil society. The opportunity was grasped and, given the compromised nature of the WSIS as a whole, the concept of communication rights probably progressed as far as it could.[2]

The circumstances, main actors, concerns, and dynamics of each phase were different, sometimes radically so. Nor can the process be characterized as one of steady progression. Each brought certain elements to the fore, achieving some success but also encountering failure. Nevertheless, overall the vicissitudes of nearly four decades of communication rights have led to many facets of the concept being explored and tested in a variety of contexts and against a diverse range of experiences. The fact that it has survived thus far, often against the extreme opposition of entrenched interests, is testimony to at least some degree of robustness and relevance of the core concept.

The world was not standing still during this period of experimentation and development, however. Earthshaking events impacted greatly on the directions taken by the debate, while the communications arena itself also saw great change. The Cold War was a major, largely regrettable influence during the NWICO phase, but there is no prospect in the foreseeable future of such a singular global political dynamic and subsequent implosion, with little directly to do with communication rights. The events of September 2001 in the United States triggered a series of actions and processes that have had serious impact on a range of human rights across the world, continuing to this day. Ultimately of more significance in the evolution of the communication rights debate, however, were trends and processes in the sphere of communication on a global scale. The "social cycle of communication," as described in Chapter 1, has been shaped and often misshapen by a number of interrelated developments at the global level:

- Communication between people, individually and as communities, has become more subject to technological mediation, particularly in poorer countries, where radio, television, and telecommunications continue to expand their coverage and accessibility.
- A wider range of media have opened up for people and communities seeking to have their voices heard, especially the Internet but also through the growth of various grassroots and community-based forms of interaction.
- Some critically important vehicles of mediation, especially mainstream media in the form of radio and television but also increasingly the Internet, have become more concentrated in ownership and control and more centralized in organization.
- Communication has been rapidly transformed into a commodified form, in both commercial and non-commercial interactions (including advertising and selling, as well as mass media content).
- Tendencies toward the homogenization of communication forms have continued, for example, in the form of the ongoing disappearance of marginal languages.
- The right to access and use creative knowledge has been ever more curtailed as the period of copyright monopoly has grown longer and its scope has been considerably reinforced in the digital era.

On balance, the collective impact of these factors on communication rights has been negative over the past few decades, but there is potential for some of them to enrich the social cycle of communication. The negative balance sheet is partly a result of changes in the level and nature of governance internationally. Compared with the early 1970s, international forums for discussion of communication issues between governments that also involve other actors, such as civil society and private sector organizations, have become fewer and weaker, to some extent as a result of the NWICO debate but largely because of the growth in corporate power globally and the strength of the neoliberal agenda. The influence of UN organizations such as the

International Telecommunication Union (ITU) and UNESCO has diminished. (A rare recent exception is the Internet Governance Forum process emerging from the WSIS, where a new and potentially innovative venue has emerged under the auspices of the United Nations, although it is not a decision-making body and its scope is limited to Internet governance.) The waning influence of United Nations intergovernmental organizations at a time of rapid globalization of communication and media technologies and industries has been accompanied by a related growth in influence of an unconstrained corporate sector facilitated by market-driven international organizations such as the World Trade Organization (WTO) and the World Bank (Ó Siochrú and Girard 2002).

Four Decades of Exploration

The processes and dynamics just described greatly shaped the debate on communication rights and the right to communicate, and the focus of each phase, as well as the participants and protagonists, was very much a product of its day.

The impetus for the first phase, from 1969 to the time UNESCO took up the debate, came primarily from early manifestations of the global communications revolution just getting underway. The belief was that the growing power and reach of the instruments of communication would inevitably lead to a change in the means of control over the means of communication, which in turn would demand a new and "more extensive right than man's right to information." Jean D'Arcy's seminal article, "Direct Broadcast Satellites and the Right to Communicate" (1969, 9), concluded: "If we bear in mind that social structures are created for man and that any attempt to maintain them once they have outlived their usefulness is bound to end in violence, we shall see that the direct broadcast satellite and its associated technology will lead to infinitely greater communication possibilities, to a real right to communicate in all its forms. On this road, time itself is of secondary importance; what counts is the will to get there in the end."

D'Arcy (1981, 2) argued a form of determinism, but one ultimately driven by people's desire and will to communicate, realized in the context of social structures that individuals collectively comprise and generate: "There are two forces at work: that which impels the individual, for his very existence's sake, to assert his right to communicate, thereby forming, through the communication established with his fellows, a society; and that which drives the society thus formed to work out, in order to be able to function and express itself, ever more elaborate means of communication leading to even more highly developed social structures."

Much of this first phase of discussion centred on ways in which this basic notion could be fleshed out in the context of human rights. The main aim was to reach agreement on a definition of the right to communicate with the intention of proposing its incorporation into the *Universal Declaration of Human Rights* or its adoption by the UN as a separate definition (Fisher 2002).

Implied in D'Arcy's formulation is that society is quite unproblematically constituted by the aggregation of individuals, that the whole is not that much greater than, or at least different from, the sum of its parts. This is questionable in a couple of ways, and problems emerged very quickly as the debate moved into its second phase within UNESCO.

The first difficulty encountered was the aggregate expression of individuals in the form of the nation-state, decidedly constituting more than the sum of its parts and with its own historical and political dynamics above and beyond individuals. In the context of the Cold War, most countries were associated with one side or the other in diametrically opposed dynamics, a struggle first and foremost between states. This opposition was also deeply embedded in the distinctive language of rights of each of the two blocs, and the great efforts devoted to coming up with a definition of a right to communicate that could bridge that gap tended, in the end, only to accentuate the differences. A fundamental question focused on the interpretation of individual versus collective rights. For instance, in the key area of freedom of expression, although all sides acknowledged the right to freedom of expression, the issue was whether the locus of this right resides with the individual, as in "everyone has the right to freedom of opinion and expression," or whether it is a right conferred by the state, as in "freedom of the press, freedom of speech shall be guaranteed by law." As Desmond Fisher (1982, 24) puts it: "The differences between the two concepts are fundamental and perhaps, too great to bridge. One, by recognising a right, places limits on the authority of the state; the other establishes the state as the guarantor and, therefore, the arbiter of freedoms. The first locates the right in the individual; the second accords it to amorphous groups such as 'society,' 'all persons' or 'the citizens.'"[3]

In the end, this tension proved to be a major factor in the breakdown of the NWICO and the subsequent fallout.

Although by now shorn of its global geopolitical distractions, a further limitation of D'Arcy's concept came to the fore gradually in the third phase, when civil society organizations picked up the communication rights idea and moved it forward. This was because the notion of society as constituted as an aggregation of individuals also ignores the structural imbalances inherent in the now-dominant capitalist system, both within and between countries and reinforced under the ascendant neoliberal order. The focus of debate during this period turned to these differences, and most of the statements from the MacBride Roundtables on Communication, which convened annually from 1989 to 1998, highlighted issues such as the growing concentration of media ownership in a few corporations, systematic exclusion of poor people and women in communication, and ready access to the affluent few (Traber and Nordenstreng 1992, especially 24-32). In effect, this led to a greater focus on social justice and also to consideration of the role of media and communication in wider cultural issues and determinations, beyond the idea of "cultural imperialism" and toward that of the influence of media on the culture of everyday life, identity, and existence.

Ostensibly, the theme adopted by communication rights activists in the fourth phase, specifically by those who came together as the Communication Rights in the Information Society (CRIS) campaign in the WSIS, was a straightforward declaration that since communication must evidently be at the heart of any information society (information being useless until it is communicated), the recognition of communication rights was an obvious constituent requirement. In reality, this was just a foot in the door, a starting point for what was a somewhat diverse, pragmatic, and even opportunistic approach. From the outset, the WSIS maintained the rhetoric of a deep-seated social, cultural, political, and economic transformation of society.[4] As the process unfolded, however, a narrow focus on technology, infrastructure, and a neoliberal approach became evident; many possible information societies contracted into one aspect and one vision. Such extravagant claims regarding the deeply transformative potential of information technology offered an array of possibilities for arguing the case for communication rights. For if the information society is indeed so significant, and if information and knowledge dissemination are at the heart of it, then surely the WSIS must go far beyond discussing the extension of information and communication technology infrastructure and use? Surely, all forms of media and communication, and all aspects of the creation, circulation, and management of knowledge, should be encompassed by the summit? Convincing governments and precipitating action were never going to be straightforward, however, since the WSIS itself was deeply compromised: most of those involved understood that it could not possibly deliver on its promises, given the extremely narrow terms within which any solution could be sought, both ideologically and in terms of the influence that the WSIS could hope to bring to bear subsequently on international institutions and actors (Ó Siochrú 2004b).

What the WSIS did offer was an opportunity to reach a much wider civil society audience, including a diverse constituency involved in communication issues as well as a chance to sound out more sympathetic governments on issues of communication.

During the preparatory and side events of the WSIS, communication rights were debated in several contexts. Human rights emerged as a contentious issue at an early stage, but this time between civil society organizations themselves rather than between civil society organizations and governments or between governments themselves. The NGO ARTICLE 19 published a highly critical comment on a draft CRIS campaign position, leading to a public debate on the right to communicate and what it might mean. The subsequent interaction of both sides proved enlightening, and an accommodation was in effect reached.[5]

As expected, the right to communicate barely impinged on the official intergovernmental negotiating and drafting process of the WSIS.[6] At one point in July 2003, an ad hoc working group was formed to consider wording that included the phrase "right to communicate" as part of the summit's official declaration.[7] The final formulation, interestingly, echoed certain phrases of the NWICO era,[8] but explicit reference to the right to communicate was dropped. Paragraph 4 of the WSIS Phase I Declaration of Principles reads: "Communication is a fundamental social process, a basic human need and the foundation of all social organization. It is central to the information society" (ITU 2003b). Since the right to communicate was not an established right, however, it could not be mentioned in an official WSIS declaration.[9]

The greatest impact in terms of communication rights at the WSIS was undoubtedly the extent to which the concept came to be widely discussed and accepted among a broad range of actors in civil society. The WSIS – and not insignificant credit must go to the CRIS campaign for this – brought together sections of civil society involved in communications that hitherto were barely aware of UN processes and global governance institutions. They came from very different areas – activists in open source software, privacy, copyright, and human rights working alongside practitioners in community radio, development communication, and rural telecommunications – many for the first time encountering issues beyond their own particular spheres. Although it would be an exaggeration to say that they united under the idea of communication rights, it is at least true that the term became for many a broad umbrella covering a range of issues that had to do with communication and development in the widest sense. This was evident also in the success of many of the side events, including the World Forum on Communication Rights held alongside the first phase of the WSIS in Geneva in December 2003. Thus, communication rights, like the CRIS campaign itself, acted more as the unifying idea of a process around which civil society groups organized than as the subject of a focused debate.

Apart from the WSIS, other arenas reinforced the idea of communication rights as a concept capable of bringing together disparate groups under a single umbrella, at least in the right context. Between 2002 and 2005, communication rights were represented at successive World Social Forums, sometimes prominently and always attracting a diverse group of activists concerned with media and communication. But the implementation of the Communication Rights Assessment Framework and Toolkit (CRAFT) on communication rights in four countries in 2004 was probably most revealing of this effort. Those implementing the framework, which involved research and action across a range of communication areas, confirmed that the process helped to build bridges between a broad range of groups, stimulated broad debate on communication, and enabled the identification of key common areas and the development of strategies for action.[10]

The WSIS and its preparatory meetings provided a ready-made and ongoing forum for the various elements and concerns of communications rights to come together, develop positions, and engage with other actors. Although the process of establishing communications rights is now a few years into a new and critical phase, its shape is not yet fully defined, offering interested parties an opportunity to significantly influence it.

Taking Stock and Moving Forward

What do these issues, debates, outcomes, and processes tell us about communication rights today, and whether and how they can move forward? What is the legacy of these four decades, and how can the experiences best be utilized? Sorting through them chronologically reveals a lot of useful material and several directions that might be taken.

The idea that much human endeavour is motivated by a deep-seated desire to communicate, which in turn leads to elaborate social institutional structures and the need for ever more sophisticated communication technologies, was not unique to D'Arcy and was widespread in different forms from the late 1960s onwards. For instance, it was and remains an ongoing preoccupation in the sphere of engaged philosophy.[11] Although it might be academically interesting to pursue these angles in more depth, an absence of articulated and elaborate philosophical underpinnings is not at this point inhibiting the advance of communication rights. Consideration of the encounter between the impetus for communication rights outlined above and the real world of national/global politics and of injustice may yield more, beginning with the interaction with human rights dimensions.

The Human Rights Debate

Initially, as we saw, discussion on communication rights focused on the question of the collective versus individual expression of human rights at the state level, especially on freedom of expression and related rights (Fisher 1982). With the demise of most state regimes espousing this particular collective view (the most significant exception being China), and given that this issue as it relates to national constitutions no longer resonates in international institutions in relation to communication rights, the intergovernmental argument is currently redundant.

Communication rights have a more complex relationship with wider human rights constituencies in civil society, beyond freedom of expression and related issues. Successfully bringing arguments to wider civil society might create opportunities for communication rights advocates to make common cause on areas of overlapping interest. Existing human rights, mutually reinforced in national and international law, are potent weapons in the hands of activists and advocates at national and international levels, even where their observance and potential for enforcement leave a lot to be desired.

Yet the general, or "core," human rights arena is unlikely to be the central ground on which communication rights can be fought and won. Those at the forefront of human rights struggles, waged on many fronts and in many arenas, still confront strong resistance to their efforts to incorporate core human rights into national law and enforcement systems; internationally, it is an uphill struggle to create and consolidate legal instruments and institutions that can address human rights beyond national boundaries. Seeking recognition of a right to communicate, or of communication rights as a distinct combination of existing rights, does not always resonate compellingly in the turmoil of efforts to confront crimes against humanity and gross breaches of basic human rights. This was the experience, for instance, of the CRIS campaign in its attempt to encourage NGOs such as Amnesty International (as well as the UN High Commissioner for Human Rights) to become involved in communication rights issues in the WSIS. This is not because of an inherent weakness in arguments for communication rights. Rather, this sphere understandably tends to be populated by activists, lawyers, and institutions concerned primarily with "frontline" human rights issues.

If the general human rights arena is unlikely to advance the case for communication rights, the specific subgroup of freedom of expression and related rights, on the other hand, is certainly relevant even – or rather especially – with the demise of the Cold War division on this. The significance of the debate at the WSIS, in which ARTICLE 19 and the CRIS campaign could reach a rapprochement on key contentious questions, was that it cleared an obstacle to debate with the wider freedom of expression community. This was useful and is still relevant.

The arguments described in Chapter 1 concerning the "generational" approach to human rights tend to further distance and insulate the debate on communication rights within this subgroup from the divisive issue of individual versus collective rights. If mainstream human rights thinking has indeed already moved in this direction, this is a useful corrective that merits further examination and explication in order to build a comprehensive foundation for the deployment of the human rights arguments and to deflect what may be regarded at this point as spurious objections relating to individual versus collective rights.

This clears the path for what is among the most powerful of arguments that can be made for communication rights, strongly advocated here and at many points in the debate over the last decade: that freedom of expression, even where fully protected to the highest standards, is simply incapable, in the context of today's media and communication structures, of guaranteeing that everyone's voice can be heard in society. This core argument immediately draws attention to the multiple structures and forces that in practice limit freedom of expression for most people while augmenting it disproportionately for a powerful minority. It holds that the ideal of freedom of expression cannot be realized unless these issues are addressed and that addressing them demands the recognition of a broader concept, that of communication rights.

By its very nature, this argument also points beyond human rights toward another strand of thinking on communication rights, one that has been growing in importance ever since the communication rights impetus moved to civil society and away from governments: communication rights as a matter of social justice. In fact, the "unfulfilled freedom of expression" argument is perhaps more likely to be taken up by those working in the context of social justice – motivated by the persistence of real inequalities and power imbalances – than by those promoting freedom of expression within the current rights regime.

Social Justice

The social justice paradigm differs from that of the rights paradigm in a critical respect.

Human rights are anchored securely in the existing International Bill of Rights.[12] From this perspective, even if boundaries are stretched, as they are with some interpretations of communication rights, progress is necessarily incremental and cannot stray far from this baseline. Partly this is tactical: the International Bill of Rights has the virtue of being a legally recognized instrument nominally adhered to by virtually every government in the world. This makes it a powerful weapon. The focus is on implementing what already exists in law; hence the term "human rights" seems almost "apolitical," a neutral term that summons up images of lawyers, rational argument, and adjudication within existing systems.

The social justice approach, on the other hand, begins not with the idea of rights but with evident realities and verifiable injustices. It is concerned more with the actual conditions that people live in than with the set of legal circumstances that, in principle, should lead to or encourage certain outcomes. What is required is enforcement of justice for people who have been denied the means to achieve their rights in practice – economic, social, cultural, civil, and political – not equality before the law in relation to these rights. Social justice conjures up visions of marches, demonstrations, direct action – ultimately people taking matters into their own hands and responding in a direct and visceral manner. From the perspective of a government, social justice threatens the status quo; from the point of view of civil society, it can, for that very reason, be empowering and motivating.

The difference between social justice and human rights is not just about a demand for effective enforcement. At its base, a social justice approach holds out the possibility that the fundamental structures of society, such as those governing ownership of the means of production or the global terms of trade, may require radical change before justice can be achieved. The human rights perspective does not. The current regime was carefully circumscribed at the time of its drafting in the mid-twentieth century to exclude such radical possibilities. This is not necessarily a criticism: were basic human rights being formulated by the governments of today, they would undoubtedly be even narrower. Any global legal structure formulated by governments will inevitably be similarly constrained, with strong downward pressure toward the lowest common denominator. Advocates of social justice, however, are free to seek the full range of solutions that appear necessary to right the wrongs that exist.

Aligning communication rights more closely with the social justice approach was extensively discussed and ultimately agreed upon by the CRIS campaign toward the end of the WSIS, with human rights and social justice often mentioned in the same breath.[13] The explicit rationale for this was in part to facilitate alliances between rights-based groups and those pursuing more radical social justice agendas, such as questioning the very basis and legitimacy of the neoliberal paradigm shaping the communication agenda. This was driven by a perception that gaps in the rights regime per se were not among the main barriers to achieving communication rights in practice, and that working from a social justice perspective allowed for a wider range and depth of possible responses and strategies.

Development Paradigm

Another possibility emerges in relation to arguing the case for communication rights in the context of the development paradigm – that is, in the context of states, international organizations, and processes concerned (at least ostensibly) with improving the economic, social, and political prospects of poorer countries and communities within them. Of course, the second phase of communication rights – the NWICO and the wider New International Economic Order (NIEO) – can be read as being concerned with development and, indeed, with shifting the terms of the development paradigm. But the approach to development today could not be further from this, with the transformation of the global development context in the neoliberal image during the intervening period and the relationships between rich and poor countries.

There is some evidence of a growing awareness among mainstream actors of the role of media and communication in development. This comes from a few directions. Independent media are recognized as a key factor in good governance, increasingly seen by major donor countries as a critical requirement of development. Furthermore, the idea of giving excluded communities "voice" through media, particularly community media, is gaining ground. A recent guidebook funded by the World Bank on policy, law, and regulation for the broadcasting sector in a development context draws attention to a significant and growing interest in these concepts.[14] Direct links and references are made to the idea of the public sphere as a central tenet of democracy. In addition, many media development practitioners and writers, such as those pursuing a communication for social change approach,[15] argue that the communication process has a key role in empowerment and in identity and cultural formation.

Thus, various components of communication rights are gradually making an appearance in the development literature and practice based on a growing understanding of the central role that communication can play in sustainable development processes.

At this time, it is difficult to see communication rights playing a central role in the context of the main dynamics of mainstream development organizations, except possibly in reinforcing certain arguments. Rather, any influence on development dynamics is likely to come tangentially from local or international interests' arguing from rights and social justice positions in areas where these intersect with development concerns. Nevertheless, this may change.

Communication Rights as Animator

Having considered the potential for the concept of communication rights within the substantive approaches of human rights, social justice, and development, we return to their process-oriented role, referred to several times earlier. Communication rights have been used not only as a body of specific ideas but also as a means of animating a process within the domain loosely circumscribed by the concept. The multidimensional nature of communication rights can have a specific value in bringing together a diversity of groups under a single umbrella, and enabling a degree of convergence of agendas and actions. This was the case especially in the WSIS among civil society organizations, in some World Social Forum activities, and in some of the countries where the CRAFT has been implemented.

This specific character of communication rights can be analyzed as one of a set of factors that potentially contribute to the emergence and mobilization of advocacy campaigns and movements at national and international levels.[16] One of the key challenges of mobilization is the need to "frame" the issue in a manner that will resonate with as wide a constituency as possible, most immediately with "adjacent" advocacy groups involved in wider media, communication, and cultural issues around the world. "Cognitive framing" is an attempt to enable actors outside an immediate advocacy group to comprehend the arguments presented within their own context and can encourage and guide collaborative action. The goal is to undertake and disseminate interpretative work that can engage wider advocacy networks and ultimately public understanding, by achieving both internal coherence and alignment with key components of the broader political culture. Examples might include the manner in which environmental issues were first framed (for instance, "save the whale/planet") and the reframing of "female circumcision" into the more accurate, and effective, "genital mutilation." These examples illustrate the role that emotive factors can play in successfully framing an issue, but other factors are also important. For instance, the frame should be capable of pointing to a logical progression demonstrating that a problem is not inevitable, that those responsible can be identified, and that credible solutions can be designed, proposed, and implemented. Of course, not all of this can be contained within a single phrase, but the frame chosen should lend itself readily to such elaboration.

The range of issues and global processes covered by communication rights and influencing the social communication cycle does not, at the intuitive level, immediately comply with this scheme. Framing is most easily achieved where there is a simple and direct connection between the source of the problem and the victim. But there is very seldom a direct and obvious link between negative communication trends and their victims. There are few smoking guns, no images of children dying from media and communication malnutrition. Only in very exceptional circumstances do media extract a direct human toll.[17] Just as the processes and multiple actors influencing the social cycle of communication are themselves interrelated, so any attempt to explicate the issues in clear terms must be relatively complex.

Thus, the challenge facing those arguing for communication rights as a cognitive frame is that the concept is highly compressed, containing a wealth of issues that require significant unpacking before they resonate more widely: there appears to be too large a chasm between such a condensed concept and the issues it attempts to connote; too many dots to join, too many uncertainties, choices, and twists for it to resonate in the right direction – indeed, in the several directions needed – from so many different starting points.

The effectiveness of the term "communication rights" derives in part from this complexity, however.

For those who rallied around communication rights before and during the WSIS, for the many hundreds participating in the World Forum on

Communication Rights and sessions at the World Social Forum, and for those who became involved in national-level advocacy of communication rights through implementation of the CRAFT, complexity was the issue. Although each might be involved in one area – community radio, copyright constraints, cultural homogenization – most were keenly aware that their area intersected with a much wider set of communication processes and that a resolution might demand wider coordinated action.[18] To take a few examples, most are aware, at least, of the growing corporate control globally of knowledge generation and communication processes of all kinds; would understand that the WTO is playing a much larger role in governing trade relations and in restructuring and constraining national media sectors; and would recognize a connection between these processes and the commodification of all communication forms in everyday life. What the concept of communication rights offers is a frame wide enough to encompass such diversity and complexity, one capable of sparking connections in diverse yet complementary directions. Even if it does not immediately boil down into simple propositions and identify culprits and solutions, it creates the basis for dialogue and fosters a common recognition of the complexity of any solution. At the same time, the concept manages to retain its integrity and direct appeal: that everyone has the right to communicate, to be listened to, and to be heard.

What is appealing about the concept of communication rights is this combination of a generic but meaningful specific appeal that can be resolved quickly, with the aid of the social cycle of communication concept or the communication rights assessment framework, into a range of complex generalities needed to address the root of the problem. The concept, if properly elucidated, carries the user from the particular to the general and back to the particular, but now enriched with connections to other particulars.

Communication rights is thus a useful frame for those already involved in and concerned about specific areas of social communication processes, and a useful conceptual space within which they can begin to collectively tease out the interconnections between different communication issues and processes and explore the wider picture. Groups and individuals coming from human rights, social justice, or development perspectives on communication, to name a few, can meet on the common ground of communication rights and explore ways to learn, collaborate, and move forward together.

While the concept of communication rights thus potentially offers an effective cognitive frame for activists and practitioners in a number of inter-related areas, the job of reaching, motivating, and influencing wider audiences and the public requires additional and more specific conceptual and analytical effort. Ideally, the concept of cognitive framing as a means of involving and motivating wider publics concerning an issue involves direct and explicit logical links between issues and solutions, something that as we noted is extremely difficult to establish in the sphere of communication. To achieve it, the concept of communication rights must be resolved into a more detailed array of current key issues, and each of these must be explained in its own right – each specific issue being framed in a direct and widely comprehensible manner but within the wider framework. Examples might include "building the public sphere," "giving voice to the people," "expanding the public domain," "enclosure and the public commons," "saving the legacy of linguistic diversity," "civil rights in media," "reversing media pollution," "media justice," and any number of other issues or "subframes" that can both directly assist in illuminating a particular question and act as a springboard into the common complex of issues surrounding social communication.[19]

Of course, this process of resolving communication rights into constituent parts depends largely on which groups of activists and practitioners recognize the concept's potential as a means to achieve their own ends and on how well those promoting communication rights can reach out to them through means such as the CRAFT. The ultimate effectiveness of the combined effort will also depend on, among other things, the topicality of the key issues selected and their potential to mobilize wider publics and influence policy.

At this point, however, it is perhaps sufficient to establish the credentials of communication rights as a potential cognitive frame in the wider sphere of social communication.

The Experience of Implementing the Framework

Going beyond these more or less theoretical considerations, the implementation of the CRAFT in four countries gives us a glimpse of what communication rights might mean in practice as a mobilizing tool. All four research-and-advocacy-oriented NGOs or networks that undertook the work described some of their experiences of the process.

In Brazil, a loose network of media/communication activists and NGOs called Intervozes oversaw the work and through the process gained significantly in internal cohesion: "Through this rich interaction between organizations and specialists, the team believes that the concept of communication rights, broad as it is, greatly assists the development of actions among them, allowing them to realize that all are participating in the same struggle ... Communication rights relate to many different aspects, but they must always be observed as a whole" (Intervozes 2005a, 5).

In the Philippines, too, the NGO leading the work, the Centre for Media Alternatives, remarked: "We feel that the Research project had a positive impact in integrating various threads of advocacies under the Communication Rights umbrella. This was positively seen by the fact that different constituencies – media rights advocates, ICT for Development practitioners, telco regulators, NGOs using online tools ... began to see the thread of their issues as being interrelated, at least on the conceptual level" (Somera and Alegre 2005, 6).

In Colombia, an NGO promoting human rights and peace coordinated the work and described a process of interaction between academic research and grassroots organizations that led to "opening a space for communication as a right, institutionally and within the framework of the demands of diverse grass-roots sectors" (Planet Peace Project n.d.a, 5). The human rights agenda in Colombia is already closely linked to social justice.

These experiences tend to validate the efficacy of the concept of communication rights in terms of its potential to open a common space and create a lexicon for discussion of a range of communication issues. But the CRAFT was also implemented through a specific process, more or less similar in each country. This involved a number of workshops where the issues were raised, interviews and consultations, a verification process that brought the main stakeholders together, and the selection of priorities for future action. In some cases, such as Kenya and the Philippines, those involved included senior policy makers, media/communication practitioners, advocacy NGOs, academics, and others. This process of implementing the CRAFT became a key initial part of the advocacy activity.

Brazil reported that the "research report was political enough to unify those interested in communication rights and wide enough to unite actors of several different areas." It continued: "In the long term, however, it could be interesting to use this generic framework as a tool for political intervention in the communication rights status quo. The idea of creating committees or organisations councils could be evaluated, or even high-level panels linked to communication rights, that could analyse the situation regarding each approached issue (not only as a validation process, but a broad view of the data and figures). That would allow an effective link between research and direct action" (Intervozes 2005a, 5).

Somewhat similarly, in Kenya, where the work was undertaken by key members of a multi-stakeholder advocacy network, consideration was given to repeating the process as part of an advocacy effort: "Generally the team believes that the framework will eventually add impetus to advocacy efforts in communications rights. We anticipate that the status review, if updated, will play a significant role in creating a linkage between hitherto disparate sectors: information and telecommunications, broadcasting regulation and communication rights in general" (Gatheru and Mureithi n.d., 3).

Based on the process, the teams concluded the work with the identification of a small number of priority areas. The selection rationale varied but consensus on the gravity of the issue in terms of processes of social communication and the potential it offered for advocacy across a broad collaborative front were common to all of them.

Each of the four teams had implemented a common or "generic" version of the communication rights framework, and a final event brought together all the teams to compare results and plan follow-up. There was agreement that the work had enabled them to develop a common language and understanding of communication rights, facilitating later collaboration at the international level within the context of the WSIS and elsewhere.

As a whole, the experience of implementing the communication rights framework not only confirmed the potential of the concept of communication rights as an animator of collaborative advocacy at the national and international levels but also underlined the role of designing a process specifically to realize this potential.

The deployment of the CRAFT framework in this book differs in some ways from its earlier use. The process here was more research oriented and academic in nature and lacked a direct advocacy aspect. The CRAFT itself acknowledges that there are two distinct approaches to assessing communication rights (CRIS 2005a, 53). The four initial countries implementing the framework adopted the "mobilization approach," pursuing the process of research, drafting, and verification primarily to generate a common understanding of the concept and begin the process of mobilizing major stakeholders, especially civil society, around it. The other approach is the "political-influence approach." Here the emphasis is on the credibility of the research and on an objective, dispassionate, and nonpartisan approach, the impact of which comes from presenting evidence that is not easy to ignore and difficult to refute.

This book fits squarely in the latter tradition. The vertical and horizontal planes bring both breadth and depth to the discussion of communication rights in Canada. In terms of the rigour and thoroughness of research, it goes well beyond what has been achieved elsewhere and provides a wealth of material that can be drawn upon by a range of actors who might take this forward. It summarizes succinctly and with originality the history of communication rights both internationally and in Canada and clearly delineates the contours of the concept. It systematically assesses the key components of communication rights in Canada beyond the formal legal level, moving toward what the reality is on the ground. It delves in depth into a number of critical areas, gaining insight through original empirical research and interaction. And it proposes a range of practical and far-reaching suggestions for enhancing communication rights in Canada and bringing them to the forefront of practice in this area.

PART 2

Communication Rights in Canada – An Assessment

3
The Horizontal View

Marc Raboy and Jeremy Shtern

As the universal communication rights framework described in Part 1 has emerged over the past sixty years, Canada has proudly signed the international instruments on which it is based. Universal communication rights must therefore be seen as intrinsically Canadian communication rights, and the notion of communication rights, in this respect, relates immediately to a set of existing human rights promised to all Canadians. These commitments, however, are in many cases repeated, further elaborated, and even occasionally circumvented or contradicted through domestic human rights law and communication policy, not only through the structure of the Canadian policy framework for governing communication but also in the practices associated with them.[1]

The task of assessing communication rights in Canada thus involves mapping and evaluating the various domestic laws and policies that impact communication in Canada.

As a basis for assessing the extent to which Canada's legal framework is adequate to the diverse purposes that we might imagine for law and public policy in supporting democratic communication under contemporary conditions, the approach adopted in this study is concerned not only with the analytical question of the extent to which this framework guarantees communication rights to Canadians but also with the empirical question of the degree to which communication rights are actually realized on the ground. Toward these ends, we conducted an assessment of the current state of communication rights in Canada, using the Communication Rights Assessment Framework and Toolkit (CRAFT).

As explained in the Introduction and discussed in Chapter 2, the CRAFT is a methodological tool developed by the Communication Rights in the Information Society (CRIS) campaign to structure and guide inquiries by civil society groups into the status of communication rights in a given society. In the Introduction, we introduced the CRAFT, described how we adapted and employed it, and reflected on how it shaped our assessment of communication rights in Canada.

In this chapter, we present the results of our CRAFT assessment on the state of a series of issues fundamental to communication rights in Canada: freedom of expression; freedom of the press and media; access to information; diversity of content in the media and plurality of media sources; access to the means of communication; access to knowledge; right to equality before the law, to one's honour and reputation, and to protection against unwarranted damage to them; the right to privacy; minority cultural and linguistic rights; and the right to self-determination and to take part in government.

Later, in the subsequent chapters of Part 2, we will return to look at the state of communication rights in each of the five principal thematic areas that fed our assessment: media, access, Internet, privacy, and copyright.

Freedom of Expression

Section 2(b) of Canada's most important human rights document, the *Canadian Charter of Rights and Freedoms,* establishes the right to "freedom of thought, belief, opinion and expression, including freedom of the press and other media of communication."[2] Section 1 of the *Charter* establishes that all *Charter* rights are subject to "reasonable limits prescribed by law as can be demonstrably justified in a free and democratic society." Supreme Court of Canada jurisprudence accepts limits on *Charter* rights where they deal with pressing and substantial social problems to which the government's response is reasonably and demonstrably justified (Trudel 1984). With regard to freedom of expression, such responses are viewed as "reasonable" where they do what is required in order to pursue truth, political or social participation, and self-fulfillment, but no more (Moon 2008; see also *R. v. Zundel* and *Ross v. New Brunswick School District No. 15*).[3]

In his treatise *The Constitutional Protection of Freedom of Expression,* Moon (2000, 40) describes section 2(b) of the *Charter* as an individualistic understanding of freedom of expression. "The Supreme Court of Canada," he maintains, "like most contemporary commentators, draws on both listener-centred and speaker-centred accounts of the value of freedom of expression." This would seem to imply that there might be some scope for approaching expression as a communicative process within the application of freedom of expression by Canadian courts. Furthermore, commentators point to the judgment in the case of *R.W.D.S.U., Local 558 v. Pepsi-Cola Canada Beverages*

(West) Ltd.,[4] where Chief Justice McLachlin and Justice LeBel, writing for the Supreme Court of Canada, argued that freedom of expression "is fundamental not only to the identity and self-worth of individual workers and the strength of their collective effort, but also to the functioning of a democratic society" (paragraph 69). This has been interpreted by some commentators as indication that juridical application of *Charter* section 2(b) approaches it as a fundamental Canadian value that should be distinguished from concern for the economy and individual economic concerns. Schneiderman (2004, 12), for instance, makes the case that "Chief Justice McLachlin and Justice LeBel, writing for the Court, distinguished between 'fundamental Canadian value[s],' like freedom of expression, and those diverse interests served by the common law and 'not engaged by the *Charter*. Salient among these are the life of the economy and individual economic interests' (see also *R.W.D.S.U. v. Pepsi-Cola Canada* 2002 at para 44)."

Thus, an argument can be made that conventional interpretation of *Charter* section 2(b) as applied to the Canadian legal system at present is more dynamic and robust than the one-way treatment of freedom of expression that we discussed in the Introduction. *Charter* section 2(b) cannot be conflated with the right to communicate, however; it does not address the entire process of communication in society in a cyclical and holistic fashion.

Moon (2000, 41) points out that, in spite of acknowledgment in Canadian jurisprudence that *Charter* section 2(b) applies to both speakers and listeners, "the court's focus on the individual interests of the speaker and/or listener misses the communicative relationship that joins the interests of speaker and listener." Schneiderman (2004, 12), meanwhile, qualifies his endorsement of the broad notion of freedom of expression advocated by the *R.W.D.S.U. v. Pepsi-Cola Canada* decision with the caveat that "the Court, however, has not always been faithful to these presuppositions."

The recent case law around the efforts of the Adbusters Media Foundation to procure advertising time for its anti-consumerist message is one of the strongest examples of the difficulty that Canadians can face when trying to exercise their freedom of expression in the Canadian media and of the distinction between *Charter* section 2(b) and the ambitious claims of a right to communicate.

Adbusters is a not-for-profit organization founded in 1989 and based in Vancouver.[5] The organization is highly critical of the place of advertising and consumption in North American culture and has produced over the years a number of television spots that question these practices. Adbusters was repeatedly informed by the major private and public Canadian networks that the ads were not appropriate for commercial television. In the end, with a couple of exceptions, none of the spots was ever aired.

The business of selling advertising is a crucial revenue stream for commercial and public broadcasters in Canada. Communication firms should not, however, be required to air any and all advertising that they are presented with. Broadcasters should be able to reject potential advertising customers if, for instance, they are not willing or able to pay for the time they are requesting, or if the ads they are hoping to air are not of acceptably professional production values. In the case of Adbusters, however, these issues were not in play. The Adbusters advertisements were professionally produced, and the organization had every intention of paying the commercial rate to have them broadcast on Canadian television.

Furthermore, there are a variety of rules that restrict the ability of communication firms to accept advertising in certain situations, even if they wanted to. It is illegal, for example, to use the media to disseminate hate speech in Canada (see Moon 2008), and during elections the *Canada Elections Act* regulates the advertising time that each political party is permitted to purchase and prohibits third-party groups from buying political advertisements (part 16).[6] These were not issues in the *Adbusters* case. Rather, Adbusters alleged that its spots were rejected because the "anti-consumerist message of the advertisements was inconsistent with the [networks'] business models and [with] their perception of the preferences of their commercial clientele" (see *Adbusters Media Foundation v. Canadian Broadcasting Corporation*).[7]

The level of discretionary censorship and self-interest that Canadian broadcasters seem to be able to exercise in keeping the gates to Canada's mass media system should raise concerns about the diversity of voices in the public sphere. Arguing that the refusal to accept its ads was a violation of the group's freedom of expression, Adbusters undertook legal action against two Canadian broadcasters (CanWest Global Television and the Canadian Broadcasting Corporation [CBC]) in 2005. The organization argued that, by denying access to publicly regulated frequencies, the broadcasters were practising arbitrary, self-interested censorship of public speech, in violation of *Charter* section 2(b). In a 2008 decision, Justice Ehrcke of the British Columbia Supreme Court supported an earlier 1995 ruling of Justice Holmes that Canadian commercial broadcasters, despite being licensed by a government agency, are also private entities engaged in commercial activities and thus should not be subject to *Charter* section 2(b) claims; and that "the Charter does not apply to the CBC either as a governmental body or as a broad-caster generally" (*Adbusters Media Foundation v. Canadian Broadcasting Corporation*, paragraph 26; *Adbusters Media Foundation v. Canadian Broadcasting Corp.*,[8] paragraph 48).

This is a key point in that a defining characteristic of the *Charter*'s legal personality is the principle established in the landmark 1990 case of *McKinney v. University of Guelph*, where Justice La Forest ruled that "the Charter is confined to government action ... the Charter is essentially an instrument for checking the powers of government over the individual" (paragraph 261).[9] In his 1995 ruling, Justice Holmes reiterated that, no matter how close the administrative links are between the organization in question and the government, "the conduct in issue of the entity in question" must be found to be "governmental in nature to give rise to Charter application" (paragraph 31). On this basis, Justice Holmes determined that the CBC and CanWest were not exercising governmental functions in their dealings with Adbusters.[10]

In other words, the essentially commercial activity that constitutes the majority of the activities of the Canadian media, including those of the national public broadcaster, are not seen as being governmental in nature by the courts and are therefore not subject to *Charter* scrutiny. Effectively, this means that *Charter* section 2(b) does not guarantee freedom of expression through the media, even through the public broadcaster, even for Canadians who are willing and able to pay for advertising. The judgment thus confirmed the property right of media owners to decide what was in their interests to publish.[11]

The *Adbusters* case raises many questions. *Adbusters* magazine editor-in-chief Kalle Lasn (as quoted in the 2008 decision), for one, wonders why CanWest and the CBC are "selling as much time as they possibly can to corporations, while fighting expensive legal actions to keep citizen-produced messages off the air?" In asking, "Why doesn't the Canadian Charter apply to the most powerful social communications medium of our age – television?" Lasn argues that "this case goes to the very heart of what our democracy is all about." The *Adbusters* case goes a long way to get to the heart of what communication rights and the right to communicate are all about as well.

The constitutional guarantee of freedom of expression alone does not determine the robustness of free speech. While it is perhaps more dramatic to imagine that governments need to employ shock troops and use coercive power backed by the threat of violence in order to constrain or censor the free expression of their citizenry, the fragility of free speech on the ground in

Canada is also to be seen in the everyday workings of government. The episode of Bill C-10 underlines how the realization of communication rights can be at stake in all areas of government policy making. Bill C-10 incited public outcry about government efforts to censor artistic expression in Canada through, of all things, an amendment to the *Income Tax Act*.[12]

Domestic film and television productions receive significant government subsidies in Canada, as well as tax credits to help defray the costs of production. Bill C-10, an omnibus bill amending the *Income Tax Act*, was presented to Parliament in October 2007. Section 12 of the bill would allow the heritage minister to deny tax credits to certain productions on the basis of the morality of their content, even after federal agencies responsible for subsidies, such as Telefilm Canada and the Canadian Television Fund, had already invested in the production.

Then Heritage Minister Josée Verner has said that "Bill C-10 has nothing to do with censorship and everything to do with the integrity of the tax system ... The goal is to ensure public trust in how tax dollars are spent" (quoted in Noakes 2008) and to create a process in which the government of Canada is able to "take fiscal measures to make sure that the Canadian taxpayers' money won't fund extreme violence, child pornography or something like that" (quoted in Worboy 2008).

Under Bill C-10, the decision to withhold tax credits would be made by representatives of the Heritage and Justice departments (Canada 2007a). Given the structure of Canadian film and television production deals – where tax credits can spell the difference between a sure loss and a chance to turn a profit – a decision to withhold tax credits would essentially ensure that a project would never see the light of day. Insidiously, the *possibility* of such a decision would have a chilling effect on freedom of expression by steering artists and producers away from themes and contents that could be seen as problematic by the Heritage and Justice departments.[13] Bill C-10 also includes the potential for after-the-fact direct censorship in the ability of a tax-credit ruling to bankrupt an ongoing project and prevent it from being completed.[14]

Pointing out that laws already exist to prohibit offensive media content, and reiterating that such laws have been adopted and balanced against freedom of expression through due process and not by virtue of summary decisions made by politicians and civil servants, legal scholar Pierre Trudel (2008) calls Bill C-10 "an unjustifiable violation of the freedom of expression." The reaction of Canadian film director David Cronenberg, who has forged much of his international reputation as one of the pre-eminent art house filmmakers of his generation by exploring edgy themes in his often sexually explicit and graphically violent films, was more visceral: "It sounds like something they do in Beijing" (quoted in CBC News 2008b).

There is certainly a larger issue at stake in this discussion about the lack of enthusiasm that the Canadian public outside of Quebec has shown for the art house, *auteur* material that is regularly produced by taxpayer-subsidized Canadian filmmakers. The controversy that was created when the government attempted to use Bill C-10 to define the mainstream for Canadian film production in moral rather than market-based terms underscores two points that are crucial in evaluating the realization of freedom of expression in Canada. First, because of extensive government intervention in the sphere of cultural production, as well as the high stakes of Canadian identity politics, freedom of expression in Canada is particularly contingent upon what we call "flanking rights," and these are often dependent on regulations and policies in a variety of areas not directly covered by the *Charter*. Bill C-10 should be seen not as an isolated issue but as one iteration of a type of policy controversy wherein the limits of what constitutes acceptable politicization of freedom of expression are at stake. Second, Canadians may be free to say what they choose on a soapbox or in their bedrooms, but access and capacity to use our system of mass communication is not universal or guaranteed. To the extent that technologically mediated communication in a modern society depends on such access, formal recognition of the right to freedom of expression, as precious as it is, is insufficient.

Freedom of the Press and of Media

Freedom of the press is addressed in section 2(b) of the *Canadian Charter of Rights and Freedoms*, which includes "other media of communication." The idea that freedom of the press applies to "other media of communication" as well has been the accepted understanding of freedom of the press in Canada since the 1979 case of *CKOY Ltd. v. R.*, in which Justice Spence declared: "I am ready to assume that the broadcasting media may be presumed to be defined within the word 'press' in matters related to freedom of the press" (14) (see also Trudel 1984).[15]

As we discuss in Chapter 4, the Canadian press has not been subjected to formal legal constraint except in situations deemed to be of national emergency. Our assessment suggests, however, that freedom of the press in Canada is currently undermined by the absence of effective policy responses to related developments, including structural forces within the media industries, the emergence of new media platforms, and the post-9/11 security environment.

The highly concentrated ownership of the Canadian media makes journalists vulnerable to various strong-arm tactics that undermine their journalistic integrity; permanent positions are subject to economic rationalization and freelancers have little bargaining power where there is little competition for their services. Journalists have little leverage to negotiate final editorial say and who controls the copyright to their work. This is discussed in greater detail in Chapter 8.

A series of recent cases discussed in Chapter 4 illustrate how the work of professional journalists is being undermined by post-9/11 security measures in Canada. The crucially important ability of journalists to protect the confidentiality of their would-be-anonymous sources in particular is undermined by legislation such as the *Security of Information Act*.[16] Nowhere do the policies and institutions regulating communication in Canada focus explicitly on protecting journalists and ensuring that the guarantee of a free and independent press and media declared in the *Charter* is actually enforced (see Schultz 2005 and Canada 2006b).

Furthermore, the emergence of new newsgathering and diffusion practices that are intimately linked to the Internet and mobile technologies demands a reconsideration of who is entitled to claim freedom of the press in Canada. In Chapter 6, we discuss the case of Charles LeBlanc, a Saint John resident who keeps a blog dedicated to his observations and criticisms of the activities of the New Brunswick provincial legislature. In 2006, LeBlanc's pictures were erased and he was arrested and charged with obstruction while covering a conference in Saint John after police summarily decided that he was a protester and not a journalist – and hence not entitled to freedom of the press.

Overall, the inability to draw on an explicit framework that would allow journalists and press freedom activists to respond effectively to a changing media landscape reveals how precarious the protection of freedom of the press is in Canadian law and policy. In the 2006 edition of the "World Press Freedom Index" compiled by the international NGO Reporters Without Borders, Canada tied for sixteenth place (with Austria and Bolivia) in terms of "the degree of freedom journalists and news organizations enjoy in each country, and the efforts made by the state to respect and ensure respect for this freedom" (Reporters Without Borders 2006). By 2009, Canada had dropped to nineteenth spot (Reporters Without Borders 2009).

Access to Information

The *Access to Information Act* aims to provide every Canadian with the right of access to records (in any format) held under the control of a government institution, subject to certain specific and limited exceptions.[17] An officer of Parliament, the information commissioner of Canada, monitors the government's role in the realization of this communication right. That said, the 1985 *Access to Information Act* was, from the start, poorly administered and prone to the creation of loopholes through which government could shirk its responsibility for making information publicly accessible. Suggestions from Information Commissioner John Reid for improving the act's performance were largely ignored, and most of Reid's recommendations have since been redirected into a draft document that appears destined to be dampened by committee deliberations (Panetta and Bronskill 2006).

The Conservative government of Stephen Harper came to power in 2006 with a mandate that included making changes to the *Access to Information Act* as part of an election platform built around increased government transparency and accountability. However, the resulting *Federal Accountability Act*, which does increase the number of government agencies responsible to the *Access to Information Act*, largely fails to address current problems such as the failure or refusal of civil servants to create information in the first place.[18] (No information equals no need to respond to access to information requests.) These modifications also contain ten new loopholes that enable civil servants to deny requests, according to the British Columbia Freedom of Information and Privacy Association (2005).

Furthermore, in April 2008, the Harper government instructed the civil service to cease updating the Co-ordination of Access to Information Requests System (CAIRS). The CAIRS registry is an electronic list of nearly every access to information request filed with federal departments and agencies. Because its usefulness stems from its near-comprehensive coverage, the cease-updating order effectively renders it irrelevant. Within government, the CAIRS was used by civil servants to keep track of requests and coordinate the government's response between agencies to the release of potentially sensitive information. CAIRS was also used by journalists, experts, and the public "to do statistical studies, submit new requests with fine-tuned wordings and discover obscure documents – often using the resulting information against the government" (CBC News 2008e). While criticism of this move from the political opposition was predictably topical and measured,[19] a press release of the Canadian Association of Journalists (2008) underlined that there were real issues of accountability at stake here and argued that "without updates to the database, it will become only easier over time for federal departments to delay, obfuscate and potentially with-hold valuable government information."

Not all government information is freely and easily available to Canadians at present, and placing a Freedom of Information request in Canada can be prohibitively complicated, time consuming, and costly for individuals, as-suming that the information requested does not fall through one of the many loopholes that mean the request can be refused.

Diversity of Content in the Media and Plurality of Media Sources

On the premise that spectrum frequency is a scarce resource and therefore must be administered as public property,[20] the *Broadcasting Act* outlines a series of policy prescriptions directed at ensuring that Canadian broadcasting emanates from a plurality of sources and presents diverse content. As discussed in Chapter 4, the mixed system approach recognizes the importance of pub-lic service and community broadcasting alongside privately owned broadcast-ing and promises a diversity of institutional structures and objectives among Canadian broadcast sources. The national public broadcaster, the CBC, is responsible for ensuring geographical as well as linguistic diversity in both the source and content of broadcasting available in Canada.[21] The comple-mentary role assigned to alternative and community broadcasting represents an effort to ensure diversity through the programming of content genres and subject matter as well as marginal views that are largely ignored by mainstream broadcasters.[22] The *Canadian Multiculturalism Act* provides an overall frame-work for the promotion of ethnocultural and racial diversity in Canada.[23] The *Broadcasting Act* is more specific, mandating broadcasting to facilitate expressions of citizenship through debate, dialogue, and exchange. The *Can-adian Multiculturalism Act* positively affirms diversity as a "fundamental characteristic of Canadian heritage and identity" as well as "an invaluable resource in the shaping of Canada's future," but it is short on specifying implementation mechanisms (section 3(1)(b)). The *Broadcasting Act* translates that affirmation into a set of policy objectives for broadcasting,[24] as well as qualified language on the specific importance of programming that reflects Canada's Aboriginal cultures.[25]

There are no policies aimed at ensuring any kind of source or content diversity with regard to other Canadian media, such as newspapers and websites. Except for the market considerations provided under competition law, which essentially target advertising, Canada had, until very recently, no legislation, regulation, or policy guidelines regarding the concentration of media ownership. In this respect, Canada stood apart from most comparable countries (including the United States), where thresholds limiting market share and especially cross-media ownership are common. These typically consider the impact of high levels of media concentration on the plurality and diversity of the available range of information.

This framework, as we discuss in Chapter 4, has been stunningly unsuccessful in promoting diversity within Canadian media.

Ownership of the Canadian media is highly concentrated in a handful of companies. For example, in the newspaper industry, four groups control over 80 percent of the English-language market. A single company owns all the English-language dailies in many Canadian markets, including Vancouver. Cross-media ownership is increasingly common and problematic; CanWest Global Communications and CTVglobemedia each own one of Canada's two national newspapers as well as one of Canada's two English-language national commercial television networks.[26] In Quebec, a single company, Quebecor, dominates the market in newspapers, television, Internet service, and cable (Centre d'études sur les médias 2008).

Canadians working outside of the corporate media empires struggle to have their voices heard in Canadian media. Community broadcasting is one area where Canadian media could be diversified through the interventions of non-corporate voices and individual citizens. Despite its designation by the *Broadcasting Act* as one of the three components (with public and private broadcasting) of Canada's national broadcasting system, however, not-for-profit community broadcasters receive no funding from the federal government, and the Canadian Radio-television and Telecommunications Commission (CRTC) and Industry Canada do not reserve radio spectrum for their use. Struggling to support permanent staff, forced to use equipment that is often outdated or inadequate, and squeezed by the demands for ever more spectrum space that commercial broadcasters are making in every large Canadian city,[27] community broadcasting as presently configured has a far less pronounced impact on the diversity of the Canadian mediascape than apparently envisioned in the *Broadcasting Act*.

Broadcast content that is independently produced to be aired on commercial or publicly owned media is another area where a greater degree of diversity could be achieved. As we discuss in Chapter 8, however, an overly cautious approach to copyright clearance on the part of commercial broadcasters and public agencies such as the National Film Board (NFB) often imposes extensive financial and human resource demands on independent production efforts to secure clearances that should arguably be considered fair dealing. Corporate media firms often employ in-house counsel to negotiate usage terms with rights holders, as well as research staffs to track down rights holders, and have budgetary flexibility to cover rights clearance fees as required. Artists and smaller producers, on the other hand, are simply unable to meet these demands and are consequently unable to effectively realize their rights to fair dealing.

The critiques are no less severe with regard to levels of diversity of content in the Canadian media. Despite the CBC's mandate as specified by the *Broadcasting Act*, regional diversity at the national public broadcaster has diminished seriously as a result of budget cuts beginning in 1990. As discussed in Chapter 4, the House of Commons Standing Committee on Canadian Heritage found the *Broadcasting Act*'s qualified treatment of the role of Aboriginal cultural programming to be "discriminatory" and recommended the removal of the qualifying phrase "as resources become available for the purpose" from the act (Canada 2003c). Many commentators argue that minorities more generally are chronically under-represented and misrepresented in Canadian media (e.g., Henry and Tator 2000; Fleras and Kunz 2001; Mahtani 2001) and that there is an absence in the media of coverage of issues dealing with the experienced reality of systemic racism in Canadian society (Henry and Tator 2000; Bullock and Jafri 2001). In addition, since 9/11, there has been a perceived return to Orientalist stereotyping of minorities in Canadian media, affecting representation of Arabs, South Asians, and Muslims in particular (Jiwani 2005). Overall, gaps in representation have encouraged minority publics in Canada to seek out other media forms that better resonate with their cosmopolitan experiences (Karim 2006; Ojo 2006).

From a structural standpoint, the *Broadcasting Act* provides that different social groups, including women, should be fairly represented among media employees at every level, but there are no mechanisms for verifying and monitoring the extent to which this goal is being achieved.

Access to the Means of Communication
The concept of universality has been widely accepted as an intrinsic facet of the Canadian identity. As discussed in Chapters 5 and 6, communication

policy in Canada has aggressively pursued this ideal, and penetration of communication technologies in Canada is relatively high.

Through a historic combination of private sector growth and government support, Canada has one of the highest levels of penetration of telephony, household cable, and satellite television in the world. Furthermore, the Canadian government set out a course for data networking early in the history of what was to become the Internet. The build-out of the US-funded Advanced Research Projects Agency Network (ARPANET) – the principal ancestor of the Internet – started in 1969. The defunct Science Council of Canada (1971, 4) issued a proposal for the establishment of "a nationwide system of computer communication networks" only two years later. By June 2005, Canada was among the top six Organisation for Economic Co-operation and Development (OECD) countries in broadband Internet subscriber rates, with 19.2 broadband Internet subscriptions reported per 100 Canadians (OECD 2005), and Canada initiated several funding programs to create Internet access in public spaces, such as schools and libraries, as well as community access points, particularly in rural and remote areas. The 2007 Canadian Internet Usage Survey (CIUS) conducted by Statistics Canada placed the percentage of Internet users at 73 percent (or 19.2 million) of Canadians aged sixteen and older (Statistics Canada 2008).[28]

Proactive steps have been taken to extend the principle of universal access both across existing and onto emerging technical platforms for communication. Our studies, however, reinforced the point that access in Canadian communication policy is often too narrowly focused on provision of technology and neglects the need to develop the capacity within individuals and communities for making meaningful use of the technologies provided. In addition, where access to relevant media in Canada is less than universal, it tends to be the already marginalized (poor, isolated, disabled, and so on) who go without. A variety of digital divide studies in Canada have come to the same conclusions: access is determined by socioeconomics – income, education, geography, gender, and age (Dickinson and Ellison 1999; Dickinson and Sciadas 1999; Sciadas 2002). Statistics Canada reports that domestic access to information and communication technologies (ICTs) increases with income and education, the presence of children, and living in urban environments. Despite the continual increase in various income groups' gaining access to the Internet, there is a persistent divide between those in the highest and those in the lowest income levels. Chapter 5 underscores the necessity of reconceptualizing the digital divide as a social divide, and the importance of incorporating integration of ICTs with other skills and activities in people's daily lives, a perspective that receives scant attention from policy makers in Canada.

By promoting the principle of "technology neutrality," the CRTC (2005b, paragraph 130) has declared that regulation should focus on "core principles that can be adapted to changing technologies." This approach has been used to ensure that Voice over Internet Protocol (Voice over IP, or VoIP) telephony is subject to the same obligations to universal service as traditional fixed-line telephony. As discussed in Chapter 6, however, the CRTC's hearings on network traffic shaping were presented with persistent claims that the non-neutral networks that Canadian cable and telecom companies aspire to enforce would violate the universal service elements of Canadian telecommunication policy (see also Chapter 9). The challenges posed to communication rights by these developments are further problematized by the fact that they occur against the backdrop of a diminishing government commitment to maintaining universal access with regard to already established ICTs.

For example, as discussed in Chapter 5, numerous existing connectivity funding schemes, such as SchoolNet and the Community Access Program (CAP), have suffered drastic budget cuts in recent years as part of a move toward cutting off such funding entirely, despite the fact that the Internet continues to evolve and that, as we discuss in Chapter 6, in order to have effective access to knowledge using Web 2.0 technologies, people are being required to obtain Internet services with higher data transmission rates. Such higher-bandwidth Internet service is more expensive and less universally available in Canada, meaning that some of the same people who are currently able to access the Internet as a result of having been provided with service even a few years ago through these programs may soon find themselves effectively disconnected. It is telling that by 2007 Canada had fallen to tenth place among OECD countries in terms of broadband subscribers per 100 inhabitants, a drop of four positions in two years (OECD 2007b).

The 2009 federal budget pledged $225 million for extending broadband infrastructure through public/private partnerships (PPPs). While this was a welcome development, the funding falls short of what commentators are calling for and what the Harper government promised in its 2008 campaign. It also remains to be seen whether, after some twenty years of practice in "connecting Canadians," these funds will be allocated in a way that substantively addresses Canada's digital divides, or whether the focus will once again be on simply improving technology penetration statistics.

The need to ensure that often expensive commitments to universal service endure as changing communication technologies demand reinvestment in communication infrastructure is a fundamental communication rights issue in Canada and is evident across Canada's system of mass communication. The CBC presents another striking example of how fickle these commitments can be.

After many decades and at great cost, the CBC finally, in the 1970s, extended its national coverage to all communities with a population of 500 or more. As we discuss in Chapter 4, however, during the CRTC's latest review of television regulations, the CBC asked to be freed from its over-the-air (OTA) television delivery obligations, arguing that OTA broadcast is a more costly and less efficient means for reaching most of the population than cable or satellite (CRTC 2006b; see CBC/Radio-Canada 2006). While this may be true, it raises a serious concern about universality of service: why should people be required to pay for a private delivery service in order to receive publicly funded and technically available broadcast signals? Thus, while there are clearly opportunities and challenges related to Internet access in Canada, it is important to be vigilant in ensuring that "old media" continue to figure in discussions about universal access to communication in Canada and in ensuring real measures in support of policy rhetoric.

Access to Knowledge

Canada's national strategic and policy orientation toward knowledge creation, dissemination, and use is evident only upon examination of a series of often disparate policy initiatives. In practice, policy's impact on enriching the public domain, satisfying the various needs for knowledge, and encouraging creativity from all sectors of society in Canada is inconsistent.

Partly because education falls under provincial jurisdiction in Canada, there is more emphasis at the federal level on knowledge creation than on dissemination and use. Exceptions include projects such as the Department of Canadian Heritage's Canadian Culture Online, the NFB's "Citizenshift," and the Virtual Museum of Canada. Overall, however, policies for ensuring that publicly funded knowledge and information are publicly available in Canada are sporadic and, where they exist, are often poorly supported by practical measures. For instance, government information is made public, but it is not made available in "the public domain" in a copyright sense: Crown copyright vests ownership in the Crown for fifty years after creation. Public service media and other publicly funded Canadian media content are not, at present, effectively archived in a publicly available format.[29] Both the Canadian Institutes of Health Research and the Social Sciences and Humanities Research Council of Canada are proposing that projects they fund be published in "open access"[30] form, but these proposals have not yet been implemented. Meanwhile, many individual universities are putting much more emphasis on commercialization than on non-commercial dissemination. Open access permits the government or other creators who receive public funding to prevent unauthorized commercial use of material, while encouraging all other uses. Open access should be a policy priority in this area, but it is not clear that Canada is effectively moving in this direction at present.

In our assessment, Canada's existing copyright law addresses issues surrounding the generation and communication of knowledge reasonably fairly (e.g., support for "fair dealing" with copyrighted material, constraints on digital rights management, and recognition and protection of the "moral rights" of authors). The push behind copyright reform over the past few years, however, has been the need to harmonize Canadian law with relatively regressive US legislation and to ratify and implement the World Intellectual Property Organization (WIPO) copyright and performances and phonograms treaties. Bill C-61, a controversial piece of legislation that borrows extensively from the US *Digital Millennium Copyright Act (DMCA)*, was introduced by the Harper government in June 2008 but died on the Order Paper when an election was called (see Canada 2008a).[31] Chapter 8 describes how critics and copyright activists succeeded in mobilizing a formidable public campaign in opposition to Bill C-61 but suggests that this bill was just the latest in a series of troubling indications that future copyright legislation in Canada may not respect a balanced approach between user and producer rights.

Additionally, research conducted with artists and creators in Canada for the study presented in Chapter 8 reveals that Canadians are constrained by misconceptions of the law and often do not claim the communication rights to which they are entitled in this area. Similarly, it is often the case that broadcasters and other risk-averse gatekeepers in the social cycle of communication enforce copyright standards that are more restrictive than the actual statutes themselves. The question of what flanking communication rights need to be secured in order to guarantee the fair enjoyment of copyright needs to be considered.

At present, affordable access to the various means of sharing knowledge is not equitably distributed across all groups in society. As discussed earlier, there are significant access divides in Canada that contribute to the further marginalization of already marginalized groups. Access to the means of sharing knowledge is particularly problematic for residents of Canada's North. The combination of large areas to cover and low population densities leads to a situation in which the cost of new communication infrastructure is extremely high.

With regard to broadcast media, opportunities for developing skills and capacities to utilize media and communication technologies are relatively widespread in Canada. For instance, in the early 1970s, the NFB's Challenge for Change program kick-started an effort to make video technology and skills available to all. Today, video and film resource centres exist in most medium to large Canadian cities and offer affordable training and facilities for media creation. In addition, many less formal video and film collectives have been formed over the past ten years. One project that addresses issues of technology and marginality is HomelessnessNation.org, which has developed an online community for homeless youth in Montreal, Toronto, and Vancouver, providing resources and training through local community centres and case workers. Training in radio operation, production, and journalism is available from every community radio station in Canada, as part of its mandate.

Overall, however, there is a history of non-involvement on the part of government in this area. This is particularly evident with regard to Internet access initiatives, where Canadian programs operate with too narrow a focus on augmenting penetration rates and have neglected to make skills training a funding condition or priority. In the Community Access Program (CAP), discussed in Chapter 5, money was allocated to expand technical infrastructure, whereas training, although clearly a required parallel activity, was not considered something to be funded. This means that communities shoulder the brunt of the financial and institutional burden of helping people develop the capacity to make meaningful use of the technologies. The role played by the group *Communautique* in Quebec has been one positive example of how this largely ad hoc arrangement can work (see Proulx and Lecomte 2005).

Right to Equality before the Law, to One's Honour and Reputation, and to Protection against Unwarranted Damage to Them

The *Charter* makes strong statements about the right to equality before the law.[32] The right to one's honour and reputation and to protection against unwarranted damage to them is not explicitly addressed in the *Charter* but is very clearly guaranteed in the *Universal Declaration of Human Rights (UDHR)* and the *International Covenant on Civil and Political Rights (ICCPR)*, which

Canada has signed and ratified.[33] The realization of this most fundamental human right is increasingly contingent, however, on questions about enforcement and redress that are raised when information that affects an individual's honour and reputation is diffused through the media, particularly when this information might be false or unreliable and the resulting damage to the person's reputation unwarranted. The fallout from recent cases, such as the campaign against Maher Arar and the abuse directed toward minority groups by radio "shock jock" Jeff Fillion, reveals the limited range of Canada's policy toolkit in addressing the impact of the Canadian media on individuals' honour and reputation. Overall, the law in this area has yet to come to terms with the full potential impact of the media.

Maher Arar, a dual citizen of Syria and Canada, was arrested at New York's John F. Kennedy International Airport in 2002, held for thirteen days, and questioned by US Homeland Security personnel. He was then sent to Syria, where he was detained, interrogated, and tortured for a year before being released to Canada. All because his name was on a "watch list" of suspected terrorists, an association that was proven to have been baseless when, in 2006, the report of an official Canadian inquiry exonerated Arar and reprobated the RCMP for releasing false information to American authorities, who still claim that Arar is a threat (Canada 2006c, 2006g; MacCharles 2009).[34]

Among the many communication rights issues raised by the Arar case is the intentional release of false information by government security officials to the media and other entities. In spite of Arar's very public exoneration and a $10 million reparation payment by the Canadian government, the US government has kept Arar on a watch list and continues to deny him entry into the United States (Center for Constitutional Rights 2008). Thus, effectively, Arar's honour and reputation were tarnished beyond repair by irresponsible and baseless actions taken by agents of the Canadian government. There is little that Arar can do to ensure that the story of his innocence is as widely circulated by the media as the coverage of the original false accusations against him. It is arguable that the high media profile of the story that outlined the case against Arar placed the US government in a position where it cannot now publicly acknowledge his exoneration without creating an undesirable political controversy. In other words, Arar's unfairly tarnished reputation is being held hostage by the notoriety created by false media coverage.

Conversely, there is the case in which the CRTC's 2004 decision not to renew the broadcasting licence of radio station CHOI-FM held an individual media firm and its professionals accountable for repeated instances of abusive programming. In an unprecedented decision, the CRTC cited *Charter* section 15 and the unique role that the media play in the realization of the right of individuals to honour and dignity. Despite the fact that "the interveners who supported the renewal of CHOI-FM's licence based their support primarily on the principle of freedom of expression," the CRTC insisted that the link between the media and individual reputations is such that the "use [of] the airwaves to make personal attacks ... may be of grave psychological and social consequences for the person or members of the targeted group." In its decision not to renew CHOI's licence, the CRTC maintained that "the principle of freedom of expression, which both protects those who express their views and those who hear them ... recognizes the right of licensees, through their employees, to criticize and question on air the actions of individuals, groups and institutions in the community," but that "the derision, hostility and abuse encouraged by such remarks have a severely negative impact on the targeted group or individual's self-worth, human dignity and social acceptance within society. This harm undermines the equality rights of those targeted, whereas the broadcasting policy for Canada states that those rights should be reflected in the programming offered by the Canadian broadcasting system ... Protecting an individual's good reputation is therefore of fundamental importance in our free and democratic society" (CRTC 2004a).

The CRTC decision was upheld by the Federal Court of Appeal. Meanwhile, one of the parties targeted by CHOI-FM who figured in the CRTC decision, television meteorologist Sophie Chiasson, successfully sued CHOI talk show host Jeff Fillion, his co-presenters, and CHOI-FM's parent company, Genex, for defamation of character and received a judgment of $425,000 (*Chiasson v. Fillion*).[35] In effect, Chiasson received vindication by virtue of two separate days in court (at the CRTC and the Quebec Superior Court).

Overall, the entire process of holding CHOI-FM accountable for its use of the media to mount gratuitous attacks against the reputation and honour of specific groups and individuals spanned over three years. Questions should be asked, going forward, about whether this system is sufficiently responsive to the task of enforcing the right to honour, dignity, and reputation in relation to media and communication and adequate in terms of the redress it offers to those wrongly attacked.

Right to Privacy

There is no explicit constitutional right to privacy in Canada, although sections 7[36] and 8[37] of the *Charter* have been interpreted by the Supreme Court of Canada (in *R. v. Duarte*)[38] to protect against "unreasonable" invasions of privacy. Overall, as discussed in Chapter 7, Canadian federal legislative protection of privacy is a patchwork, in that it involves a number of different institutions and policy frameworks, including:

- the *Privacy Act*,[39] which applies only to the federal public sector in relation to data collection, placing limitations on the collection, use, disclosure, and disposal of personal information held by the federal government and federal agencies
- the *Personal Information Protection and Electronic Documents Act (PIPEDA)*,[40] which applies to the federally regulated private sector with respect to the collection, use, and disclosure of personal information, but only for the transaction of commercial activities
- the Office of the Privacy Commissioner (OPC), which investigates any complaints from individuals who feel that their privacy rights have been violated under *PIPEDA*.

Discussion of privacy as a communication right in Canada must not be limited to these statutes, however, as it implicates a variety of distinct policy frameworks and institutional and industrial stakeholders, depending on the circumstances surrounding a specific issue or complaint. For instance, with regard to privacy of communication, the *Telecommunications Act*[41] defines policy objectives in economic, social, and technical areas, including "to contribute to the protection of the privacy of persons" (section 7(i)).

Our assessment is that this complex system is underfunded and poorly suited to the current environment. Enforcement is poor and opportunities for redress are unsatisfactory. Greater coordination is required, not only between the various pieces of privacy legislation but also in terms of better integration of privacy policy within the regulatory framework of communication in Canada. Post-9/11 security pressures and an increasing reliance on data storage practices that involve firms based in other countries and global communication networks are fundamentally undermining the right to privacy in Canada. In 2000, the Senate Standing Committee on Social Affairs, Science, and Technology recommended the creation of a *Charter of Privacy Rights* that would be a quasi-constitutional document providing an overarching legislative framework for the general protection of privacy (Canada 2001f). Further policy development of an explicit and meta-level framework around Canadians' right to privacy is clearly required (see Chapter 7).

In addition, however, our assessment found no consensus on how the use of technologies with built-in capacities for surveillance should be regulated in Canada, despite the potential of the ever more ubiquitous use of such technologies to create a chilling effect on Canadians' freedom of expression, movement, and association. For instance:

* The Privacy Commissioner of Canada has called for anti-spam legislation (see Canada 2007d), but there has been no concrete follow-up action in this area.
* Expressing an unwillingness to horse-trade their privacy rights and skepticism over the real crime-fighting benefits of video surveillance, residents of certain Canadian cities, including Brockville and Peterborough, Ontario, have successfully mounted organized resistance to pressure from local authorities to expand closed circuit TV (CCTV) surveillance of public places (see Hier et al. 2007). Still, the push to link up police forces with what one newspaper article called their "trusty partner" (Appleby and Freeman 2009) and make CCTV surveillance of public spaces ubiquitous moves forward unabated in other Canadian cities, such as Winnipeg, Manitoba (see Winnipeg Police Service n.d.); Toronto, Ontario (see Toronto Police Service n.d.; Appleby and Freeman 2009); and Vancouver, Surrey, and Kelowna, British Columbia (see Mertl 2008).
* The increasing and mundane uses of radio frequency identification (RFID) to track everything from clothing to money present significant possibilities for coordinating and tracking individuals' consumption and mobility, with or without their knowledge. RFID tags can be embedded in objects without the knowledge of those who purchase them. Tags do not require line of sight and can be read at a distance and, as such, can be rendered invisible, making it impossible for an individual to know whether he or she is being scanned or tracked. Embedded RFID tags enable individuals to be traced spatially, temporally, and uniquely, presenting opportunities for monitoring and profiling them. Additional information may also be revealed by digitally mapping movements and interactions. The data generated through RFID may be stored and aggregated with additional information, facilitating the ability to identify and track individuals (Canada 2006a).
* RFID is already being used to trace and organize movements of people between the US and Canada (Peslak 2005). Two border crossing programs, NEXUS (frequent visitors) and FAST (commercial trucks), oblige

users to pre-apply for RFID-embedded identification cards that ensure access to special lanes for card users, bypassing long queues (Gorham 2006). There is no clear consensus between industry and government, however, on the extent to which RFID should be used and regulated. Studies of related industries indicate that self-regulation is not sufficient to ensure observance of privacy protection principles (cf. CIPPIC 2006).

• Electronic mail is a particularly insecure form of communication; thus, ethical and legal issues concerning the privacy of e-mail used for communication in the workplace are quite complex. E-mail can create an electronic trail that can discourage secure communications. Although e-mail should be considered private communication between the sender and the recipient, it can be easily forwarded to and exchanged with others without the consent of the original sender, and can therefore be easily taken out of context. Users of e-mail can be subjected to breaches of confidentiality of their communication. For instance, employers can easily monitor e-mail users.

In the summer of 2009, the social networking site Facebook agreed, in response to a critical report produced by the OPC and in consultation with OPC officials, to implement a new series of privacy policies regarding, among other issues, its sharing of personal information with external firms that develop games, puzzles, and other applications for Facebook sites (see Canada 2009e). The case illustrated that Canadian public authorities, and the OPC in particular, are indeed capable of influencing seemingly borderless forms of digital communication. The OPC intervention was triggered by a complaint filed by the Canadian Internet Policy and Public Interest Clinic (CIPPIC), an independent organization based at the University of Ottawa, thus further illustrating what can be accomplished when well-resourced civil society groups are able to push public authorities to defend the communication rights of Canadians.

Minority Cultural and Linguistic Rights

Official bilingualism is a foundational governance principle in Canada, and human rights protection for linguistic duality is explicit and strong.[42] Policies that derive from or are designed to reinforce official bilingualism are embedded, at every level, in the framework governing media and communications in Canada. Through policies such as the CBC's mandate to "contribute to shared national consciousness and identity" *(Broadcasting Act)*, communication rights in Canada are intimately tied to cultural development. Such ambitions are clearly fraught with difficulty, however; whatever the CBC may or may not be contributing in this area, it is doing separately in English and in French.

While Canada's official bilingualism framework is often acknowledged as a model worldwide, from the communication rights perspective there is clear room for improvement. We question whether Canada's media system is optimally structured for filling this role, and underline the fact that, regarding the media at least, the promotion of French/English linguistic duality in Canada often ignores members of official language minority groups in Quebec and the rest of Canada, Aboriginal people, recent immigrants, and other cultural communities with needs for services and programming in languages other than English and French.

On the basis of the Commission on Accommodation Practices Related to Cultural Differences, convened by the government of Quebec in early 2007 and commonly referred to as the Bouchard-Taylor Commission on reasonable accommodation, some troubling observations can be made about the role that the Canadian media play with respect to cultural diversity in Canada.

The Bouchard-Taylor Commission heard a spectrum of views from and regarding Quebec immigrants and minorities, ranging from alienation to acceptance. It also heard a series of highly mediated xenophobic diatribes that mischaracterized and stereotyped various ethnic groups, including some with long-established histories in Quebec. Clearly, the media cannot be held accountable for every nasty uninformed opinion, but the hearings raised some relevant questions about media's role as a potential platform for reasoned public discussion of issues of cultural difference. In its report, the commission suggested that "if we can speak of an 'accommodation crisis,' it is essentially from the standpoint of perceptions" (Bouchard and Taylor 2008, 13).

As we discuss in Chapter 4, while media are perceived to be a powerful tool in suggesting what it means to be Canadian, research suggests that ethnic and racial minorities are under- and misrepresented in the Canadian media and that issues dealing with the experienced reality of systemic racism in Canadian society receive scant attention.

In a more concrete way, the media's treatment of the context that led to the Bouchard-Taylor Commission hearings also raised fundamental questions about the aptitude of the Canadian media for reporting on the complex issues surrounding cultural difference and for informing and facilitating the sort of public reflection that might meaningfully help to resolve them.

The Bouchard-Taylor Commission conducted in-depth research on a series of controversies that had garnered media attention and fed the sense that government action on the issue of reasonable accommodation was required. It noted what it called "striking distortions" between the facts and mediated public perceptions in fifteen of the twenty-one cases examined, and concluded that "the negative perception of accommodation often stemmed from an erroneous or partial perception of practices in the field. Had the public been more familiar with such practices perhaps there would not have been an accommodation crisis" (Bouchard and Taylor 2008, 22).

The commission was no less critical of the media coverage of the hearings themselves, lamenting the tendency to sensationalize the handful of inflammatory, controversial interventions without contextualizing them as exceptions to the generally well-prepared and moderate remarks of ordinary citizens that made up the vast majority of comments (Heinrich and Dufour 2008, 38-39).

Did the Canadian media merely drop the ball on the Bouchard-Taylor Commission hearings by not realizing what the real significance was until they were over? Or does the twenty-four-hour news cycle reduce storytelling to a search for hot-button issues and rerunnable footage? Are the media capable of capturing the rich and nuanced machinations of a complex, multifaceted, and ambiguous issue such as the place of ethnic and cultural minorities in a diverse community? For those who harbour hopes that media coverage of public affairs can help sustain democratic dialogue and deliberation, this is precisely the sort of issue where we require more from our media.

The representation of immigrants, cultural communities, and Canadians of various backgrounds in the Canadian media needs to be reconsidered, particularly within the more esoteric high-policy goal of presenting a convincing narrative about a harmonious and universally accepted Canadian identity. Whether one looks at census statistics or demographic projections, or uses intuitive common sense, it is clear that Canadian "multiculturalism" is neither a recent nor a passing phenomenon.

In other areas, however, the conventional view that the role of the Canadian media ought to be limited to the two official languages seems to be in retreat. The report of the 2004 Panel on Access to Third-Language Public Television Services observed that "the provision of third-language services has been a success, and Canada has one of the more diverse ranges of such services in the world" (Canada 2004c). The number of ethnic digital services reporting to the CRTC in 2003 and 2004 was four; this increased to seventeen in 2005 (CRTC 2006c), and the number has continued to rise. Still, most third-language broadcasters approved by the CRTC do not have a carrier and are therefore inaccessible to Canadians. The CRTC oversees a situation that is nominally open to outside voices, but in general it promotes only communication that has a Canadian corporate sponsor. This approach toward third-language broadcasting (and broadcasting from non-Canadian sources in English or French as well) leads to sometimes conflicting results. For example:

- As recently as December 2006, the CRTC granted nine Chinese satellite television stations eligibility for carriage in Canada. Within weeks, Rogers Communications, a leading cable company, announced a Chinese Great Wall TV package, offering these channels to its digital subscribers. To ensure that Canadian Chinese-language channels remain competitive, the CRTC ordered Rogers to sell its package only to subscribers who already pay for and receive existing Canadian-based Chinese-language services.
- In 2004, the CRTC approved the international Arabic-language satellite service Al Jazeera for carriage in Canada, but made it the responsibility of any cable or satellite distributor that opts to offer the controversial network to alter or delete "abusive comment" from Al Jazeera programs. This required a special dispensation granting distributors exceptional censorship power that is otherwise forbidden. Given the human and technology resource demands and the potential public relations nightmares, these conditions made it highly unlikely from the start – despite the approval of the CRTC – that any Canadian cable or satellite service provider would offer Al Jazeera to its customers (see Dakroury 2005).[43]

On the other hand, in one justly celebrated example, the Aboriginal Peoples Television Network (APTN) received Category 1 status from the CRTC in February 1999, making it part of the basic cable package for all Canadians. This bold step placed Canada at the forefront of Aboriginal broadcasting worldwide (see Roth 2005). Overall, our view is that questions regarding linguistic and cultural broadcasting need to be dealt with in a larger consideration of how broadcasting should be contributing to the cultural development objectives of Canadian society and the communication rights of Canadians.

Generally speaking, however, assuring the communication rights of Aboriginal Canadians and other inhabitants of the far North has been an ongoing policy challenge. Access issues related to the cost of connecting the North have disproportionately impacted access to knowledge creation and sharing opportunities available to Aboriginal Canadians. Despite the existence of numerous programs designed to fund universal access in northern Canada, many communities remain excluded. This is most evident where efforts have been undertaken by rural communities themselves to develop their own community Internet service providers with little or no funding from the federal government. Many projects by Aboriginal and rural communities are currently in various stages of developing networks that will provide wireless broadband access and accompanying distance programs in areas such as education and health care.

Opportunities for the development of community broadcasting are much more limited in rural areas and particularly in northern Canada. While community broadcasting has been afforded right-to-carriage by cable, it has been denied such right over satellite, which is generally a favourable mode of distribution in large areas with low population density. While many Canadian community radio stations broadcast online, creators' rights groups have begun to develop new rates that will cause further financial hardship to many broadcasters.

A Right to Self-Determination and to Take Part in Government

Formal access to the policy-making process has to be underscored as a significant aspect of the Canadian communication rights framework. Canada has a laudable history of public consultation on communication policy development.

Canadian media policy has generally been developed in an open framework (see Raboy 1995a, 1995b). The *Broadcasting Act* provides for a public voice in the policy process;[44] all decisions, reports, and calls for hearings of the CRTC are posted on the commission's website; and the CRTC is required by law to support a public consultation process. In addition to the CRTC's statutory obligations, public comments are regularly sought by policy-making bodies. Some recent examples include, notably, the CRTC's proceeding on VoIP telephone services in which incumbent telecommunications providers and VoIP providers alike gave input on various topics, including network neutrality (see, for instance, CRTC 2004e). There was extensive public/expert participation in the review of *PIPEDA* (see Lawson 2005). In its various reviews of legislation falling within its scope, such as broadcasting and copyright, the House of Commons Standing Committee on Canadian Heritage regularly invites public submissions (cf. Canada 2004b).

Overall, however, we have to question whether these actions and statements of principle are adequately supported by mechanisms to ensure that public participation is possible and open to all Canadians. The 2003 report of the Standing Committee on Canadian Heritage, *Our Cultural Sovereignty: The Second Century of Canadian Broadcasting*, noted that there are difficulties for citizens trying to participate in CRTC broadcast hearings and recommended public funding support, as is available on the telecom side (Canada 2003b). This is a perennial sore point – for example, the object of a private member's bill by Senator Sheila Finestone in 2001 (see Canada 2001a) – but it has never been addressed by government. On the contrary, the government, in its response to *Our Cultural Sovereignty*, explicitly stated that it would not consider funding support for participants in broadcast hearings but would allocate any available funding to Canadian content production instead (Canada 2003c). There is a need for increased recognition and integration of nongovernmental and community groups in the policy process.[45]

Furthermore, there is alarming evidence that the role of public consultation in communication policy development in Canada has been effectively diminished in recent years. Communication scholars in Canada have been highly critical of the weak role of public consultation in the development of ICT policies,[46] and our assessment points to other areas in which the shrinking role of public consultation is troubling.

The efforts of Canadian civil society groups in this area have led to various initiatives, both inside and outside formal government channels, as well as varying degrees of satisfaction with the openness of government to their inputs. As discussed in Chapter 4, civil society groups working within the consultation process were the driving force behind getting recognition of the importance of the multicultural and multiracial nature of Canadian society, as well as of community broadcasting, in the 1991 *Broadcasting Act*. In making decisions like the one to end CAP (discussed in Chapter 5), however, the government regularly ignores the voiced concerns of civil society groups.

Overall, we are left wondering where public involvement in communication policy making is heading in Canada and whether it will continue to play a crucial role in the realization of communication rights. Public consultation may be fast becoming a cynical form of window dressing that does nothing more than rubberstamp preordained agendas and waste the time and resources of those who manage to participate. There is a clear need to develop meaningful participation of civil society in policy processes in Canada and to define its role and identify how it can be supported.

4
Media

Marc Raboy

Origins of the Press in Canada

The Canadian media were born in paradox. Canada's first newspapers, established in the colonies of British North America beginning with the *Halifax*
Gazette in 1752, were operated by printers and earned most of their revenue
by publishing government material. The early printer-editors were, according
to Kesterton (1969), "quasi-civil servants" and their journals contained little
unofficial content. This would change dramatically in the wake of the American Revolution. While a good part of the foundation of what would become
Canada was based, on the one hand, on loyalists to the Crown of England
fleeing the liberal republicanism of pamphleteers such as Thomas Paine and,
on the other hand, on the conservative Catholicism left over from the recently vanquished French regime, the media soon took on a distinctly op-
positional tone.

Fleury Mesplet, also a printer but one whose interests were more political than entrepreneurial, was recruited in Lyon by Benjamin Franklin and
brought to America to serve the revolutionary cause. From his Philadelphia
workshop, Mesplet addressed a proselytizing appeal to the inhabitants of the
province of Quebec in 1774. It failed to stir them, but Mesplet nonetheless
received a $200 grant two years later from the First Congress of the United
States of America to found a printing shop in Montreal, then occupied by
American troops. In 1777, he created *La Gazette du Commerce et Littéraire* of
Montreal, the direct forebear of a newspaper that still exists today, the *Montreal Gazette*, although that organ has arguably come a long way from its
revolutionary origins. Mesplet's *Gazette* was banned by the British governor
of Lower Canada and Mesplet was thrown in jail, thus ending an adventure
rich in irony for what it says about the paradoxical origins of the Canadian
media, their underlying political agendas, their role in constructing democracy,
government attempts to influence them, and our peculiar national question,

not to mention how Canadians have come to understand the parallel notions of communication rights and the right to communicate.

A highly political "opinion press" closely associated with democratic currents flourished in Canada throughout the nineteenth century. In Quebec alone, 104 newspapers were created between 1805 and 1838. Needless to say, this press defined itself largely in opposition to the colonial government of the period, from which it expected no favours and accepted no interference. The role of the press would change radically by the end of the century, with the social and economic transformations brought on by industrialization, urbanization, and the spread of literacy. By the turn of the twentieth century, Canada had a nascent popular commercial press that largely followed the model developed in the United States, as well as a small but influential radical press. Although Canada, historically, did not have the equivalent of the US First Amendment,[1] which guarantees the freedom of speech and of the press, the press in Canada has not been subjected to legal constraint except in situations deemed to be of national emergency. The 1914 *War Measures Act* gave power to the Governor in Council in situations of "invasion, apprehended war or insurrection."[2] It was used in 1970 during the October Crisis in Quebec, after the Front de Libération du Québec (FLQ) kidnapped Quebec Vice-Premier and Minister of Labour Pierre Laporte and British Trade Commissioner James Cross. The act was replaced in 1988 by a more limited and structured law called the *Emergencies Act*.[3] That said, the press in Canada is as free, or not as free, as any other in the Western world.

Press freedom in Canada today has to be seen through the prism of the *Canadian Charter of Rights and Freedoms*.[4] Section 2(b) of the *Charter* states: "Everyone has the following fundamental freedoms: ... freedom of thought, belief, opinion and expression, including freedom of the press and other media of communication." As we shall see, this is not identical to the freedom, or right, to communicate. But it is a valid starting point for examining the state of communication rights with respect to the media as institutions.

What Do We Mean by Freedom of the Press in Canada?

The *Charter* did not step into a void.[5] Jurisprudence built on the division of powers to establish what has been referred to as an "implied bill of rights" had previously carved out a particular status for political speech in Canada. The implied bill of rights was rooted in the Supreme Court of Canada's 1938 holding that the 1937 province of Alberta *Accurate News and Information Act*, which would have forced newspapers to publish government comment, was *ultra vires* because the importance of the "free public discussion of affairs" to the democratic system was such that it exceeded provincial jurisdiction over property and civil rights and fell under the federal duty to ensure peace, order, and good government *(Reference Re Alberta Statutes)*.[6] This jurisprudential background has infused both statute and case law relating to the press and other media of communication.[7]

Prior to adoption of the *Charter*, federal[8] and some provincial[9] bills of rights had already provided similar rights, but because these were not constitutionally entrenched, the state was in a position to overrule them in subsequent statute, making them of limited use against public parties. Opposability to private parties was similarly limited insofar as communication takes place in a market framework, giving the speaker the option to speak elsewhere, and jurisprudence had not developed a scarcity doctrine finding a political/economic rationale for elevating speech rights above property rights in concentrated markets. By entrenching a right to freedom of the press and other media of communication against state actors, therefore, the *Charter* has shaped the regulatory framework for the media sector by preventing a variety of prior restraints and holding any censorious or prohibitive schemes to a high standard.

The most interesting test of the effectiveness of this protection in recent years has come in the case of the Ottawa journalist Juliet O'Neill, whose home and office were raided by RCMP officers looking for information regarding the source for an article that she had written about Maher Arar, a Canadian citizen deported to Syria by US authorities in 2002. O'Neill published an article in the *Ottawa Citizen* on 8 November 2003, detailing the circumstantial evidence, false allegations, and coerced confessions contained in a series of documents that Canadian security services apparently leaked in the weeks leading to Arar's return to Canada. It cited an unnamed "security source" who went into operational detail about an ongoing investigation into alleged terrorist activity in the Ottawa area in explaining the leaks as a case of the government's wanting to avoid a public inquiry at all costs in defence of this ongoing investigation (see O'Neill 2003). In the early hours of 21 January 2004, RCMP officers raided O'Neill's home and office and confiscated her address books, Rolodex, and computer files as well as other personal possessions (see *O'Neill v. Canada (Attorney General)*).[10] The RCMP raid was conducted using warrants obtained under the sweeping powers granted to the police by amendments to Canada's *Security of Information Act* that were hastily enacted after the 11 September 2001 terrorist attacks against the United States.[11]

Although there was much criticism of the raid, which led to renewed calls for a public inquiry into the Arar affair, the more important issue for our purposes centres on the quality of media treatment of the events. An article published in the December/January 2007 issue of *The Walrus* magazine denounced the poor judgment of journalists and editors who perpetuated the false story about Arar's alleged connection to al-Qaeda (see Mitrovica 2007). By publishing anonymous information and subsequently continuing to protect their sources, even after the information they provided was found to be false, the news media helped propagate and perpetuate the claims of the RCMP and the Canadian Security Intelligence Service (CSIS) about Arar's supposed guilt. The Arar case thus underscores the complex, often contradictory, relationship between law, state intervention, and media practice that characterizes much of the communication rights environment.

On 5 February 2004, Justice Dennis O'Connor, associate chief justice of Ontario, was commissioned by the federal government to conduct an inquiry into the actions of Canadian officials in relation to Arar. He concluded that the RCMP did indeed provide "American authorities with information about Mr. Arar which was inaccurate, portrayed him in an unfair fashion and overstated his importance to the investigation," some of which had the potential to create serious consequences for him (Canada 2006d). He also stated in his three-volume report that "labels have a way of sticking to individuals, reputations are easily damaged and when labels are inaccurate, serious unfairness to individuals can result" (Canada 2006g). More than 2,500 articles of all sorts about Arar were published between 2002 and 2006. In September 2006, Justice O'Connor cleared Arar of all terrorism allegations, stating that he was "able to say categorically that there is no evidence to indicate that Mr. Arar has committed any offence or that his activities constitute a threat to the security of Canada" (Canada 2006d).

Another prominent case involved a reporter for the *Hamilton Spectator*, Ken Peters, who was found guilty on 7 December 2004 of contempt of court for refusing to divulge a source. In 1995, Peters obtained documents regarding a series of problems at a Hamilton, Ontario, nursing home (see Peters 1995). After officials launched a malpractice investigation that was chronicled by Peters (working the *Spectator*'s municipal beat), the nursing home brought a libel suit against the City of Hamilton and Halton Region, alleging in essence that information reported by Peters that should have stayed confidential was harming its business. During the trial, Peters was asked to name the person who had provided the information, but he refused. Although the source came forward voluntarily later on, Peters remained in contempt of court and was fined $31,600. The international NGO Reporters Without Borders condemned the arrest as "a dangerous precedent" (see CBC News 2004a; Reporters Without Borders Canada 2004).

Each of these two recent challenges to the ability of journalists to protect the confidentiality of their sources was subject to court challenge. On 17 March 2008, the Ontario Court of Appeal set aside the contempt of court charge against Peters, recognizing that punishing journalists who refused to name sources was unconstitutional and had a chilling effect on reporting.[12] But while the appeal decision was hailed as "an important step forward for the ability of journalists to protect sources to whom they have promised confidentiality" (Canadian Journalists for Free Expression 2008), media advocacy groups and press organizations said that it did not go far enough and "stopped short of enshrining an absolute right to protect sources" (Canadian Press 2009). On 19 October 2008, the Superior Court of the province of Ontario ruled that, while someone who had authorized access to secret information had illegally taken it and, acting unlawfully by breaching *Security of Information Act* provisions, given it to O'Neill, the RCMP, in investigating that instance of criminal activity, implied that O'Neill was herself the target of a criminal investigation in order to secure warrants to search and question her. This amounted to what the court termed intimidation of the press and an infringement of the constitutional right of freedom of the press, in that it "chilled media reports on the Arar matter specifically and had a general chilling effect on political and investigative reporting." As a result of these findings, the court struck down the so-called anti-leakage suite of post-9/11 amendments to the *Security of Information Act* as direct violations of the *Charter* (*O'Neill v. Canada*, paragraph 31).

The O'Neill and Peters cases reignited calls for Canadian statutory guarantees similar to those provided under US state "press shield" laws. These cases demonstrated how Canadian case law balances the importance of journalists' source confidentiality, which can be considered an essential element of speech, against circumstances in which state intrusion – particularly in the context of gathering criminal evidence – would be justified. There is, however, no statutory support for protection of journalists in Canada.[13]

The *Final Report on the Canadian News Media*, tabled by the Senate Standing Committee on Transport and Communications in June 2006, noted that "no constitutional, *Charter* or legal protection for journalists who refuse to give the names of sources" currently exists in Canada (Canada 2006b, section

C1). To the extent that this is true, it also limits all Canadians' right to freedom of expression as defined by article 19 of the *Universal Declaration of Human Rights (UDHR)* (see Chapter 1).[14] Therefore, the question remains, where should Canada draw the line to strike the best balance between journalistic freedom and the law?

Concentration of Ownership as a Restriction on Freedom of Speech

Article 19 is the minimum internationally accepted standard for freedom of expression. It is used, generally, to advocate for media freedom from government interference. As we see from the text, however, this right applies to *everyone*, not only those with direct access to the media. From a communication rights perspective, the right "to seek, receive and impart" information is particularly important. It implies a right of access to all available information as well as a right to communicate dialogically.

Canada, as a signatory to the *UDHR*, recognizes this right. It is arguably, however, a passive right for Canadians, as Canadian law makes no provision to ensure that it is effectively realized. The *Charter* offers no details on how these freedoms are to be preserved or enforced, yet they are obviously seen as a vital link to a healthy democracy. Free market enthusiasts and the media industries often interpret the "freedom" of the *Charter* to mean the right of unfettered media ownership.

Media ownership in Canada is regulated by the federal Competition Bureau and (for broadcast media) the Canadian Radio-television and Telecommunications Commission (CRTC). Historically, these agencies have examined media mergers and acquisitions on a case-by-case basis and the CRTC, in particular, has tended to approve these as being in the public interest. This stands in stark contrast to Canada's strong position on limiting foreign ownership of Canadian media to a minority stake. It raises a number of problems that we will examine in turn below.

On 15 January 2008, the CRTC made a historic announcement in deciding to change its approach to broadcast media ownership. Up to that time, except for the market considerations provided under competition law, Canada had no legislation, regulation, or policy guidelines regarding concentration of media ownership. In this respect, it stood apart from most comparable countries (including the United States), where thresholds limiting market share and especially cross-media ownership are common. These thresholds typically consider the impact of high levels of media concentration on the plurality and diversity of the available range of information. Official inquiries held by a long trail of parliamentary committees and a royal commission have drawn attention to this problem and proposed a range of approaches, but no government agency had acted upon it until now.[15] Before we discuss the new initiative, it is important to understand the unique context in which media in Canada had been operating.

Increased concentration and decreased competition in the newspaper industry in the 1960s and 1970s prompted two federal government inquiries: the 1969-70 Special Senate Committee on Mass Media, chaired by Senator Keith Davey (see Canada 1970) and the 1980-81 Royal Commission on Newspapers, chaired by former senior civil servant Tom Kent (see Canada 1981). The Kent Commission proposed a Canada Newspaper Act, to balance the rights and responsibilities of a free press, and a Press Ownership Review Board, to correct the worst cases of corporate concentration and cross-media ownership. These studies fuelled considerable debate and continue to provide scholars with a basis for criticism of media performance, but the Canadian government largely ignored their findings and recommendations and has steadfastly refused to regulate the newspaper industry, treating freedom of the press as a right belonging to those who own one.

Provincial government inquiries, such as that of the 2003 Quebec parliamentary committee on the quality and diversity of information (Comité conseil sur la qualité et la diversité de l'information), also added to the number of studies that skirt the decision whether to intervene regarding media consolidation. The Quebec committee proposed a dozen recommendations but no coercive measures to address the situation. It proposed a fund to assist independent media and emphasized self-regulatory measures to improve journalistic standards, but did not take on the real issue: the fact that 97 percent of the daily newspaper market in Quebec is controlled by two companies (Saint-Jean 2003a, 2003b). And this situation exists not only in the province of Quebec.

The daily newspaper industry in Canada remains highly concentrated; nationally, four newspaper groups control over 80 percent of the English-language newspaper market. Regionally and linguistically, concentration is even more radical. Vancouver's two dailies are both owned by CanWest Global Communications Corporation, the country's largest newspaper publisher. In some smaller provinces, it is common for all of the available daily newspapers to be owned by a single company. Cross-media ownership is increasingly problematic. The owners of Canada's two national newspapers, CanWest and CTVglobemedia, also own English Canada's two national television networks,

Global and CTV. In Quebec, newspaper ownership is dominated by two conglomerates, Power Corporation of Canada and Quebecor (which also owns the main French-language television network, TVA,[16] as well as the main cable operator, Vidéotron) (Centre d'études sur les médias 2008). Concentrated ownership, the convergence of newspapers with television networks and Internet sites, and the increasingly interventionist style of a new generation of media owners have renewed interest in concentration issues.

The *Final Report on the Canadian News Media* expressed these concerns about media concentration: "As for media concentration and cross-media ownership, the current regulatory system offers little protection against particular adverse effects of ownership concentration on the diversity of voices. This absence of regulatory focus has allowed media dominance by individual players in Vancouver, Quebec and New Brunswick and could as easily occur in other Canadian markets; indeed, it has already happened in the community newspaper sector." It recommended that "a new section, dealing with mergers of news gathering organizations, be added to the Competition Act. This new section should: a) trigger automatic review of a proposed media merger if certain thresholds are reached; b) allow the appropriate ministers to order a review of proposed mergers; c) set out the process that will be followed when a merger is being reviewed, including the appointment of a panel to conduct the review" (Canada 2006b, recommendation 1).

Meanwhile, the report of the House of Commons Standing Committee on Canadian Heritage, *Our Cultural Sovereignty* (also known as the Lincoln Report after committee chair Quebec MP Clifford Lincoln), called for the CRTC to implement a clear policy of editorial independence (Canada 2003b, recommendations 11.1 and 11.2) and also recommended that "the Government of Canada issue a clear and unequivocal policy statement concerning cross-media ownership" (recommendation 11.3). The government responded to the issue of cross-media ownership first by stating that it had analyzed the situation to determine whether the effects were positive or negative considering the new platforms available to obtain information. It concluded as follows: "The Government recognizes that convergence is now a core business strategy in the information era. The Government will give further consideration to the issues involved in cross-media ownership, including practices in other countries, and notes that the Senate Committee on Transport and Communications is in the midst of a study of the Canadian news media" (Canada 2003b).

A subsequent wave of consolidation encouraged the CRTC to take a serious look at its practices in this regard.[17] From 17 to 21 September 2007, it held a public hearing on the theme *Diversity of Voices*. The proceeding brought together broadcasters, broadcast distribution undertaking owners, labour unions, and public interest groups to discuss diversity – more precisely, editorial diversity. The outcome was what the commission called a "new approach to ownership" (CRTC 2008f).

The CRTC's new policies (see CRTC 2008b) impose "limits on the ownership of broadcasting licenses to ensure that one party does not control more than 45 per cent of the total television audience share as a result of a transaction" (CRTC 2008f). Additionally, the CRTC decided that it will "not approve transactions between companies that distribute television services (such as cable or satellite companies) that would result in one person effectively controlling the delivery of programming in a market." Also, the commission will permit a person or entity to control no more than two types of media, including local radio stations, local television stations, and local newspapers. The thresholds are high enough not to affect the current Canadian situation. Furthermore, the CRTC chose not to take into account national radio, television, or newspaper undertakings. This permits empires such as CTVglobemedia, which owns Canada's premier national paper, the *Globe and Mail*, as well as twenty-seven conventional television stations, thirty-five specialty channels, thirty-five radio stations, and interests in a variety of entertainment venues, sporting teams, and production facilities, to pursue the status quo.

For most parties, these measures come much too late because the damage has already been done. Between the time of the *Diversity of Voices* hearing and the announcement of the new policies, the CRTC allowed CanWest Global to acquire the specialty services chain Alliance Atlantis. Only a few minor adjustments were made to ensure, at least on paper, that the US financial interests in this arrangement would not deteriorate into foreign control over decision making in the company. In short, one may well wonder whether Canada has made any real progress in this area. The regulator has at last recognized, however, that there *are* thresholds beyond which media consolidation is a threat to diversity, and these could very well come into play at a future date.

Why Broadcasting Is Regulated but Not the Press

Free speech and ownership issues aside, the picture shifts dramatically whether one is looking at the press or at broadcast media – radio, television, cable and satellite distributors, and, increasingly, Internet broadcasting. In short, broadcasting is distinguished from the press by virtue of its status as a public service, governed by a federal statute, the *Broadcasting Act,* and regulated by a public authority, the CRTC.[18]

Why is this the case?[19] Broadcasting, like all public discourse and communication, takes place in a particular moral and ethical environment. It exhibits certain characteristics, however, which demand some oversight by the public authorities.

The regulation of broadcasting dates from the introduction of what came to be known as radio stations in countries such as Canada, the United States, and Great Britain in the years following the First World War. Every industrialized country in the world regulates broadcasting to some extent, if only to attribute operating licences to corporate entities that are consequently entitled to use a particular broadcasting frequency for a determined period of time.

The scarcity of broadcasting frequencies is an uncontested fact that results directly from the characteristics of over-the-air broadcast technology and that results in an obvious need to "control traffic" on the radio (as well as television) airwaves. As soon as more people want to broadcast than there are frequencies, some allocation mechanism is necessary. The public character of the air and the particular nature of broadcast media are subtler notions that have been open to various degrees of interpretation (discussed below). Regulation also seeks to provide equilibrium in order to ensure the overall viability of broadcasting systems (for example, by providing for a full range of services, including public and private broadcasting, ensuring that different social groups have access to the system, regulating certain aspects of market conditions such as limits on advertising, and so on). In Canada, successive Parliaments (through successive versions of the *Broadcasting Act* and other measures) have added yet another important level of justification for regulating broadcasting: the need to promote a Canadian sense of cultural identity and protect Canada's cultural sovereignty in a world dominated by non-Canadian media messages.

How is this justified in a democracy, especially where other media (most notably the press) are not regulated? We have already mentioned the technical considerations. More important, the regulation of conventional broadcasting is justified by the particular features of the medium. These include broadcasting's pervasiveness, invasiveness, publicness, and influence (Tambini and Verhulst 2000).

Broadcasting *pervasiveness* refers to the fact that, because of frequency limitation, all broadcasting content is "everywhere" when it is being broadcast. Unlike the press, which one must actively seek out (finding the newsstand that carries the journal you are interested in, for example), anyone who has a radio or television set has immediate and direct access to *all* content that is being broadcast in his or her community at a given time, and *only* to that content.[20]

Invasiveness refers to the fact that one does not know what one is about to hear until one has actually heard it. With the press (not to mention other media, such as books, records, or cinema) one has far greater opportunity to filter and control one's consumption (as well as that of one's children, for example). With broadcasting, particularly radio, one is not always in a position to choose what one is going to be exposed to.

Broadcasting, again because it can be relatively well circumscribed (on the radio or television dial, for example), plays a particular role in public life. Its *publicness* resides in the fact that the medium enables a broadcaster, at least hypothetically, to reach all of the people all of the time. Many societies have recognized this by establishing public broadcasting organizations such as the Canadian Broadcasting Corporation (CBC) or the British Broadcasting Corporation, something that is virtually unthinkable in the area of the press.

Finally, broadcasting has great *influence*. It describes the boundaries of public experience and public debate but does so in the privacy of the home. It has a strong role in agenda setting, in framing the important issues of the day, in suggesting what it is important for people to think about. Furthermore, in every society, there are some people who receive all of their information from the broadcast media. Rare is the individual whose media consumption is exclusively limited to the press.

The German legal scholar Wolfgang Hoffmann-Riem points to two basic types of broadcast regulation: "imperative regulation with conduct control," using guidelines, requirements, orders, and prohibitions, sanctioned negatively with a range of provisions from fines to licence revocation or positively with subsidies; and "structural regulation," a general framework set up to influence the conduct of broadcasting entities, specifying basic structures and procedural rules, steering the actors toward desired goals, and generally influencing their overall development (Hoffmann-Riem 1996, 281). Many countries, including Canada, combine both.

Hoffmann-Riem, a member of Germany's Constitutional Court and one of the world's leading experts on the social basis of broadcasting regulation, has argued that a regulatory regime is necessary in order to protect what he calls society's "vulnerable values." He writes, in his classic study *Regulating Media* (1996), that the nature of broadcasting regulation in any society is influenced by the value accorded to media freedom in that society, with the important caveat that most societies value freedom of speech not as an end in itself but as a means of reaching normative objectives such as the promotion of democracy. "Therefore, mass communication is deemed to have an important sociocultural dimension. Mass media render a service to society. Government, particularly the legislature, bears the responsibility of ensuring that the processes of informing the public, exchanging ideas, and thus shaping values take place in a truly free manner and are not jeopardized either by the state or private power-holders" (268).

The notion of "vulnerable values" merits some elaboration. Broadly speaking, the term refers to values that are generally accepted by society at large but that can be considered to be at risk. Hoffmann-Riem cites twenty fields or areas that typically require protective regulatory measures in broadcasting. These include pluralism, diversity, fairness, and impartiality; public responsibility in airing different interests and countering of stereotypes; access for minorities; protection of juveniles and fostering of educational programming for children; maintenance of standards in matters of violence, sex, taste, and decency; maintenance of high-quality programming; and personal integrity. In addition to *values*, regulation can also aim to protect vulnerable social *groups:* women, children, ethnic and racial minorities, and so forth.

The need to defend vulnerable values and social groups in broadcasting, therefore, requires providing safeguards to protect those that may be generally supported by the legal and social order but are potentially placed at risk by broadcasting content. When different values collide – say, freedom of expression and the need to protect children – authorities need to find the appropriate balance point. Societies differ as to where this point lies.

The European Commission High Level Group on Audiovisual Policy articulated this issue in the following way in 1998: "The European approach has traditionally been one of balance. Recognising the role of the audiovisual media as a societal, democratic, cultural and economic factor, legislators have striven to achieve a balance between conflicting demands. For example, the right to freedom of expression has to be balanced against other rights with regard to matters such as the protection of minors, racial hatred and the right to privacy" (European Commission 1998, 5).

This echoes a growing international consensus that freedom and constraint must be balanced. According to the United Nations Educational, Scientific and Cultural Organization (UNESCO) World Commission on Culture and Development (1995, 106), "there are serious questions about media content ... The sounds and images carried by the media may offend certain deeply-held beliefs and sensitivities ... The question is, who will say 'enough' and when? How to find the dividing line between desirable freedom and unacceptable licence?"[21]

The story of the Quebec City radio station CHOI-FM is a case in point. On 13 July 2004, the CRTC denied Genex Communications Inc's request to renew the licence of CHOI-FM. Since its acquisition by Genex in 1997, the station had successfully marketed an aggressive brand of programming that led to repeated complaints from different segments of the community. Most were related to the on-air behaviour of a morning call-in radio show host, Jeff Fillion. His recurring comments were often characterized as racist, sexist, and offensive, and as using the public airwaves to verbally attack and harass people. The CRTC at first imposed conditions of licence that sought to use the Canadian Association of Broadcasters (2002) Code of Ethics to try to improve the situation, but without any impact. The station simply ignored the regulator. In 2002, the CRTC renewed CHOI's licence for a reduced period of two years. At the end of that period, a public hearing was held, at which Genex insisted that there was no problem and that it was simply filling a market demand. The CRTC refused to renew the licence and issued a call for applications to occupy the frequency. It set 31 August 2004 as the last day the station could broadcast (CRTC 2004a, 2004b).

Genex appealed, but on 1 September 2005 the Federal Court of Appeal upheld the CRTC decision. Writing on behalf of the court in *Genex Communications v. Canada (Attorney General)*, Justice J.A. Letourneau wrote:

> The appellant makes much of the guarantee of freedom of expression in paragraph 2(b) of the Charter and seems to want to treat it as unqualified, something that the courts have never recognized. I do not think I am mistaken in saying that freedom of expression, freedom of opinion and freedom of speech do not mean freedom of defamation, freedom of oppression and freedom of opprobrium. Nor do I think I am mistaken in saying that the right to freedom of expression under the Charter does not require that the State or the CRTC become accomplices in or promoters of defamatory language or violations of the rights to privacy, integrity, human dignity and reputation by forcing them to issue a broadcasting licence used for those purposes. To accept the appellant's proposition would mean using the Charter to make the State or its agencies an instrument of oppression or violation of the individual rights to human dignity,

privacy and integrity on behalf of the commercial profitability of a business. (paragraph 221)[22]

This exceptional case stands as a landmark in balancing the *Charter* right of freedom of expression and societal standards and in affirming the legitimacy of public regulation of media.

The *Broadcasting Act* as an Instrument of Communication Rights

Broadcasting in Canada is governed by the *Broadcasting Act,* which defines broadcasting not as an industry but as "a public service essential to the maintenance and enhancement of national identity and cultural sovereignty." In other words, the act defines broadcasting as a system of communication and not merely as a medium of entertainment. The CRTC is responsible for enforcing the *Broadcasting Act* and licenses both radio and television broadcasters in three distinct sectors: public broadcasting (the CBC, provincial educational broadcasters), private broadcasting (commercial services), and community broadcasting (nonprofit, community-based radio and television). The CRTC also licenses a range of cable and satellite distribution undertakings.

More detailed and specific than the *Charter,* the *Broadcasting Act* can be seen as the cornerstone of Canadian communication rights with respect to media. Struggles surrounding the writing and adoption of subsequent versions of the act, going back as early as 1932, have resulted in the recognition of broadcasting as an essential public service, of the role of national public broadcasting, of community media, and of the multicultural and multiracial nature of Canadian society as well as the special place of Aboriginal people, and in the insertion (in 1991) of a unique section that can be considered a standard-setter in the codification and normalization of communication rights. This section reads: "The Canadian broadcasting system should ... through its programming and the employment opportunities arising out of its operations, serve the needs and interests, and reflect the circumstances and aspirations, of Canadian men, women and children, including equal rights, the linguistic duality and multicultural and multiracial nature of Canadian society and the special place of aboriginal peoples within that society" (section 3(1)(d)(iii)).

The first thing to be noted about this section is that its insertion in the act was the result of a unique process of public consultation and lobbying that mobilized dozens of civil society groups and several thousand individuals over a six-year period (1985-91).[23] This process led, for example, to the differentiation, in the act, of "programming" and "employment" as distinct elements of the broadcasting system, both of which can legitimately raise normative expectations; and to the differentiation between the "multicultural" and "multiracial" nature of Canadian society (the initial version referred only to "multicultural"). The rights of children were also written into the act as a result of lobbying efforts after initial legislative omission. The formal access to the policy-making process has therefore to be underscored as a significant aspect of the Canadian communication rights framework.

Research conducted in 1998 pointed, however, to the limitations of this legal provision as an effective tool for the realization of communication rights on the ground.[24] In focus group interviews with activists who use the media but do not consider media the target of their activist efforts, the clause was dismissed by some as an empty gesture to "political correctness," while others argued that its effects, if any, were certainly not apparent on the air.[25] Because the law is expressed in the conditional mood ("should"), it was felt that such a statement did not force policy makers to specify a precise form of regulation. This portion of the law, participants in one of the group discussions agreed, is not a principled statement that assigns a mission to the broadcasting system, but rather a relatively vague definition that does not carry with it any real obligations for broadcasters:

> *Former political advisor (female), 39 years old:* The term "should" means that they're setting out a mission, here, for [the] broadcasting system ... So that's something [toward] which we can tend but where everyone knows we're not going to get there. In politics you arrange things so you don't paint yourself into a corner; you put this kind of statement in the law, and all they have to do when there's an accusation is to say, "It's true that we should have tried a bit harder, we sinned, we're sorry, we'll see what we can do." In the end, at the political level, it's perfect!

Another problem noted was that one could have a broadcasting system that meets the law's requirements but still fails to meet one's hopes and needs:

> *Former political activist (female), 40 years old:* It's true that, with a great deal of creativity, we could certainly get to a [system that meets the *Broadcasting Act*'s mandate], but would I be interested in that system? I can't say.

Some criticized what, for them, was the narrow scope of the law. Other participants felt that the law did not sufficiently constrain economic forces:

> *Political party activist (female), 25 years old:* They could have talked about how television is financed. To what point, for example, does a financial backer have the right to interfere [with programming]? They could have talked about that [in the act].

Some participants questioned the very principle behind having a law control the Canadian broadcasting system, while recognizing its possibilities:

> *Former political activist (female), 40 years old:* Something tells me that it's worth thinking about that a bit more ... [For example,] I'm pretty much in favour of [community broadcasters]. Maybe I'd change their programming; maybe I'd want to change things around. But the idea that they exist in the first place, I like that. So I don't agree with throwing [the law] out. [Certainly,] it shouldn't be a nitpicking type of regulation that operates through juxtapositions, a layer here to please one person, another layer to please someone else, and so on until it becomes a total patchwork, a kind of quilt. The pattern starts to spin out of control. It could be simplified but I think that if the State doesn't do it, who's going to give [the media system] its soul?

The individual acceptance of the status quo in broadcasting among these otherwise politicized respondents was, on the surface, surprising. At the same time, however, it was consistent with the expectations that they had exhibited with regard to the media system at large: expectations were low, and so demands were neither stringent nor exacting. Our interviewees further noted a fairly large degree of diversity in programming supply that, they felt, would be able to meet nearly anyone's needs relatively well. This observation contradicted other, rather negative judgments that they made of the "very poor" quality of the programming. What is more, when respondents did assert their identities as citizens who demand change, it was tempered by a clear sense of near-powerlessness with regard to the ability to concretely change media content. Here, too, the ultimate resolution may be to look for responses to information and entertainment needs outside the media by breaking with media-use habits – that is, by interrupting the link of familiarity with media that over time has become an almost obligatory point of passage for meeting any information and communication needs that one might experience.

> *Cultural organizer (female), 60 years old:* That's me. I'm a protester ... I ask myself, "But why is it only me, or maybe twenty other people who know all of this, when there's a whole audience out there that's hungry for this sort of thing [and has no access to it]?" ... That's why I'm demanding. It's time we stopped showing ourselves lousy television, lousy media.

> *Former political activist (female), 40 years old:* If I knew how to be more demanding of CBC without necessarily having to write to them [all the time] ... When there is really something that shocks me, I [write to them].

Another participant located a paradox in a broadcasting system searching to "reflect the circumstances" of those using it. The discussion that followed questioned the existing law and attempted to identify new principles on which to base an acceptable social check on the broadcasting system. Should "common values" be identified with all citizens, shared values to which force of law might in some way be assigned? But how would this adhesion to "common values" translate concretely into effective management of media channels and programming? Without a law, on the other hand, would the media system not become beholden to a strictly market-based logic? For the *Broadcasting Act*'s affirmation of the necessity of reflecting citizens' circumstances and aspirations, suggested one participant, might not a code of ethics be substituted, to which all media professionals would submit and whose application would guarantee the production and distribution of socially honest, fair, and nondiscriminatory programming?

> *Political party activist (female), 25 years old:* Like I said, there's a paradox there ... "Reflect the circumstances," well ... a show like "Lifestyles of the Rich and Famous" doesn't reflect circumstances, but it sure reflects aspirations! Where poor people hope to become rich, are we supposed to have shows about the rich, in order to respond to people's aspirations, or is it shows about the poor people, because those are their circumstances? I mean, it could mean anything at all

... There's another paradox: "needs and interests." They'd need to be defined, these "interests" of the population, you know? Do we do lousy shows because the population wants them, or are the shows lousy because the population laps them up?

In short, do we have the media we want or the media we deserve? Numerous ideas were expressed aimed at improving the act: that it require the establishment of a code of ethics; that the principles and values it expresses focus on quality of life; that the act also mention broadcasters' social responsibility:

Community worker (female), 43 years old: The text would have to set objectives that deal with quality of life, that aim to improve living conditions, that try to establish a balance [with regard to] social and human [values] ... [If] my interests are pornography, and my needs involve being excited, well that would certainly [fall under the law] ... [The system] could meet my needs and interests ... but is it meeting the needs and interests of improving quality of life and social balance? No ... It's too broad, and too open to interpretation.

Social worker (female), 40 years old: I'd want to see it talk more about social responsibility ... it's funny because we'd have thought it would be government telling us how we should behave but, right now, it's the markets telling us how we should behave. They've already imposed uniform needs, uniform interests and aspirations on us. In that sense, I think [that policy makers] would have a lot more impact if they talked in terms of social responsibility: we could define broadcasters' social responsibility in terms of the public; there we'd certainly need signposts.

Community worker (male), 28 years old: Canada pretends to be a democratic society. For me, democracy isn't just the choice between the blue party and then, five years later, the red party ... It's the broad participation of citizens in different organizations and from one ocean to the other, in lots of cities, in lots of environments ... If we look around across Canada, there are groups which bring together thousands of people, and I think that that kind of democracy should show up more often in the media. We should make more room for that instead of always focusing on liberal democracy, which takes all the room ... I think there'd be room for people's aspirations, to hear from the people and ... the organizations that people have created in order to have a voice, in order to have power. To my mind, the broadcasting system should be the expression of real participative democracy.

At the end of the day, it emerged from our lively discussions with these committed social activists that they had not really given much thought to media issues, although these were issues that they recognized as affecting their everyday lives and their social and political citizenship practices. One of the most telling statements we gathered was this one, reflecting at one and the same time the positive contribution of the *Broadcasting Act* and its limited effectiveness:

> *Activist theologian (male), 70 years old:* First, I didn't have any idea that [this] law existed ... If someone had told me, "Listen, here's the Canadian law," I would have said, "I don't believe you one bit" ... it's so different from what's actually visible in the media these days ... As neither a lawyer nor a specialist, I find it interesting, and I'd say that the media in general don't seem to be making much of an effort to stick to this, [especially] reflecting the circumstances and aspirations of Canadian men, women and children: that's equality at the level of rights. Not bad.

Communication Rights and "Other" Rights, or the Broader Context of Media and Communication Rights

While the *Broadcasting Act* specifies a series of rights and obligations for broadcasters, the way that these translate into actual media practice impinges forcefully on the realization of Canadians' individual and collective rights *in general.* Looking closely at how this plays out is instructive for understanding the place of communication rights in Canada.

To illustrate, let us take one eloquent example that demonstrates how different aspects of the act intersect in real life. Section 3(1)(o) of the act specifies that "programming that reflects the aboriginal cultures of Canada should be provided within the Canadian broadcasting system as resources become available for the purpose." As we saw earlier, section 3(1)(d)(iii) insists that Canadian broadcasting serve all Canadians equally. There is no legal incompatibility between these two articles of law. In practice, however, the choices made by Canadian broadcasters with respect to the way they carry out their obligations impinge upon the ability of the system to serve the different parts of its constituency. The Lincoln Report noted that the act's qualification that "programming that reflects the aboriginal cultures of Canada should be provided within the Canadian broadcasting system *as resources become available for the purpose*" detracts from another section of the act, which states that "the Canadian broadcasting system should reflect the special place of aboriginal peoples within Canadian society" (Canada 2003b, emphasis added). The same type of qualifier is found elsewhere in the act, in sections dealing with services accessible to disabled persons and linguistic duality, and also in various CRTC decisions and policy statements that privilege economic considerations over more fundamental social and cultural objectives of Canada's broadcasting policy. The resources argument is most evident in the CBC's justification for the choices it makes.

In the research described in the preceding section, we asked the Mohawk elder who participated in the study whether he felt that the Canadian broadcasting system was meeting the needs and interests of Canada's Aboriginal population. His reply:

> They may be trying to but there's always that one thing that's facing them: costs. They could do a good job, sure. They say they're going to too, too much. They had programs coming from Northern Cree settlements. I used to get up in the morning and listen to those on Sunday. I didn't understand the language but I'm getting the feel from people, listening to them, grasping what they're talking about, you know? I wish I could put myself right in there knowing the language. It's fun. They're so at ease with what they're doing. They've got their own language and that's very helpful. It's a good thing for their people, they're learning something. They're learning what's going on in the rest of the world too ... They don't see too much happening but they know what's happening from their small community.

This small tale poignantly illustrates a number of aspects of the Canadian social environment that can be addressed through the framework of communication rights. A Canadian scholar of the role of culture in governance, Robin Higham (1998), points out that the philosopher Charles Taylor (1992, 1993) has described Canada as an experiment in multinational pluralism, where the notion of "civility" is particularly valued as an approach to problem solving. "Canada may be as close as any society has come to balancing unity and diversity, to producing a society where belonging as a citizen is non-threatening to that citizen's cultural identity. Our weak spot is the fragility of that balance," writes Higham (1998, 12). Cultural diversity in the Canadian context is, in other words, to connect back to Hoffmann-Riem's approach to media regulation, a vulnerable value that requires proactive measures.

The special rights of Canada's Aboriginal people, to continue in the same domain, have in some cases been enhanced by positive media regulation. The best example of this is the CRTC's requirement that cable and satellite distributors provide the Aboriginal Peoples Television Network (APTN) to all subscribers, collect a fee, and pass it on to the broadcaster. This example – unique in the world – is in some ways a model for proactive enabling of communication rights. But how far can it extend to covering *everyone* or even to any one group's communication rights?

Linguistic duality is another aspect of the *Broadcasting Act* that appears straightforward in the text but is complex and multi-layered in practice. The act reiterates, in several places, the fundamental characteristic of Canada as a bilingual state and goes further than most federal policy texts in recognizing the asymmetrical nature of bilingualism on the ground, when it states in section 3(1)(c) that "English and French language broadcasting, while sharing common aspects, operate under different conditions and may have different requirements." This is a double-edged blade, however: on the one hand, it recognizes the autonomy and distinctiveness of each of the country's dominant linguistic groups, but, on the other hand, it opens the door to broadcasting policies that could prove to be discriminatory to minority-language communities or, on a macro scale, to French-language broadcasting nationally. What does it actually mean? Can all Canadians claim a "right" to receive broadcasting services in English and in French, and what does that mean for the communication rights of Canadians whose interests and aspirations might indicate a need or a desire for broadcasting in other languages?

To elaborate, let us look at how this plays out in the official mandate of the national public broadcaster, the CBC. Section 3(1)(m) of the act mandates the CBC to:

    (i)   be predominantly and distinctively Canadian,
  (ii) reflect Canada and its regions to national and regional audiences, while serving those regions,
 (iii) actively contribute to the flow and exchange of cultural expression,

(iv) be in English and in French, reflecting the different needs and circumstances of each official language community, including the particular needs and circumstances of English and French linguistic minorities,

(v) strive to be of equivalent quality in English and in French,

(vi) contribute to shared national consciousness and identity,

(vii) be made available throughout Canada by the most appropriate and efficient means and as resources become available for the purpose, and

(viii) reflect the multicultural and multiracial nature of Canada.

The CBC, as everyone knows, has suffered crippling budget cuts in the past two decades. In a word, it has responded to its mandated obligations, for better or for worse, by focusing on high-end, national programs at the expense of less prestigious, less visible services to local, regional, or niche publics. It is arguably "predominantly and distinctively Canadian," but its ability to serve "the special needs" of Canada's regions has becoming increasingly problematic and contested. Grassroots dissatisfaction with CBC service in and to the regions was the leitmotif of public hearings held across the country by the Lincoln Committee in 2001-03. This was particularly pronounced with respect to official language minorities, who have generally felt shortchanged by services programmed in the metropolitan centres of Montreal and Toronto.[26] The act pointedly does *not* require the CBC to provide *local* programming, and the notion of "region" in Canada is problematic at best.[27]

The CBC is mandated to "strive to be of equivalent quality in English and in French," a laudable objective that plays out in annual budget allocation exercises that take place in a total absence of transparency.[28] CBC program services are linguistically striated from the vice-president level on down, and budgets to media end up allocated roughly two-thirds to English and one-third to French – or somewhere between what would be determined by either a distribution based on demographics or a fifty-fifty split that striving "to be of equivalent quality" would seem to indicate. In other words, it is a political solution that, arguably, takes account of the different circumstances and requirements of English- and French-language broadcasting mentioned elsewhere in the act. As for the CBC's mandated obligation to "contribute to shared national consciousness and identity," it is clearly fraught with difficulty:

whatever the CBC may or may not be contributing in this area, it is doing separately, in English and in French.

The apparently innocent injunction that services "be made available throughout Canada by the most appropriate and efficient means," coupled with the previously mentioned disclaimer "as resources become available for the purpose," makes for a volatile combination in the case of the CBC. During the CRTC's 2006 review of television regulations, the CBC advocated getting out of over-the-air television delivery (CBC/Radio-Canada 2006), a costly and arguably less efficient means of reaching *most* of the population, but the only *appropriate* means of ensuring that all can have access to this national public service, as it is free of charge and available almost everywhere in Canada. After many decades and at great cost, the CBC finally, in the 1970s, extended its national over-the-air coverage to all communities with a population of 500 or more; it has now proposed to the CRTC a formula that would see it realize a substantial saving and, by its calculation, deprive *only* about 2 percent of the Canadian population of access to what should be a universal public service (CBC/Radio-Canada 2006). From a communication rights perspective, this is a damning proposition.

Another aspect that needs consideration here is the link between the multicultural mandate of Canadian broadcasting and media representation, cultural diversity, and the place of minorities in Canadian media.[29] This is relevant insofar as the success or failure of Canadian media in fulfilling this mandate can be considered either an enabling or disabling mechanism that stimulates inclusion and participation in civic life. It is thus central to the realization of communication rights.

Cultural policies in Canada are intrinsic to manifestations of cultural diversity; as such, they influence the ways in which we belong, participate, and live. In this regard, media representation of ethnic and racial minorities in Canada is one of the important ways to assess the coming together of two of Canada's most important cultural policies, in the spheres of *broadcasting* and *multiculturalism*.

The *Canadian Multiculturalism Act* provides an overall framework for the management of ethnocultural and racial diversity in Canada.[30] The *Broadcasting Act* is more focused and specific, as we have seen: it describes broadcasting as a public service and mandates broadcasting to facilitate expressions of citizenship through debate, dialogue, and exchange. Multiculturalism policy positively affirms diversity as a "fundamental characteristic of Canadian heritage and identity," as well as "an invaluable resource in the shaping of Canada's future" (see section 3(1)(b) of the *Canadian Multiculturalism Act*). The *Broadcasting Act* translates that affirmation into a set of policy objectives for broadcasting.

Much of the research on media representation of ethnic and racial minorities in Canada focuses on the chronic *under-representation* and *misrepresentation* of minorities (e.g., Henry and Tator 2000; Mahtani 2001; Fleras and Kunz 2001). Not only are minorities under-represented and misrepresented but evidence also suggests that there is an overwhelming absence in the media of issues dealing with the experienced reality of systemic racism in Canadian society (Henry and Tator 2000). Media representation of minorities also serves to shape the social and civic identities of Canadians (Mahtani 2001) and reinforces the exclusion of minorities, while at the same time suggesting what it means to be Canadian (Bullock and Jafri 2001). Since 11 September 2001, there has been a perceived return to Orientalist representations of minorities in Canadian media, affecting representation of Arabs, South Asians, and Muslims in particular (Jiwani 2005). Overall, gaps in representation have encouraged minority publics in Canada to seek out other media forms that better resonate with their cosmopolitan experiences (Karim 2006; Ojo 2006).

There is also the question of the place accorded on the air to media produced by and for the members of minority communities themselves. According to Ojo (2006), more than 250 newspapers and approximately fourteen radio stations are devoted to ethnic broadcasting in Canada. The CRTC has issued licences for dozens of specialty, pay television, and digital services representing over fifty cultures. Although this may seem like a significant amount, the literature related to the media representation of minorities is disturbing. Not only are minorities stereotypically depicted in many instances but the mere fact that minorities do not own or control the stations and are not represented in the newsrooms results in what Ojo (2006, 347) calls a "homogenization of the media landscapes." On the one hand, the chronic under- and misrepresentation of minorities in the media is indeed disabling for minority communities in Canada vis-à-vis communication rights; on the other hand, the emergence of "ethnic" media produced by and for members of these communities can be considered an enabling mechanism for these same communities and an articulation of the right to communicate.

The issue is clouded when one tries to look at it from a universalistic perspective: is the purpose of multicultural broadcasting to represent minority communities in the semiotic sense or in the political sense? Is it to strengthen their identities and capacity to participate in society as members of particular groups or to guarantee their democratic rights of citizenship? The concept of a right to communicate is compelling in this regard because it remains unclear and perhaps that is its strength.

One of the spaces that captured Canada's diversity long before it made its way into mainstream television was community radio.[31] Campus-based stations had been known in Canada since the 1920s, and in the mid-1970s community radio took off, with stations in Vancouver, Kitchener, Ottawa, and Montreal. Today, there are approximately 140 licensed community and campus-based radio stations across the country, with broadcasters in every province and territory.

The community sector, along with the private and public sectors, comprise the Canadian national broadcasting system, which is defined as follows in the *Broadcasting Act:* "The Canadian broadcasting system, operating primarily in English and French languages and comprising of public, private and community elements, makes use of radio frequencies that are public property and provides, through its programming, a public service essential to the maintenance and enhancement of national identity and cultural sovereignty" (section 3(1)(b)). Not only is there a theoretical equality between the three sectors of broadcasting but there is also a recognition (further refined through the policies specific to these sectors) that they are distinct and complementary. As with other aspects of the *Broadcasting Act,* that which appears straightforward on the surface is much more nuanced in practice. For community radio, the main problem is the use by the CRTC of the commercial ratings measurement firm BBM's definition of market as the standard unit of measurement to determine the parameters with which to evaluate the success of community radio (see CRTC 1986, paragraph 2). Community radio, however, is owned by not-for-profit organizations, which makes it difficult to understand why the CRTC defaults to commercial standards when looking at their performance.

Other issues have also weighed on the existence of these operations. Traditionally, community broadcasters were guaranteed a right of carriage over cable transmission networks, in recognition of the extension of the Canadian broadcasting system through cable FM. With the arrival of satellite radio in Canada in 2005 (see CRTC 2005a), community broadcasters hoped to stretch the system in another direction. Although the CRTC agreed that community radio on satellite was an interesting prospect, it did not guarantee carriage through this new form of technology, leaving the arrangements for potential carriage up to the different parties.

Unlike the public broadcaster, CBC/Radio-Canada, community broadcasters do not have access to reserved portions of the spectrum, making it difficult to develop in large cities where the spectrum is already saturated. In addition, it is difficult for new low-power broadcasters to penetrate markets because no protection is given to them in the event a full-power broadcaster applies for a licence that will interfere with the less powerful signal. Developmental community stations CJAI, Amherst Island Radio, located outside of Kingston, Ontario, and CFMH in Saint John, New Brunswick, faced this situation in 2007.[32]

Another important point of contention is the unequal allocation of public funding for "public media." Parliament provides CBC/Radio-Canada with $1 billion per year (in addition to which, the CBC enjoys an additional $400 million in advertising revenue), but very little is allocated to the community media infrastructure. Quebec is the only province actively funding its community media. These practices are contradictory to those of most industrialized countries, which have developed national funds to ensure the vitality of the community broadcasting system.

In spite of the inequitable regulatory environment, community broadcasting has made some progress in recent years. The uniting of Canada's three large community radio associations – National Campus and Community Radio Association (NCRA), the Association des radiodiffuseurs communautaires du Québec (ARCQ), and the Alliance canadienne des radiodiffuseurs communautaires du Canada (ARC) – provide a united front to actively develop Canada's first national funding mechanism for community radio through regular discussions with regulators and commercial broadcasters. In August 2007, the NCRA and ARC intervened in Astral Media's purchase of Standard Broadcasting and obtained $1.5 million over seven years, to be invested in the Community Radio Fund of Canada (CRFC).

As far as policy is concerned, in the summer of 2007, the Department of Canadian Heritage announced that it would invest limited funds to conduct its first-ever study of community broadcasting. Studies will be conducted in community radio and television. These studies will contribute to the comprehensive review of community broadcasting radio and television policies that the CRTC committed to undertaking in its *Diversity of Voices* decision (CRTC 2008b). In addition to an analysis of the Canadian Heritage studies, the planned CRTC review will examine licensing policies, the role of new technologies, funding sources, and national community undertakings.

The community broadcasting associations have also developed a news and program exchange network to facilitate the wider circulation of independently produced content and provide citizens with a national communication infrastructure in which they can take part. The NCRA has initiated an independent wire service available in three languages (French, English, and Spanish), called *GroundWire*.

From a communication rights perspective, the potential success of Canadian community broadcasting lies primarily in the ability of the regulator (and, by extension, the general public) to consider the broadcasting system as something broader than a simple "market." A more balanced approach striving to maintain all three sectors (public, private, and community) in the system through a variety of measures would ensure appropriate access to all citizens. Such a change in policy-making ideology and practice requires both a regulator with the vision to successfully engage civil society in its work and a civil society that is willing to engage the regulator. Consequently, key elements in developing community broadcasting include the unrelenting work of policy advocates, the growth of the Community Radio Fund of Canada, and a stronger commitment from government to invest public funds into the "third sector" of the broadcast system.

Despite the fact that CRTC proaction has been indispensable to the community broadcasting sector, it is difficult to count on this in the current environment. The CRTC was created in the late 1960s, a time when new communications technologies began developing at a rapid pace. Regulating all aspects of the broadcasting system was the CRTC's mandate, and it embodied the Canadian cultural standards to which all broadcasters should aspire (Raboy and Bonin 2008). The CRTC's role has changed through the years, however, permitting many broadcasters to consolidate and test just how far Canadians are prepared to see this institution go in balancing the objectives of Canadian content, access to the system, and letting market forces prevail.

Historically, public hearings in Canada have been powerful events – going back to the first parliamentary commission on radio in 1932, which heard Graham Spry of the Canadian Radio League tell parliamentarians that the choice between the people's interest and commercial interests was a choice between "the State or the United States." Public hearings, however flawed, are one of the best support mechanisms for communication rights. They also

provide a barometer with which to assess the performance of public authorities, as well as a window to the positions of the various players and stakes.

In February 2008, the CRTC held hearings to review the state of the Canadian Television Fund (CTF). Two large conglomerates, Shaw Communications and Quebecor, were at the heart of this review. As we discuss in
Chapter 3, the fund, which has been the bread and butter for many producers,
writers, and actors for the last decade, was publicly criticized and discredited
by the private broadcasters, who chose to withdraw their contributions, a
gesture that goes against prescribed conditions of licence and industry best
practices. The broadcasters proposed to create their own development fund
in lieu of contributing to the CTF. This battle was a further test of the power
of the CRTC, which rejected the proposal in a report released on 5 June 2008
(CRTC 2008d).

Another hearing held in 2008 reviewed the regulatory framework for
broadcast distribution undertakings (BDUs) and discretionary programming
services (see CRTC 2008g). This followed on the heels of the controversial
Dunbar and Leblanc report (2007), which suggested, among other things,
removing simultaneous substitution, a practice that has been a highly lucra-
tive cash cow for the television industry over the years, but that has proven
to add no value to Canadian content and in fact encourages conventional
broadcasters to show US programs during prime time.

But the most important part of this round of hearings, held in February
and March 2009, focused on "Canadian broadcasting in new media" (CRTC
2008a, 2008c). Seen as a revisiting of the CRTC's controversial decision not
to regulate broadcasting on the Internet (CRTC 1999), the hearing covered
a sweeping range of issues that went to the heart of defining the emerging
multi-platform media environment, touching on the definition of "new
media," funding of conventional public and private broadcasters, a floated
levy on Internet service provider (ISP) revenues to be used for supporting the
production of Canadian online content, and the exemption of mobile on-
demand broadcasting from regulation.

In its June 2009 "new" new media policy, the CRTC renewed its 1999
order making new media broadcasting exempt from regulation in Canada.
The result is, according to Abramson and Buchanan (2009), that "anyone
may continue to provide audiovisual content in Canada over the Internet –
or, assuming an authorized use of spectrum, wirelessly – without registering
with the CRTC, meeting any Canadian ownership and control requirement,

ensuring a minimum level of Canadian content, or being subject to any cross-media ownership rule." At the same time, however, the 2009 new media policy expresses uncertainty over how "new media broadcasting" ought to be defined in light of the emergence of a series of distinct and very different technical platforms (ranging in maturity, penetration, and profitability from Internet to mobile phone–based broadcasting services and including the emerging market for personal video set-top devices, and so on) and how its consumption and availability should be monitored. In response, the CRTC launched a series of follow-up proceedings and requested the Federal Court of Appeal to consider the question of whether or not the definition of a broadcaster should include Internet service providers offering access to broadcasting content (see CRTC 2009; Abramson and Buchanan 2009).

With the CRTC promising to revisit its new media policy yet again within five years or "at such time as events dictate," this proceeding promises to shake the foundations of Canadian media regulation and outline the shape of the next generation of media services. The CRTC is redefining what broadcasting means in the context of converging content and digital network technologies, as well as its own role with respect to new media. The actions taken by the CRTC in the coming years, and the quality of the public consultation that goes on with regard to them, will thus be fundamental to shaping the system and understanding exactly where it is headed and on what basis. The extent to which Canadian media are able to support communication rights will be strongly affected by the outcome of this process.

5
Access

Leslie Regan Shade

Access, Communication Rights, and the Soul of the System

Initiated and managed by Industry Canada, the Community Access Program (CAP), which commenced in 1994 as part of the Connecting Canadians agenda, provided funding for public Internet access sites in schools, community centres, libraries, and friendship centres, many of them in rural and remote regions. At one time, the various CAP sites around the country were said to have more outlets than Tim Hortons, serving over 20 million Canadians in the past decade, from British Columbia to the Far North to the Atlantic provinces. Despite this apocryphal and humorous promotional hook, used by community networking activists to rally support for a declining federal program, what cannot be discounted is the tangible "return on investment" garnered by the $340 million decade-long investment that spun and leveraged local community partnerships, bringing positive community economic development to many regions of the country (Moll 2007).

A blog initiated in early 2007 to discuss issues of community Internet projects in Canada called on the federal government to reverse its position on the closure of CAP, whose support had dwindled from $25 million in 2005 to $6.6 million in 2006, even though the decade-long costing had materialized into a fivefold investment because of the myriad partnerships and community leveraging.[1] CAP sites were a boon for local community economic development, as bloggers' comments attest.

From the Pacific Community Networks Association, a nonprofit group based in British Columbia, came the following entreaty:

> We are in danger of losing a truly Canadian resource. Meanwhile, the rest of the world is using the model and vision that our government is killing ... CAP is a successful program with a proven economic and social impact. It cuts across nearly every community in

Canada. It will be lost forever. The Conservative government has offered no new initiative to take the place of CAP. They refuse to comment on this.

Blog posts from across the country spoke of the essential role of CAP for social and economic opportunities for seniors, youth, and lower-income community members:

Elizabeth said ...
CAP is imperative to Afton, PEI. CAP is the only broadband connectivity in a 15km. radius of this community. Satellite connectivity is our only broadband resource. Dialup service is so poor that most users connect at 28.8 which is half the 56k ideal of dialup. We need CAP just to be connected. Is this government abandoning its rural citizens?

Daryl Hobbs said ...
5 years ago I set up a CAP Site at 504B Parliament for Toronto Community Housing Corp. Since then the site has been an inspiration to everyone that drops by.

Chad said ...
Through CAP, we've provided basic assistive technology to over a dozen communities across Canada, giving people with disabilities basic tools to access computer information.

Emilie and Jeff said ...
I am horrified to hear that this program might be cut. I'm very Internet dependent yet I don't possess a computer. I use the computers at the Fairfield Community Association almost daily. It is where my son goes to Preschool. In a time where energy efficiency and the environment are on top of the political heap of concerns, it seems the government has forgotten about toxic waste left behind by discarded computer hardware. Cutting this program is the equivalent of canceling the mass transit system. I am disappointed that Canada can't recognize it's own good ideas. This is more than two steps back. I am directly affected, lower income people are directly affected.

Nick said ...
CAP is absolutely essential for youth in rural communities. It creates
opportunities for us by helping to build up our experience, our skills,
and our involvement in the community.

For many front-line workers and community advocates, CAP has indeed
given what *Instant World* referred to as "soul" to their communities by providing technical and social infrastructures to citizens. Whether this soul can be
sustained with the loss of core government funding is unknown, but there
seems to be consensus that with the gradual demise of CAP, Canada's reputation as a global leader in information and communication technology (ICT)
services and access for citizens will decline. CAP is a salient example of discursive and material shifts in how ICT access policy has changed in the last
decade, from ICT access to foster and nurture participatory citizenship toward
a discourse that merely advantages consumers' access to goods and services,
discounting the political will of Canadians and performing a disservice to
our citizenry. While Chapter 4 focused on the press, broadcasting, and the
right to communicate, this chapter considers ICTs and the right to communicate. The term "ICTs" refers to the digitization of media (from using analog
to digital signals) and the attendant convergence of audio- and visual-based
content – broadcasting, audio, the Internet, and newer "Web 2.0" forms of
the Internet – which facilitate more flexibility in terms of content creation
and new platforms for distribution.

ICTs also create the potential for a more participatory user environment.
Assessing numerous quantitative and qualitative studies on Internet use in
Canada, Veenhof and colleagues (2008, 23) remark that "the Internet is
breeding a more social era, with active communication and information
seeking activities compared to the more passive traditional forms of entertainment such as television." As this chapter will argue, access to ICTs is a fundamental communication right for Canadian citizens, given the central – and,
some would argue, unavoidable – need for all citizens, regardless of age,
gender, ethnicity, linguistic background, class, and geographical location, to
be able to connect to ICTs in their everyday lives for education, work, or
leisure.

From POTS to PANS

Universal service has traditionally been the goal of North American telecommunications policy. In the United States, this concept dates back to 1907,

when Theodore Vail, then president of the American Telephone and Telegraph Company (AT&T), used the term in reference to his desire to interconnect the fragmented local telephone companies into a unified and interconnected national system (John 1999). The US *Communications Act of 1934* directed the Federal Communications Commission (FCC) to make available an efficient and nationwide wire and radio network, with universal service achieved through application of cross-subsidies made possible through the regulated monopoly scheme of the telephone industry.[2] Sixty years later, the *Telecommunications Act of 1996* expanded the concept of universal service beyond dial tone – "plain old telephone service," or POTS – to consider advanced services such as the Internet (Cooper and Kimmelman 2001).[3] Through extension of the Universal Service Fund to provide public access network services (PANS), the E-Rate Program mandated discounts for high-speed connections for schools, libraries, and rural health care centres (Hudson 2004).

In Canada, the concept of universality has been widely accepted as an intrinsic facet of Canadian identity. Historically, a commonly used measure in achieving universal service was telephone penetration – the percentage of all households that have a telephone on the premises (Schement and Forbes 2000). As Cheryl Buchwald (1997) observed, however, with the development and deployment of the Internet in Canada during the mid-1990s, Canadian policy makers became influenced by the pro-market mantra of the US as reflected starkly in the *Telecommunications Act of 1996,* and neoliberal policies touting deregulation and privatization won over the calls of public interest groups to preserve a viable and vibrant public space (Aufderheide 1999). Robert Babe (1998) has argued that Canadian telecommunications have historically been characterized by regulated monopoly firms with a distinct separation between services, technologies, and regulation, but that the new regime, starting in the late 1980s to mid-1990s until now, exists in a pastiche of convergences – among sectors, services, and technologies. The end result is globalization in a neoliberal and anti-regulatory environment, where issues of access, equity, and social justice receive scant attention.[4]

Despite a strong history of communications technologies and policies in Canada serving the needs of Canadian culture and identity, the concept of universalism in ICTs has faded as Canada has aligned itself with Western free market ideologies and, like the US, dismantled or greatly reduced federal government programs designed to bring public access to communities, schools, and other public sectors. This trend continues today, with moves by Stephen Harper's Conservative government to allow for more competitive market-led approaches in the telecommunications sector, including then Industry Minister Maxime Bernier's tabling of a policy directive ordering the Canadian Radio-television and Telecommunications Commission (CRTC) to rely on market forces to the "maximum extent feasible" in implementing the *Telecommunications Act*, and an announcement in 2008 of a possible review of foreign ownership caps (Longford et al. 2008).[5]

In considering the history of universal service and universal access in Canada, Martin Dowding (2002, 218) remarks that they "have never been clearly defined, partly because of a corporate agenda and partly because of a combination of technological, ideological, and regulatory change." Discussing the early development of "information highway" policy in the United States and Canada in the mid-1990s, Dowding differentiates between the socio-technical tradition and the newer techno-economic convergence regime. According to this distinction, the socio-technical tradition accounts for "concurrently and equitably, the needs and contributions of all society – the market, civil society, the government – and the technology created, controlled, and beneficially experienced by the whole of society." The regime of techno-economic convergence, on the other hand, "assumes first and foremost that profits realized by the private sector through the nexus of technology and the market should remain in private sector hands" (Dowding 2001, 12).

It is within this tension of differing traditions that the 1995 CRTC report *Competition and Culture on Canada's Information Highway* considered universal access and universal service, indicating "its concern that the market and those citizens affected by it are subject to two different kinds of 'access,' but mak[ing] it clear that technical, competitive market access is no more, or less, important than universal access for communities, health-care facilities and schools" (Dowding 2002, 217; see also CRTC 1995). The Canadian government's response to the final report of the Information Highway Advisory Council (IHAC), entitled *Building the Information Highway: Moving Canada into the 21st Century*, identified the need for a "national strategy for access to essential services" from the ministers of Industry and Canadian Heritage (see Canada 1996). This was reiterated in IHAC's final report (see Canada 1997a), along with recommendations for governments, industry, and public interest and consumer groups to "make community networks and public spaces sustainable," and a further recommendation for a national access advisory committee (Clement et al. 2001). While a national access strategy was never formulated per se, Industry Canada's Connectedness Agenda, a series of funded programs to provide ICT access (discussed in more detail later), was the Liberal government's response to create a semblance of universal access for Canadians. This agenda would, according to former Minister of Industry John Manley (1998), ensure that Canada become "the most connected nation in the world by the year 2000." More recently, however, faced with substantial cutbacks and elimination of some funded programs, Canada's Conservative government reneged on the country's traditional public service principles, championed the free market as the competitive saviours, and positioned Canadian citizens as mere consumers for ICT services. Placed at risk are those citizens who, for reasons of socioeconomics, culture, or geographical location, are not able to effectively procure or participate in ICTs for their personal or community betterment. In ICT access, as in other areas, the lack of a diversity of voices signals the extent to which many Canadians are not fully realizing their communication rights.

Access as a Communication Right

Various stakeholders have different conceptions of universal access to ICTs. Generally, industry defines access as an elimination of regulatory barriers to foster the development of innovative products and services in order to maximize accumulated profits and market share. Government sees itself as a facilitator, rather than as the party that could and should set universal access goals. Government has also been concerned with developing targeted programs to ensure access of ICTs to citizens that will in turn provide examples to the private sector, and perhaps eventually lead to the further commodification of government services. In contrast, the public interest sector envisions a broader notion of society and democracy through the promotion of universal access as a public good and a communication right that will achieve positive externalities. Public access, provided through a myriad of physical locations, has been championed, with advocates contending that these environments contribute toward a sustainable and vital public sphere. This vision of universal access to basic network services is seen as an elemental component of communication rights in an information society, where effective citizenship depends on ensuring that all citizens can create, and have access to, the content they need for active participation in their local communities and in their more global communities of interest (Kahin and Keller 1995; IPRP 1998; Clement et al. 2001; Walters 2001).

Achieving consensus on the fundamental values surrounding universal access among the different stakeholders is one of the most challenging ICT policy issues today. While it is acknowledged that access to networks and services should be equitable, affordable, and ubiquitous, it is also recognized that access depends on diverse physical, technical, economic, social, and cultural factors. As well, communities define access in different ways according to their everyday needs. For instance, most elementary and secondary schools will not need the same high bandwidth required by researchers in medical imaging. The disabled community will need special features to aid in accessing information that the able-bodied community takes for granted (Steinstra et al. 2007). Different individuals and groups will demand access to, and the creation of, their own idiosyncratic information content, which can require special equipment such as webcams, scanners, or other computer peripherals. Technological developments, notably Wi-Fi and mobile communications, have added to the complexity of what should be considered essential ICT tools for economic and social betterment; BlackBerrys and Internet-enabled mobiles such as the popular iPhone are now ubiquitous tools of many trades.

A Canadian legal precedent that the provision of Internet access should be considered a public good and a social utility was established by the Federal Court of Appeal in a 1996 case in which a group of community computer networks in Vancouver successfully challenged Revenue Canada's stance that nonprofit Internet service providers (ISPs) were not entitled to charitable status. Also known as FreeNets, such ISPs are typically owned and operated by a nonprofit, community-based organization whose board of directors is made up of people active in local community affairs. In 1993, the Ottawa-based National Capital FreeNet attempted to register itself as a charitable entity under the *Income Tax Act,* but the Charities Division of Revenue Canada ruled against it. The *Vancouver Regional FreeNet Assn. v. Canada (Minister of National Revenue – M.N.R.)* appeal decision overturned this ruling, affirming in the process the status of community networks as social utilities:

> The information highway is almost limitless in its scope and capacity but that is no reason for failing to recognize its vast potential for public benefit. The appellant's purpose in providing access to it is one of general public utility [paragraph 18] ... The appellant's purpose is to provide public access for the inhabitants of the lower mainland of British Columbia to the modern information highway. That is, in my view, as much a charitable purpose in the time of the second Elizabeth as was the provision of access by more conventional highways in the time of the first Queen of that name [paragraph 20].[6]

Defining and Ameliorating the "Digital Divide"

The term "digital divide" became popular in the mid-1990s as a way to describe disparities between those who had access to the Internet and those who did not. Initially, the term took on a simplistic definition, with access defined solely as access to technologies, for instance, to computers and telecommunication services. Later definitions encompassed more complex measures of access – not just access to the technical infrastructure but also access to the social infrastructure, including access to education (measures include literacy rates) and content (the ability to produce as well as to consume information). A variety of socio-demographic characteristics were recognized as increasing or inhibiting access, including income, education, gender, race, ethnicity, age, linguistic background, and geographic location (rural versus urban).

Pippa Norris (2001) has delineated a useful approach to understanding the different dimensions of the digital divide: the social divide (the gap between the information-poor and information-rich in nations); the global divide (the gap between industrialized and developing countries); and the democratic divide (those who use ICTs for civic participation versus those who are passive consumers).

The social divide. Given continuing rhetoric about increased computer and digital skills as a prerequisite for adequate participation in what is often referred to as our knowledge-based economy/society, those who cannot partake are, as many economists, pundits, politicians, and educators claim, at risk of not attaining economic success and personal advancement. Emanating from "information highway" discourse in the mid-1990s were claims that access to the Internet would enhance and improve the lives of individuals, create lifelong learning opportunities, improve job skills and career advancement, improve democratic participation in public life, enhance cultural and creative opportunities, improve access and communications for individuals with disabilities, create more efficient markets, and increase business productivity. While much of this rhetoric bordered on technological determinism, it is a truism that digital technologies have become an essential component of the lives and livelihoods of many citizens.

In the last decade, a plethora of research has examined various facets of the social digital divide in local, national, and international contexts. A focus on ameliorating the digital divide in order to provide economic and social opportunities for disadvantaged groups (children, low-income families, women) and communities (rural, remote, and inner-city) is a characteristic of this research. In their overview of digital divide literature, Brian Loader and Leigh Keeble (2004, 1) rightfully argue that this notion is "crucially bound up with debates about social exclusion, economic regeneration of deprived areas and the breakdown of social capital and community relations."[7]

The global divide. Global imbalances in access to ICTs need to be viewed both within the context of overall socioeconomic imbalances, an ongoing and persistent issue since the 1970s, and the New World Information and Communication Order (NWICO) debates (see Chapter 1), and in relation to neoliberal ideologies and practices (Thussu 2006; Pickard 2007). While digital divide studies were initially conducted in Western countries, the international promotion of electronic commerce and a liberalized telecommunication sector has led to greater recognition that the digital divide is between and among countries. So, although the 1990s witnessed a fantastic penetration rate of the Internet in the North, Southern countries have lagged behind, often in stark contrast to the North; as Campbell (2001, 121) writes, "half the world population has yet to make its first telephone call, or ... the density of telephone lines in Tokyo exceeds that of the entire continent of Africa."

For the Organisation for Economic Co-operation and Development (OECD) (2001), the fundamental barrier remains access to basic telecommunication services, and it argues that trade liberalization and increased market competition for telecommunication services are mechanisms to overcome such divides. The OECD further contends that trade liberalization has increased demand for communication services, leading to an increase in the growth of fixed and mobile access lines, alternative access technologies, Internet access and use, and lower bandwidth prices. This pro-competitive policy environment, however, reinforced by the Annex and Telecommunications Reference Papers attached to the *General Agreement on Trade in Services (GATS)*, supports commercial interests over public interests, thus lessening communication rights for many citizens and communities (Grieshaber-Otto and Sinclair 2004).[8]

Bridging the global digital divide has been the focus of many international public/private partnerships, from the 2000 *Okinawa Charter on Global Information Society* of the Group of Eight (G8) (Shade 2003)[9] to the two-phase World Summit on the Information Society (WSIS), with its focus on information and communication technologies for development (IT4D; see ITU 2003a, 2003b, 2005) amid a new multi-stakeholder semblance of governance (Raboy 2004c).

The democratic divide. Norris (2001, 12) describes this divide as the most challenging, as it "concerns the potential impact of the digital world on the distribution of power and influence in political systems ... there is growing awareness that a substantial *democratic divide* may still exist between those who do and do not use the multiple political resources available on the Internet for civic engagement."[10]

Whether or not ICTs are an appropriate tool for democratic development is controversial; for developing and least-developed countries, the arguments fracture between "cyber-enthusiasts," who firmly believe that ICTs are necessary to implement within societies, and "cyber-skeptics," who question the role of ICTs as an effective development device (Kenny 2006). Although socioeconomic indicators are a good sign of which countries and populations have access to ICTs, other variables need to be considered, including the range of human rights and civil liberties available in countries, education and literacy levels, and telecommunications availability and affordability.

Access to ICTs can bring about individual empowerment, citizen participation and advocacy, and community development. Use of ICTs to organize social justice campaigns for on-the-ground mobilization has been well documented;[11] research groups that bring together academics and community partners in order to address digital divides and contribute to policy have also been active.[12]

Organizations such as Montreal's Communautique have addressed the various digital divides across Quebec through training, policy advocacy, and dissemination of a platform for Internet citizenship, Vers une plateforme québécoise de l'Internet citoyen, while Northern Ontario's K-Net has maintained a vital multimedia portal that includes access to First Nations Schools, providing distance education so that their youth do not have to leave their homes for residential schools, and My K-Net, a precursor to popular social networking sites.[13]

There is little indication, however, that access policy in Canada has sought to address the complexities inherent in political discourses concerning the digital divide – just the opposite, in fact (Barney 2004).

Who's Connected?

The findings of digital divide studies in Canada mimic those of such studies in the US: access is determined by socioeconomics, education, geography, race, gender, and age. Statistics Canada data from the mid-1990s to the present consistently report that domestic access increases with higher income and education, the presence of children, and urban residence. Despite the continual increase in income groups gaining access to the Internet, a persistent divide exists between those in the highest and lowest incomes, with a sizeable proportion of non-users at the highest income levels (Sciadas 2002, 5; Reddick and Boucher 2002).

In January 2002, when Internet usage in Canada reached 72 percent, an Internet user was defined as someone who had had access to the Internet in the past three months at a variety of access points: home, work, school, or public access site (Reddick and Boucher 2002). Andrew Reddick's report *The Dual Digital Divide* (2000) concluded that the digital divide is a complex phenomenon that involves not only users and non-users but also two groups of non-users: those not able to connect because of socioeconomic particularities and those who have opted not to connect because of mere disinterest. In their follow-up report, Reddick and colleagues (2001, 14) reiterated the necessity to reconceptualize the digital divide as a *social* divide and to "incorporate the importance of the integration of information and communication technologies with other skills and activities in people's daily lives." Other relevant factors include "social literacy and capacity, the role of community organizations in access and training (community divides), and diversity of information" (Reddick and Boucher 2002, 12).

Reporting on Statistics Canada's Household Internet Use Survey data, Catherine Middleton and Christine Sorensen (2005, 464) argue that "the much-promoted view of Canada as one of the world's most 'connected' countries masks unequal Internet adoption patterns."[14] Internet adoption rates of households headed by lower-income, less-educated, and older Canadians are well below the Canadian average. Data from the 2005 Canadian Internet Use Survey show that 16.8 million adult Canadians (68 percent) used the Internet for personal non-business reasons during the twelve months prior to the survey and that adults residing in urban areas had higher rates of access (Ottawa-Gatineau and Calgary had the highest at 77 percent, Montreal and other urban areas were at 68 percent, and those residing in rural or small towns were at 58 percent). Once again, household income, educational levels, and urban residence were predictors of higher Internet usage (Statistics Canada 2006).

Middleton and Sorensen (2005, 475) further argue that it is important "for all Canadians to have an equal opportunity to participate in the information society" but also to have the option not to participate if it is not beneficial to them. They question what it means for Canadians to be disconnected: "Being disconnected means that citizens cannot access online resources related to health, education, and jobs, nor can they partake in the entertainment or commerce services available online." Surely this inability to connect to a myriad of information resources, whether for leisure or as a way to carry out basic citizenship duties (for example, access to government information related to citizenship and immigration, taxes, jobs, and social security), is an encroachment on our communication rights.

New digital divides include those related to broadband and Wi-Fi. December 2008 statistics from the OECD indicate that Canada is a leader among Group of Seven (G7) countries for broadband penetration and ranks tenth among OECD member countries, with 9.2 million broadband subscribers in June 2008, approximately 27.9 for every 100 inhabitants (OECD 2008). Many fear, however, that it will be difficult for Canada to remain in the top ten and that Canada's position in international rankings will slip unless there is more national competitive pricing and service options to encourage more Canadians to subscribe to broadband. This necessitates, according to Michael Geist (2007b), a reconsideration of Canada's overall federal broadband strategy; as will be discussed later in this chapter, it has, two years later, elicited some response from the federal government and led to a renewed activist agenda.

Wi-Fi provision is yet another potential new divide. Community and municipal Wi-Fi initiatives in Canada have been proliferating; networking models include hotspots, hub-and-spoke systems, and dynamic mesh. Successful initiatives include Fredericton's Fred eZone and Montreal's Île sans fil.[15] While these initiatives merge community and local content (news, culture, and so on) and are a practical mechanism for users to connect to the Internet in public spaces (libraries, cafes, community centres), access almost always depends on users' having their own laptop. Given that laptop ownership is not ubiquitous, the proliferation of Wi-Fi marks a nascent potential divide.

Closing the gaps in these penetration statistics has been the primary focus of ICT policy in Canada. Such programs have too often failed to adequately account for the cyclical nature of social communication in Canada and, while providing technological platforms, have not done enough to empower large swaths of Canadian society to claim their communication rights.

Beginning in the 1990s, Canada initiated several funding programs to create Internet access in public spaces, such as schools and libraries, and community access points, particularly in rural and remote areas. A variety of public sector and nonprofit policy initiatives were initiated to close the digital divide, through technology acquisition, education, training, and life-long learning. Corporations (including Microsoft, AT&T, Intel, Hewlett-Packard, and AOL Time Warner) established foundations to provide Internet access to local communities, typically through donations of training and used equipment.

Federal programs and policies designed to close the digital divide were organized along six pillars under the mandate of Industry Canada. Initiated in the mid-1990s, these various programs were continually refined and in some instances discontinued. Their not-so-modest goal was the creation of Canada as the most "connected" nation on earth. These programs included the aforementioned CAP, which provided community access sites for rural, remote, and urban communities; SchoolNet and First Nations SchoolNet, which connected elementary and secondary schools to the Internet; Library-Net, connecting public libraries to the Internet; VolNet, the Voluntary Sector Network Support Program, which provided Internet connectivity to voluntary organizations; the Smart Communities initiative, which involved public-private and community partnerships to support pilot projects that used the Internet to promote community economic development; Canadian Content On-line, which was designed to digitize Canadian content; and Government Online, which made a vast array of government services, as well as industry and trade material, available online.

While several hundred million dollars were spent on the Connecting Canadians agenda and programs in support of some 10,000 community ICT initiatives, the "wiring" of public schools and libraries, and the provision of broadband access to rural and remote regions, there has been scant evaluation and assessment of these programs to date, and many of them are now barely clinging to life.

From Digital Divides to Digital Capabilities

I think there is a Mercedes divide. I'd like to have one; I can't afford one. I'm not meaning to be completely flip about this. I think it's an important social issue. But it shouldn't be used to justify the notion of essentially the socialization of the deployment of the infrastructure.

– Michael Powell, Federal Communications
Commission chairman

After the "dot-com bust" of the early 2000s, many policy makers and technology pundits cheerily declared that digital divide programs and policy subsidies were no longer necessary. Their feelings were perhaps characterized by the widely quoted quip of former FCC chairman Michael Powell shown earlier. Whether or not these policy fixes will eliminate the digital divide is the subject of much research. Will the digital divide be transitory or persistent? Some contend that as the cost of computers and online access decreases, and as more schools and public institutions become wired, concern about a digital divide will become moot. After all, there will always be areas of social stratification that no amount of public subsidy can fix. Others insist, however, that if the assumption remains that basic computer skills are essential for economic success, and ICT access for participation in civic and cultural life, then we need to be concerned and diligent in preventing the information-poor from becoming further marginalized (Schement 2001).

The Bush administration's retreat from funding programs to ameliorate the digital divide was echoed in Canada's 2004 Throne Speech (see CBC News 2004b).[16] Funding for the Connecting Canadians and broadband programs was reduced, and in the midst of an economic downturn in Ottawa's high-tech sector and a prevailing discourse focusing on security enhancements in the wake of 9/11, Canada fell in step with its southern neighbour.

In 2007, OECD (2007b) broadband rankings placed the US at fifteenth place (down from fourth place in 2001) among the thirty members, a precipitous slide that renewed calls for government intervention to bring about broadband competition to ensure reliable, affordable, and ubiquitous service for the estimated 10 million American homes that remain unserved, and the additional 50 million homes that chose not to subscribe because of high costs or low speeds (Turner 2007). Seeing broadband infrastructure as an important element in reviving the US economy, the Obama administration allocated $4.5 billion to finance broadband infrastructure in order to expand access in rural and underserved parts of the US, in its $787 billion stimulus package approved by Congress in February 2009 (Hossain et al. 2009).

This initiative provided the bare minimum of support called for by many organizations. One such group, BB4US.net (the US Broadband Coalition), was formed in December 2008 to announce "A Call to Action for a National Broadband Strategy."[17] Over 125 organizations – an eclectic group consisting of a nonprofit association, major industry and telecom firms, public interest groups, academic institutions, and trade associations – called for a comprehensive national broadband strategy to ensure that "every American home, business, and public and private institution" would have access to "affordable high-speed broadband connections to the Internet," respecting net neutrality so that it is "open to all users, service providers, content providers, and application providers," in as "competitive as reasonably possible" a marketplace.

Similar concerns about plummeting access to broadband as detailed by OECD rankings were seen in Canada, which until recently had been seen both domestically and internationally as an innovator and leader in broadband access. In 2002, Canada was ranked second alongside South Korea in OECD countries for per-capita broadband subscriptions, but a mere six years later, in the summer of 2008, it had slipped to tenth (Nowak 2008). Canada now ranks behind the Scandinavian countries with 36.7 subscribers per 100 inhabitants and a population density of 126 per square kilometre.[18]

The January 2009 budget announced by the Stephen Harper's Conservative government likewise invested in broadband as a stimulus for the sagging economy. The sum of $225 million was allocated for a three-year program to extend broadband service to unserved rural and remote communities by private development administered through Industry Canada (Canada 2009a), an amount that fell far short of the $500 million to be spent over five years that the Conservatives promised in their election platform the previous fall (CBC News 2008a). Leading up to the budget, public interest groups advocated the development of a pan-Canadian National Inclusion Strategy to ensure appropriate broadband infrastructure development and the creation of community-based programs in order to remedy what the Canadian Centre for Policy Alternatives (CCPA) (2009, 52) Alternative Federal Budget cited as the "37% of Canadian communities, many of them in rural and remote areas" that in 2007 were "still unserved by broadband," with many communities erroneously classified as already being served by broadband. The CCPA estimated that a $2 billion investment over five years could "ensure that every Canadian has access to sufficient broadband to allow effective participation in the social, political, and economic life in the 21st century" (52).

Academics have offered trenchant critiques on the tendency for access policy to employ the concept of the digital divide oversimplistically and have long pointed to the need to go beyond mere penetration statistics in developing access policy. David Gunkel (2003, 517) especially argues that we need to be cognizant of how technological determinism is implicated in digital divide discourses. Daniel Paré (2004, 97) demonstrates that it is important to consider not only access to technology and infrastructure but also what people want to do with technologies and how they currently use them: "Policy choices and programmes must be made in accordance with the motivations of technology users, not on abstract assessments of techno-logical potential and its supposedly uniform imperatives and impacts." Neil Selwyn (2004, 351) reconstructs the notion of digital divide "as a hierarchy of access to various forms of technology in various contexts, resulting in differing levels of engagement and consequences," and he presents four stages in the digital divide: formal/theoretical access, effective access and use, en-gagement, and outcomes and consequences.

Reliance on measuring the digital divide only by its technical infrastruc-ture, and in using quantitative measures for assessing quality of services and social benefits, is only one side of understanding the divide; basic social issues inhibiting access need to be considered. Robin Mansell (2001, 56) emphasizes this point when she calls for the adoption of a social capabilities approach: "These capabilities include general education and technical competencies, the institutions that influence abilities to finance and operate modern organ-izations, and the political and social factors that influence risks, incentives, and personal rewards including social esteem."

Rhae Adams (2001, 7) echoes this concern, arguing that we need to move "beyond numbers" and strive for richer analyses that add "the sociocultural perspective and what is termed the 'experience-near' understanding of divide manifestations." Mark Warschauer (2003) also argues that we need a more critical conceptualization of the digital divide that encompasses technology for social inclusion, referring to the extent to which families and communities can participate in society in an autonomous fashion. Social inclusion is the ability to access, adapt, and create new knowledge using ICTs.

Access to economic resources, health, education, housing, culture, and civic engagement are all elements, with literacy a key element. Effective use of ICTs, defined by Michael Gurstein (2003) as "the capacity and opportun-ity to successfully integrate ICTs into the accomplishment of self or collab-oratively identified goals," thus involves a model that accounts for physical resources (telecommunications and computers), digital resources (relevant content in diverse languages), human resources (literacy and education), and social resources (community and institutional support).

Going from a concept of digital divides to digital capabilities necessitates interrogating the texture of communication rights and entitlements within a capabilities approach. Nicholas Garnham (1997, 32), critical of quantitative modes of communication indicators, says that what the capabilities approach "highlights is that access is not enough. In evaluating levels of entitlement we need to take into account both the range of communication options made available, and these must be real options not mere choices between products and services with minimal real differences, and the ability of people actually to make use of these options, to achieve the relevant functionings."

Too often, ICT policy discourse frames "functionings" as the ability to purchase and consume products and services – consumer rights – rather than as citizens' rights – the ability to access ICTs in order to create and participate meaningfully in democratic public life. Livingstone and Lunt (2007, 53) write that contemporary policy discourse tosses about the terms citizen and consumer interchangeably, and they rightfully interrogate what this entails: "Is 'consumer' taking over from 'citizen' in the communications sector, as suggested by the ubiquitous discourse of choice and empowerment? Does the 'citizen' have a voice in regulatory debates, or is this subordinated to the market?"

As has been demonstrated, Canadian public policy on ICTs has shifted from a sense of citizen-based universality to a regime of market-generated rules (Birdsall 2000; Moll and Shade 2001a, 2001b). The emphasis has been on the development of programs and policies fixated on the technical, rather than the social, infrastructure. Demonstrative of this shift is the 2006 final report of the Telecommunications Policy Review Panel (TPRP), the first major public review of Canada's telecommunications policy framework since 1993 (see Sinclair et al. 2006).

The TPRP studied three specific areas related to increasing changes in technology, consumer demand, and market structure – regulation, access, and ICT adoption – and was dominated by industry and government concerns with competitiveness, productivity, and deregulation. Throughout the TPRP final report, there are sixty-nine references to "consumers" compared with seven to "citizens" and eight to the conflation of "citizen-consumers" (and two to "citizens and businesses"). The panel was forthright in acknowledging that its proposals "seek to accelerate the pace of deregulation of competitive telecommunications markets" through reliance on "market forces" that will thus "strengthen and better target regulatory approaches to achieve important social objectives and protect consumers' interests in the more competitive environment" (Sinclair et al. 2006, 3).

Not surprisingly, the TPRP final report called for less regulation and in-creased reliance on market forces in order to promote the growth and competitiveness of Canada's telecommunications industry. Many community organizations are rightfully concerned that this avowedly market-based tilt coupled with a belief in open markets (and less foreign ownership restrictions) will not lead to more universality of technology, services, and content. Rather, this sensibility ushers in an unprecedented attempt to diminish the ability of Canadian citizens, through public regulatory bodies like the CRTC, to ensure that Canada's telecommunications system meets the needs of all Canadians. The TPRP process also revealed the fragmented, isolated, and ad hoc nature of public interest and community technology organizations in Canada as far as their ability to intervene effectively in such policy discussions is concerned (Moll and Shade 2008).

Amid this neoliberal and highly politicized mindset, more than ever access to ICTs must be seen as a constituent element of communication rights and reoriented towards social policy. As argued in Chapter 4, the political economy of media in Canada, characterized by increased concentration, conglomeration, and cross-media ownership, privileges corporate voices, thus muffling the diversity of citizens' voices. This requires a more complex understanding of the digital divide and of the roles that ICT access policy play in the realization of communication rights in Canada.

The Access Rainbow: A Socio-Technical Model

Access to the Internet is multifaceted, encompassing an overlapping mixture of technical, economic, and social infrastructures. An integrated model, the "Access Rainbow," proposes a socio-technical architecture for analyzing and discussing access to network services (Clement and Shade 2000). The lower layers of the rainbow emphasize the technical aspects constituting access, while the upper layers highlight the explicitly social aspects. All the layers are interrelated and necessary in order to meet the needs of the content/service layer.

Technical factors include carriage facilities (those that store, serve, or carry information, such as telephone, cable Internet, satellite, and wireless transmission); physical devices (telephone terminal equipment, modems, cable modems, personal digital assistants, personal computers, and Web televisions); and software tools (browsers, e-mailers, search engines, authoring and editing tools, groupware). Also key are the content and services that people find useful, such as telephone enhancements, the World Wide Web, and e-mail. Content and services need to be affordable, reliable, usable, diverse, secure, and privacy-enhancing in order to meet quality-of-service standards.

FIGURE 2

The Access Rainbow model

The Access Rainbow model for analyzing and
discussing access to network services
(Clement and Shade 2000).

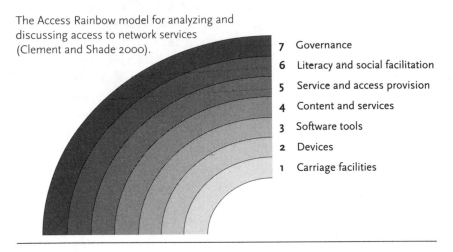

7   Governance

6   Literacy and social facilitation

5   Service and access provision

4   Content and services

3   Software tools

2   Devices

1   Carriage facilities

Aspects of the social infrastructure include services and access provision – the organizations that provide network services and access to users, including employers, educational institutions, ISPs, telecommunications companies, community networks, public libraries, Internet-enabled cafes, and various other community organizations. Literacy and social facilitation – the skills people need to take full advantage of ICTs – are crucial. Acquiring these skills is largely a social process involving a combination of formal and informal methods within the context of supportive learning environments. The means for acquiring network skills need to be affordable, readily available, attuned to the learners' varied life situations, and sensitive to differences in language, culture, physical ability, and gender.

And finally, the central challenge of governance – how decisions are made concerning the development and operation of the Internet – is to foster a democratic process that enables all ICT stakeholders to participate equitably in policy making. Table 1 provides an overview of the layers that encompass this holistic view of access.

Foregrounding the Citizen

While there are many challenges to ensuring meaningful and sustained public access to ICTs and enshrining this as a fundamental communication right

TABLE 1

Access Rainbow summary

Layer	Description	Essential aspects	Gaps	Key policy questions
7. GOVERNANCE How decisions are made concerning the design, development, operation, and policy of ICTs	ICT development implicates an array of local, national, and international stakeholders differently placed in terms of their ability to contribute effectively toward decision-making and policy processes. A central challenge of governance is to foster democratic processes allowing all stakeholders to become informed of the issues and participate equitably in choosing from among alternatives.	• Public consultation process • Citizen education • Research and social impact assessment • Creation of new institutions (e.g., National and Regional Access Councils) • Concept of the electronic commons	Almost everyone is left out except those with a large financial stake in the industry or those entrenched within government.	• How will the public be involved meaningfully in the decision making? • How will decision making be better informed through research (e.g., impact assessments)? • What role will the current regulatory bodies (e.g., CRTC and FCC) have? • What new institutions will be created? • How effective is multi-stakeholder policy? • How will the pressures of globalization and deep integration be dealt with?
6. LITERACY/SOCIAL FACILITATION The skills citizens need to take full advantage of ICTs, together with the learning facilitation and resources to acquire these skills	ICTs are complex and rapidly changing technologies requiring a range of skills to use effectively, especially when creating new content. Acquiring these skills is largely a social process	• Basic literacy, numeracy, and media-savvy skills • Computer literacy (keyboarding, Web navigation)	• Unemployed • Lower income • Non-English speakers • Cultural and visible minorities • Women	• How will training and education be funded? • What is the role of local community organizations in providing training and support?

▲

▲ TABLE 1

Layer	Description	Essential aspects	Gaps	Key policy questions
	involving a combination of formal and informal methods within the context of supportive learning environments.	• "Local experts" in workplace, home, or neighbourhood	• Socially isolated • Cognitive differences	• How will indigenous and local content be created that is meaningful for communities?
5. SERVICE PROVIDERS The organizations that provide network services and access to users	• Most users gain access through employers or educational institutions that provide a range of access services. • Individual subscribers also need affordable, ongoing relations with network service organizations. • Wi-Fi hotspots in public spaces and in cafes, airports, and other retail establishments are increasingly common. • Municipal Wi-Fi ventures are increasingly common.	• Local public access points such as libraries, schools, hospitals, daycares, post offices, and community centres • Affordable	• Unemployed • Low income • Rural/remote • Ethnic/linguistic minorities • New "Wi-Fi divides" of those who do not own a laptop computer	• How will the host (public/nonprofit institution) be sustained? • How do they participate in governance? • Are the providers responsible for the content that goes over their pipes? • Do the providers adhere to net neutrality provisions?

4. CONTENT/SERVICES The actual information and communication services that citizens find useful	The central role of ICTs is to facilitate access to a wide range of information and communication services that citizens find valuable in their daily lives as producers, consumers, and caregivers.	• E-mail • World Wide Web content (search engines, weather, job banks, government information, civic/local events, blogs, video, entertainment) • E-commerce • Integration with mobile devices	• Low income • Non-English speakers • Disabled • Children/elderly • Cultural and visible minorities	• Are the content and services reliable, usable, diverse (culturally, linguistically, politically), secure, privacy-enhancing, text-only-compatible, individually filterable, censorship-free? • Is content accessible for people with physical and cognitive disabilities? • What intellectual property rights do users have with regard to user-generated content? • Does content adhere to privacy practices (e.g., PIPEDA)?
3. SOFTWARE TOOLS The programs that operate the devices and make connections to services	Software is the critical ingredient that extends ICTs. These tools, undergoing rapid development and convergence, are increasingly embedded in a growing range of devices.	• Web browser • E-mail program • Authoring tool • Encryption and other privacy enablers	• Disabled • Non-English speakers • Low income	• Are major software tools easy for everyone to learn and use? • Are they affordable and interoperable? • Are open-source options available? • Are they privacy-enabling? • Are they available in languages other than English?

▲

▼ TABLE 1

Layer	Description	Essential aspects	Gaps	Key policy questions
2. DEVICES The actual physical devices that people operate	Contrary to the general trend of convergence seen in carriage media, digital and wireless convergence create a widening mix of capabilities, prices, and sizes.	• Workstations • Net PCs • Public kiosks • Mobile devices • Universal design features	• Low income • Disabled • Handicapped • Rural	• Are the devices affordable? • Are the devices interoperable with other devices, and do they avoid rapid obsolescence? • Are they easy to use, especially for people with disabilities? • Are the ICTs close to where people need them?
1. CARRIAGE The facilities that store, serve, or carry information	• The Internet is the most prominent of digital information infrastructures, with previous analog devices being converted to digital. • Mobile and Wi-Fi devices are increasingly common.	• Telephone (affordable, single-party service, digital dial tone, ADSL, ISDN, phone number portability) • Cable with modem • Internet connection locally • Mobile phones and devices with number portability	• Low income • Rural/remote ("high-cost areas")	• Are there new support mechanisms to supplement or replace internal cross-subsidization? • Are penetration rates a suitable measure of access? • How can one ensure the inter-operability of the networks? • What is the minimal "essential bandwidth"? • Is public spectrum available?

SOURCE: Updated from Clement and Shade 2000.

for all Canadians, rather than merely bemoaning governmental retreat from public access funding programs and policy making that inadequately engages Canadians, let us consider a few positive actions that illustrate the fortitude of many Canadian citizens in pushing for ICT access for all. The use of social networking sites (SNS) to raise awareness and mobilize against government funding cuts has been illustrated in this chapter's discussion of CAP through the example of the blogosphere. Facebook has also been used to mobilize in the same fashion (Geist 2007a). As discussed in Chapter 6, net neutrality as an access issue is an emerging and controversial topic in Canada. The Campaign for Democratic Media (CDM), a national nonprofit organization whose goals are to support the development of a democratic media system in Canada, initiated a "Stop the Throttler" campaign in response to Bell Canada's use of traffic shaping to limit how subscribers can access Web content.[19] Besides a Facebook page, a YouTube video was used to educate the public about the issues, and the CDM website provided information on contacts at Bell Canada and the federal Competition Bureau. Often done rather crudely and humorously, the low-cost creation and dissemination of such public service announcements can educate the public about complex policy issues that impact their everyday use of ICTs and galvanize them into action.

CDM later formed a coalition, Save Our Net, that brought together individuals, nonprofit organizations, labour groups, media groups, Internet service providers, and political parties, including the Green Party and the New Democratic Party, to campaign for net neutrality provisions and mobilize support for this through CRTC hearings held in July 2009.[20] The net neutrality campaign is a salient example of how Canadian citizens mobilize for often very esoteric yet crucially important digital inclusion policies (Shade 2008).

Another example of citizen activism for digital inclusion is the creation of the Internet for Everyone campaign, launched in October 2008 in order to catalyze debates during the latest federal election on the development of a national broadband strategy and continuation of federal funding programs for community Internet access such as CAP. The group quickly mobilized over 60 Francophone and Anglophone organizations and almost 160 Francophone and Anglophone individuals to join forces "to promote open access to Internet as a basic right for all Canadians":

ACCESS
Everyone, in rural and remote regions as well as urban regions, must have high-speed Internet access.

INCLUSION
Citizens of all ages, all abilities and all socio-economic levels
should be included in the information age.

OPENNESS
Online communications should be free from any kind of
discrimination.

INNOVATION
The Internet must continue to create jobs, foster innovation and
stimulate economic growth starting from the community level.[21]

Broadband access and its provision has raised numerous issues with
respect to access. Analyzing broadband usage patterns in Canadian households, Middleton and Ellison (2008) argue that we need to look not just at
connection speeds but also at the intensity of usage, as these "measures of
scope and intensity create valuable new insights, with important implications
for equal access and participation in an information society" (21). While
many urban areas in Canada are relatively well served, broadband access in
remote, rural, and northern regions of Canada is an access issue that needs
to be addressed. Whether or not the recently announced infusion of funds
for rural and remote broadband as part of the Conservative government's
Economic Action Plan will spur private companies to partner with the government in support of broadband connectivity in regions that may not have a
guaranteed return on investment is unknown at this time (see Canada 2009b).
   The fact, however, that a debate on the intricacies of broadband speed,
depth, and reach has made its way onto the political agenda – albeit not with
the intensity that many activists would prefer – and that citizens have become
more cognizant of the diverse dimensions of ICT access, from broadband
speed to net neutrality (as discussed further in Chapter 6) to copyright reform
(Chapter 8), bodes well for the near future of ICT policy making in the public interest. Here is where the power of citizens to effect change through innovative and creative capacity building using ICTs is amply demonstrated.

6

Internet

William J. McIver Jr.

The analysis of communication rights – or a unified right to communicate – in the context of new information and communication technologies (ICTs) is continually confronted by two situations. First, certain aspects of new ICTs may reproduce an existing mode of communication about which potential threats and violations of norms are well understood. For example, the applicability of privacy protections to Internet-based telephony can be seen as a natural extension of the norms around previous forms of telephony.[1] Second, a new ICT is also likely to produce potential modes of communication, interactions, or conditions that were not contemplated during its design. Such potentials are referred to as "affordances" in human-computer interaction and design research (Norman 2002). A new ICT offers affordances in the sense that it makes possible certain actions through its properties. The potentials for such actions may be readily apparent, as in the reproduction of an existing mode of communication; or, more importantly, the potentials may be latent. For example, while the applicability of privacy protections to Internet-based telephony may have been readily apparent, technical properties unique to the new form of telephony have given various actors new methods of violating privacy that may or may not have been apparent to the public or to regulators.

The general problem posed by the existence of technological affordances in communication rights is not new (McIver and Birdsall 2004). Jean D'Arcy's (1969) introduction of the notion of a right to communicate can be seen as emanating from the identification of new affordances offered by satellite-based communications technologies (see Chapter 1). Fundamental properties of the Internet have enabled an environment in which affordances that challenge existing norms and human rights codes are produced more rapidly than in earlier communication technology frameworks such as analog telephony or telegraphy (McIver and Birdsall 2004). Further, these same properties have enabled the production of higher-order affordances – affordances resulting from the combination of other affordances – which are increasing the complexity of addressing communication rights. For example, as we will discuss later in this chapter, non-neutral network policies result in higher-order impacts on various types of Internet applications.

This chapter will examine communication rights in the context of three Internet technology areas: the practice of network traffic shaping; the broad area of Semantic Web and Web 2.0 applications; and Internet telephony. These three areas are linked through the layered architecture of Internet applications. Internet applications depend fundamentally on the exchange of data through functionality provided by technologies at lower layers of the Internet. Thus, technologies that are implemented at higher layers are partially an expression of the functionality presented and constraints posed by lower layers. For example, network traffic shaping involves layers of functionality upon which Semantic Web, Web 2.0, and Internet telephony applications depend. Each of these technology areas presents different affordances to different actors, resulting in sites of conflict around communication rights. Semantic Web, Web 2.0, and Internet telephony have enabled the expansion of social and political communication for individuals, with significant reductions in cost barriers in many cases. Network traffic shaping capabilities – a form of control over Internet data exchange – are actionable by the state and private sector network operators and, objectively, present both barriers and benefits to citizens.

Canadian Internet Policy Objectives

The impacts of Internet technologies on communication rights in Canada must be examined in the context of the country's policy objectives. The Canadian government set out a course for data networking early in the history of what was to become the Internet. The build-out of the US-funded ARPANET – the principal ancestor of the Internet – began in 1969. The defunct Science Council of Canada (1971, 4) issued a proposal for the establishment of "a nationwide system of computer communication networks" only two years later.[2] This proposal articulated a policy approach meant to ensure Canadian control over its networks in the face of market forces, stating in part: "A 'laissez-faire' attitude will eventually result in the supply of most computing and information services via spur lines from U.S. computer communications networks." The proposal called for equitable access to these networks, stating: "The system of networks should not be allowed to practice 'cream-skimming'

by concentrating exclusively on the densely populated, highly profitable regions of Canada. It must link all important centres in Canada in order to bring
computing and information services to the greatest number of Canadians."

Two decades later, the 1993 Canadian *Telecommunications Act* defined a
broad and overlapping set of policy objectives in economic, social, and technical areas for telephony in Canada.[3] Although the Internet as we know it
today was still in its infancy, a number of these policy objectives relate to
social communication, the complex of rights relating to communication, and
– indirectly – the Internet itself. These include:

* strengthening the "social and economic fabric of Canada" (section 7(a))
* making possible "reliable and affordable telecommunications services"
  to Canadians in both "urban and rural areas" (section 7(b))
* fostering the creation of innovative ICT services in Canada through
  "research and development" (section 7(g))
* responding to "the economic and social requirements of users of telecommunications services" (section 7(h))
* supporting privacy protections for users of ICT (section 7(i)).

The requirements of the *Telecommunications Act* coupled with the emergence of new Internet-based communications technologies continues to
create new conditions under which existing rights can be challenged. The
Canadian government recognized the need to update its telecommunication
policy framework given new technological and market realities, and it formed
a Telecommunications Policy Review Panel (TPRP) in 2005. Although the
TPRP review, was, as discussed in Chapter 5, hardly framed around communication rights, some of the recommendations from its final report are
nonetheless revealing about the challenges that the diffusion of Internet
technologies pose to existing telecommunications policies in Canada (see
Sinclair et al. 2006).

Traffic Shaping, Network Neutrality, and Communication Rights

The Internet consists of many separately managed networks that are interconnected, hence "Inter" and "net." The networks that participate in the Internet are implemented with hardware and software from a variety of sources.
The ability of diverse networks to interoperate to form the Internet has been
made possible by a common set of technical protocols to which vendors and
network operators adhere. Transmission Control Protocol/Internet Protocol

(TCP/IP) and the Domain Name System (DNS) are key examples. Thus, the operation of the Internet has depended in large part on the cooperative implementation and equitable use of protocols among its constituent networks.

NETWORK TRAFFIC SHAPING

One dimension of the Internet's operation where cooperation and equity are most relevant is the handling of data packets as they cross individual networks from sender to receiver. Network traffic shaping is the practice of controlling the flow of packets through a network based on the type of data they contain, current network conditions, and other constraints. Packets are the basic unit of transmission for any type of data sent across a network, including e-mail messages, audio and video files, and documents.

Packet flows are "shaped" in the sense that they are handled in a differential manner according to their volumes or the types of data they contain. There are several basic traffic shaping policies. Some types of packets may be given priority over others so that they will reach their destinations with shorter delays. This practice is sometimes referred to as "throttling." Limits may be placed on the volume of certain types of packets to preserve a network's channel capacity (also known as "bandwidth") for other types of packets or certain classes of users of a network. Some types of packets may be blocked altogether by a network operator. Any type of packet that is not explicitly prioritized must be handled within whatever network capacity remains after the data packets that have been given priority are transmitted.

Traffic shaping is often necessary in managing a network. Each network has practical limits with regard to the volume and arrival frequency of packets that it can service effectively. When a network's channel capacity is approached or exceeded, the quality of service (QoS) that it supports decreases and services may eventually cease to function altogether. E-mail messages, for example, might be delayed significantly.

Traffic shaping provides an operator with the ability to maintain a certain QoS offered by its network under a heavy load. For example, a provider of real-time voice or video communication services will want to prioritize traffic generated by those services over others, given that delays and interruptions in natural language are less tolerable than those that might occur with e-mail. An operator might also choose to limit the amount of data that any one user can transfer, to ensure a minimal QoS to everyone on its network. Some networks shape traffic based on time of day, so that more stringent policies are implemented during times when heavier loads are expected.

Finally, organizations must use traffic shaping if they wish to respond to the arrival on their networks of undesirable data from other networks. If a user engages in illegal music or video file sharing, their Internet service provider may face legal threats. Independent of their legal status, music and video files may be less desirable because they are orders of magnitude larger than typical webpage transfers or e-mail messages. Networks now commonly experience performance problems related to the transfer of video and audio files. Traffic shaping allows an operator to constrain or block undesirable data outright to prevent unwanted activities on its network. One recent example is Ohio University's effort (2007) to address both legal threats and performance problems caused by music file sharing. The university was classified in 2007 by the Recording Industry Association of America (RIAA) as one of the top institutions where music piracy was taking place. As a result, it decided to block all peer-to-peer (P2P) traffic on its network.

Traffic shaping is of interest here because its use has come to be seen – under the term "network neutrality" – as antithetical to communication rights.

NETWORK NEUTRALITY

The concept of network neutrality has arisen in recent years as a framework for describing the practice of traffic shaping in the context of the interconnected networks that make up the Internet. Network neutrality is a traffic shaping policy whereby all data are treated equally in terms of restrictions and costs for their transit across a network. Controversy has arisen in recent years around non-neutral network practices proposed by commercial Internet service providers.

The concepts of network neutrality and network traffic shaping are often conflated, which is improper. The two must be examined as distinct, though potentially interrelated, concepts. Network traffic shaping refers mainly to the technical dimension of routing content across networks. Network neutrality refers mainly to a set of principles pertaining to network operators: a network operator should not discriminate between data packets sent by or destined for its users; a network operator should provide full, nondiscriminatory transit for data packets sent by and destined for other networks; and network operators should have limited liability for the data they permit across their networks (Mueller 2007).

Supporters of network neutrality link the characteristics of TCP/IP with network neutrality in explaining the essential strengths and the successes of the Internet. One perspective is that network neutrality relates to the

FIGURE 3

Sending packets over interconnected networks

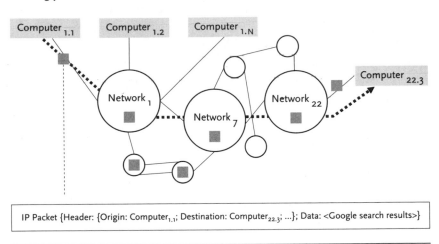

IP Packet {Header: {Origin: Computer$_{1.1}$; Destination: Computer$_{22.3}$; ...}; Data: <Google search results>}

operationalization of the TCP/IP suite of Internet protocols. From the example depicted in Figure 3, the message sent from Computer$_{1.1}$ to Computer$_{1.2}$ traverses only Network$_1$, which connects the origin and destination computers. At minimum, the devices on Network$_1$ must examine the address on the message to route it to Computer$_{1.2}$. Network$_1$ may choose to do more, however. It may give preferential or prejudicial treatment to the delivery of the message based on its origin or destination addresses, depending on the policies of the owners of the network. Further, Network$_1$ might choose to examine the contents of the message and give preferential or prejudicial treatment to its delivery. A network neutral approach would be to deliver the message without prejudice as to its origin, destination, or content.

A network neutral approach is key to enabling the commonly held notion that telecommunication common carriers should provide transmission services to the public without discrimination. According to Noam (1994, paragraph 8), common carriage principles were developed "to guarantee that no customer seeking service upon reasonable demand, willing and able to pay the established price, however set, would be denied lawful use of the service or would otherwise be discriminated against." Noam cites US legal precedent in stating that the "prohibition on unreasonable discrimination is the most important component of the common carrier obligation" (paragraph 20).

The development of common carriage principles began well before the regulation of telecommunication services, with origins that predate early English common law. These principles eventually supported the development of telecommunication networks by giving carriers certain benefits, such as physical rights-of-way and monopoly protections, in exchange for the anti-discrimination restrictions placed on them. Common carriage was applied to telecommunications as early as 1848 in the context of telegraphy and was a key part of the US *Communications Act of 1934* (Noam 1994).[4] It also exists within Canadian law.

The 1993 Canadian *Telecommunications Act* states that no "Canadian carrier shall, in relation to the provision of a telecommunications service or the charging of a rate for it, unjustly discriminate or give an undue or unreasonable preference toward any person, including itself, or subject any person to an undue or unreasonable disadvantage" (section 27(2)). The act frames its obligation to protect consumers against discrimination, unjust and unreasonable rates, and preference or disadvantage as solely a function of Canadian carriers' being subject to sufficient competition (section 35(1)).

Frequently, arguments for network neutrality are given at an engineering level in terms of its importance to innovation. This has been derived mostly from the "end-to-end" (e2e) principle in the design of the Internet (Saltzer et al. 1984). The e2e argument applies to communications in general, not just the Internet. It addresses the engineering dilemma of where to place data communications services, such as message ordering, filtering, or error detection, when they can either be implemented in a network or be made the responsibility of the systems that use the network. The e2e principle holds that as long as sufficient basic data communications functionality exists at a lower layer, advanced functionality can and should be added later at higher layers. The implication is that the network should not discriminate between the types of applications it is serving. One example of advanced functionality in this context would be specialized methods for handling packets containing specific data types, such as voice or video. The e2e principle holds that advanced functionality is best implemented above the basic service layer of the network, inside the specific applications that require it.

The consequences of nondiscrimination from an e2e perspective must be viewed not from isolated perspectives regarding specific technologies but from the standpoint of its impacts on performance and innovation across the whole Internet "ecology." Saltzer and colleagues (1984, 9) showed that this approach is necessary to achieve optimal modularity and economy in developing software, where complex and expensive functionality need not be designed ahead of time and then locked into the lower layers of a network. The authors described this as "a kind of 'Occam's razor' when it comes to choosing the functions to be provided in a communication subsystem." The use of the e2e principle has been cited as a major factor in enabling the rapid evolution of online services. An example of what has been made possible by the end-to-end principle is the relative ease with which TCP/IP has been able to support higher-level protocols that are the basis for the Web, such as the Hypertext Transfer Protocol (HTTP). Google (2007, paragraph 2) has stated that network neutrality has "allowed many companies, including Google, to launch, grow, and innovate" because of this principle.

Fundamental aspects of the Internet's architecture are being re-examined, including the appropriateness of the e2e principle across all classes of services (Clark 2005; Clark et al. 2003). Security and mobility, for example, have been shown to be ill served by the current Internet architecture. Proposals for addressing these shortcomings have included re-examining adherence to the e2e principle for all services (Feldman 2007). While not an immediate challenge to network neutrality, the potential impacts of these efforts – known as the "Clean Slate approach" – should be studied by policy makers.

NON-NEUTRAL NETWORK POLICIES
Arguments for non-neutral network policies have originated from major commercial Internet service providers (ISPs) such as telephone and cable television companies. Many of these ISPs do not simply provide their customers with access to the Internet. They offer content-based services of their own and view them as complementary to their data communications product offerings. Services include e-mail, website hosting, news feeds, and music downloading. The business proposition is that content-based services make their core products – data communications services – more attractive. Conflicts of interest are seen by ISPs where third-party content providers are concerned. Popular examples include Google.com, YouTube.com, Yahoo. com, Vonage.com, and Skype.com. When a customer of an ISP accesses a third-party content provider, the resulting data are communicated over the ISP's network infrastructure. Thus, the packets from the third party "compete" with the ISP's own content, potentially slowing down the network where data-intensive content such as video is concerned. An ISP may also view third-party content providers as getting a "free ride," since they do not invest

in network construction and operation. This position is exemplified by Edward Whitacre (quoted in O'Connell 2005), chief executive officer of SBC Telecommunications, a peer of Verizon:

> How do you think they're going to get to customers? Through a broadband pipe. Cable companies have them. We have them. Now what they would like to do is use my pipes free, but I ain't going to let them do that because we have spent this capital and we have to have a return on it. So there's going to have to be some mechanism for these people who use these pipes to pay for the portion they're using. Why should they be allowed to use my pipes?
>
> The Internet can't be free in that sense, because we and the cable companies have made an investment and for a Google or Yahoo! or Vonage or anybody to expect to use these pipes [for] free is nuts!

There have been many developments concerning the practice of non-neutral network policy by the private sector since Whitacre's comments in 2005. Comcast Corporation, one of the largest residential Internet service providers in the US, retreated from its policy of restricting data in its network resulting from the popular peer-to-peer BitTorrent protocol, which is used most often to download large video and audio files (Comcast 2008). In Canada, Bell Canada acknowledged its practice of restricting P2P data on its Sympatico Internet Service (CBC News 2008c). The most important policy developments in Canada have stemmed from a complaint filed with the Canadian Radio-television and Telecommunications Commission (CRTC) in April 2008 against Bell Canada by the Canadian Association of Internet Providers (CAIP) (see CRTC 2008i).

CAIP's membership includes ISPs who buy wholesale Internet services from companies such as Bell Canada for resale as a retail service to their customers. CAIP claimed that Bell Canada's traffic shaping policies for its wholesale Asymmetric Digital Subscriber Line (ADSL) Internet service violates several parts of the *Telecommunications Act* in that they, among other things: (1) are not part of the conditions established under the tariff approved by the CRTC for the wholesale Internet service in question; (2) result in a form of unjust control and influence over content of public telecommunications and its meaning; and (3) result in a form of unjust discrimination toward certain users of their services (CRTC 2008j). Some parties testified that data transfer rates over Bell's ADSL service used through these ISPs were reduced

significantly for P2P applications due to traffic shaping. This is seen as problematic because the files are typically very large, which can cause congestion,
and many of these files are in violation of copyright laws. Complainants
against Bell disputed claims by Bell that its customers were the cause of congestion or even that there was congestion.

Bell Canada argued that its traffic shaping policies were not in violation
of the tariff, in part because: (1) the tariff specifies only the upper and lower
bounds on communication rates guaranteed to wholesale subscribers, and
(2) traffic shaping is necessary for the company to "ensure fair and propor-
tionate use of its network as specified in its Commission-approved Terms of
Service." It claimed that its network experiences congestion due to the use of
peer-to-peer technologies by the retail customers of the ISPs who buy their
wholesale service (CRTC 2008j, section (I).16).

The CRTC (2008j) denied CAIP's complaint, saying, in summary, that
Bell had demonstrated that: (1) P2P data transfers contributed disproportion-
ate load and congestion on Bell's network; (2) traffic shaping was the only
practical method of managing its network under such load conditions; and
(3) Bell applied traffic shaping equally to its own retail customers and those
of the ISPs who buy their wholesale ADSL service.

The CRTC did find that Bell's introduction of traffic shaping caused
impacts of such significance on the retail customers of the ISPs who buy their
wholesale ADSL service that advance notice should have been given. Ironic-
ally, the CRTC did not find this lack of notice to be in violation of its earlier
requirements to provide advance notice of changes.

The most important outcome of the decision is that the CRTC initiated
a consultation process and scheduled a hearing for July 2009 on network
neutrality, in recognition that these issues were not satisfactorily resolved by
this first round of hearings (CRTC 2008h).

Major concerns remain over large carriers' use of traffic shaping despite
the CRTC 2008-108 decision (CRTC 2008j). The major carriers do not apply
traffic shaping in a manner that is transparent to the public, as evidenced by
testimony for the CRTC 2008-108 decision. Traffic shaping prevents customers from making full use of services at advertised rates. P2P technologies are
objectively legitimate and ideal technologies for transferring large files. The
presumption that P2P file transfers and other data-rich technologies suggest
illegal or undesirable activities is not warranted. Rich data types, such as
video and audio, are now common for legal data transfers over the Internet;
thus, traffic shaping policies have the effect of undue discrimination against

communications that are constitutionally protected. Finally, carriers who sell wholesale services to companies with which they compete for retail customers in the same class of services enjoy an unreasonable competitive advantage in establishing network policies, especially when they can do so in nontransparent ways.

Responses to this consultation yielded some unexpected arguments against network neutrality regulations as well as arguments in support of ISPs' rights to employ traffic shaping and blocking policies with regard to data coming from some ISPs and content providers who compete against the major network operators. Companies representing these points of view see such policies as providing valid and necessary tools for controlling unwanted content, including viruses, spam, child pornography, and illegally copied content (Anderson 2009).

The CRTC policy on network traffic shaping was announced in October 2009 (CRTC 2009c). It includes a blanket prohibition on content-blocking. Other forms of traffic shaping are condoned conditionally; for example, ISPs are permitted to shape traffic if prior notice is given and a grace period is observed and wholesale traffic can be shaped more aggressively than retail traffic, provided prior regulatory approval is granted. The policy also establishes a complaint-based process for challenging traffic management practices as unnecessary or disproportional, but in the assessment of Abramson, Buchanan, and Intven (2009), "private citizens and individual consumers without legal training or firsthand familiarity with Commission proceedings may find it very time-consuming to prepare a review application in a way that complies with CRTC procedural rules and standards of evidence." Thus, the CRTC set some ground rules about when traffic shaping is and is not permitted and provided some measure of transparency and accountability around it. This is nonetheless far removed from the ideal of net neutrality.

NETWORK NEUTRALITY AND THE PROCESS OF SOCIAL COMMUNICATION

Network neutrality, as shown earlier, is often framed in a market context, with a communication rights dialectic pitting the rights of individuals to enjoy completely unfettered data packet exchange against entities motivated to impose cost-based traffic shaping policies. Non-neutral network policies are often seen as cost barriers to social communication processes. Some Canadian Internet telephone companies have stated that those who want to use their services should have to pay a premium to their Internet service providers (CRTC 2006d). Depending on how such policies are implemented, those who do not pay for premium services could experience poor voice quality or outright blocking of voice data. The CRTC has not found this to be true thus far (CRTC 2006d, 2008j).

Mueller (2007) and others argue that competition based on tiered service could yield positive impacts on Internet access for all users, even those who may not be able to afford top-tier services. These potentials, according to Mueller, include overall improvement in bandwidth availability as operators upgrade their networks to compete in tiered service markets, which is then expected to reduce bandwidth costs for everyone due to overall increases in network capacity.

A reliance on market-based solutions to ensure network access and network neutrality would be problematic, both in terms of market dynamics and existing legal frameworks. Evidence shows that both market and political forces have at times encouraged non-neutral network policies. Van Schewick and Farber (2009) have documented a series of recent cases in North America where network operators have implemented traffic shaping policies to thwart competition or to block Web content for political reasons.

Slater and Wu (2008) have pointed out that growth in broadband has traditionally been slow relative to other aspects of computing, such as processing power. The expected returns on the large investments required to grow bandwidth may not be sufficient to motivate carriers who worry about maximizing returns on investment from existing infrastructure and avoiding new competition. Providing larger bandwidth to consumers has made it possible for third parties to compete against carriers over their own networks. Skype and Vonage are examples of Internet-based telecommunications services that effectively compete against the telephony services offered by the carriers who also offer Internet services.

Competition has historically not guaranteed network access by people in rural and remote regions, where infrastructure development costs are usually higher due to geography and potential profits are lower due to sparse consumer markets. Governments have historically had to subsidize such services.

Competition has also not been a reliable force for the introduction of life-critical communications services. The extension of wireline 9-1-1 emergency services to wireless telephony is a prime example, where Canada lags behind the US; interventions by government, in this case in the form of the CRTC, have often been necessary to force carriers to make such infrastructure improvements.[5]

Van Schewick and Farber (2009) point out that antitrust law may be too narrowly defined to include certain types of anti-competitive behaviour involving non-neutral network policies. Under US law, for example, traffic shaping policies would have to be shown to create or provide the potential for monopoly power in order to be found anti-competitive. In this case, some traffic shaping policies may fall short of providing ISPs with monopoly power but are still harmful to their competitors, as some earlier examples have shown. Indeed, a 2007 study on network neutrality by the Organisation for Economic Co-operation and Development (OECD), discussed later, calls for a re-examination of competition laws.

Market-based network neutrality protections are also not likely to be stable. Defenders of network neutrality change positions for business reasons. Google, an early and outspoken defender of network neutrality, has recently announced an effort to arrange preferential treatment for the transmission of its data – search results and advertisements – with selected telecommunications companies (Kumar and Rhoads 2008).[6]

Some network traffic shaping policies may transcend competitive practices, leaving consumers without recourse, as has been pointed out by van Schewick. If all network operators within a market decide to block P2P services, for example, then changing one's ISP will not be an option for obtaining those services.

From the perspective of the practical social communications needs that all citizens have, non-neutral network policies are unjust barriers, with exceptions discussed below. While network neutrality is often discussed in the context of non–life-critical communications, such as the downloading of movies and music for entertainment, the Internet is becoming the medium through which increasing amounts of life-critical communication takes place. Non-neutral services will be unacceptable in this context to the extent that they create either economic or operational barriers to communication. For example, we anticipate a time in the near future where the 9-1-1 system will benefit from the use of two-way video communication between citizens in need and emergency responders. Nondiscriminatory treatment of such data will then be necessary if people are not to be put at risk. Some people will not be able to afford the QoS necessary to exchange life-critical information.

Non-neutral network policies are not necessarily discriminatory in an economic sense. Sometimes such policies are actually necessary to guarantee adequate QoS for critical communication needs. Rural and remote Aboriginal communities in Canada present one such setting where the dominant market-based, binary framing of network traffic shaping is not appropriate. The Keewaytinook Okimakanak (KO) First Nations tribal council, which is composed of seven First Nations in northern Ontario, formed the Kuhkenah Network (K-Net) in the late 1990s to address major gaps in telecommunications between its communities that were arguably completely outside the norms of most communities in Canada at the time. The only telephone service that many members of these First Nations had prior to K-Net was through their local tribal council offices. K-Net, a TCP/IP-based network implemented with a sophisticated hybrid architecture of satellite communications and landlines, brought Internet access to homes that did not even have telephones. Thus, and in contrast to non-rural and less remote parts of Canada, Internet access became the life-critical medium for most communication throughout the KO communities. Unique also to the KO communities is the fact that the use of video and voice communications over the Internet is far more common than in most other parts of Canada, where e-mail and Web accesses are still prevalent. In this case, the affordance of telephony over the Internet was not one of several alternatives but the only practical communications service between KO communities and the outside world.

It is in this context that network traffic shaping is seen by K-Net administrators as a vital tool for preserving their community members' abilities to communicate effectively (O'Donnell et al. 2007). Since K-Net hosts many data-intensive video conferencing and voice communication sessions concerning life-critical matters such as health care and governance, it is critical that network QoS be managed in a highly disciplined way. Inappropriate use of the network could conceivably present life-threatening situations to the citizens of the KO First Nations, for example, by preventing emergency communications from taking place.

The most ominous example of non-neutral network policies is the use by governments of packet filtering to implement censorship and surveillance (Human Rights Watch 2006). Deibert and colleagues (2008) have shown how many countries use packet filtering to prevent their citizens from exchanging news with the outside world. Human rights groups are thus prevented from reporting on events within their own countries to people outside their countries, and they are also prevented from accessing news sources other than their state-controlled media. One affordance that packetized communications offer in a unique form of censorship is the implementation of efficient content substitution. By examining packet contents, origins, and destinations, a network operator can decide whether to add or substitute information on its way to a recipient. Rogers Cable has reportedly experimented with content substitution whereby commercial messages are added to Google search results (Geist 2007c). Content filtering prevents people and communities from exchanging life-critical information. Content substitution results in inaccurate communications and reduces the confidence that people have in the information they request.

IMPACTS OF NETWORK TRAFFIC SHAPING POLICY ON COMMUNICATION RIGHTS IN CANADA

Non-technical arguments for network neutrality are usually given in terms of a user's rights. Google (2007, paragraph 2) has described network neutrality as allowing people to take "control of what content they view and what applications they use on the Internet."

Non-neutral network policies might be interpreted as infringements on the exercise of civil rights in Canadian society. One approach is to link guarantees in the *Canadian Charter of Rights and Freedoms* with the intent of Canadian telecommunication policy.[7] Section 2(b) of the *Charter* provides for the "freedom of the press and other media of communication." Freedom here could be interpreted broadly to include a positive right of equal access to media of communication. The *Telecommunications Act*, for its part, does not refer explicitly to the *Charter* as the basis for its objectives, but it does make clear that the act is rooted in supporting the "essential role" of telecommunication in "the maintenance of Canada's identity and sovereignty" (section 7). Further, the act includes the objective of rendering "reliable and affordable telecommunications," as discussed earlier (section 7(b)). There are arguments that non-neutral network policies have the potential to prevent the attainment of this objective (see Geist 2004).

The implications of network neutrality or non-neutrality become more complex and potentially disruptive when multiple networks are interconnected. Messages might need to traverse multiple networks to reach their destinations. Senders might know and be prepared for the consequences of their own network's policies, but they would not make use of a network if they could not be certain of the network's policies regarding their data.

Revisiting the example depicted in Figure 3, suppose a packet is to be sent from $Computer_{1.1}$ on $Network_1$ to $Computer_{22.3}$ on $Network_{22}$ via another network that connects $Network_1$ and $Network_{22}$, $Network_7$ (see Figure 4). At minimum, $Network_1$, $Network_7$, and $Network_{22}$ must examine the address of the message to determine how to route it properly from $Computer_{1.1}$ to

FIGURE 4

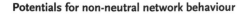

Potentials for non-neutral network behaviour

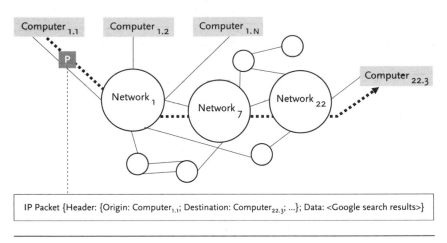

IP Packet {Header: {Origin: Computer$_{1.1}$; Destination: Computer$_{22.3}$; ...}; Data: <Google search results>}

Computer$_{22.3}$. Network$_7$ and Network$_{22}$ would be non-neutral if they refused to assist in the delivery of the packet on the basis of the type of data it contains or the IP addresses indicating its origin or destination. It is also possible that some packets making up a single message will take different routes to the destination. Each packet could be subjected to different network neutrality policies as they cross each of these networks.

The impacts of non-neutral network policies extend to international contexts. A number of popular services running on top of the TCP/IP protocol suite – and, as such, susceptible to non-neutral policies – are often used for communication across Canadian borders. For example, Voice over Internet Protocol (VoIP) services, such as Skype, have become attractive substitutes for traditional international long distance calling for many people because of their low costs.

International Internet data traffic traverses multiple jurisdictions, each with its own network neutrality policies (if any). Thus, a policy framework for Canada would not be sufficient to address impacts felt within its borders. Mueller (2007, 1) sees network neutrality as a "global principle for Internet governance." Discussion of network neutrality has taken place at the international level within the OECD. The OECD's Working Party on Telecommunication and Information Services Policies of the Committee for

Information, Computer and Communications Policy (CISP) issued a report called *Internet Traffic Prioritization* (OECD 2007a). The government of Canada is represented on the CISP as an OECD member state. Among the CISP's key findings were that: (1) network service providers should operate in a manner that is transparent to customers with respect to network traffic shaping policies and their expected impacts; (2) antitrust laws must be re-examined in the context of traffic shaping concepts and realities; and (3) entry into the broadband market should be made easier to encourage competition. The OECD report does not deal with cross-border issues of network neutrality, however.

Non-neutral network policies might be interpreted in the international dimension of communication rights as a corollary to domestic human rights interpretations. In this context, such policies might be seen as infringements of articles 19 and 27 of the *Universal Declaration of Human Rights (UDHR)*.[8]

The CRTC has supported public consultation processes on issues relating to network neutrality. Comments were sought, in particular, for its proceeding on VoIP services. Canadian incumbent (i.e., established) telecommunications providers and VoIP providers gave input on various topics, including network neutrality (CRTC 2004c, 2004d, 2004e). By using these submissions as a basis for accentuating the principle of technology neutrality, however, the CRTC largely steered clear of adopting a position on the issues related to network traffic shaping until its 2008-108 decision (CRTC 2008j) and the consultation and hearing process that concluded in July 2009 (CRTC 2008h, 2009c).

Semantic Web and Web 2.0 Technologies

The Semantic Web and Web 2.0 are related and competing research and development movements attempting to improve the usefulness of the World Wide Web. The Semantic Web aims to change the way information is represented on the Web to enable computers in ways that are more useful to humans (Berners-Lee et al. 2001). The initial approach to sharing information on the Web has been human-oriented in that Web documents have been defined largely in terms of their structure and visual presentation and less so with respect to the meaning of their content. Information represented in this way is difficult for machines to process and thus limits the ways in which it can be searched, interpreted, and used. For example, search engines cannot reliably search for Web pages by their authors' names because that information is often not explicitly represented. A software agent cannot reliably interpret the contents of travellers' Web pages for their opinions on hotels without being told how to locate it within a page and how it should be evaluated. How is a machine to understand the differences or similarities between "the hotel was decent" and "I found it to be clean but overpriced" and generate a recommendation?

Web 2.0 generally refers to human-oriented techniques for improving the usability of Web content and to an evolving set of business models that depend on these techniques. Web 2.0 shares some of the technologies for representing content developed for the Semantic Web, but it depends largely on the interaction of humans to process information in ways that make it more useful to whole communities. O'Reilly (2005, section 2, paragraph 24) has characterized Web 2.0 as a "harnessing [of] collective intelligence." If a software agent cannot be made to locate and process information intelligently, software can make it easier for larger numbers of humans to collaborate in carrying out such tasks. This is known as "collaborative filtering."

Web 2.0 encompasses blog systems, social networking services, "mash-ups," and rich Internet applications (RIAs). The essential contribution of Web 2.0 technologies to blog systems is the concept of tagging, which allows human authors and readers to categorize entries so as to make searching more effective. Web services help people establish social networks on the Internet, including facilities for finding people with common interests, managing contact lists, and analyzing one's own network. Tagging and social networking should be seen as new forms of communication subject to protection.

A mash-up is a process of combining two or more existing Web services to form a new service to solve a specific problem. A well-known example is the combination of Google's traditional search service with its mapping service to allow users to either locate information geographically or to locate geographic information associated with other forms of information. For example, one can ask to see certain kinds of businesses near a certain address, along with opinions about them. This is an example of a service that is dependent on the cooperation of multiple users, in this case to contribute opinions and rankings.

RIAs are provided by Web services running in users' Web browsers, but they provide interactivity and functionality that are similar to those found in traditional applications resident on personal computers. RIAs do not just mimic traditional applications. The Web dimension of RIAs enables real-time collaboration and remote storage of documents. A well-known example of an RIA is Google Docs, a Web-based service that enables people to edit documents and spreadsheets.

SEMANTIC WEB, WEB 2.0, AND THE PROCESS OF SOCIAL COMMUNICATION
Traditional knowledge creation is being supported and extended by Semantic Web and Web 2.0 technologies. Researchers, writers, composers, and artists can collaborate with others over the Internet in more sophisticated ways using these technologies. RIAs exist that support real-time collaborative text editing. Photographers are using blogging systems to display their work and to enable people to search their portfolios. Web 2.0 technologies are offering new affordances in the area of knowledge creation. The tagging facilities in blogging systems have made it possible for communities of scholars to semi-automatically generate taxonomies of any knowledge space. These have been termed "folksonomies."

Distribution of knowledge using Web 2.0 technologies is being accomplished on multiple levels. Interpersonal and group communication occurs using blogs, chat, and e-mail RIAs. Gatekeeping is achieved using access controls and editorial functions on shared knowledge spaces such as blogs. Filtering takes place through collaboration, as discussed earlier. Gatekeeping and filtering are thus barriers to communication; they deny or remove access to knowledge. In contrast, many Web 2.0 technologies support dissemination and distribution processes whereby knowledge is promoted and recommended to people on the basis of voting or sophisticated processing of their predefined preferences.

Practical access to knowledge using Web 2.0 technologies generally requires only a personal computer with a web browser and Internet service, but the necessary characteristics of Internet service are changing. Documents containing only text and images were once the dominant form of web content, but video and audio are now prevalent. This type of content can be orders of magnitude larger than text documents. Thus, to have effective access to knowledge using web 2.0 technologies, people are being required to obtain Internet services that permit higher data transmission rates. Some Web 2.0 services may require the installation of software in addition to the web browser. In contrast to communication costs, software costs are often not a barrier in web 2.0. The dominant Web 2.0 business model provides software and access to data for free, with the objective of generating revenue from the viewing of web content through advertising and by stimulating sales of products and services through that content.

The capacity to use knowledge accessed via Web 2.0 technologies is limited largely by their ease of use and, in some cases, by the user's ability to install the necessary software. The usability of Web 2.0 technologies, including web browsers and RIAs, is generally no worse than that of traditional PC applications.

Use and interaction of knowledge via Web 2.0 technologies takes place in the context of the public sphere, business activities, identity formation, and cultural activities. In the public sphere, Web 2.0 technologies are supporting democratic processes and social organization. The functionality provided in social networking and blogging systems have been combined to support political campaigns and other forms of activism.

In terms of business activities, Web 2.0 as a movement has fostered an inversion of the dominant business relationship between software and data. Profit in Web 2.0 enterprises is now generated from data and not from the software used to process them. For example, people submit music recordings and opinions on music to the Canadian inDiscover.net web service for free.[9] The service then offers collaborative filtering services for free using those recordings and opinions to help people buy music they will like.

Identity and cultural formation are also facilitated by social networking services. One example is Cyber Yugoslavia, a website that serves as a virtual nation for those who had been citizens of the former Yugoslavia.[10]

The process of social learning within social communication is not automatically supported by Web 2.0 technologies; this depends on their application. Communities are using the functionality discussed earlier, such as social networking and collaborative filtering tools for problem solving.[11]

Impacts of Semantic Web and Web 2.0 Technologies on Communication Rights in Canada

Semantic Web and other Web 2.0 technologies have the technical potential to reduce communication barriers and invigorate the public sphere. RIAs and Web 2.0 are now discussed in terms of "cloud computing," whereby applications are made freely available to users not on their own computers but instead in the "cloud" that is the Internet (Baker 2007). This trend could reduce some communication costs for users, since it will reduce the need to invest in certain types of software necessary for communication via the web.

Significant efforts have been made to apply Web 2.0 technologies to increase the exercise of democratic and consensual participation in society. They provide new modes of communication and interaction for community activism, elected officials, and the electorate. The Crossing Boundaries National Council (CBNC) has sponsored projects in the use of ICTs to enhance democratic participation as part of a broader mandate.[12] New Brunswick MLA Jody Carr and Saskatchewan MLA Doreen Hamilton piloted CBNC's "Wired Elected Official" system (CBNC 2007). This suite of advanced web tools includes managing constituents' files, performing online consultations with citizens, and publishing content. The CBNC's (2007, 6) own evaluation of the project claims that the system "improved effectiveness and efficiency" of elected officials and their constituency office staff and that "citizens value the additional communication channels and the improved responsiveness."

Web 2.0 technologies have provided new modes for communicating knowledge, many of which have enabled citizens to sidestep traditional media such as news organizations. Older media have often operated as gatekeepers and filters. Objectively, gatekeeping and filtering functions are necessary for some media, such as enforcing a discipline in the reporting of news, even if they are not always performed in an ideal manner. Some argue that many such gatekeepers have often prevented or failed to enable the communication of useful knowledge. Market forces are identified as a major factor. In many cases, market forces have led to uncompetitive environments and to a reduction in original content formation, such as in-house reporting and the reporting of local news. These have resulted in a lack of diversity of content.

The key affordance offered by Web 2.0 mechanisms such as blogging, content management, and video upload systems is enabling people with Internet access to communicate with a wide range of people in forms that were once the sole province of traditional media. The Canadian member websites of the global Independent Media Center (IMC) are examples.[13] "Indymedia" has provided a mechanism for people to publish news content that may otherwise not be published by mainstream media organizations.

Semantic Web and Web 2.0 technologies have offered only technical potential for improving access to mass media by communities and individuals and for invigorating democratic processes in society. In reality, these technologies have not helped people fully achieve their transformative potentials. They have arguably weakened quality journalism and replaced it with a flood of amateur commentary and junk information in the form of blogs, websites, text message broadcasts, videos, junk e-mail, and other new media. While these technologies have made significant impacts on certain types of political engagement, most prominently fundraising, the evidence that they have made significant, positive, transformative impacts on political participation is still unclear (Muhlberger forthcoming).

One civil rights issue involving Web 2.0 services is the question of data ownership. The blogosphere and other segments of the Web 2.0 sector, such as web-based e-mail services, Internet chat facilities, and free web content hosting services, all have a critical dependence on the externalization of personal or community knowledge. That is, they exist only through individuals or groups of people contributing and managing personal data via their web services. O'Reilly (2005, section 1, paragraph 21) cites this as a central tenet of Web 2.0: "The service automatically gets better the more people use it." Massive numbers of users now regularly externalize detailed personal knowledge by "posting" text, pictures, video, and audio on web services owned and controlled by someone else. Technorati.com, a highly recognized monitor of the blogosphere, stated as of 26 May 2006 that they were monitoring 41.2 million blogging sites having 2.4 billion links.[14] O'Reilly (2005, section 3, paragraph 2) eventually asks: "Who owns the data?" This was also the subject of a high-level discussion at the 2006 World Wide Web Consortium (W3C) Technical Plenary and WG Week, the main forum for working groups and interest groups within the consortium (W3C 2006).

The initial assumption in popular Web 2.0 services, such as Blogger.com, MySpace.com, and Facebook.com, was that users would retain ownership and copyright of data that they input. Blogger.com (n.d., article 6), a popular blog hosting site owned by Google, declares that it "claims no ownership or control over any content submitted, posted or displayed by you." MySpace. com (2006, article 6.1) also affirms in its terms of service that the users "continue to retain all ownership rights" of content they post on the site. The original terms of service for Facebook.com (2008, paragraph 5) imply that users own their own data: "All content on the Web site ... are the proprietary property of the Company, its Users or its licensors with all rights reserved." More recently, however, Facebook tried to quietly change its data ownership policies to require that users agree to license ownership of the data they create in perpetuity to the company (EPIC 2009). This was seen as an attempt to derive even more commercial value from users' data. Public pressure and an impending complaint to the US Federal Trade Commission forced Facebook to restore its original terms of service, although questions have been raised about how Facebook operates in the gray areas of such statements.

A complaint was filed with the Office of the Privacy Commissioner of Canada (OPC) in 2008 by the Canadian Internet Policy and Public Interest Clinic (CIPPIC) against Facebook, alleging that Facebook did not adequately inform members about how their personal information was shared with third parties (see CIPPIC 2008). The OPC's investigation of the CIPPIC complaint underlined a series of areas in which the policies of Facebook did not conform with Canadian law. In response to the OPC report (see Denhem 2009), rather than obfuscate the requests of the OPC or simply marginalize the Canadian market for its product, Facebook, working in close consultation with OPC officials, developed a strategy aimed at improving its performance in privacy protection, particularly with regard to the sharing of user information with third-party application developers; the ability of users to deactivate their accounts; and the protection of the privacy of people who decline invitations to join the social network as well as deceased users. While her office has jurisdiction over Canada only, Privacy Commissioner Jennifer Stoddart points out that "these changes mean that the privacy of 200 million Facebook users in Canada and around the world will be far better protected" (Canada 2009e).

Although separate, the question of data ownership is a related issue, and the CIPPIC complaint should raise questions about Facebook's performance in this area and also illustrate what can be accomplished – even in regard to the realization of communication rights in relation to the sort of seemingly borderless communication supported by the Internet – when well-organized civil society organizations use the machinery of democratic governance to push public authorities to confront powerful gatekeepers such as multinational communication firms.

Work-related blogging is now a common activity. The copyright and contents of employee blogs that are managed by an organization's systems may be owned by that organization. Hewlett-Packard, for example, owns the copyrights and data for blogs created by its employees using its corporate facilities (Foley 2005). Employees are equally capable of using a third-party blogging service outside the control of their employer. In these cases, it is becoming common for employers to issue guidelines concerning their employees' responsibilities when discussing corporate matters in their blogs. Examples of prominent corporations that apply these policies include Yahoo! (n.d.), Sun Microsystems (n.d.), and Microsoft (Weil 2005).

Another communication rights question that has arisen is whether the Web 2.0-enabled endeavours such as blogging can be classified as journalistic activities with the civil rights protections it is afforded in Canada and other countries. One case is that of Charles LeBlanc, a self-professed blogger who has been a frequent observer of the New Brunswick legislature. He was arrested and charged with obstruction in June 2006, while taking pictures at a business conference in Saint John, New Brunswick (CBC News 2006a). Police erased his photographs. He was apparently viewed by police as a protester. LeBlanc claims to have told them that he was a "blogger," implying that he should be afforded the same status as traditional, credentialled journalists at the event. LeBlanc's claim was challenged in provincial court. The court's decision in November 2007 was that LeBlanc should be recognized as a journalist, and the charges against him were dismissed (Austen 2006).

Independent of data ownership and civil rights issues, users are likely to have limited control over the data they create and manage using commercial Web 2.0 services. Many common software applications store data in file formats that can be transported easily between computers and that can often be used by different applications. For example, the applications Microsoft Word, OpenOffice, NeoOffice, and TextEdit are all capable of sharing documents in several common formats, and those documents can be transferred between computers with ease. This is often not the case with the data that users enter into their blogs and other types of Web 2.0 services. While much of the underlying technologies used to implement blogging systems are nonproprietary – Extensible Markup Language (XML) and Hypertext Transfer Protocol (HTTP), for example – there is not yet agreement on higher-level formats for storing blog information. There is also no agreement on communication protocols for transferring blog data between different systems. Blogger.com (n.d.), one of the most popular blogging sites in the world, states: "Blogger does not have an export or download function. However, you can use the following instructions to create a single file with all your posts which you may publish and then copy to your own computer for use as desired." This is followed by a process that average users would probably find to be complex. Arguably, such knowledge management arrangements are not yet engineered with the communication and data rights of users in mind.

Internet Telephony

The Internet has enabled the creation of a new type of telephony known as Voice over Internet Protocol (VoIP). Instead of delivering voice in analog form, as is still done in large parts of the public switched telephone network (PSTN), VoIP converts voice to packets and sends them via the Internet – and sometimes over the PSTN – to their destination.

VoIP services are attractive because they offer inexpensive long distance calls and because a subscriber's telephone number or user identifier is not

FIGURE 5

Categories of VoIP service

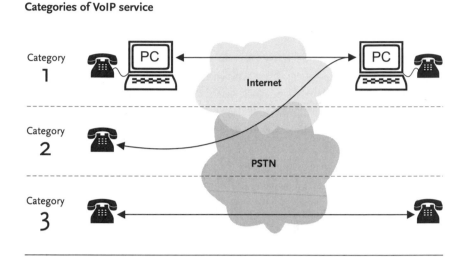

tied to a specific location. VoIP allows telephone services to be delivered wherever there is Internet access. Compared with mobile telephony, VoIP services are not tied to a specific device, and there is no home calling area where roaming charges are concerned. One's telephone number need not be dependent on a physical location or a home area in the context of mobile telephony. The location-independent nature of VoIP has enabled competition in traditional local and long distance telephone markets, where barriers to competition have been based largely on physical access to facilities. In the case of rural and remote communities such as the First Nations represented by the Keewaytinook Okimakanak, VoIP is a life-critical service.

VoIP comes in several forms, as depicted in Figure 5. The CRTC (2005d, paragraph 29) defines Category 1 VoIP services as allowing users to communicate between PCs over an Internet connection. Category 2 VoIP services allow users to communicate in either direction between PCs over an Internet connection and telephones on a public switched telephone network. Category 3 VoIP services allow users to communicate between telephones, and other devices, on a public switched telephone network.[15] These categories represent affordances stemming from the layered architecture of the Internet, which has provided a nexus for the integration of different forms of communication, in this case, the bridging of new and older forms of telephony.

An example of a Category 1 service is Skype-to-Skype calls, where all voice data are transmitted through the Internet. An example of a Category 2 service is SkypeOut, where voice data are exchanged between a device on the Internet and a device, such as a telephone or fax machine, on the traditional public switched telephone network.[16] Examples of Category 3 services are traditional telephone services offered by Vonage and Primus, which are implemented by using traditional public switched telephone networks managed by incumbent carriers, such as BellAliant.[17] Incumbents such as Telus offer Category 3 services. Some services, such as Skype and Vonage, offer integrated services that fit in both Category 1 and 2.

Canada was early among nations to develop a regulatory framework for VoIP (Lemay-Yates Associates 2005). The distinctions between categories of VoIP were central to the creation of a regulatory framework. If VoIP is equivalent to "plain old telephone service," or "POTS," the logic goes, it should be regulated in the same way.

The CRTC (2005d, paragraph 113) determined that VoIP Categories 2 and 3 are equivalent to POTS since they provide "two-way, real-time voice communications to and/or from anyone on the PSTN." This is an example of technology-neutral regulation. Category 1 services were viewed as Internet services under the framework, which are exempt from regulation under this framework. The decision included the following regulations:

- extension of local number portability obligations for incumbents to VoIP service providers
- equal ability of VoIP providers and incumbents to assign telephone numbers
- equal requirements for accessing incumbent facilities and providing access to others for network interconnection purposes
- requirement for VoIP providers to file tariffs like incumbents (paragraphs 213, 214, 225, 242, 326).

VoIP services under Categories 2 and 3 were also found to be eligible to make contributions to the CRTC's national fund, which is intended to subsidize the high-cost rural and remote services (CRTC 2005d, paragraph 14). Any company with annual revenues over $10 million must pay a percentage of those revenues into the fund. This helps to support Canada's telecommunication policy objectives, as discussed earlier in this chapter. Also, given that

Category 2 and 3 services are viewed as equivalent to POTS, they must also abide by the 9-1-1 emergency requirements laid out under an earlier CRTC telecom decision (see CRTC 2005c).

INTERNET TELEPHONY AND THE PROCESS OF SOCIAL COMMUNICATION

VoIP subscriber services offer yet another medium of interpersonal communication through which knowledge can be delivered. It is important in this respect because of the advantages it provides over landline and mobile telephony. These include location independence, landline independence, elimination of mobile telephony roaming charges, and advanced calling services. Since VoIP services are implemented using the Internet, services can be provided in a largely location-independent manner, unlike landline telephony, which depends on a fixed PSTN infrastructure. A subscriber needs only to have access to Internet service to place and receive VoIP calls. The subscriber's VoIP service provider can map the traditional telephone number that the subscriber was assigned to the specific Internet address being used at the moment. For example, if a VoIP subscriber from New Brunswick connects to his or her service from an airport lounge in Bangkok, anyone calling the VoIP-enabled phone number in the New Brunswick area code can be routed transparently and at no additional cost for many VoIP services to that computer in Thailand. This can be done because the VoIP software that subscribers use notifies the service of the subscriber's location. Some VoIP services, such as Skype, allow calls between computers at no cost.

The other advantages of VoIP are related to location independence. Since VoIP requires only Internet access, subscribers can potentially avoid paying for traditional landline telephony services altogether. It is often the case, however, that VoIP subscribers must obtain Internet services from local telephone companies. Thus, telephony costs must sometimes be factored into the overall cost of VoIP services. The advantage of VoIP over mobile telephony is that the costs of roaming are potentially greatly reduced. When away from their local calling area, subscribers incur only the cost of Internet access when they initiate and receive VoIP calls. Thus, per-call mobile telephone roaming charges can be replaced by a short-term Internet access fee (such as in an airport lounge). The cost of that fee amortized over each VoIP call becomes the effective roaming charge, with corresponding economies of scale. The combination of routing and parallelism capabilities offered by the Internet has enabled companies providing VoIP services to offer average subscribers a wide array of advanced calling services at a relatively low cost. These include the ability to ring multiple numbers in parallel or to automatically dial a list of telephone numbers in sequence (e.g., a priority list) until the call is answered. Many of these services were previously affordable only to large organizations, and some were not practical prior to VoIP.

The requirements for accessing and using VoIP services are modest for those already using computers and the Internet. Access to VoIP requires a subscription with a service provider and an Internet service with a channel capacity of greater than 2 megabits per second – typical high-speed or broadband. High-speed service is required for reasonable quality. VoIP services are relatively easy to use for those familiar with computer applications. In most cases, direct use of software is not necessary, since traditional telephone handsets and dial keypads are used for basic calling.

IMPACTS OF INTERNET TELEPHONY ON COMMUNICATION RIGHTS IN CANADA

The advantages of VoIP over previous forms of telephony are making possible the dissemination of knowledge for subscribers at lower costs and in more sophisticated ways than allowed by landline and mobile telephony. This has enabled individuals and organizations alike to reduce the cost of communicating knowledge. In many cases, VoIP can bridge communications between other forms of telephony and computers, thus extending the abilities of older communication technologies in disseminating and distributing knowledge.

Current usage rates show that VoIP is an attractive mode of communication in Canadian households. Statistics Canada (2007) reported in a December 2006 survey that 10.6 percent of Canadian households had VoIP or cable telephone service. The proportion of Quebec and Alberta households was over 13 percent. These penetration rates are remarkable because residential VoIP services have been available for less than five years in Canada. In comparison, the same survey reported that landline and mobile telephone services were used by 90.5 percent and 66.8 percent of Canadian households, respectively.

There has been concern over the potential for incumbents to use their networks and customer accounts in ways that would prejudice competitive VoIP providers (Geist 2004). Claims of network non-neutrality regarding VoIP have been reported following the creation of this framework (Geist 2005c). Shaw Communications Inc., Rogers Communications Inc., and Vidéotron – all cable companies as well as incumbent Canadian ISPs – have been accused of, and/or found to be, shaping Internet traffic over their networks where VoIP is concerned. Shaw proposed a $10 fee to guarantee quality of service for its customers who use VoIP.

Potential infringements on civil rights as a result of network traffic shaping are directly related to VoIP services. VoIP services that are not provided by incumbent telephone carriers have been threatened with non-neutral network policies by incumbents. These incumbents would discriminate against third-party VoIP data crossing their networks. Some incumbents have demanded that premiums be paid by subscribers who wish to use third-party VoIP services. Such actions could constitute barriers to "reliable and affordable" communication as guaranteed by the *Telecommunications Act*.

As discussed in the context of network traffic shaping, there have been public consultations related to VoIP. These have resulted in a technologically neutral view of VoIP relative to traditional telephony in the CRTC's VoIP decision (2005d), which did not deal with the potential impacts of non-neutral network policies on VoIP.

Another risk with new types of telephony such as VoIP (and mobile telephony before it) is the introduction of gaps in access to emergency services. In particular, 9-1-1 services were not accessible in earlier offerings. The CRTC addressed this in a decision requiring VoIP service providers to fulfill the same emergency service obligations that other carriers have (CRTC 2005c).[18]

Communication Rights and Regulatory Challenges in Canada

The affordances offered by Internet-based ICTs have, to some extent, reproduced existing modes of social communication, such as basic telephony and postal communications. Internet-based ICTs have also made possible extraordinarily novel and powerful modes of communication. Web 2.0, social networking, and variations on Internet telephony now enable more far-reaching and sophisticated communication, knowledge sharing, and collaboration than at any time in history. Individuals and communities can now use Internet technologies to communicate in text, audio, or video with millions of other similarly equipped people around the world at relatively low cost. The average users or their communities can now also publish or produce their own news, research, literature, movies, or music and distribute them to millions of others at relatively low cost, whereas before, corporate media served as gatekeepers for these types of communications, preventing most of these same people from communicating in these ways.

These new affordances have created conditions that require societies to re-examine both communication rights and telecommunications policy. These novel communication technologies do not give rise to the need for fundamental rights beyond those already recognized under the umbrella of communication rights as much as they create new conditions under which existing rights can be challenged. Any new technology-specific affordance that can be exploited in a way that violates communication rights can be mapped onto a communication rights framework in a technology-independent way. We do not need to map new rights onto specific technologies. For example, as we saw earlier, network operators could now use network traffic shaping to impede those telephone communications that are based on VoIP. This potential to interfere with communications depends on a new affordance made possible by a new set of technologies, but acts of interference using this affordance would still be reducible to an analysis of communication rights violations held in common with earlier forms of telephony. Existing human rights, such as article 19 of the *Universal Declaration of Human Rights*, provide a technology-neutral basis and language by which to conduct this analysis. Thus, one of the critical functions that a communication rights framework must implement with regard to Internet policy is ongoing monitoring for new conditions that infringe upon communication rights. The variety of attitudes of ISPs toward network neutrality and consumer rights, as seen in the comments submitted to the CRTC's consultation on network neutrality, combined with the potential impacts of Internet-based ICTs on social communication, underscores the need for a set of inalienable communication rights.

Canadian telecommunications policy, on the other hand, is not congruent with our communication rights framework. This chapter has surveyed a variety of new conditions created by Internet-based ICTs that have challenged existing telecommunications policies.[19] What we have also seen is that Canada cannot depend on competition alone to achieve and preserve the social aspects of its telecommunications policy objectives and thereby guarantee adequate communication rights. Governments and the policies they make must balance markets with mechanisms that require telecommunications companies to operate in a transparent manner so that people know what types of services they are entitled to receive and what types of services are being denied or restricted. This is the norm today in general commerce, and many people do not otherwise have the technical expertise or the resources to determine these facts for themselves.

7
Privacy

.. *Leslie Regan Shade*

> But though we tend to take it for granted, privacy – the right to
> control access to ourselves and to personal information about us
> – is at the very core of our lives. It is a fundamental human right
> precisely because it is an innate human need, an essential condi-
> tion of our freedom, our dignity and our sense of well-being.
>
> – Office of the Privacy Commissioner of Canada

Reporting to Parliament for 2001-02, George Radwanski, then Privacy Commissioner of Canada, issued a scathing critique of recent initiatives and their
potential impact on the privacy and security rights of the Canadian public.
"The fundamental human right of privacy in Canada is under assault as never
before," he wrote, and unless the government reversed its legislative course,
"we are on a path that may well lead to the permanent loss not only of privacy
rights that we take for granted but also of important elements of freedom as
we now know it" (OPC 2002, 1). Under the pretext of "anti-terrorism," Radwanski argued, the government's initiatives in the collection and uses of
personal information could "establish a devastatingly dangerous new principle of acceptable privacy invasion" (2).

More than seven years after Radwanski's report, his concerns about privacy
rights are still relevant. Bureaucratic and governmental prevalence and dependence on information and communication technologies (ICTs), with
their qualities of facile mobility and informational aggregation, create new
concerns "about information that is not sensitive and intimate and that may
be collected in public," troubling traditional theories of informational privacy
(Austin 2003, 128-29). Consider the following recent news reports about
perceptions of privacy and intended or unintentional privacy violations,

aided and abetted by emergent uses of digital technologies and a political environment conducive to supporting a "homeland security" complex:

- Maher Arar, a dual citizen of Syria and Canada, was arrested at JFK International Airport in 2002 because his name was on a "watch list" of suspected terrorists.[1] After he was held for thirteen days and questioned by American Homeland Security personnel, the Immigration and Naturalization Service (INS) sent him on an executive jet off to Syria, where it knew he would be tortured. After a year, he was released to Canada, and in 2006 the final report of the O'Connor commission of inquiry exonerated Arar and blamed the RCMP for releasing false information to American authorities, who still claim that Arar is a terrorist (Canada 2006c, 2006g). Among the many issues the case raises is the intentional release of false information to the media and other entities by government security officials in violation of Arar's privacy rights (Canada 2004f; see also Chapter 4).
- A March 2006 EKOS Research Associates survey for the Office of the Privacy Commissioner (OPC) revealed that Canadians are very concerned about the privacy of their personal information, with seven in ten believing that it is less protected than before. Privacy is "one of the most important issues facing our country in the next ten years," according to two-thirds of Canadians, but most do not believe that governments or businesses take seriously the protection of personal privacy. Canadians are ignorant of existing privacy laws and institutions, with a mere one in five reporting a "clear" awareness of privacy laws. Most Canadians agree that technological changes will warrant updated privacy legislation, and they want to be able to take control of their personal information, including the ability to turn off built-in tracking devices. The survey also revealed an "impressive awareness of the *USA PATRIOT Act* and the privacy issues it raises," with "more Canadians report[ing] a high level of recall of privacy-related concerns with the *PATRIOT Act* than with the Canadian privacy laws" (EKOS 2006).[2]
- "I'm accused of something I didn't do. It's not me. I have the same name, that's it," said Alistair Butt, a fifteen-year-old top student in Orleans, Ontario. Alistair's name appeared on a new "no-fly" list (the Passenger Protect program) initiated by the Canadian government in conformity with US security laws. Said his mother: "Canada is telling him he's guilty until proven innocent every time he flies" (CBC News 2007).

In February 2009, the first remote-controlled Predator aircraft, a surveil-lance drone known for its use in Afghanistan and Iraq, took off in South Dakota to patrol a 370-kilometre stretch of land along the southern Manitoba border, to test its resilience against harsh Prairie winters. Said Manitoba MLA Cliff Graydon whose own farm will be in the line of surveillance: "Privacy is the biggest concern ... many of my constituents already have fences up for privacy on the ground. Now they'll have someone up in the sky watching them. How would you like someone staring in your window all day?" (White 2009). Part of the Northern Border Air Wing plan, recommended by the US 9/11 Commission amid concerns over border security with respect to drug smuggling, guns, and terrorism, the Predator is restricted from flying closer than 16 kilometres to the Canadian border, but "that still leaves a roughly 24-km swath of Canadian borderland open to U.S. government eyes" (White 2009).

Despite Canadians' claims that they are concerned about their personal privacy, the OPC survey highlights how surprisingly ignorant they are of privacy legislation. Media coverage of the O'Connor Commission report on the Arar case in September 2006 alerted the public to various privacy viola-tions by multiple law enforcement jurisdictions (as well as the lax journalis-tic coverage of the case prior to the commission – see Mitrovica 2007; the press implications of the Arar case are discussed more extensively in Chapter 4) under the pretext of national and global security. The Predator drone case highlights the porousness of national borders thanks to sophisticated sur-veillance systems that could have unanticipated consequences for the privacy of innocent bystanders. Alistair Butt's plight raised awareness of the folly of "no-fly" lists and the fact that it could happen to any of us unfortunate enough to share our name with a person deemed suspicious by law enforcement agencies. The Arar and Butt cases point to unintended and egregious instan-ces wherein violations of informational privacy led to unfortunate and serious consequences for the livelihoods and personal integrity of citizens and their families. They also highlight the value of considering Nissenbaum's model of informational privacy, which she develops around the notion of context-ual integrity. Contextual integrity should be the benchmark of privacy, "defined as compatibility with presiding norms of information appropriateness and distribution" (Nissenbaum 2004, 137). Violations of privacy involve variables that are situationally dependent, "the nature of the information in relation to that context; the roles of agents receiving information; their relationships to information subjects; on what terms the information is shared by the subject; and the terms of further dissemination" (137-38). Contextual integrity is used to explain our increasing unease with pervasive forms of public surveillance, defined as involving "a new technology that expands the capacity to observe people; gather information about them; and process, analyze, retrieve, and disseminate it" (116).

Almost forty years ago, the government of Canada initiated a high-level study to investigate the status and future of telecommunications in Canada. Looking broadly at the social, policy, and technical challenges of telecommunications, *Instant World*, the report of the official government-sponsored study group known as the Telecommission, was prescient, progressive, and insightful in its call for a right to communicate (Canada 1971). Many of the insights contained in *Instant World* as well as its contributions to the development of the right to communicate are discussed in greater detail in the Introduction to this book. The centrality of privacy to *Instant World*'s notion of the right to communicate and the derivative conclusion that the right to privacy is among the most fundamental and precarious of communication rights warrant further discussion.

Instant World discussed the efficacy of establishing a right to privacy, pointing to the dilemma involving conflicts between the public "right to know" versus the individual "right to be private," with some seeing the "right to privacy" as "an elitist attitude towards the power of information, especially information about rich and powerful people" (42). The report questioned what privacy rights the less powerful in society ("welfare recipients, the out-patient at a public clinic, or the indigent senior citizen") would have. There was widespread consensus that a legal concept of "invasion of privacy" should be introduced into both provincial and federal Canadian law, and that the "right to communicate"

> should imply a complementary right not to be communicated about involuntarily, a recognition that there exists a private "domain," within which the individual will either refuse to communicate, or will do so only reluctantly and to a limited audience. There is no simple answer to the nature of this "domain," which entails the desire to be left in peace by one's neighbours and the community, to be detached or offbeat, to be anonymous in public, to communicate

confidentially – in short, to disconnect at will. These needs are, for many people, basic to personal equilibrium and peace of mind. (Canada 1971, 45-46)

Vast technological innovations since the days of *Instant World* have created an amplified blurriness between the public and private realms: our tolerance for revealing more about our personal lives, in daily interactions or online, has increased amid the supposed anonymity of the Internet; the mainstream media's insatiability in providing audiences with heightened tabloidization and titillation detracts from investigative journalism in the public interest; and our ability to be "detached or offbeat" is countered by the ability of governments and security agencies to track and monitor our everyday movements in case we pose "threats" to national security. Since *Instant World* was released, the need for privacy rights is increased by the development of intrusive technologies of surveillance and a political climate suffused with a homeland security mentality. Regan (2004), commenting on the *PATRIOT Act*'s impact on various public sectors (financial, educational, transportation, and library), argues that there has been a muddying of privacy versus security concerns, an increased sectoral reduction in privacy concerns, and an expansion of governmental authority with "government's ill-conceived assemblage of unmanageable amounts of information," creating massive surveillance systems instead of what were formerly streamlined records management systems (490).

The idea of a right to privacy resurfaced in the late 1990s with a proposal for a Canadian charter of privacy rights promoted by then Senator Sheila Finestone, who passed away in June 2009. This chapter traces the debate generated by that proposal, and prolongs it by arguing that the challenges of emergent material technologies coupled with political technologies of regulation and governance necessitate a reconsideration of a privacy rights platform for the twenty-first century.

Privacy as a Human Right
Interpretations of privacy depend upon myriad sociocultural contexts, socioeconomic differences, gender, the space of privacy ("real" space versus online), and delineations of privacy as a claim, entitlement, or right. Colin Bennett and Charles Raab (2006, xv) argue that privacy-related problems "are as much political and public policy issues as they are legal and technological ones."

Privacy debates must therefore interrogate changes in privacy protection due to technological accelerations, the globalization of policy instruments for the protection of personal information, and comparative perspectives on privacy governance, all subsumed within a "policy sector" consisting of "the collection of laws, codes, guidelines, conventions, and practices that together regulate the processing of personal information" (xix).

Valerie Steeves (2006) demarcates four ways to consider privacy: (1) as an essential facet of the democratic process (integral to individual freedom and autonomy, intrinsic to citizenship); (2) as a social value (allowing one to define and control one's personal relationships); (3) as data protection (the right of access to personal and reliable data); and (4) as a human right. Considering privacy as a human right recognizes it as an important element of civil liberties and a necessary component of a communication rights framework. As Gus Hosein (2006, x) argues, "a regard for privacy is a belief that we must maintain human dignity, and that this is the core objective of human rights." Hosein adds that because it is "tightly intertwined with our sense of right and wrong, our moralities ... privacy can be seen as a core protection of individual autonomy and human agency."

Privacy as a human right is linked to the development of international human rights legislation after the Second World War and global responses against the legacy of Nazism and fascism. Article 12 of the United Nations *Universal Declaration of Human Rights (UDHR)* states: "No one shall be subjected to arbitrary interference with his privacy, family, home or correspondence."[3] As discussed in the Introduction and in Chapter 1, Canada has signed and ratified both the *UDHR* and the *International Covenant on Civil and Political Rights,* which reiterates the guarantee of the right to privacy.[4]

Canadian federal privacy legislation is a patchwork of protections. There is no explicit constitutional right to privacy, although sections 7 (which states that "everyone has the right to life, liberty and security of the person and the right not to be deprived thereof except in accordance with the principles of fundamental justice") and 8 ("everyone has the right to be secure against unreasonable search or seizure") of the *Canadian Charter of Rights and Freedoms*[5] have been interpreted by the Supreme Court of Canada (in *R. v. Duarte*)[6] to protect against "unreasonable" invasions of privacy. Canada's two pieces of federal privacy legislation are limited in terms of privacy rights. The *Privacy Act* applies only to the federal public sector in relation to data collection, placing limitations on the collection, use, disclosure, and disposal of personal information held by the federal government and federal agencies.[7] The

Personal Information Protection and Electronic Documents Act (PIPEDA) applies to the federally regulated private sector with respect to the collection, use, and disclosure of personal information, but only for the transaction of commercial activities.[8]

Whither Privacy Rights?

Although there is no explicit recognition of privacy as a human right, but only a court precedence for a "reasonable expectation" of privacy,[9] the vexing issue remains: in an ever-shifting digital world, with slippery boundaries and jurisdictional challenges, what is a reasonable expectation of privacy? With regard to communication rights and the right to communicate, fundamental freedoms of expression have been curtailed by recent acts, including the *Antiterrorism Act*, which limits access to information and threatens privacy rights.[10]

As we have seen in Chapter 1, article 19 of the *UDHR* guarantees freedom of opinion and expression. These ideals are reflected in the *Charter*, which guarantees rights and freedoms subject only to reasonable legal limits that can be demonstrably justified in a free and democratic society (section 1). Fundamental freedoms include freedom of conscience and religion, freedoms of thought, belief, opinion, and expression, including freedom of the press and other media of communication, freedom of peaceful assembly, and freedom of association (section 2(a)-(d)). The *Charter* also ensures individuals the right to be secure against unreasonable search or seizure (section 8). The guarantee of these rights and freedoms does not deny the existence of other rights and freedoms (section 26).

Toward a Privacy Rights Charter: Senator Finestone's Private Bill (2000)

In 2000, Senator Sheila Finestone introduced a *Privacy Rights Charter* (Bill S-27) in the Canadian Senate. It was delayed by a federal election before its reintroduction as Bill S-21 in 2001 (Canada 2001b; see also Canada 2001d, 367-71). When Finestone retired from the Senate in 2002, the bill did not find significant support, and it was eventually dropped from the Order Paper.

As a Member of Parliament, Finestone had chaired a 1997 committee on human rights and the status of disabled persons to examine the privacy implications of developing technologies. A prescient report for its time, *Privacy: Where Do We Draw the Line?* (Canada 1997b) was the product of a parliamentary committee that travelled across Canada seeking broad public input into the pressing and emergent privacy issues of the day, such as genetic testing, smart cards/biometric encryption, and video surveillance. The committee was discerning in its recognition of the need to go beyond a consideration of privacy as mere data protection and thus as an individual right, to considering it as a collective responsibility of society and as a human right and social value: "Canadians see privacy not just as an individual right, but as part of our social or collective value system ... Canadians view privacy as far more than the right to be left alone, or to control who knows what about us. It is an essential part of the consensus that enables us not only to define what we do in our own space, but also to determine how we interact with others – either with trust, openness and a sense of freedom, or with distrust, fear, and a sense of insecurity" (6).

In 2000, the Standing Committee on Social Affairs, Science, and Technology of the Senate recommended the creation of a Charter of Privacy Rights that would be a quasi-constitutional document providing an overarching legislative framework for the general protection of privacy. Although committee members supported a full constitutional right to privacy, they considered the constitutional amendment process too cumbersome to deal with the urgent need to establish general privacy principles. The Privacy Rights Charter therefore "became the embodiment of this proposed quasi-constitutional document" (Oscapella 2000). The Privacy Rights Charter was designed to go beyond the then newly launched *PIPEDA* and establish rights related to the collection, use, and disclosure of personal information, and rights of physical privacy, freedom from surveillance, and freedom from the monitoring and interception of private communications. In essence, the Privacy Rights Charter "would act as umbrella legislation, under which the *Privacy Act* and *PIPEDA*, and such other existing and future specialized privacy legislation would constitute the different spokes; it would set out the governing principles on privacy in Canada" (Canada 2001f). In the Thirteenth Report of the Senate Standing Committee, Marjory LeBreton described Senator Finestone's overview of the Privacy Rights Charter:

> She underlined that while privacy is a fundamental human right, it is not an absolute or inflexible right. Under section 1 of the Canadian Charter of Rights and Freedoms, it is subject to such reasonable legal limits as can be demonstrably justified in a free and democratic society. Senator Finestone explained that the bill is intended to set out an explicit legal right to privacy – something Canadian law does not currently contemplate – while giving effect to the principle that privacy is essential to an individual's dignity, integrity, autonomy,

well-being and freedom, and to the full and meaningful exercise of
human rights and freedoms. She described how the bill would apply
to all persons and matters coming within the legislative authority of
Parliament by protecting against, for example, genetic discrimination
and infringements on freedom from surveillance. Senator Finestone
noted that the bill would be paramount over other ordinary legislation and would necessitate a review of existing, as well as all new,
federal legislation to ensure compliance with the bill. She did not
consider grandfathering existing legislative provisions an option as
it would amount to giving statutes enacted before the bill a special,
unjustified immunity from review under the bill. (Canada 2001f)

Concerns were raised in the committee that the bill would muddy the
interaction between the right to privacy, the *Criminal Code,* and the burden of
proof, referred to as "the obligation to affirmatively prove that what one is
doing is lawful as opposed to being able to do as one pleases as long as it is
not unlawful" (Canada 2001f).[11] The committee was also concerned about the
role of the federal Privacy Commissioner in relation to the bill, particularly
with respect to establishing a complaints process separate from that of the
Privacy Act, with the potential to undermine or compete with rulings, raising
questions of precedence. The committee was also keen to see the Privacy Commissioner be more active in the application of a Privacy Rights Charter.

Ursula Franklin (1996) argues that privacy needs to be approached from
a rights-affirming and people-centred perspective, rather than from the needs
of the marketplace: "When human rights informs the language in which the
discussion among you and the general public and Parliament takes place,
you speak then, rightfully about *citizens* and all that comes with that. On the
other hand, if the emphasis is primarily on the protection of *data,* one does
look at a market model, one does look at an economic model, and all the
things you've heard about the new economy. Then it is the language of the
market that informs your discourse."

Validating Franklin's citizen-centric model was the approach adapted in
the Privacy Rights Charter and its predecessor report, whose principles were
included in section 2:

(a) privacy is essential to an individual's dignity, integrity,
     autonomy, well-being and freedom, and to the full and
     meaningful exercise of human rights and freedoms;

(b) there is a legal right to privacy;

(c) an infringement of the right to privacy, to be lawful, must be justifiable. (Canada 2001b)

According to section 3, every individual has a right to privacy, including:

(a) physical privacy;

(b) freedom from surveillance;

(c) freedom from monitoring or interception of their private communications; and

(d) freedom from the collection, use and disclosure of their personal information. (Canada 2001b)

Federal elections, Finestone's retirement from the Senate, perhaps weariness from the collapsing tech boom, hopes and attendant beliefs in market competition, and the ascendancy of the consumer-oriented *PIPEDA* served to dampen enthusiasm for pushing forward with a Privacy Rights Charter.

Privacy and ICTs – New Challenges and Trends

Globalization, convergence, and the malleability of multimedia have created a fascinating and often conflicted landscape in which individual privacy is rapidly eroding. Some critics contend that we have entered a surveillance society, where our everyday actions – from surfing the Web to registering our automobiles – have come under the eye of Big Brother (Lyon 2003). The accumulation of technologies and administrative procedures in our daily lives is what Carolyn Bassett (2007, 83) dubs the "total surveillance trajectory," an ensemble of "material technologies (surveillance systems including CCTV, data-mining practices, data-retention/tapping techniques), political technologies (regulation, governance), and in a series of discourses around privacy, security, safety, on the one hand, and control, efficiency, and convenience on the other."

In her 2005-06 *Annual Report to Parliament* (OPC 2006b), Privacy Commissioner Jennifer Stoddart commented on the ubiquity and stealth of digital technologies in penetrating and threatening personal privacy. Digitization has created "limitless storage capacities, limitless transmission capacity, limitless data mining capacity ... the challenge of protecting data is increasingly globalized, because actions in one distant part of the world now may directly impact the privacy of Canadians" (1-2). New variations in ICTs create multifaceted and integrated databases and hypertextual modes of information. One of their characteristics is their two-sided nature: they have the ability to empower citizens through access to valuable information, but at the same time they make citizens vulnerable to surveillance manipulation through personal information gathered by search engines and data mining. This information can be collected and stored to create detailed profiles of user tastes and preferences in shopping, reading, and other habits, which is all of great value to corporations that rely upon mass marketing. The risk of adding this information to commercial databases has become a focus of consumer activism (Chester 2007).

Children and youth are particularly vulnerable to privacy threats, including the capture of data from their web surfing by marketers using increasingly stealthy methods; such data mining raises important ethical issues about children's rights to privacy and freedom of expression (Grimes and Shade 2005). As a response to these trends, the US *Children's Online Privacy Protection Act (COPPA)* was enacted in 1998 and became effective in 2000 to protect children's privacy on the Internet by regulating the collection of personal information from children under the age of thirteen.[12] Canada has no such legislation, although the *Canadian Code of Practice for Consumer Protection in Electronic Commerce* provides some principles for online communication with children (see Canada 2004a). The code, endorsed by federal, provincial, and territorial ministers responsible for consumer affairs, is open to endorsement by the private sector and consumer organizations interested in endorsing best practices for e-commerce.

Marc Rotenberg, executive director of the Electronic Privacy Information Center (EPIC) in Washington, DC, identified the following emerging privacy issues, which are exacerbated by Web 2.0 applications:[13] DNA databases, deployment of RFID (radio frequency identification – a small identifier tag using radiowaves affixed to products, people, or animals), social networking sites, identity management, and pervasive surveillance. Privacy research is crucial, he added, in order to preserve important social values, to answer broad questions, to assess emerging issues, to enable oversight, and to formulate effective policy proposals (Rotenberg 2007).

Privacy Rights after 9/11
In his 2001-02 *Annual Report to Parliament*, Privacy Commissioner Radwanski warned that "any intrusions or limitations on the fundamental human right

of privacy that are imposed as a purported wartime measure against terrorism will likely never be rescinded. What we are confronting is the prospect of a permanent redefinition of Canadian society" (OPC 2002, 16).

Rather than give up individual and collective privacy freedoms for the illusion of security, Radwanski proposed that any new "security" measure must meet the following four-part test:

1   It must be demonstrably necessary in order to meet some specific need.
2   It must be demonstrably likely to be effective in achieving its intended purpose. In other words, it must be likely to actually make us significantly safer, not just make us feel safer.
3   The intrusion of privacy must be proportional to the security benefit to be derived.
4   It must be demonstrable that no other, less privacy-intrusive, measure would suffice to achieve the same purpose. (OPC 2002, 17)

After the 11 September 2001 terrorist attacks in New York City and Washington, DC, governments internationally introduced new legislation and policy measures to counter alleged terrorist threats and beef up public security to provide a semblance of safety for their citizens. In the process, however, privacy rights became collateral goods, a fact that galvanized many privacy rights organizations to mount new educational campaigns to roll back heightened surveillance measures. Barry Steinhardt (2003), associate director of the American Civil Liberties Union (ACLU) comments that in the US, although privacy laws are less robust than they used to be, the fact that many citizens, privacy advocates, and politicians are "resisting incursions" on privacy is a good sign (and Steinhardt's article was written before media such as the *New York Times* reported on the Bush administration's authorization of widespread wiretapping by the National Security Agency (NSA) without prior approval from the Foreign Intelligence Surveillance Court (FISC), an event that further alarmed Americans – see Risen 2005). As many have observed, increased surveillance measures do not necessarily translate into higher levels of societal security; it is therefore harder to justify constraints in human rights (Peissl 2003). Bennett and French (2003, 10) argue that after 9/11, Canada was forced to go along with the US on the privacy front, despite its progressive move toward alignment with European Union (EU) privacy policies: "11 September has convinced many American policy makers that American security is only as strong as that of the longest undefended border in the world. And those arguments have obviously had a powerful influence on the Canadian federal government."

In *Illusions of Security*, Maureen Webb (2007) provides a panoramic overview and scathing critique of the political economy of the global corporate security complex engendered and intensified by the Bush administration's "war on terror" and its brazen abrogation of legal and legislative privacy and human rights. Measures undertaken without public, let alone legislative, consultation have created a moral morass that "only creates illusions of security. Illusions that do little to catch or stop terrorists and that ensnare the innocent, divert resources away from better initiatives, obscure our public policy debates, and betray our real personal and collective security" (235). Webb details a startling array of secretive and stealth initiatives by governments under the guise of pre-emption that range from extraordinary rendition (wherein untried terrorism suspects are sent to other countries to be interrogated under less humane conditions, e.g., use of torture); arbitrary detention (detaining persons with no legal cause); warrantless domestic wiretapping of citizen's telephone conversations without court sanction and with the complicity of the NSA and major telecommunications carriers; the use of biometric technologies to ferret out and register aliens and immigrants; enhanced technology for surveillance, including biometrics and facial recognition software and identity cards; restrictions on mobility, including enhanced tracking of travel (advance passenger information, passenger name record, no-fly lists, the Canada-US Smart Border Action Plan); and coordinated data mining across national boundaries.

In response to the abrogation of civil rights, the International Campaign against Mass Surveillance (ICAMS) was formed in 2005 with the support of almost 100 international groups, including its founders the ACLU, Focus on the Global South, the Friends' Committee on National Legislation, the International Civil Liberties Monitoring Group, and Statewatch. Its campaign declaration stated: "All data collection, storage, use, analysis, data mining and sharing practices that erode or are contrary to existing data protection, privacy and other human rights laws and standards must stop immediately. Governments must resist efforts by the United States and other countries to pressure them into weakening their existing privacy standards."[14]

The declaration also called for the rights of individuals to adjust and redress false personal data; for allowing the international transfer of personal data between countries only under internationally recognized data protection principles; for governments to stop the collection of "wholesale and indiscriminate" information on citizens, especially its acquisition from private companies; and for governments to halt the implementation of biometric passports and passenger name record information "until the issue has been openly debated at the national level and privacy and other human rights protections are established."

Two controversial pieces of Canadian legislation, the *Anti-terrorism Act* and the Lawful Access proposals, both introduced after 9/11, highlight why civil liberties groups are concerned about the curtailing of fundamental privacy rights. Other concerns emanate from free trade provisions that allow for the outsourcing of Canadian information by US private corporations that operate in Canada, which are subject to US legislation such as the *PATRIOT Act*.

Anti-terrorism Act

The *Anti-terrorism Act* substantially amended the *Criminal Code*, broadening offences related to terrorism. An omnibus piece of legislation, it also amended the *Official Secrets Act* (now the *Security of Information Act*),[15] the *Canada Evidence Act*,[16] the *Proceeds of Crime (Money Laundering) and Terrorist Financing Act*,[17] and the *Charities Registration (Security Information) Act*.[18] Changes to section 38.13 of the *Canada Evidence Act* altered legislation dealing with disclosure of information to individuals involved in legal proceedings that could injure national defence or security or that would encroach on the public interest. This necessitated amendments to the *Access to Information Act* (adding sections 69.1(1) and (2)),[19] *PIPEDA* (adding sections 4.1(1) to (4)), and the *Privacy Act* (adding sections 70.1(1) to (4)) that prevented or stopped disclosure of information to individual requests under certain circumstances. The definition of "terrorist activity" in the *Criminal Code* was broadened, with potential applications to situations not commonly considered to be terrorist-related.

When the *Anti-terrorism Act* was enacted, then Justice Minister Irwin Cotler argued, amid civil liberties critiques that it went too far in allowing for warrantless arrests and limiting the right to remain silent, that these "measures go to the core of protecting our rights and that's the right to life, liberty, and security of the person ... anti-terrorism legislation is profoundly human rights legislation and human security legislation. There's no contradiction between the protection of national security and the protection of human rights" (MacLeod 2004, A1).

One year later, the Privacy Commissioner argued that *PIPEDA* was weakened by legislation included in the *Anti-terrorism Act*. Specifically, the *Proceeds of Crime (Money Laundering) and Terrorist Financing Act* mandated that financial institutions disclose personal information to the Financial Transactions and Reports Analysis Centre of Canada; Bill C-44, amending the *Aeronautics Act*,[20] required that Canadian air carriers must disclose passenger information to foreign customs and immigrations departments; and the *Public Safety Act* required that air carriers and aviation reservation systems disclose passenger and crew information to the RCMP and the Canadian Security Intelligence Service (CSIS) (OPC 2006a).[21]

When the *Anti-terrorism Act* was enacted by Parliament in 2001, two controversial provisions, created under the guise of public safety, were recognized as being extraordinary enough that they were enacted with safeguards, including execution only with the approval of an elected political officer (federal justice minister or provincial attorney general) and with a five-year sunset clause. The two provisions were the preventive detention power (allowing authorities to arrest suspected terrorists without a warrant and detain them for up to twelve months without laying any charges) and the investigative hearing procedures (used to force any suspected conspirator to testify about terrorist plots). Since 2001, these provisions have never been invoked. In February 2007, they were excised in a parliamentary vote after the Opposition defeated a Conservative motion to renew the extraordinary legal powers of authorities to detain and interrogate suspected terrorists (Sallot 2007, A1).

Lawful Access

"Lawful access" refers to the lawful interception of communications and lawful search and seizure of information. The interception of information is possible only with legal authority such as a court order executed within a particular time frame. Lawful interception includes telephones, wireless technologies, cellular phones, pagers, satellite communications, and the Internet. Only law enforcement and national security agencies (RCMP, CSIS, municipal and provincial police forces, and the Competition Bureau) are able to request lawful access (Canada 2005d). Given that law enforcement has not yet demonstrated the inadequacy of current laws, however, these new powers have little judicial oversight and may be unnecessary (Geist 2005a).

The Lawful Access proposals, designed to bring Canada into compliance with the Council of Europe's *Convention on Cybercrime*, will change some of the safeguards that currently limit the privilege of information access.[22] Lawful access heightens surveillance powers through modifications to interception capability, access to subscriber data through warrantless searches, changes to preservation and production orders, and increased access to e-mail. Amplified interception capabilities would require telecommunications service providers to increase interception capabilities on networks when they are upgraded, which the Privacy Commissioner believes could result in elevated usage (OPC 2005). Mandating that subscriber data be handed over to law enforcement even without judicial authorization would eradicate current safeguards that protect privacy. The Privacy Commissioner argues that each request for access needs to be justified and allowed only for those with supervisory responsibilities; that links between the identity of the account user and IP address are not precise; and that therefore accessing subscriber data without a warrant will be fruitless (OPC 2005).

Lawful Access proposals also include lower thresholds for obtaining telecommunications tracking (determining the location of an individual) and transmission (identifying origin, type, direction, date, time, and other aspects of the communication) data (cf. Canada 2002a). Lowering the grounds from "reasonable grounds to believe offence has/will be committed" to "reasonable grounds to suspect" dramatically changes the circumstances where judicial authorization must be sought, potentially leading to more intrusive measures. Lawful Access proposals also call for lower privacy standards for e-mail in temporary storage at Internet service providers (ISPs), as e-mail can be considered either a private communication or a document. Requirements governing the interception of private communication are more burdensome than requirements for seizing a document. Lawful Access proposals interpret an e-mail as a document when stored at the ISP of either the sender or the recipient, and thus subject to less stringent requirements for seizure of this communication. The Privacy Commissioner believes that all e-mail should be considered private communication (OPC 2005). Many experts believe that Lawful Access proposals are not constitutional and will face challenge and scrutiny from the Canadian courts (Geist 2005a). The Canadian Internet Policy and Public Interest Clinic compiled civil society responses and critiques to the Lawful Access proposals, including the following (CIPPIC 2007):

- The government has still not provided clear evidence justifying the need for these additional powers. Without such justification, we should not be eroding civil liberties.

- There is inadequate oversight of law enforcement use of these powers, so as to prevent and punish abuse. If police are given additional powers, oversight bodies must be created and/or better empowered to keep such powers in check. Current oversight mechanisms are inadequate for this purpose and need to be supplemented.
- No police searches of any sort should be permitted without judicial authorization.
- Access to Subscriber Data without warrant: Police should not be able to access subscriber name and address merely upon request, without any kind of justification, let alone judicial authorization.
- Compelling Interception Capability: The Lawful Access proposals would effectively cause a reconstruction of network architecture, from one that currently supports a degree of anonymity to one that facilitates surveillance and identification. This will be true generally, not just for law enforcement. Under the new architecture, individual telecommunications users would be much more easily identified and pursued for purposes that may be legitimate or illegitimate.

In February 2009, reports surfaced that the Harper government was planning on reintroducing aspects of the Lawful Access proposals, particularly wiretapping laws, giving law enforcement officials the ability to access information from Internet service providers. Privacy Commissioner Stoddart called this potential move a "serious step forward toward mass surveillance," and CIPPIC staff attorney Kris Klein commented that ISPs would be able to harvest retroactive conversations: "I think that's a huge move towards the totalitarian state where everybody is eavesdropping on one another and handing over information to the police" (CBC News 2009).

Indeed, the Lawful Access proposals were reintroduced by the government in June 2009. Bill C-46, *The Investigative Powers for the Twenty-First Century (IP21C) Act* (see Canada 2009b), and Bill C-47, *The Technical Assistance for Law Enforcement in the 21st Century Act* (see Canada 2009c), mirror the previous Lawful Access proposals. Bill C-46 is aimed at updating law enforcement tools by allowing law enforcement agencies to apply for orders requiring service providers to provide them with transmission data sent or received through the Internet or telephone; allowing law enforcement agencies to apply for preservation orders requiring service providers to retain data related to specific communications or to an individual subscriber; criminalizing online or telephonic arrangements or agreements for the sexual exploitation of a child; and revising the system of tracking warrants to allow for the remote activation of tracking devices in equipment including mobile phones (Canada 2009b). Bill C-47 imposes legal obligations for telecommunications service providers to include interception capabilities in their networks. The possibility of new surveillance mechanisms being embedded in the Internet by legislative fiat has concerned many public interest groups such as CIPPIC; these concerns align with those of many ISPs, who fear that providing tapping capability could both raise costs and drive customers away (Canada 2009c).

Deep Integration, Outsourcing, and Transborder Data Flows

"Deep integration" refers to the further harmonization of the security systems and economies of the United States and Canada. For Maude Barlow (2005, 15) of the Council of Canadians, deep integration poses grave threats to Canadian sovereignty and cultural identity, given the dominance of the US free market economy: "The dramatic increase in Canada's reliance on U.S. markets for economic survival has also subjected all Canadian laws, practices, and regulations, including government spending, to the test of whether they violate American business interests. This in turn has limited Canada's ability to maintain social, cultural, and environmental policies that are in the interest of Canadian citizens." Barlow contends that the Canadian government has made "a serious commitment" to "create a North American fortress with a common economic, security, resource, regulatory, and foreign-policy framework ... driven by the mutual interests of big business on both sides of the border, and the foreign policy and security hawks in the White House who want a compliant and well-behaved Canada" (30). Like Webb (2007), Barlow is concerned with heightened surveillance measures, noting that "governments are aggressively using information gathered and shared through electronic systems to crack down on dissent, close borders to refugees and activists, and seize and detain people without reasonable grounds" (Barlow 2005, 91-92). The security of Canadians' personal information is at stake; for "information technology companies such as Lockheed Martin, LexisNexis, ChoicePoint, Accenture, Computer Sciences, and Acxiom, the war on terror has been a boon," and "by contracting with private corporations, government agencies gain access to databases they would not, under privacy and other laws, be able to maintain themselves" (95). The cross-border economic integration achieved so far further undermines the belief that personal information is absolutely secure and private.

Concern over transborder data flows is exacerbated by the increased contracting of government services to companies that are either located outside Canada or located inside Canada but owned by a foreign national. Information created, managed, and maintained by these companies are not subject to Canada's privacy legislation but may be confiscated and used by foreign governments without Canada's knowledge or consent. Canada's privacy legislation does not extend across its borders, and there is currently no redress for privacy violations that originate in foreign jurisdictions (Perkins 2006). The Privacy Commissioner does not feel that she has jurisdiction to act outside Canada, but she has recently called for her office to have greater powers to enforce privacy legislation, and to have the ability to coordinate investigation efforts with foreign privacy commissioners (OPC 2006c). Many Canadians fear that legislation such as the *PATRIOT Act* may be leveraged by foreign governments to access their personal information (OPC 2006b). These concerns were heightened when the Office of the Information and Privacy Commissioner of British Columbia (OIPCBC) released a report, *Privacy and the USA Patriot Act* (2004), triggered by a BC Government and Service Employees' Union lawsuit that alleged that the provincial government under Premier Gordon Campbell was handing over responsibility for confidential records to American corporations, such as IBM and MAXIMUS, which had been shortlisted to bid for administrative contracts for the BC Medical Services Plan and PharmaCare. The OIPCBC, under Information and Privacy Commissioner David Loukidelis, issued strong recommendations to dampen the free flow of such confidential information in order to protect personal privacy.

The *PATRIOT Act* allows American security officials such as the Federal Bureau of Investigation to access information held by corporations that operate in the US. As a result of the concerns and recommendations contained in the OIPCBC report, the Privacy Commissioner of Canada announced in January 2005 government amendments to future federal contracts to counter US powers under anti-terrorism laws. Canadian federal agencies and departments have therefore been asked to conduct an assessment of risks to Canadian information that is released to US companies carrying out contract work.

The BC and federal privacy commissioners acknowledge that possible use of the *PATRIOT Act* or other means by a foreign entity in order to access information about Canadians is part of a larger problem involving transborder flows (Canada 2006e).

A more recent issue regarding transborder data and privacy concerns arose, also in BC, when the Canada Border Services Agency decided to repatriate a database containing personal information on its citizens that were stored on RFIDs. These citizens were participating in an "enhanced" driver's licence pilot project related to Canada-US border crossings (Beeby 2009).

Privacy, a Fundamental Communication Right

On 18 September 2006, the government released its official report on the case of Maher Arar.[23] The commission of inquiry, led by Dennis O'Connor, cleared Arar of all terrorism charges and found that actions, including various privacy breaches by Canadian officials, likely led to his ordeal through extraordinary rendition. The report accused the RCMP of passing erroneous and unfair information to US officials that probably led to his deportation and torture in Syria. The twenty-three recommendations contained in the O'Connor Commission's report centred on improvements to the RCMP and their sharing of information with international security agencies (Canada 2006c, 2006g).

For the Canadian public, the plight of Maher Arar and media coverage of the O'Connor recommendations starkly illustrated the perils of the "new normal" of homeland security: the routine roughshod activities of security entities, the failure of cross-border intelligence, extraordinary rendition's menacing of lives and livelihoods, and the egregious nature of racial profiling. Legislation such as the *PATRIOT Act* and the *Anti-terrorism Act*, and the Lawful Access proposals, give intelligence agencies greater authority to track individuals suspected of terrorist activities; privacy advocates and civil libertarians are justly concerned that these laws will push citizen's rights into a precarious situation. The public interest implications of such anti-terrorism legislation are therefore unprecedented. How can and should privacy rights of citizens be protected in our current era of globalization? How can citizens' rights to privacy be strengthened in a climate of heightened security concerns in the wake of geopolitical instability? How can the Canadian government protect its informational sovereignty, given the slippery nature of transborder data flows? What are appropriate processes for information sharing among governments? How can governments trust other governments that have questionable human rights records?

Returning to Nissenbaum's (2004, 118-19) notion of contextual integrity, "it expresses a right to privacy in terms of dichotomies – sensitive and non-sensitive, private and public, government and private." Contextual integrity is not just the purview of law and policy; normative dimensions of etiquette and morality are configured here. When norms of public surveillance are violated through systematic pervasiveness, however, and "when strong incentives of self-interest are behind these violations, when the parties involved are of radically unequal power and wealth, then the violations take on political significance and call for political response" (139).

As has been argued in this chapter, emergent technological, legal/legislative, and political/sovereignty issues that arose in after 9/11 underscore the need for a basic privacy right. These days, one can be considered "offbeat" by governments and security establishments, not on the basis of quirkiness and charming idiosyncrasies but because of the colour of one's skin, or one's religion or nationality. Privacy rights are intrinsic to communication rights, and policy debates geared toward recognizing and implementing a Canadian Charter of Privacy Rights should be renewed. It is time to engage in widespread public debate on the privacy rights of Canadians in an effort to recognize the essential nature of privacy as a human right integral to one's "dignity, integrity, autonomy, well-being and freedom, and to the full and meaningful exercise of human rights and freedoms" (Canada 2001b).

8
Copyright

Laura J. Murray

> So long as it remains undisclosed, the fruit of the creative act –
> the text or image of composition or contraption – possesses the
> status of a secret: confected in private, it remains the absolute and
> exclusive property of its creator. Yet the society at large cannot
> benefit from the work of creative people unless that work is
> published. In the long-term interests of the public, copyrights
> and patents create a temporary bubble of exclusivity around
> published artifacts and public inventions: the physical text or
> object can be bought, owned, borrowed, lent, sold, or destroyed,
> but never copied, at least not beyond the allowances of fair uses,
> without the creator's permission. This monopoly privilege should
> not be so extensive that it chills public discourse through the
> privatization of ideas. Nor should it be perpetual, lest it prevent
> future creators from building on past creations and thereby injure
> the public good. But it cannot be so perfunctory or so brief that
> creators are better off guarding their innovations in secret or
> ceasing to innovate altogether. Embodying these delicate balances,
> intellectual property is a frail gondola that ferries innovation from
> the private to the public sphere, from the genius to the commons.
>
> – Paul Saint-Amour, *The Copywrights: Intellectual
> Property and the Literary Imagination*

Copyright, as Saint-Amour presents it, is a vehicle for moving knowledge
between individuals and the wider world. From this perspective, the marvel
of copyright is that it enables a person to make intellectual or creative work
public without giving it away. Saint-Amour's vision contrasts markedly with

today's dominant copyright rhetoric, in which copyright is seen primarily as a tool for preventing appropriation of private property, or as a machine for turning public goods into private goods. For the cultural industries, of course, it stands to reason that cultural expressions are commodities first and foremost. But the capitalist view of copyright is bolstered by a long-standing and pervasive view of the nature of creativity, in which the lone genius "expresses" his mind into words or images, pouring out the rich wine of poetry from within. Here, too, Saint-Amour demurs, evoking instead the social nature of knowledge production.

Indeed, we could say that for Saint-Amour – as for the authors of this book – *communication* is a more powerful concept than *expression* for understanding and developing democracy and culture. Copyright exists not only to encourage creative production but also to encourage *dissemination* of ideas. What is more, these two functions are inseparable: as John Dewey (1927, 176) wrote, "knowledge cooped up in a private consciousness is a myth, and knowledge of social phenomena is peculiarly dependent upon dissemination, for only by distribution can such knowledge be either obtained or tested." Or, in the words of the Campaign for Communication Rights in the Information Society (CRIS 2005a, 21), "communication rights demand that the conditions needed for a positive cycle of communication are, in practice, created. This cycle involves a process not only of seeking, receiving and imparting, but of listening and being heard, understanding, learning, creating and responding." It is in the cycle of publicity and reflection and reinvention (see Figure 1 in the Introduction) that cultural and intellectual inventiveness takes place. Undue constraints on this cycle impose costs on the group, even if they present benefits for some individuals.

Part 1 of this book offers a critical review of the debate over the relative merits of the freedom of expression and communication rights frameworks. Copyright debates show a range of ways of handling this dilemma. In the policy realm, the goal is often framed as a balancing of multiple rights to freedom of expression: those of the maker of copyrighted works, those of their owners, those of their custodians, and those of their users. In this view, there are many freedoms of expression to be accommodated to each other. There are two major limitations to this approach, however. First, it may fail to acknowledge that the right, say, to parody a piece of corporate art as an assertion of freedom of expression is meaningful only if accompanied by the right and ability to disseminate that parody with a power somewhat equivalent to the reach of the original. Freedom of expression in one's own bedroom is simply not a very expansive freedom. Furthermore, the "competing freedom of expression" formula pits one stakeholder against another, rather than acknowledging or insisting that all are part of a cycle of knowledge reception and production, and that each party in fact occupies several roles in this cycle: we are all at once (or could be enabled to be) creators, receivers, and transmitters of human expression and knowledge.

What we could call a "communication cycle" view of cultural production is increasingly entering into copyright discussions in Canada and elsewhere. At a grassroots level, it appears in blogs and other outlets associated with free software, appropriation art, free culture, and consumers' rights movements, where certain forms of copyright law are represented as barriers to innovation. The Creative Commons licence – which allows creators to, for example, permit non-commercial use of their work without closing off the possibility of profiting from commercial use – also asserts the value of free circulation rather than control. In academic circles, Canada's prominent intellectual property scholars are showing that in order to go beyond merely declaring intersecting or conflicting rights to freedom of expression, we must engage with media ownership, copyright and corporate law, international trade agreements, the technical structure of the Internet, and so on.[1] The communication cycle view of copyright can be found as well in a series of recent Supreme Court of Canada cases. For example, in *Théberge v. Galerie d'art du Petit Champlain*, the court observed: "Excessive control by holders of copyrights and other forms of intellectual property may unduly limit the ability of the public domain to incorporate and embellish creative innovation in the long-term interests of society as a whole, or create practical obstacles to proper utilization" (paragraph 32).[2] However, Canada's most recent piece of copyright legislation, Bill C-61, introduced in June 2008 and abandoned upon the fall election, manifested a vision of copyright antithetical to a communication rights perspective.

This chapter offers a preliminary assessment of copyright's relationship to communication rights in Canada at present. This is not a simple relationship. While the role of copyright does not often make itself felt as starkly or visibly as censorship or barriers to access to the airwaves, copyright has the capacity both to enable and to hamper the exercise of communication rights by citizens. It might *enable* individuals by offering them ways to fund their efforts at public communication. It might also enable them by allowing them to maintain and defend the integrity of their communication, and its attribution to its origin (or, if the originator wishes, its anonymity). Finally, it might enable the exercise of communication rights by giving citizens access to a broad range of ideas and knowledge, by facilitating their interaction with these materials, and by facilitating their transmission of these interventions to others. On the other hand, copyright might *hamper* the exercise of communication rights if it does not provide financial support for the creativity of citizens or does not allow individuals of ordinary means to access legal advice and procedures. It might hamper them if it does not protect the integrity and attribution of works – or their anonymity. It might hamper them by imposing limitations on access to ideas and knowledge or limitations on citizens' ability to create or disseminate materials built upon or responding to the work of others.

In the development of this chapter, these various possibilities were assessed through a combination of research into the development and state of law and policy and also through interviews to illuminate artists' experiences of this law and policy. A fuller investigation would also examine the experiences of a wider range of artists and other Canadians: teachers, students, ordinary consumers, and people in different demographic groupings, for example. But artists with some experience of copyright were a particularly rich place to start.

Existing Statute and Case Law: Users' Rights

A great deal of communication is quotation: human expression emerges out of implicit or explicit references to ideas and expressions of others.[3] This may be especially true of political communication, which needs to be able to hold public icons and powerful figures to account for their stated views. Thus, a central issue for communication rights is the extent to which people are free to reference the words (or images or sounds) of others. In terms of copyright, this ability is regulated through the mechanisms of the substantiality requirement, the copyright term, and the provision of "fair dealing," along with more specific exceptions.

Substantiality Requirement

The *Copyright Act* of Canada grants copyright only to "works or any substantial part thereof" (section 3).[4] That is, use of "nonsubstantial" portions of copyrighted material are not infringing. Recent case law has understood substantiality to be both a matter of quantity and quality; that is, there is no set formula for determining whether the threshold has been met.[5] The advantage to this from the point of view of communication rights is that reasonably generous uses might be considered "nonsubstantial," depending on other factors such as the effect of the use on the work, the proportion of the use, and so on. The disadvantage is that there is a high degree of uncertainty. In practice, publishers and broadcasters do not ever mention the substantiality requirement and require clearance for all uses; even more important, the lawyers for the errors and omissions insurance demanded before broadcast consider all uses to be substantial.

Copyright Term

Canada's copyright term remains at fifty years after the death of the author, unlike in other jurisdictions, where the term lasts up to seventy (United States, Europe) or even 100 years after the author's death (Mexico). This shorter term is good for the exercise of communication rights: it means that less material is under the umbrella of copyright and more material can be freely used without permission or payment (see Boyle 2003). As one of our interviewees, a theatre director, said:

> I don't want to characterize myself in an unpleasant way, but a theatre artist of my sort does a little bit sit like a vulture, watching for the fifty year period to expire after the author's death, because there are different things that one is then able to do in creating a new work out of that. The Master Builder [by Henrik Ibsen, 1892], that I'm doing right now, I've written my own adaptation of it and I've changed it quite a bit actually ... the work suddenly gains a new kind of relevance and appeal. My job as a director with any play is to provide a kind of conduit between the author's imagination and the audience, and the art demands a certain amount of freedom in how I judge is best to do that.[6]

In late 2008, this same director directed an early play by Bertolt Brecht, who died in 1956. Unlike directors in the United States and Europe, he was free to devise an adaptation suited to his artistic purposes.[7]

Fair Dealing and Other Exceptions

Section 29 of the Canadian *Copyright Act* states: "Fair dealing for the purpose of research or private study does not infringe copyright." Sections 29.1 and

29.2 list criticism or review and news reporting, respectively, as other allow-able purposes, with the added requirement of naming the source.

Throughout the twentieth century, fair dealing was generally understood as a limited defence that should be construed narrowly. In *Michelin v. CAW*, the Federal Court concluded that fair dealing provisions "should be restrict-ively interpreted as exceptions," and barred the Canadian Auto Workers from reproducing the image of the "Bibendum" (generally known as the Michelin Man) in their unionization drive posters (II.ii).[8] In the section of the case dealing with the union's claim that its freedom of expression had been ham-pered, in violation of section 2(b) of the *Canadian Charter of Rights and Freedoms*,[9] the court even went so far as to say: "I agree with the plaintiff's submission that the defendants are not permitted to appropriate the plaintiff's private property – the 'Bibendum' copyright – as a vehicle for conveying their anti-Michelin message. Thus, the defendants' expression is ... not protected under the umbrella of paragraph 2(b)" (*Michelin*, III.A.ii).

Although Michelin remains the most prominent Canadian parody case, scholars have roundly criticized it as "no longer ... good law,"[10] and subse-quent Supreme Court of Canada cases have departed markedly from its logic. Most importantly, in *CCH Canadian Ltd. v. Law Society of Upper Can-ada*, the Supreme Court of Canada ruled that the Law Society's library did not infringe copyright when it faxed legal materials to its members and let them use photocopy machines.[11] It made a number of points that clearly expand the scope of fair dealing from what it had been believed to entail. First, the court clarified, the nature and character of the fair dealing defence: "Procedurally, a defendant is required to prove that his or her dealing with a work has been fair; however, the fair dealing exception is perhaps more properly understood as an integral part of the *Copyright Act* than simply a defence ... The fair dealing exception, like other exceptions in the *Copyright Act*, is a user's right. In order to maintain the proper balance between the rights of a copyright owner and users' interests, it must not be interpreted restrictively" (paragraph 48). In the same paragraph, the court went on to quote, and adopt, legal scholar David Vaver's observation (2000) that "user rights are not just loopholes. Both owner rights and user rights should therefore be given the fair and balanced reading that befits remedial legisla-tion" (paragraph 48).

Together with the decisions rendered by the Supreme Court of Canada in the *Théberge* and *Society of Composers, Authors and Music Publishers of Can-ada v. Canadian Assn. of Internet Providers*[12] cases, the *CCH Canadian* case articulates the idea of users' rights and also asserts the need for careful balancing of interests. This might suggest a very favourable environment for communication rights in the Canadian courts where commentary on or reuse of copyrighted materials is concerned.

Nonetheless, the lack of a high court ruling on parody appears to have left Michelin some power; it was recently followed by a ruling in British Columbia that freedom of expression was not a pertinent issue in the case of CanWest Global Communications against two parodists of the *Vancouver Sun* (Murray and Berggold 2009). This case remains to be settled. And Canadian "fair dealing" remains quite a narrow provision compared with American "fair use" in that it can be practised only for the purposes of criticism, review, research, private study, or news reporting: quite a number of artistic or consumer practices may not be included in these categories. Section 107 of the US *Copyright Act of 1976* lists "purposes *such as* criticism, comment, news reporting, teaching (including multiple copies for classroom use), scholarship, or research," allowing the courts more latitude about appropriate categories of legitimate fair use.[13] Increasing numbers of scholars and stakeholder associations have been calling for a "flexible fair dealing" formulation in the Canadian statute.[14]

In addition to fair dealing, the Canadian *Copyright Act* includes various specific exceptions for private, library, and educational use. For example, it is not infringement to reproduce copyrighted material in an examination or to show a news program taped off television within a month of its taping, if rules regarding the keeping of proper records are observed.[15] While such exceptions may in some ways facilitate the exercise of communication rights, they are very narrow and specific and may cause more problems than they solve. The so-called private copying exception has been especially controversial: it allows certain copying of music without permission, but only in exchange for the payment of a levy on blank media.[16]

MORAL RIGHTS

Moral rights are essentially three: the right of integrity, the right of attribution, and the right of association.[17] Only creators have them (i.e., corporate or employer owners do not), and they may be waived but not transferred. The right of integrity allows a creator to act in defence of the original form of his or her work. Except in the case of unique works of visual art, it is infringed only when it damages the honour or reputation of the author. In *Snow v. The*

Eaton Centre Ltd., the Ontario High Court of Justice accepted the artist's subjective opinion that his reputation had been damaged when his sculpture was altered, and the case preceded an amendment to the *Copyright Act* that specifically protects unique works of visual art (section 28.2(2)) so moral rights in those type of works are even clearer now.[18] In *Prise de Parole Inc. v. Guérin éditeur Ltée*, on the other hand, the court would have required some objective evidence in order to make a finding for moral rights infringement when a book was abridged without permission.[19] The *Théberge* court also seemed to set a high bar for damage to reputation, expressing skepticism that an artist who had licensed thousands of cards and stationery products could have his reputation damaged by canvasback reproductions. It is clear, therefore, that some sort of objective evidence is probably necessary to assert the right of integrity, but this does not seem unreasonable.

On right of attribution, the *Copyright Act* notes that attribution must be practised "where reasonable in the circumstances," which permits needed flexibility for follow-on creators.

In practice and in terms of case law, moral rights do not seem very strong in Canada. In the few cases that have been heard, courts appeared reluctant to weigh them very heavily. A moderate moral rights regime may seem most conducive to the exercise of communication rights, because excessively strong moral rights would impair the ability of follow-on creators, parodists, and other commentators. And yet there is cause for concern in the imbalance of power between a small number of large media outlets and the large number of freelancers: contracts with publishers, broadcasters, and even government routinely require moral rights to be waived altogether, and freelancers, researchers, and employees have little bargaining power (see, for example, PWAC 2007). Improvement in this situation would require regulation of concentration of media ownership rather than a shift in copyright law, as is also indicated by the discussion in Chapter 4.

Legislation and Legislative Reform

For the past ten years, Canada's *Copyright Act* has been said to stand on the verge of change. When substantial alterations were made to the law in 1997, a provision for a review of the act within five years was included in the legislation. Furthermore, Canada's signing of the 1996 *World Intellectual Property Organization (WIPO) Copyright Treaty*[20] and *WIPO Performances and Phonograms Treaty*[21] left unfinished the question or process of implementing these so-called Internet treaties. Meanwhile, the Office of the United States Trade Representative, along with the music recording industry, rallied to promote an American-style implementation of these treaties (often known as "WIPO plus"). In this context, from 2001 through 2004, the Canadian government engaged in consultation on copyright issues and produced a series of studies and policy statements.[22] Among these, the report of the House of Commons Standing Committee on Canadian Heritage, the so-called Bulte Report, drew quite a volume of public critique for its failure to recognize users' rights (Canada 2004d).[23] In 2005, the minority Liberal government introduced Bill C-60, an imperfect piece of legislation nonetheless more moderate than the Bulte Report, which died on the Order Paper in 2005 when the government fell (see Canada 2005a).

The change to a Conservative minority government delayed copyright policy once again, but in June 2008 the government introduced Bill C-61 (Canada 2008a). This bill, too, died on the Order Paper when an election was called. In the wake of public consultations in the summer of 2009, the Conservatives are poised to introduce copyright legislation once again, and so C-61 still merits attention as a benchmark for the next attempt at copyright reform.

In terms of communication rights, Bill C-61's most significant provision was the outlawing of the circumvention of technical protection measures on digital materials, a provision that would have nullified users' rights in those materials. Here, the bill followed the 1998 US *Digital Millennium Copyright Act* despite extensive documentation that this law has had a serious chilling effect on freedom of expression and research (Electronic Frontier Foundation 2007).[24] A wide range of educational, research, and artistic practices would have been suffocated by Bill C-61; for example, taking clips from DVDs for fair dealing purposes such as research or criticism would become illegal.

Bill C-61 did offer various specific exceptions for consumers and educators, but within the communication rights framework all of these appear extremely problematic. For example, consumers were given the right to format-shift and time-shift legally acquired materials in private, but only in private. Thus, for example, if one were to put a track from a CD on a hard drive (a shift of format) and then give away the CD, one would fall outside the exception. Such limitations are one way of meeting the WIPO requirement that "making available" be a right reserved for owners. However, the strategy of meeting WIPO obligations through specific constrained exceptions explicitly locks consumers into precisely that role: they must receive but never circulate or respond to cultural material that enters their home. Similarly, educational exceptions were burdened with unworkable constraints. An exception permitting some use of copyrighted materials in distance education without permission would have required the institution to prevent duplication of those materials, to limit access to the duration of the course, and to destroy all the materials within thirty days of the final exam. An exception for a digital interlibrary loan required that the materials be encoded to prevent duplication and also that they evaporate within five days of sending. Clearly, "communication" is not being enabled by such provisions.

It might be noted that Bill C-61 did not contain copyright term extension despite international pressure on that front; neither did it feature a system by which Internet service providers would be immune from liability only if they removed materials from their servers that copyright owners alleged to be infringing. "Notice and takedown," as it is called, would give rights holders even more power than they already have to dictate the law without judicial review. These are some areas where Canada may be steering away from policy harmful to communication rights.

While the bill died for parliamentary reasons rather than on its own merits, it is important to observe that it provoked considerable public controversy. In the years preceding its introduction, library, museum, and educational organizations had been repeatedly articulating their concerns about copyright policy (see CARL 2008; CAUT 2008; CFHSS 2007). In addition, the Canadian Music Creators' Coalition (CMMC 2007), the Appropriation Art Coalition (2008), and the Documentary Organization of Canada (DOC 2006) all made it clear that their copyright interests differed from those of the big American record labels, and pointed out that US and Canadian interests ought to be better distinguished. But it may have taken 90,000 Canadian consumers angry about not being able to transfer their cellphones to new service providers or to watch imported DVDs to get the Conservatives' attention. Those were the members of the Facebook group Fair Copyright for Canada, created in December 2007 by scholar and activist Michael Geist when the Conservatives were indicating that legislation was imminent. The Facebook group appears to have been effective in delaying the introduction of legislation at that time. When the bill was introduced in June 2008, the Facebook group grew further and shifted into high gear once again in its resistance to the "Canadian DMCA," despite time-shifting and format-shifting exceptions and limitations on statutory damages for downloading, provisions that seemed designed to allay consumer fears.[25]

Surely the Conservatives' consultation initiative of summer 2009 was at least in part an attempt to pre-empt such consumer-rights wildfires.[26] But if copyright has become a hot-button issue, it remains to be seen whether public concerns over access to information, freedom of expression, and consumer rights will affect future legislation in any serious way. When any legislation does appear, it will likely be larded with exceptions, to indicate awareness of public interest concerns; in some versions, these exceptions might actually be useful to the public. The New Democratic Party will continue to champion users' rights and criticize any bill that does not adequately address them, but it is not likely that either the Liberals or the Conservatives will ever present a bill that fully integrates and features users' rights.

Partly this is because the international context is as important as the domestic context in determining the future of Canadian copyright policy.[27] Canada is party to and compliant with the *Berne Convention for the Protection of Literary and Artistic Works.*[28] It has signed the WIPO "Internet treaties" of 1996 as well. Neither the Berne nor the WIPO treaties contain effective enforcement mechanisms; furthermore, the fact that Canada signed the 1996 treaties does not commit it to implement them or to implement them in any particular way: the treaties actually permit considerable national variation.[29] However, the World Trade Organization's (WTO) *Agreement on Trade-Related Aspects of Intellectual Property Rights* contains standards for the protection of intellectual property, including copyright, that go well beyond the standards contained in the *Berne Convention.*[30] This agreement *is* enforceable as part of the overall apparatus of the WTO and is subject to the same dispute settlement provisions as the other trade agreements, such as the *General Agreement on Tariffs and Trade*[31] and the *General Agreement on Trade in Services (GATS).*[32]

As recently as 2001, in its "Framework for Copyright Reform," the Liberal government reviewed the many recent changes to the copyright statute and stated: "As a result of all these amendments, Canada's *Copyright Act* is now consistent with our international obligations" (Canada 2001e). Such resolve has been foundering, however, in the face of repeated American assertions to the contrary. The United States Trade Representative has stated that "the United States will use the Out-of-Cycle review to monitor Canada's progress in providing an adequate and effective IPR protection regime that is consistent with its international obligations and its advanced level of economic development, including improved border enforcement, ratification and implementation of the WIPO Internet Treaties, and strong data protection"

(US 2006). This claim is essentially bullying: it has not been confirmed by the WTO and does not accord with scholarly evaluation of Canada's compliance (Tawfik 2005). It may work nonetheless to move Canada's law toward the American "WIPO plus" standard, since maintaining good trade relations with the US is likely to outweigh calls for a Canada-specific copyright regime, especially in difficult economic times.[33]

Citizens' Perceptions

For most people at most junctures in life, the law is what they think it is. Most artists, teachers, and citizens going about their daily lives do not have direct contact with the *Copyright Act* or indeed with copyright lawyers. They may hear rumours about copyright reform, but they are unlikely to keep track of what happens during committee hearings or in the parliamentary system. So while the legal situation described in the two preceding sections exists, it does not necessarily resemble the working reality of most Canadians.

To test the hypothesis of a disconnect between law and practice, we interviewed some thirty artists about their experiences with copyright law. It is difficult to generalize from the interviews, which were broad-ranging and loosely organized. The interviews did confirm, however, that most of the foregoing description of the law and pending legislation is effectively irrelevant to the ordinary practice of artists in Canada. Artists do not have full or balanced sources of information on copyright, and this study's sample, at least, has very negative perceptions of copyright's utility. In fact, the vast majority of this sample of Canadian artists acts as though Canada had already passed American-style legislation.[34] The exception is a small number of activist artists who understand the specifics of the functioning of collectives or fee negotiations, or of Canada's "fair dealing" provision, which is a much less resilient shelter for artists than it is for academics, journalists, and hobbyists.

Owners' Rights

Earlier in this chapter, it was suggested that copyright's ability to provide financial support for creative activity would be one measure of its contribution to communication rights. Clearly, copyright underwrites Canadian cultural industries, multimillion-dollar operations. But the question here is whether it is key to supporting *creators* of various sorts. Few of the interviewees are making a substantial portion of their direct income from sales or licensing. Several were grateful for the share of their income that did come via collective organizations such as the Society of Composers, Authors and Music Publishers of Canada (SOCAN), Canadian Artists' Representation/Le Front des artistes canadiens (CARFAC), and the Alliance of Canadian Cinema, Television and Radio Artists (ACTRA), and they saw those organizations as important tools for artists' rights.[35] Others seemed to feel distaste for the whole idea of owners' rights. A craftsperson said, "I like designing things, and I like making things, but I don't actually feel that proprietary about them. And that may have to do with being immersed in folk music for as long as I have: I believe in variations on a theme. And people just taking something and changing it."[36]

Some felt that copyright was irrelevant at their career stage,[37] given the essentially non-commercial nature of their work[38] or because they had academic salaries. Others observed that they earned more from grants than they ever would from licensing fees. This may be especially true for expensive media such as film. A media artist said: "I have sold a documentary I did last year, a one hour documentary, to Bravo. I think I'm getting $5000 for national broadcast. This thing cost 30, 40 thousand dollars to make, so the potential to make a huge amount of money is not very great. Most of us make our money through grants at the front end, and so copyright as a control measure at the tail end doesn't really affect our incomes very much."[39]

There was widespread concern among interviewees about the role of large corporations in mediating artists' access to audiences and markets. Thus, a performance artist wondered whether she had the right to use a television clip of a performance of her own work. A musician spoke about the risk for musicians who speak out against record labels who hold rights in their own work.[40] One interviewee noted that while various individuals have appropriated his work unfairly, "corporate media outlets ... will do whatever they can, will bend over backwards to use the bare minimum amount of my work on the air so they don't have to pay me a cent."[41] There was some concern about a general lack of respect for moral rights, and an Aboriginal interviewee argued that increased recognition of indigenous customary laws is necessary in Canada.[42] From other research, it is clear that journalists face problems controlling their rights in a corporate, media-concentrated market.[43]

All in all, there was a high degree of criticism and even cynicism about copyright law as an enabler of creative communication, and pessimism about its ability to mediate relationships and transactions in the art world. While a couple of interviewees were optimistic that copyright law could be reformed in such a way as to improve the situation, this was definitely a minority opinion.[44]

Users' Rights

Artists are of course users of the work of others, especially in a day and age when major trends in music and the visual arts, both commercial and non-commercial, manifest an aesthetic and politics of appropriation. Among our interviewees, we found more widespread and vehement concern about users' rights than about owners' rights.

Anger was expressed over copyright's lack of discernment between kinds of reproduction: "Copyright law as it exists right now, there doesn't seem to be any difference between bootlegging ... and collage, like Negativland, or any of the early Dadaist collages."[45] Appropriation was described as a survival skill in a world where commercial products inundate all citizens without their permission: "The fact of the matter is that Paris Hilton is everywhere: she's on all the newsstands, all the news racks, on the TV, on the radio ... My consciousness, that belongs to me, and Paris Hilton is in it and she didn't have my permission. And so to suggest that these images and these sounds that bombard my public experience daily, don't belong to me in any way ... to me that is just insane."[46]

Another artist described working with "an image [from Hollywood cinema] that would replay in my mind in different ways and I felt like I really wanted to get inside that image since it was inside of me and explore it my own way." This process provoked "a consideration of what and how these images in popular culture and images that become part of our cultural texts do somehow become my building blocks for expression, for language."[47] In fact, these sorts of concerns blossomed in 2005 into a new artists' alliance, "Appropriation Art," led by artist-curators Sarah Joyce and Gordon Huggan, who were initially motivated by a sense of legal vulnerability as they prepared for a multi-site exhibit of appropriation art. As Huggan said, "we thought it was either we change our work or we change the legislation. So we decided to change the law."[48] Within three weeks, Joyce and Huggan had garnered some 600 signatures on a petition, some of them representing large organizational memberships.

While the sense of illegitimacy of rights ownership by large commercial enterprises was widespread among interviewees, others had more practical complaints about the logistical difficulty of locating rights holders and the financial cost of clearing rights. After an account of a wild-goose chase over rights to one line of song lyrics, one filmmaker analyzed it this way: "It struck me that copyright really is meant to work from corporation to corporation. Filmmakers like me, well for one we don't have producers, generally, and two, the dividends are so small for the copyright holding companies like Sony that they don't really want to deal with us. So it's easier for them to say no, you don't have permission than to go through this elaborate process which then will give them something like 200 dollars in the end ... because you know, independent producers can't afford to pay more."[49] Publicly owned media came in for special criticism for their high prices for rights clearance: "I think about how CBC is a public institution and these are news images of public figures: this is just history really. You know, if I was writing an academic treatise I could quote without having to pay any royalties [laughs], whereas when I made this film (and it was an historical film) then I had to get all sorts of permissions, they had to approve of what I'm doing ... and this is a public institution. It should really belong to everybody."[50] The National Film Board (NFB) was also singled out: "The problem when you're dealing with government is that the political drift of the last twenty years has forced them all to think like they're businesses. So they've created this confused mentality within every government department: they've got all this cost recovery bullshit. If I make a film with the film board and I want to use film board imagery, the film is still going to be charged."[51]

Our interviewees' impressions about the law are based on some mixture of experience, fact, and a generalized feeling of outrage. Whether or not they are always factually correct in all their details, they feel that the system is not working. In this context, artists described making decisions based on their moral codes, community practice, and their assessment of risk. For example, one said: "I purposely picked a image that I know this photographer got well paid. And I just took a chance. Otherwise I just don't use the image."[52] A curator explained: "I also make another judgment which has to do with common use. I've read about [copyright]; I've read material that is intended to advise people in positions like my own; but then I also often look at what existing practices are and that becomes a real measure of how I function."[53] A filmmaker also emphasized that the arts world is not one of wanton piracy: "It has to be recognized that another ethos is at play here. It's not that people want to steal the work of other artists. There would be some exceptions ... but it's generally only commercial work that is appropriated."[54]

As an indicator of the existence of a distinct arts ethos about users' rights, there was a fairly widespread idea that one should have more rights to use without permission if one transformed the material to a high degree: "Sampling is an art, and if you treat the sample with the highest regard and respect, and your own creativity is in that same echelon, you can create some really cool stuff. For example, Amon Tobin – he'll sample something but you'll have no idea what it is because he's cut it up into such tiny pieces, he's stretched it out, he's played with the melody, he's taken it and messed with it, creating something entirely new, and that's kind of cool."[55]

None of the people interviewed had actually been sued for infringement, although two had received lawyers' letters that later amounted to nothing. One artist had cancelled a show when a lawyer advised her that she was infringing Disney's copyright: "I was a little bit nervous about someone actually phoning up Disney and saying that Diana Thorneycroft has done a drawing of Mickey Mouse hanging from a noose, so after [a lawyer] said you are infringing on copyright, and not only that but now that you know what you know they could sue you for punitive damages as well, I pulled the other work, and I just did a generic cow, and Raggedy Andy, and a snowman, and things like that."[56] This artist has since exhibited her work publicly, however, without any legal action being taken.

ACCESS TO INFORMATION ABOUT THE LAW AND TO THE LAW ITSELF

Access to information about the law was sorely lacking for our interviewees. Many of them were aware of this problem. For example: "Every craft show when there's quiet times, which there always are, we talk about these things in the aisles ... who is stealing what, and whose ideas are too close to whose. And basically, there isn't a mechanism that anyone understands for protecting yourself ... there may be, but none of us know it and we all just sort of believe some things to be true and believe other things not to be true. We may be believing little bits of US copyright law to be applicable; whether it is or not I don't know."[57] Even in a crisis, artists did not have easy access to legal advice: "I e-mailed Negativland about it because I didn't know what to do. And they told me just to ignore it [laughs]. They said that they knew people who had received these scary letters, and they just ignored them and nothing ever happened."[58]

In some cases, a decision was made not to study up on copyright. One artist said: "I'd rather spend my time making more work than going down some legal rabbit hole."[59] Another said: "I could go and look at the law; you're right. But it might say something that I'm not comfortable with. And so what I am more interested in is, are we, all the individuals involved in this, comfortable and satisfied with this solution that we've come to, and here let's sign a paper."[60] The widespread perception was that the law was unfair and impenetrable – although it is interesting that in this example the individual turned to contract law as a preferable alternative to copyright law.

Little correct knowledge of fair dealing or moral rights was represented in our sample. This might be "blamed" partly on artists' cast of mind, but it might also be argued that the law has an obligation and perhaps even, for its own legitimacy, a need to reach out in the direction of artists. Copyright education might be understood not as the replacement of community norms with "correct" law but as the facilitation of dialogue between norms and law so that citizens could have some involvement in crafting a just and socially functional law. Roderick Macdonald (2002, 28) puts it this way:

> Today, there is a popular belief that law is just a formalized way of issuing written orders. The idea is that because people cannot be trusted to do what is right, society needs to regulate their conduct in detail. On this view, law is like a command. It works best when it is used to tell people exactly what to do, and forces them to do it. But there is another way to think about law. Because most people act responsibly most of the time, society only needs to establish a general framework of rules. Law is most successful when it gives people guidelines about appropriate conduct toward others, as well as a structure within which they can pursue their own goals while still respecting these guidelines. The choice between these two conceptions of law's ambitions has important consequences for the way legislation is designed and implemented.

The law of cultural circulation must be informed by non-market customs and ethical norms. It might be said that many of the judgments made by individuals about "users' rights" are self-serving – but then if the law is not serving these situations it is only appropriate that individuals develop their own decision-making practices. The decision-making practices, in fact, represent long-standing economies of creativity that are no less legitimate than the black-letter law.

One group deserves special mention when it comes to information about the law: documentary filmmakers. Because of their relationship with the broadcast industry, they have no dearth of information about copyright – in fact, they are deluged by it – but, as they are increasingly aware, it comes from a very biased source:

The way it works is our lawyer will go through a production and they'll flag: they'll say this, this, this, and this are a problem. Change 'em. And so I might want something to be in and even a commissioning editor at a broadcasting company might want something to be in, but both of us are overruled by first, the corporate policy of the broadcaster that you must have this insurance, and finally by a lawyer in the employ of an insurance company. Needless to say all of this is outside of the law. Lawyers aren't necessarily trying to protect you from a judge: they're trying to protect their own clients from a lawsuit that will cost them money.[61]

Clearly, as confirmed by a recent study of documentary practice in Canada, this sector is in crisis: rights are unaffordable, and the very process of clearing them is impinging upon documentarists' creative and political autonomy (Knopf 2006).

Finally, we must turn to the question of access to the law itself: can "ordinary" Canadian artists, or citizens more generally, actually get to court to defend their owners' or users' rights – or, more broadly, their communication rights? Certainly they do not perceive that they can. One artist spoke of the prohibitive cost of pursuing infringement in court: "If my neighbour violated my copyright ... I would just go and talk to her maybe ... maybe not. I would just be like, that's weird. If Bell Canada violated my copyright, what would I do? They're huge. I just went through a legal process of dealing with my landlord this year and that was hell. That was like a part time job. I don't have time for that, really. Suing people for copyright violation is something for rich people. You know, it's not accessible."[62]

Indeed, despite the rather generous language about "balance" and "users' rights" in the courts, litigation is simply *financially* out of reach of most people as a way of asserting copyright when a major power or resource differential is at issue. Relationships between "equals" can be effectively arranged via contract, and arts organizations, for example, could help develop templates for such. In the case of a corporation's infringement of an individual's copyright, the one hope would be pro bono legal assistance – and hopefully a victory to reduce such actions in the future. The same would apply when "ordinary citizens" are pursued or intimidated by large rights holders. In both kinds of "David and Goliath" cases, citizens' communication rights can sometimes be upheld by publicity in the court of public opinion: one of our interviewees had great success through this route, with the result that CTV backed down from its intimidation once it was made to look ridiculous in public, and no lawyers were needed. There is, however, a widespread sense of vulnerability among artists that is well founded, given that an intellectual property lawyer at a large firm charges in the vicinity of $500 an hour.

Toward Citizen-Friendly Copyright in Canada

> When I was in Iran, a few years back, these Iranian filmmakers said to me that in their opinion, economic imperatives did as much to censor art in North America as political imperatives did in the Middle East. And at that time I thought that they meant that moviemaking was largely commercial undertaking in the West – and you always had to think about making stuff so that it would make money. But my encounters with copyright in the past little while have shown me that copyright can be used to control knowledge, and information, and experience, and consciousness just as much as politics does, and propaganda and so forth in Iran.
>
> – Matthew Rankin, filmmaker

> I do think that this is a very interesting question that you bring up ... and much more in a sense proactive to say, well, we don't only have the right to make this work, we should actually have the right to distribute it.
>
> – Johanna Householder, media artist

Copyright, of course, is only one factor in the total universe of underpinnings to communication rights. In Canada, however, where direct state control over freedom of expression is less prevalent than it is in some other jurisdictions, copyright is often experienced as a serious bottleneck in freedom of expression. The Canadian copyright statute, combined with recent case law, is more conducive to the exercise of communication rights than American copyright laws. That said, the particular attention paid to artists in this study makes it clear that fair dealing as it exists provides uneven shelter, facilitating the exercise of communication rights for academics and journalists more than it does for artists. More research would have to be done to confirm general public attitudes toward, and knowledge of, copyright law in Canada. Based on research so far, we can propose that confusion between American and Canadian law, combined with lack of effective public education on copyright, and intimidation and propaganda by large rights owners (and the concentration of media ownership that makes such behaviour possible), produces a general public fear and cynicism – all of which mask Canadian copyright's more citizen-friendly features.

PART 3

Policy Recommendations and Alternative Frameworks

9
Fixing Communication Rights in Canada

Marc Raboy and Jeremy Shtern

The objective of our assessment of communication rights in Canada was to underline areas of communication law and policy requiring further intervention on the part of activists and scholars and reform on the part of policy makers – in terms of specific issues, the overall policy framework, and the very legal principles that define and orient this system. In Part 3, we reflect on the current state of the art in law and policy for communication in Canada and on where and how our assessment underlines the need for rethinking and renewal.

Our assessment of communication rights in Canada addresses the entire legal environment that impacts the social cycle of communication as an integrated whole rather than as a series of distinct policy areas. We encountered a series of cross-cutting policy problems that are more or less common throughout this system. In this chapter, we offer policy recommendations that are similarly intended as system-wide initiatives.

Some issues have fallen through the cracks of Canadian communication policy and need to be addressed or redressed. In some areas, policy exists but needs to be radically reconstituted, as it is clearly inadequate to the current environment. Elsewhere, there are significant gaps between the often laudable principles espoused by Canadian communication policies and the opportunities actually available to Canadians for realizing their communication rights on the ground.

In certain areas, such gaps relate to a lack of concrete provisions on how the rights that are promised should be realized. For example, moral rights should protect creators from use of their work by others that will damage their honour or reputation; in practice, many creators are forced to waive their moral rights as part of a contract to publish or broadcast a work. The caveat "where resources are available" as well as the use of the conditional mode in phrases such as "the Canadian broadcasting system *should*" are, as we have seen, particularly popular qualifiers in the *Broadcasting Act*.[1] Even where such qualifying language is not used explicitly, gaps between stated policies and realities on the ground in Canada can often be traced to the absence of explicit mention of concrete schemes for financially supporting such policy objectives and the programs created in their pursuit.

In some areas, these gaps relate not to the absence of policy but to the existence of countervailing measures in other areas that undermine explicit-ly stated policy objectives. For instance, while Canada likes to pat itself on the back for the role that public funding for arts and culture plays in sup-porting widespread creativity, the absence of open-access requirements for public institutions means that Canadians are dependent on the goodwill of organizations such as the National Film Board (NFB) and the Canadian Broadcasting Corporation (CBC) to make available content that the public has paid to create. Another example: community media are acknowledged by the *Broadcasting Act* as a crucial element of broadcasting but receive in-sufficient financial and regulatory support.

In some instances, we observed strongly declared communication rights that are intentionally undermined by policies that contain built-in capabilities for circumscription or non-compliance. This is the case, as we discussed, in the relationship between the right of access to information and the *Federal Accountability Act*, which, while ostensibly designed to help remedy the faults of earlier legislation, actually created new loopholes through which civil servants are able to deny freedom of information requests (British Columbia Freedom of Information and Privacy Association 2005).[2]

Reaction to the CHOI-FM case discussed in Chapter 4 is perhaps the most vivid reflection of the gap between the declarative strength of law and policy and the realization of communication rights on the ground in Canada, despite the fact that we have pointed to it as a largely positive example of the real-ization of communication rights. The actions of the Canadian Radio-television and Telecommunications Commission (CRTC) in that case were contested because they were unprecedented and highly controversial, particularly with regard to their alleged implications for freedom of speech in Canada. What the CRTC did was entirely in line with the letter and spirit of the *Broadcasting Act*, however (Raboy 2004a, 2006; see also CRTC 2004a). The very fact that this case required a controversial precedent-setting decision despite the lack of ambiguity surrounding the authority of the CRTC is an example of how communication rights that are declared in Canadian law and policy are not always regularly enforced on the ground.

The relationship between policy and practice in the area of communication has clearly deteriorated over a sustained period in which important policy principles have been undermined by a lack of enforcement and a lack of administrative support, to the point where they are routinely ignored by industry stakeholders, poorly understood by the public, and controversial when public authorities do choose to intervene.

In many respects, we have to question the integrity of Canada's commitment to the realization of communication rights. It is significant that problems appear to recur and cut across not only specific areas of communication rights separately but also the various industrial sectors, institutions, and policy frameworks that make up Canada's communication system as a whole. Overall, the system lacks coherence and coordination, and steps need to be undertaken to eliminate parallel and conflicting principles.

In response, we recommend the following general guidelines for reforming communication law and policy in Canada:

- Increase monitoring, analysis, and enforcement of communication rights.
- Develop and organize the civil society sector around communication rights issues.
- Raise public awareness of what policy and the media should be doing for citizens.
- Diversify the media and bring them closer to people.
- Let Canadians use their media.
- Widen the (Inter)net of communication rights in Canada.
- Re-examine the policy linkages between cultural nationalism, globalization, and multiculturalism.
- Reframe fundamental principles of freedom of expression in Canada.

Government, the communication industries, civil society, and the public are all culpable, to varying degrees, in the malaise affecting communication rights in Canada at present. Each has a role to play in the blueprint that we propose for realizing them, again in varying degrees.

Monitor, Analyze, and Enforce Communication Rights

Before thinking about new policy in the effort to recapture communication rights, Canada should actually use the policies it already has. In order to address the numerous gaps that we observed between the declarative strength of communication rights in Canadian law and policy and their realization on the ground, we recommend the further development of analysis and monitoring functions across the spectrum of Canadian communication policy making that would evaluate and ensure, on an ongoing basis, that existing Canadian policy objectives related to communication rights are being met, or at least report on how they are not. As a starting point, we recommend that the *Broadcasting Act* be amended so that the qualifier "as resources become available" be removed each and every time it occurs.

The *Broadcasting Act* provides guidelines to ensure that different social groups, including women, are fairly represented among media employees at every level, but there is no body or individual charged with keeping an accounting of who is employed by the Canadian media.[3] Even if such analysis were available, it is not clear who would enforce this provision with regard to Canada's media companies and how. Elsewhere, the CRTC and Competition Bureau regularly impose conditions on mergers between media corporations that are designed to ensure that, for instance, the *Toronto Star* and the *Globe and Mail* endure as independent and diverse voices in the Canadian mediascape, even as they are fused together within the same media conglomerate. Once this type of media merger is approved, however (and no matter how controversial, they are always approved in the end), there is a total absence of formal analysis and ongoing monitoring of whether or not the conditions imposed are being adhered to and, more fundamentally, whether they are actually succeeding in ensuring the diversity of voices within the Canadian media.[4]

The research and analysis capacity that would be required to carry out this mandate does not exist at present within the agencies involved in communication policy in Canada. The ability of the CRTC, for instance, to take on such functions is limited. At the same time, where analysis and monitoring functions do exist, there is no guarantee that such empirically grounded recommendations will have any effect on policy development. We saw, for instance, how recommendations of the Privacy Commissioner of Canada were bogged down, circumvented, and eventually largely ignored. Thus, this is not merely a question of advocating that more government ombudsmen be created. Not only is the potential impact of such an avenue limited, it is also easily refuted with the standard response "nice idea, no budget."[5]

Instead, we propose a coordinated approach to analysis and monitoring that involves government, academic, activist, and industry stakeholders. There is a vibrant communication policy research community in Canada that often has little direct interaction with the day-to-day regulation of Canadian media (see Sinclair et al. 2006). Closer collaboration between government and university-based researchers in a variety of disciplines could help develop an informal analysis and monitoring capacity with regard to the performance of the Canadian media in relation to key communication policy objectives (see Abramson et al. 2008). Public pressure is required in order to ensure that the government acts on such evidence, and organized advocacy groups can work in partnership with academic researchers to bring issues of non-compliance with communication rights policies to the attention of policy makers, directly or through pressure campaigns.

Through self-regulatory and co-regulatory regimes such as the Canadian Broadcast Standards Council (CBSC), enforcement of the rules that apply to the Canadian media is increasingly being devolved from public authorities to the media industry itself. At present, such bodies deal with complaints as they are forwarded to them, do not conduct much research of their own, and see little research presented to them or brought to their attention in their public proceedings (Abramson et al. 2008). It stands to reason that, in exchange for the increased autonomy afforded by self-regulation, the Canadian media should be required to fund, consider, and regularly act on analysis based on independent monitoring of compliance with the actual policy framework in which they operate.

Increased analysis, monitoring, and enforcement of existing policy are required in order to realize the communication rights that are promised to Canadians. Public authorities alone do not have the capacity to carry out this function, the political will to acknowledge it, or increasingly – where the media are concerned at least – the direct authority to act. Government does, however, retain the sole responsibility for ensuring that its policy objectives are met. We strongly recommend a coordinated and multi-stakeholder effort to monitor and analyze the realization of communication policy objectives in Canada and a pragmatic approach to closing the gap between declarative strength and on-the-ground reality of communication rights.

Develop the Civil Society Sector
What we propose above would represent a first step toward building up the civil society sector in Canada. More is needed toward these ends. Canadian nongovernmental organizations (NGOs) are active, well-organized, well-funded, and effective participants in the international policy processes that are increasingly formalizing the participation of civil society in communication governance globally. Furthermore, publicly funded Canadian Crown

corporations such as the International Development Research Centre (IDRC) fund international NGOs. With regard to domestic policy development, however, civil society is poorly defined and its role in the policy development process is largely unclear. Dedicated funding for public interest advocacy of the type that is available to US civil society organizations from private organizations such as the Ford Foundation or to European NGOs in the form of direct government subsidies simply does not exist in Canada on the same scale.

There are, nonetheless, a wide variety of vibrant groups that have organized in Canada around communication rights issues. As in the case of training programs for information and communication technologies (ICTs), such groups are increasingly relied upon for the achievement of crucial policy objectives linked to communication rights. Greater coordination is required between these groups, however. Overall, we recommend a serious process of reflection on the role of civil society groups within the Canadian communication policy framework, and consideration of how the important work they do and could be doing can be better supported and accounted for by public authorities.

Canadians appear to have little recourse for claiming their rights with respect to the media. The increased coordination and involvement of civil society in the policy process could perhaps provide some counterbalance to the impact of the diminishing role of public consultation. For example, the impact of a complaint filed by the Canadian Internet Policy and Public Interest Clinic (CIPPIC) with the Office of the Privacy Commissioner (OPC) against the social networking site Facebook (discussed in Chapter 6) underlines the importance of the civil society/public authority nexus and its potential to counterbalance the rising power of private multinational communication firms alongside the diminishing opportunities for public intervention that are associated with globalization of the media sector. The OPC's investigation of the CIPPIC complaint found a series of areas in which the policies of Facebook were not in compliance with Canadian law. In response to the OPC report (see Denhem 2009), Facebook, working in close consultation with OPC officials, developed a strategy aimed at improving its performance in privacy protection in a series of areas identified by the complaint and subsequent investigation. Pushed into action by a research-based complaint that had been meticulously put together by a well-resourced, focused civil society organization, an agency of the government of Canada was able to take steps toward securing the communication rights of Canadians by putting pressure on a private communication firm with considerable market power. The OPC/ Facebook case illustrates how the communication rights of Canadians can be realized despite the globalization and tendency toward deregulation of the media sector. It also underlines the extent to which such progress is contingent not only on responsive and committed government agencies but also on well-resourced civil society organizations.

To be clear, though, operationalizing this sort of multi-stakeholder governance arrangement as part of a policy response designed to counterbalance the impact of globalization and deregulation must not come at the expense of the direct link between media and the public that should be provided by policy consultation. Aside from representing the viewpoints of various communities, an adequately resourced civil society sector could also reinforce the public consultation process by, for instance, circulating information regarding media policy issues that do not make it into the coverage offered by most conventional media, particularly opinions that are critical of the commercial media,[6] and by facilitating the increased participation of marginalized groups that would otherwise be unable to attend CRTC hearings and other consultations.

Generally speaking, the civil society sector has been a key driver in the push for the realization of communication rights internationally and in other countries. A reinforced civil society sector could accomplish a lot by working in partnership with government in Canada. As was the case at the international level, a crucial first step is getting Canadians who are interested and actively engaged in social justice issues to go beyond the view that media are value-free containers of information and to begin seeing mass communication systems as an environment that is shaped by politics and power relations and is fundamental to modern life.

From our assessment, it is clear that a number of civil society groups are active in Canada where media and communication issues are concerned, although linkages between them and coordination of a united front are not terribly strong. This can be explained in part by the lack of dedicated funding; many groups stretch their human and financial resources to the limit trying to stay operational and fulfill their own mandates on a day-to-day basis and simply do not have the luxury of looking further afield. The scarcity of funding further diminishes the prospects for the sort of larger-scale cooperation that would be required in order to attract more widespread attention to communication rights issues and to address such a diffuse subject on the scope and scale that is required. Canadian activists and civil society groups themselves need to seek out more opportunities for collaborative projects and coordinated action in this area.

The government can contribute by recognizing the role played by civil society in meeting the objectives of communication policy in Canada and by funding the domestic activities of Canadian civil society groups. Such funding could, and probably should, also come from the commercial communication sector to fulfill the public interest responsibilities that they themselves are ill equipped to perform through their self-regulatory bodies. This necessitates awareness on the part of civil society groups about the need to organize broad networks of activism around communication rights issues, and to make groups working in other areas aware of the stakes and the opportunities for change in the communication system. As we saw in Chapters 4 and 8, this awareness is not always in the foreground. Raising awareness may involve something of a shift in culture among civil society groups and the creation of an umbrella organization that could bring them all together.[7]

As we saw with the attempt to introduce Canadian copyright legislation mirroring the US *Digital Millennium Copyright Act (DMCA)*, however, Canadian civil society can effectively mobilize public opinion in the area of communication rights in ways that can cause delays and adjustments to legislation and/or force the government to go back to the drawing board.[8] Arguably, the public opinion that was mobilized against the Canadian version of the *DMCA* may prevent the drafting of draconian copyright legislation that would be harmful to the realization of communication rights in Canada. In copyright and many other areas of communication policy making, however, users are also consumers, and lower prices can often placate the public without addressing the more principled but harder-to-grasp angle of users' rights. Like copyright, many communication rights issues also have global policy dimensions that create barriers to entry for non-specialist audiences, constrain the choices that are actually available to domestic government agencies, and do not typically gain much traction in the Canadian media. It is questionable, in other words, whether the approach taken by the handful of Canadian civil society groups in mobilizing public opinion with the goal of keeping the government from passing a really unpalatable piece of copyright legislation could ever be used to encourage the government to produce proactive legislation in favour of communication rights in Canada.

As we have seen throughout our assessment, legislation that appears to be good for communication rights does not always lead to their realization on the ground. This is not a reason to stop trying; intervening in policy processes to advocate for public Internet concerns and organizing Canadians to ensure that their voices are heard by government agencies and politicians should remain important roles for NGOs and civil society groups in Canada. Civil society activism neither is nor should be confined to debates over legislation, however. Non-legislative activism is just as important, probably more so.

In each of the areas examined by our vertical studies, Canadian civil society groups can and do contribute to the realization of communication rights through initiatives that focus on education, training, literacy, awareness, and development of fair practices within existing policy frameworks. Greater governmental recognition of and support for the important roles filled by civil society in Canada and greater coordination among existing NGOs and civil society actors are required to ensure that the needs and interests of citizens are heard in vibrant democratic debate concerning communication rights issues in the political sphere. Only in this way can the guarantees of communication rights that have been made across the law and policy framework for human rights, media, and communication in Canada be realized on the ground.

Raise Public Awareness of What Policy and the Media Should Be Doing for Citizens

Part of the role of civil society should be to help educate Canadians about their communication rights and how to claim them. Our assessment suggests that, in areas such as media privacy, copyright, and media diversity, Canadians are often unaware of their rights. Media literacy is a rapidly expanding area of education in most Canadian provinces. We recommend that media literacy education be augmented by direct reference to communication rights concerns, with detailed information on how such rights can be articulated and claimed by all Canadians. But in order for this to happen, it needs to be supported, for example, by creating opportunities for knowledge transfer between communication specialists and educators as well as through the production of handbooks, curriculum modules, and other educational resources.

Cooperation among provinces on the issue of media education has resulted in its being granted official status across the country. With regard to copyright, however, our study reveals that laws in Canada are less of a restriction on the exercise of freedom of expression than are people's misconceptions and lack of understanding about the laws. Existing copyright law in Canada is relatively fair in the balance it strikes between users and producers; the challenge is to overcome a lack of awareness of the possibilities it offers for realizing users' rights.

While a focus on the public education system may help future generations of Canadians understand and exercise their communication rights, there are practitioners and citizens whose crucial roles in the social cycle of communication are undermined by a lack of awareness. Chapter 8 underlined how serious this situation is with regard to copyright in particular. Thus, parallel to general efforts to reinforce media education, we underline the need for arts organizations and community organizations of different sorts to generate "best practices" documents,[9] conduct inquiries into the legal status of the practice of their members,[10] and engage in the creation of unbiased materials for the education of creators, educators, and other gatekeepers about the law, especially about users' rights and about the differences between Canadian and US law.[11]

Chapter 7 meanwhile, cites a March 2006 EKOS Research Associates survey that finds that "Canadians are ignorant of existing privacy laws and institutions, with a mere one in five reporting a 'clear' awareness of privacy laws," as well as a study conducted by Shade and colleagues (2005) that concludes that children, when queried about their knowledge of Internet-related privacy issues, evidenced little critical concern. Chapter 4 reports similar widespread ignorance about the provisions of the *Broadcasting Act* among otherwise highly aware citizens. These data appear to cast doubt on whether the media education available in Canada is adequate for equipping citizens to realize their communication rights.

Thus, educational materials concerning communication rights issues need to be created. Provincial and local educational authorities should consider how such materials can be better integrated into existing media literacy curricula. Our study points to copyright, privacy, and broadcasting policy as three areas where misconceptions and a lack of understanding are currently having a particularly negative impact on the exercise of communication rights in Canada.

Diversify the Media and Bring Them Closer to People

While Canadians need to be made more aware of their communication rights, they also need to be empowered to make claims about them on the Canadian media. There is a great gap separating the Canadian media from Canadians. It needs to be closed. The core of this problem is a lack of diversity in the Canadian media: ownership diversity, geographic diversity, cultural diversity, and programming diversity. All of these issues should be addressed.

Part of this distance relates to the fact that the Canadian media are owned by a relatively small number of corporations. The communication rights issues stemming from the concentration of media ownership in Canada are discussed at length in Chapter 4, as is the CRTC's new policy approach that aims to set some boundaries around media concentration in Canada (see CRTC 2008b; Bonin 2008). This approach, however, reifies the existing levels of concentration, which are among the highest in the developed world. It also applies only to the broadcast sector. The regulatory framework for broadcasting does not address the high degree of ownership concentration in the Canadian press and does not take into account the full extent of cross-media ownership – the extent to which media conglomerates are increasingly looking for synergies and opportunities for vertical integration by combining broadcasting properties with newspapers, telecommunications, and online services.[12] Cross-media ownership can dramatically reduce the diversity of voices in the Canadian media, where information and opinion is recycled and repurposed for parallel, simultaneous distribution on various platforms.

Canadian journalists in particular are voicing concern about the conflicts of interest that such repurposing of content can create. For example, Le Journal de Montréal is part of Quebecor Media, as are (besides numerous other communication platforms) the TVA television network, Vidéotron Cable and Internet, the Archambault chain of music and video retailers, and the canoe.ca Web portal. Star Académie, the French-language Quebec version of American Idol is a TVA show that is tied in to and marketed across services and content available on all of these Quebecor platforms. In 2005, an association of Le Journal de Montréal journalists filed a complaint against the paper's directors with the Quebec Press Council, alleging that, in being asked to cover the buzz around Star Académie as news, they were being placed in a conflict of interest (Conseil de presse du Québec 2005; see also Cauchon 2005).

This type of conflict is becoming increasingly frequent in cases where it is unclear to what extent the news presented by the Canadian media is there because it is newsworthy or because corporations want to capitalize on the free publicity that news coverage generates for cross-promoting their various divisions. For example, while editorial decisions to do a feature on the CTV national news about how parent company CTVglobemedia has acquired the rights to the Hockey Night in Canada theme song for sister stations The Sports Network (TSN) and Réseau des Sports (RDS) at the expense of rival CBC may make for good marketing strategy, they also arguably create cynicism among the public that undermines the credibility of journalists trying to carry out their crucial role in a democratic society (see CTV 2008). It is not clear at present to what extent cross-media ownership undermines public trust in Canadian journalists. Nor is there any clear policy on acceptable thresholds for cross-media ownership in Canada.

Thus, we recommend that the approach taken by the CRTC to ensure the diversity of voices (CRTC 2008b) be buttressed by three key complementary measures:

- *Regulation of cross-media ownership.* There should be a diversity of voices in Canadian communication, not just in Canadian broadcasting. In consultation with the public and with industry stakeholders – including journalists' unions and professional associations – the formulas should evolve over time to take a more explicit and critical accounting of cross-media ownership.

- *Ongoing assessment of the impacts of thresholds.* If the policy on diversity of voices is to be read at face value, the CRTC feels that concentration of media ownership has not yet reached a problem threshold. The existence of the diversity of voices framework, however, is a meaningful statement on behalf of the CRTC that concentrated ownership of the media is something that Canada should be concerned about. This is important because the position of Canadian media conglomerates is that concentration of media ownership is not a problem per se.[13] This is easier to refute now that the CRTC itself appears to have accepted that highly concentrated media ownership has an undesirable impact on the communication rights of Canadians. While this principle represents a normative statement, the idea that the problem will kick in at the exact thresholds identified by the CRTC requires further exploration. We recommend a study on current media ownership structures that would seek to determine the impact of various levels of media concentration. The objective of this study would be to establish the point at which the disadvantages of media ownership concentration begin to outweigh the advantages of the corporate synergies that it might create. Now that Canadian media policy has confirmed that ownership concentration beyond a certain threshold can have a negative effect, it is important to be vigilant in monitoring not only future mergers but also the performance of existing media conglomerates.

* *Foreign ownership restrictions.* Existing foreign ownership provisions regarding Canadian broadcasting and telecommunications companies
  should be maintained. Recent government reports on this question have
  come to different conclusions. The Standing Committee on Canadian
  Heritage report *Our Cultural Sovereignty,* also known as the Lincoln Report
  after committee chair Quebec MP Clifford Lincoln (Canada 2003b),
  called unequivocally for maintaining current foreign ownership restrictions, while the more recent report of the Telecommunications Policy
  Review Panel (TPRP) advocated the removal of foreign ownership restrictions in the telecom sector. The TPRP noted, moreover, that given the
  current levels of consolidation in the global communication industry, it
  would be very difficult to maintain foreign ownership restrictions in
  Canadian broadcasting, precisely what the Canadian Heritage report had
  feared (Sinclair et al. 2006). Such a move would further restrict both the
  diversity of Canadian voices within the Canadian media and the ability
  of Canadians to communicate in the public sphere.

A greater degree of cultural diversity in the employment practices of the
Canadian media as well as in the spectrum of programs and services offered
would help bring the media closer to the increasingly diverse population of
Canada. Cultural diversity is discussed in far greater detail as a component of
a separate recommendation on the objectives of media policy in Canada, but
it is important to note here that Canadian media often reflect an unrepre-
sentative view of the Canadian population and that this creates a natural
barrier between many Canadians and their communication rights.

Community media provide an important but underutilized element of
diversity in the Canadian media, particularly as commercial and public
broadcasters are increasingly centralized in Toronto and Montreal. Yet, as we
discuss in Chapter 4, the money, spectrum space, and political will that are
devoted to community media in Canada do not match the rhetoric used to
describe them in the *Broadcasting Act.*

As we describe in Chapter 4, a series of new initiatives on community
broadcasting were launched in 2007-08, including the $1.5 million Commun-
ity Radio Fund of Canada (CRFC), a Department of Canadian Heritage-
funded study of community broadcasting, and plans for a CRTC review of
various elements related to community media policy. These are promising
developments, but it is too early to tell what impact they will have. It is
clear, however, that greater support for community broadcasting could both

diversify the Canadian media and bring them closer to people. Thus, we reiterate that vigilance is required to ensure that these developments are followed up and that the opportunities for building up third-sector broadcasting in Canada are maximized. To these ends, we recommend the following:

- The federal government should implement the 2003 recommendation of the Standing Committee on Canadian Heritage to create a fund to facilitate the production of local, community, and regional radio and television programming.
- The *Broadcasting Act* should be amended to:
  - recognize the category of not-for-profit broadcasting as an integral part of the Canadian system
  - clarify the CBC's responsibilities regarding local and regional broadcasting
- Federal and provincial governments should recognize the importance of community media by providing appropriate mechanisms for its support.

The cost of public involvement in the development of Canada's ICT policies has contributed to a sense that individual Canadians are increasingly unable to have their voices heard by government agencies and lack an institutional space in which they can lay claim to their communication rights. Accordingly:

- The federal government should implement the 2003 recommendation of the Standing Committee on Canadian Heritage regarding the awarding of expenses to interveners in CRTC broadcasting proceedings.
- To the maximum extent feasible, the CRTC should partner with other government departments engaged in communication policy to ensure that the CRTC public consultation apparatus is applied to all Canadian government communication policy development.

Let Canadians Use Their Media

Through public broadcasting, public subsidies for film and television production (through the Canadian Television Fund and other mechanisms), and a host of arts, media, and Canadian culture programs, Canadian citizens' tax dollars pay for a significant amount of media content. The principle behind cultural policy frameworks such as Canadian content rules is that this content has an ethical and cultural value to democracy, social cohesion, and education in Canada that transcends its market value. Yet, our ability to access cultural creation that we subsidize through the NFB and the CBC is limited by copyright law and contingent on the willingness and initiative of these public agencies themselves.

It stands to reason that there would be similar non-market value to Canadian democracy, social cohesion, and education by allowing Canadians to use publicly funded cultural products as the basis of further creative activity. It stands to reason that the ability to use and share deconstructions, commentaries, and expressions related to the iconic imagery of "Canadianness" only adds value to these cultural policy objectives. But restrictive copyright laws that apply to government information and publicly funded cultural products prevent this sort of creative activity and, in particular, make it impossible to communicate such sentiments legally. If the cultural value of producing Canadian content justifies a framework of public subsidies that are purposely removed from the marketplace for cultural products in the first place, why are market-based copyright laws then applied to the access, use, and sharing of publicly funded Canadian content? While this logic seems to fail the rather abstract cultural benefits tests, it also fails at a much more concrete level: generally, people who pay for something should expect to have access to it and to be permitted to use it.

Remedying this situation requires bold moves by public institutions in Canada, including, but not limited to, the CBC, the NFB, museums, and educational institutions. These organizations should embody a strong public interest view of copyright. For example, the CBC should make its audiovisual archives available to Canadians for free, and libraries ought to at least make their public domain collections available for free. The principle is simple: publicly funded cultural products in Canada should be freely available for use by the Canadian public.

The role of copyright and crucial access to knowledge issues in the social cycle of communication is, of course, more complicated when the discussion is enlarged to include more than the cultural products produced by public institutions. There is a tendency to conflate communication rights with a demand for the right to untrammelled access to pirated copyright material. This, in our view, ignores the crucial role that the incentive to create plays in the cyclical process of communication in society. The interviews with creators and artists reported in Chapter 8 revealed the extent to which copyright enables, where it does not restrict. Thus, copyright is a question of balance, and we recommend action on many fronts to resist legislative changes and international agreements undertaken by government that will damage the balance between creators, owners, and users of copyrighted material.

At the same time, we underline the importance of similarly broad action to promote positive legislative changes to enhance citizens' ability to communicate within a copyright framework – such as abolishing Crown copyright and expanding the legal definition of fair dealing to one that is enforceable on the ground – as well as in other areas, including expanding granting programs for education and the arts and enhancing Canadians' access to the means of communication. In parallel, it is imperative that there be civil society efforts to articulate or design counterpart mechanisms that, alongside copyright, can help to spread and motivate knowledge and expression. (Creative Commons is a well-known example; others include academic citation, various "folk" culture economies, and Aboriginal traditional knowledge.)

Widen the (Inter)net of Communication Rights in Canada

The rapid diffusion and adoption of the Internet and other digital ICTs challenge the basis of much communication policy making in Canada (see Raboy and Shtern 2005). As we have discussed at various points in this book, there are numerous communication rights questions whose implications for Internet policy in Canada remain unaddressed: questions about network neutrality, about what access means as Internet services become increasingly broadband-dependent, about whether bloggers are entitled to enjoy the same protections as professional journalists, about privacy, copyright and, more broadly speaking, the interaction of the Internet with conventional media in Canada.

This confusion can hardly be attributed to a lack of policy attention to the subject. In the recent past, Canada has undergone extensive reviews of its broadcasting and telecommunications policies. Both the Lincoln and TPRP reports were premised on a need for fundamental change in Canadian communication policy in order to respond to new technological developments, technological convergence, and globalization (see Canada 2003b; Sinclair et al. 2006). The CRTC, for its part, has sought to come to terms with, for example, the place of broadcasting in the new media environment (CRTC 1999) and with the convergence of telephony and networked computing through Voice over Internet Protocol (VoIP) (CRTC 2004e). As this volume entered production, the CRTC had recently concluded a public hearing and released new policies on the regulation of new media broadcasting (see CRTC 2008a, 2009a; see also Chapter 4), and network neutrality ("network traffic management," in CRTC terminology) (see CRTC 2008h, 2009c; Chapters 5 and 6). These CRTC hearings seem likely to fill in some of the blanks that cloud our understanding of how the Internet does and could contribute to the realization of the communication rights of Canadians.

There is every reason to be encouraged by these developments and to push for outcomes that support the realization of communication rights within these and other proceedings. These are narrowly defined, highly technical hearings on specific questions being held by one regulatory agency. The issue of regulating new media broadcasting in Canada is often framed in terms of the need to figure out how Canadian content rules can endure in the age of digital technologies (see the CRTC new media [1999] and satellite radio [2005a] decisions). As we discuss in greater detail later in this chapter, this sort of narrow focus on conventional visions of national sovereignty and approaches to nation building is counterproductive in the current communication environment. This is not to say that existing policy frameworks for the Canadian media should just be abandoned; rather, the focus should be more broadly on reconsideration of how public service obligations – of which Canadian content is but one part – should be reconstituted. For example, it is important to reassess the role of public broadcasting on the Internet as has been done, for example, in the United Kingdom (see Tambini and Cowling 2004; also http://www.bbccharterreview.org.uk). The issue of network traffic management, in particular, is playing a catalytic role by introducing public interest concerns into debates over Internet management and policy. A hot-button issue for the media reform movement in the United States, network neutrality legislation was one of Barack Obama's early campaign promises and, now that he is president, it is point 1 of his plan for technology and innovation policy (Huffington Post 2007; Organizing for America n.d.). This may have raised the profile of the issue in Canada, but in any case, the Bell Canada throttling episode and subsequent Canadian Association of Internet Providers (CAIP) submission to the CRTC (see Chapter 8) drew considerable public and political attention to the issue:

• The New Democratic Party (see Canada 2008b), the House of Commons Standing Committee on Canadian Heritage (see Canada 2008c; Geist 2008a), the National Union of Public and General Employees, the

Canadian Internet Policy and Public Interest Clinic (see CRTC 2008e), and others are all calling for legislation that will enshrine net neutrality.
- CAIP's application to the CRTC drew letters of support from Primus Telecommunications Canada Inc., the Toronto-based cooperative Internet service provider Wireless Nomad, and over 1,100 individuals (see CRTC 2008e).
- Facebook groups have sprung up, and over 11,000 Canadians have signed a petition in favour of net neutrality legislation. A protest rally for network neutrality supporters was held on Parliament Hill on 27 May 2008 (see Geist 2008b; CBC News 2008d).

The campaign to establish the principle of network neutrality in law has mobilized public and political opinion to a degree that rarely occurs in Canadian communication policy making. The CRTC's answer to the question of the conditions under which ISPs should and should not be able to shape traffic on their networks includes undeniable free expression, privacy, and consumer rights dimensions. Yet the absolute normative dimensions involved in many blanket calls for network neutrality ignore evidence that some form of traffic shaping is required in order to design, maintain, and optimize the performance of networks (McTaggart 2006) and that, as we discussed with regard to the K-Net case in Chapter 8, traffic shaping may be required in certain cases in order to ensure that there is sufficient bandwidth for life-critical communication over the Internet. Network neutrality – a concept that has arguably given voice to previously unfocused public angst about the absence of a space in which the public's interest in the management of the Internet is discussed – can be a means to the realization of communication rights, but it is at present miscast as an end. In the absence of a broader policy debate about communication rights and the Internet, the battle over network neutrality has in some respects become the war over the public's interest in the management of the Internet.

Beyond these narrowly focused proceedings that are confined to the jurisdiction of the CRTC, there is little evidence of a clear and coordinated approach to how communication policy in Canada is adapting to the Internet or to how the public interest concerns traditionally associated with the regulation of communication technologies in Canada are being effectively addressed in this new context.

This point was underlined by the regulatory policy announced by the CRTC at the conclusion of its hearings on broadcasting in new media in June

2009. As we discussed in Chapter 4, the CRTC requested the help of the Federal Court of Appeal to adequately define the term "new media" for policy purposes. In its new regulatory policy for broadcasting in new media, the CRTC (2009, section 73) emphasized that

> several parties also raised new media issues that were outside the scope of the Proceeding or otherwise beyond the Commission's jurisdiction under the Act, including copyright legislation, privacy, taxation policy, broadband infrastructure, spectrum management, digital archiving of cultural works and converged legislation for broadcasting and telecommunications. These topics were mentioned as part of a broader discussion on new media issues that merit comprehensive deliberations.

Recognizing that "issues raised in relation to matters of taxation, copyright, privacy, spectrum management, and convergence of broadcasting and telecommunications industries, among others, are all interrelated and warrant a coordinated approach" (section 76), the CRTC called for the government of Canada to develop a national digital strategy (section 78).[14]

In other words, we lack the development of an overarching framework for regulation of the Internet in Canada that weighs in on controversial and problematic issues such as privacy rights, digital copyright concerns, freedom of expression issues related to network management, pricing and consumer issues, and access to communication technologies and training in their use – in short, a framework that connects all the various government departments and agencies that oversee these related functions.

Thus, we recommend, in light of the new media broadcasting policy review and the network traffic management proceeding, that a multi-stakeholder Canadian Internet Governance Forum (CIGF) be convened. Globally, the Internet Governance Forum (IGF) process was created as an output of the UN World Summit on the Information Society as a non-binding space for dialogue where problems, best practices, and emerging issues pertinent to the links between public policy and the Internet can be discussed informally by industry, government, and civil society – including the public, the technical community, and individual Internet users.[15] Part of the idea behind a domestic IGF is that not only would it address concerns that are specific to the management of Canadian Internet resources but, by virtue of informal links with the UN-sponsored IGF process, it would be one possible way for discussion of local Internet issues to move to the wider global context – as it necessarily must, if there is to be any meaningful discussion of the Internet. This format would have the advantage of discussing domestic Internet issues within a framework that reflects the larger global policy environment for Internet governance, and the reverse is also true. A Canadian IGF would contribute to more transparent, informed policy development with regard to the positions adopted by the government of Canada in the IGF, in the International Telecommunication Union (ITU), on the Governmental Advisory Committee (GAC) of the Internet Corporation for Assigned Names and Numbers (ICANN), and in the other intergovernmental forums where global Internet governance is discussed.[16]

Since the abolition of the federal Department of Communication in 1993, Canada has lacked a single, cross-cutting agency for oversight of communication rights. This is a general concern, and one that is particularly evident and problematic with regard to Canadian government policy for the Internet. As alluded to by the CRTC, the Internet is clearly, in policy terms, a cross-cutting issue and one that could do with greater coordination within the government of Canada. Convening a CIGF is one potential way of accomplishing this, but perhaps more is required, particularly to ensure the meaningful participation of all of the silos in which Internet policy development occurs in the Canadian government. For example, ICT training in Canada is another area that lacks a generalized and organized overall approach. To these ends, we recommend that the national digital strategy being called for by the CRTC be accompanied by the creation of a permanent special office for Internet policy whose responsibilities would include:

- ensuring coordination and exchange between various government agencies involved in Internet policy making
- convening and chairing the CIGF
- identifying areas in which Canada has no effective policy framework
- identifying emerging Internet policy challenges
- consulting and including industry, civil society, and the Canadian public in discussions on these and other Internet policy questions
- ensuring that Canadian Internet policy stakeholders are aware of discussions, trends, and developments in global Internet governance and policy, and that the views of such stakeholders are effectively taken into account in discussions of the positions that Canada will adopt in international forums where global Internet governance and policy issues are discussed.[17]

A guiding principle in these discussions should be the need to rethink ICT policy and reorient it toward social policy. At the same time, the government should acknowledge, as a broad goal, the need to extend Canada's media policy toolkit to include the Internet:

- The *Broadcasting Act* should be amended to include unambiguous reference to the CRTC's jurisdiction over regulation of Internet broadcasting.
- There should be a policy of continued investment in and support for ICT programs across the country, with consideration of differential access needs based on geographic location (rural, remote, urban), language (French, English, indigenous languages, immigrant and diasporic needs), gender, race and ethnicity, class and socioeconomic status, disabilities, and so on.
- Access to ICTs must be seen as a multidimensional process encompassing both the social and technical infrastructures intrinsic to communication rights and access not just to reception and consumption of information and knowledge but also to their production and dissemination.
- There should be funding and planning for training in digital literacy and use of ICTs as a component of Internet access programs.
- The impacts of heightened media concentration in Canada on Internet access, service pricing, and availability should be closely monitored.
- Canada must undertake a review of the social objectives of its telecommunication policy. The current objectives, as stated in paragraph 7 of the *Telecommunications Act,* do not address a number of critical areas, including: (1) protection against policies that might hinder free expression and communication; (2) services for the disabled; (3) data privacy concerns; and (4) balancing the act's objective of fostering "increased reliance on market forces" with non-market considerations and equal input from non-commercial stakeholders.[18]
- Canada should consider implementing legislation similar to the US *Children's Online Privacy Protection Act of 1998 (COPPA),* which provides safeguards to protect children's privacy on the Internet by regulating the collection of personal information from children under thirteen years of age.[19]
- The general principle of nondiscrimination as understood from common carriage principles should be articulated in a way that is affirmative, technologically neutral, and independent of competition. As discussed earlier, the *Telecommunications Act* of 1993 frames its obligations to

protect consumers from discrimination solely in terms of ensuring adequate competition between telecommunication common carriers. This has left a regulatory void in which carriers can – and do – implement discriminatory practices until there is a regulatory response, usually due to public pressure. This has been seen most clearly in the context of discriminatory network traffic shaping. Clear rules should be established about the situations in which network traffic shaping is permitted by ISPs, to ensure that such practices occur in a transparent, accountable fashion that is clearly communicated to users.

- Questions have been raised about the ownership and control of data that people contribute to Web 2.0 and social networking services. Telecommunication policy must be expanded to address these questions. Web 2.0 and social networking services are arguably common carriers; they provide regular service to customers, and they solicit business from the general public. These services should therefore be obligated to define clear policies in terms of the ownership and portability of their data. The latter is conceptually no different from mobile telephone number portability rights enacted in the US and Canada in recent years.
- Policy and programs must provide continued investment in and support for ICT programs across the country.
- Social and policy objectives must be expanded to address the needs of the disabled, the privacy and security concerns of ICT users, community needs for emergency information services, and continuing gaps in telecommunication services to rural and remote communities. Social communication cannot be fully realized until all members of a community who wish to communicate have the ability to do so. Advanced ICTs present affordances that can address the needs of the disabled as never before. Emergency services must be an integral part of a communication rights framework since new ICTs often introduce gaps in emergency services. More specific policy development is needed in this area in Canada.

As a cross-cutting framework, the CIGF would be a venue for discussing Internet policy issues that Canadians are passionately concerned about today, such as network neutrality, Canadian content online, and digital media copyright issues. Its added value would be that all stakeholders could address policy issues, industry conflicts, and public complaints in a suitably broad and multifaceted discussion.

Re-examine Policy Linkages between Cultural Nationalism, Globalization, and Multiculturalism

The realization of communication rights in Canada is at present highly contingent upon factors that are not limited to the political borders of Canada and not confined to the jurisdiction of Canadian law and policy.

For instance, the evolution of cultural diversity in Canada has created a rapidly expanding demand for diasporic media, while the diffusion of both old and new media plugs Canadians into a global system of mass communication over which the Canadian government has little direct jurisdiction. This creates both conceptual and pragmatic problems for Canadian communication policy. For instance, while Canada's ability to shape the Internet might be limited, it provides carriage for television, radio, and telecommunication services that are subject to regulation in Canada. It also creates very concrete challenges to the communication rights of Canadians. In Chapter 7, we saw how problematic the routine practice of contracting out government services to non-Canadian companies and companies with offices outside Canada is for the privacy of Canadians. In certain cases, the personal information that Canadian citizens submit to the Canadian government may be subject to investigation by US authorities under the *USA PATRIOT Act* when such companies have US-based offices (as they typically do).[20]

While global practice with regard to media and communication is challenging Canadian national policy, a larger impact of globalization is the emergence of communication issues that have clearly international dimensions. Thus, all the uncertainty over the enforcement of traditional Canadian media and communication objectives in the context of an increasingly globally constituted environment for communication practices and services is accompanied by an increase in intergovernmental and intercorporate global policy making in this area. We are witnessing the emergence of new international institutions and regimes of media and communication governance that create additional levels of complication and confusion with regard to where Canada stands on communication rights issues. With regard to the World Intellectual Property Organization (WIPO) treaties, for instance, rather than openly opposing the US position, Canada has opted for a heel-dragging strategy in order to maintain an independent position. Canada spent more than six years in "active consideration" of whether and how to implement the WIPO treaties. Canadian autonomy was arguably always going to be limited, however; the US government and the Hollywood and American music lobbies exert pressure on the Canadian government to reform domestic copyright in their image, and the Canadian government may simply not consider copyright an important enough issue to defend against US complaints, given the range of possible disputes between the two countries. In other words, the introduction of parallel international policy frameworks ties the hands of the Canadian government domestically in this area.

With regard to other international policy questions, Canadian positions show little consistency between domestic and global policy approaches, and nothing that resembles a uniform view of Canada's vision of global communication governance. For example, Canada was a central actor in the elaboration and adoption of the UN Educational, Scientific, and Cultural Organization's (UNESCO) *Convention on the Protection and Promotion of the Diversity of Cultural Expressions* and a key player in the World Summit on the Information Society (see Shtern 2006).[21] Yet, while the Canadian delegation to UNESCO was the driving force behind the elaboration, adoption, and eventual ratification of the highly interventionist and protectionist convention, Canada advocated a self-regulatory and market-based approach to Internet governance during the WSIS. Generally, while Canada has fought hard to "keep culture off the table" in global trade negotiations, domestic cultural policies in areas such as community media, public service broadcasting, and copyright are increasingly shifting toward market-based paradigms.

Developments related to media globalization are compromising the realization of communication rights in Canada in a number of ways, a handful of which are underlined in our Communication Rights Assessment Framework and Toolkit (CRAFT) assessment (see Chapter 3). There is little evidence, as we have seen, of anything more than a series of ad hoc responses on the part of communication policy in Canada to these rapidly emerging structural changes.

As a first step toward clearing up this uncertainty, we recommend that international commitments be implemented in domestic policy with adequate recognition of the range of options that such agreements permit. Despite the government's claims that its hands are tied by international commitments, balance in Canadian copyright law, for example, could be maximized by focusing on the choices that exist within the WIPO treaties.

What is really required however is a coordinated effort to rethink and adapt the ensemble of Canadian laws and policies to these contemporary realities. The starting point for this must be a frank assessment of how appropriate policy objectives linked to national sovereignty and cultural nationalism are as defining principles for governing this increasingly globally constituted area of policy and practice.

Generally speaking, communication policy in Canada has been intimately tied to concerns about cultural development and national sovereignty; to the ongoing project of forging a national identity across linguistic, cultural, and regional divides; and, in turn, to the protection of this fragile entity from being subsumed by our neighbour to the south. This is most famously captured in early Canadian media activist Graham Spry's famous rallying cry for the raison d'être of public service broadcasting in Canada: "The State or the United States" (Raboy 1990).

Historically, sovereignty concerns have played an important driving role in communication policy development in Canada, and concerns about sovereignty rights have in many respects (but not at all exclusively) substituted for concerns about what we are calling communication rights.[22] That said, as we well know, sovereignty rights are generally and broadly under attack in Canada and elsewhere in light of "globalization" as well as single-superpower hegemony. The *Bell ExpressVu Limited Partnership v. Rex* case is a clear example of how maintaining the principle of national sovereignty in the context of globalization leads to messy policy making that satisfies no one.[23]

As media and communication practices are changing, laws and policies from outside Canada are exerting more and more influence on whether or not Canadians are able to claim and realize their communication rights. In this environment, our assessment also underlined how Canadian sovereignty over the country's communication system is being diminished. There are two choices here: attempt to bring policy frameworks more in line with the contemporary realities of a globally constituted sector or surrender the ability to act in a fatalistic nod to the inevitability of globalization. We also have to recognize that securing the communication rights of Canadians will not always align neatly with the sovereignty and nation-building concerns of the government.

The *Telecommunications Act*, for instance, addresses several issues of national interest among its objectives, including the safeguarding of Canadian society (section 7(a)), the promotion of Canadian ownership of carriers (section 7(d)), and the promotion of the use of Canadian facilities for intra-Canadian communication (section 7(e)). In considering the relative merits of securing communication rights versus protecting national sovereignty interests in the context of globalization, it is important to understand that these objectives are promotional expressions that straddle what Krasner (1999) defined as domestic sovereignty and interdependence sovereignty. Domestic sovereignty refers to the recognition of the right of some supreme authority within the state to exercise control within its territory. Interdependence sovereignty refers to control by the state of the movement of material, information, or people across its borders. The *Telecommunications Act* lacks protective expressions relative to these understandings of sovereignty, including protections for rights of communication and data privacy for Canadian citizens and residents.

The ability to claim that the government of Canada should have made more of an effort to locate a Canadian-based facility for data storage provides little recourse to a Canadian citizen who is unfortunate enough to find herself at the end of a chain of events in which the US government takes issue with something that it finds in personal data that is being stored – under contract with the government of Canada – somewhere in the US. Even if the US Department of Homeland Security were to agree that, indeed, under the *Telecommunications Act*, Canada *was required* to look harder for domestic contractors to handle data storage, it is highly unlikely that the department would be willing to disregard the information that it had discovered, and hard to imagine that the case of the Canadian citizen under investigation would be strengthened in any way. Clearly, this Canadian policy framework is inadequate to deal with the complexities introduced by the Canadian government's need to rely on the use of modern ICTs that operate in a highly integrated global economy.

A policy remedy for this situation could address the violation of Canadian sovereignty by introducing a more detailed series of claims about the need to promote the "use of Canadian facilities for intra-Canadian communication." This would probably involve withdrawing the procurement of such services from the open market and subsidizing the building of entirely Canadian firms to take on this role. This expensive and cumbersome exercise could ensure the protection of Canadian sovereignty interests, but this is only one scenario in which global market forces and international communication platforms might combine to undermine such interests. Performing similar workarounds in every such case would not only be expensive but also require a significant renationalization of both Canadian communication infrastructure and economic policy – all in the name of dealing with the principle of sovereignty rather than real-world violations of the rights of a Canadian citizen.

Alternatively, the government of Canada could accept that there are transnational dimensions to such transactions and that such global dimensions inherently undermine claims to sovereignty, and direct policy development toward the real problem (the potential for the rights of Canadian citizens to be violated as a result of such transactions) rather than the symptom (the perception that Canadian sovereignty is being diminished in the process). This is the approach we recommend.

In other words, the *Telecommunications Act* should be reviewed in the context of the growing deterritorialization of information with Internet technologies. Of particular concern should be the data privacy rights afforded Canadian citizens in light of the cross-border management of Canadian data. The following measures should be considered:

- The *Privacy Act* should be extended to protect Canadian information created, managed, and maintained by foreign companies.[24]
- All data collection, storage, use, analysis, and data mining and sharing practices that erode or are contrary to existing data protection, privacy, and other human rights laws and standards should cease immediately. The government must resist efforts by the United States and other countries to pressure it into weakening its existing privacy standards.
- Canadian citizens, civil society organizations, and public authorities need to give consideration to the International Campaign against Mass Surveillance declaration (ICAMS n.d.).
- There should be a more transparent process in the collection, retention, and use of Canadian information by the US government under legislation such as the *USA PATRIOT Act*.[25]

There are other clear examples of areas where Canadian law and policy impact the social cycle of communication and where choices may have to be made between the sovereignty interests of the Canadian state and the communication rights of Canadians.

For instance, the *Broadcasting Act*'s provisions concerning public service broadcasting as well as the entire suite of Canadian content regulations, content-producing government agencies, and production subsidies programs also directly reflect an attempt by Canada to use media and communication

policy in the interest of protecting sovereignty and building a Canadian nation. Chapter 4 addressed a series of issues related to the regulatory framework for minority-language broadcasting. Within this complex and sluggish
system has emerged a thriving gray and black market in satellite services in
Canada (as we saw with the *Bell ExpressVu Limited Partnership* case) that fundamentally undermines the sovereignty and nation-building objectives of
Canadian communication policy. Not only does the availability of such
unlicensed broadcast signals to people living in Canada – and their use by
as much as 10 percent of the population – constitute an incursion on Canadian jurisdiction over the broadcasting available on Canadian territory but
such services also do not necessarily include domestic programming such
as CBC/Radio-Canada or CRTC-sanctioned minority-language channels. The
popularity of illegal satellite services, in other words, means that public
service obligations, Canadian content rules, and the entire toolkit of measures
intended to use broadcasting as a vehicle for maintaining and strengthening
Canada's cultural fabric and shared national consciousness (as mandated
by the *Broadcasting Act*) are being bypassed by a substantial portion of the
population.

From a cultural nationalist perspective, this practice would be defined as
a policy problem. Again, however, the availability of global media is not restricted to illegal satellite services; if the gray and black satellite markets were
shut down, many of their former users would seek out and find the same
content on the Internet, in video shops, or elsewhere. The question has to be
asked, therefore, whether this is a problem that can ever be effectively solved
by policy intervention or development. From a communication rights perspective, the practices themselves are not the problem but an indication that
the sovereignty concerns and preoccupations of the *Broadcasting Act* are in-
compatible with the social cycle of communication in an increasingly culturally diverse Canada. In particular, as we have discussed, Canadian media too
often gloss over or fail to address the issues of particular concern to immigrants
and cultural communities.

Thus, to bring Canadian cultural policy more in line with the challenges
of globalization, Canada can attempt to reassert its sovereignty by shutting
down gray and black market satellite services, or it can come to terms with
the idea that securing the communication rights of Canadians involves more
than promoting Canadian media content and services. If a substantial segment
of the population is going to access media from outside of Canada whether
or not they have been approved by the CRTC, it may make more sense to

approve them for carriage in Canada and deal with the associated sover-eignty concerns by bundling in Canadian services. We recommend that the *Broadcasting Act* be amended to recognize the value of non-Canadian and third-language broadcasting to Canadians.

In our view, this would be more pragmatic than the current approach, which effectively drives vast swaths of the Canadian population to opt for illegal behaviour in order to get the programming they want – undermining the very objectives of Canadian broadcasting policy in the process. From a communication rights perspective, reassessment of how broadcasting policy can be brought more in line with the demands of increasing global flows of people and media content would indicate that a firm commitment on the part of Canadian content producers and networks to better reflect and prob-lematize the experiences of ethnic minorities and recent immigrants is re-quired. The alternative, to continue to stubbornly chase conventional cultural nationalist objectives by presenting a whitewashed image of Canada that glosses over the conflicts and tensions surrounding integration and ac-commodation, only neglects the communication rights of many Canadians.

Strategically, the best way to protect and promote conventional Canadian communication policy concerns could very well be to frame them in a right-to-communicate perspective rather than a national-sovereignty perspective. At the centre of this should be a shift in media policy emphasis from nation building to promotion of diversity and multiple forms of citizenship. In other words, rather than structuring communication policy making around the need to promote and protect an elusive Canadian national identity, the ideal role for media and communication regulation in the context of globalization should be to support cultural diversity to ensure that all Canadian citizens are able to engage, in their own ways, in the public sphere.

Reframe Fundamental Principles of Freedom of Expression in Canada

In a report prepared for the Canadian Human Rights Commission, juridical scholar and free speech expert Richard Moon (2008, 21) wrote: "Freedom of expression is a moral or political right that is constitutionally protected in Canada. However, the proper scope and limits of the freedom should not be debated exclusively in legal or constitutional terms and should not simply be left to the courts for resolution. A determination by the courts that a par-ticular law is consistent with the *Charter* should not terminate public debate about its wisdom as public policy, including whether it pays adequate respect to important rights and interests such as freedom of expression."

Our assessment underlines the fact that a lack of legislative support for section 2(b) of the *Canadian Charter of Rights and Freedoms* means that freedom of expression in Canada is being squeezed at the margins.[26]

From Communication Rights to a Right to Communicate?

At present, the functions, institutions, and policies that shape communication in Canada are pulling in different directions and lack coherence about what exactly Canadians are entitled to from their communication system. Overall, there is clearly a great deal in flux at present, as well as significant, parallel activity in a number of areas. Seen through the prism of communication rights, all these activities affect the social cycle of communication and are thus related concerns being shaped by common trends. Canadian civil society groups have mobilized and are working on the ground regarding issues such as community and alternative media, civic networking, and network neutrality. Much of this policy activity and activist mobilization has occurred on a largely ad hoc, uncoordinated basis, however, and without a coherent overall framework that articulates the priorities for communication in Canada as well as the rights of citizens and the responsibilities of governments and corporations.

Each of the policy recommendations discussed in this chapter represents a measure that would contribute to the realization of communication rights in Canada. Welcome though they may be, we have to ask whether this series of reforms alone would be sufficient. It is telling that, in spite of the volume and the stakes of recent policy activity in the area of communication, Canadian public opinion is not being meaningfully mobilized, except possibly with regard to copyright reform and network neutrality. The concern that Canadians have expressed for the social justice implications of policies in areas such as health care and protection of the environment has dominated recent Canadian election campaigns, but media and communication issues have yet to seriously influence Canadian electoral politics (Fremeth 2006; Abramson et al. 2008). In this chapter, we have offered a series of policy recommendations aimed at facilitating the realization of communication rights in Canada. In Chapter 10, we will consider whether, in parallel, the establishment of a Canadian right to communicate can and should be considered.

10
Toward a Canadian Right to Communicate

Marc Raboy and Jeremy Shtern

The establishment of a Canadian right to communicate (R2C) would provide a clear guiding principle for both communication policy making in Canada and the positions that Canada takes on the international scene. At the same time, it would require that the logic of communication policy reflect the entire social cycle of communication, giving Canadians an easily identifiable legal tool for making claims about what they can and should expect from their media and communication system.

As outlined in Part 1 of this book, the social cycle of communication represents a multifaceted, dialogic process that encompasses notions such as the right to be heard and understood, to learn, to respond, and to share as well as to seek, receive, and impart ideas and information. It thus refers to a much broader process and set of activities than those conventionally associated with the universally accepted right to freedom of expression. During the past forty years, the idea of a right to communicate has taken shape as technology, politics, and the culture of human rights have evolved. In most jurisdictions, however, communication rights remain focused on the fundamental but limited right to freedom of expression.

It is no longer clear that a legal framework based strictly on freedom of expression is adequate for the diverse purposes we might imagine for supporting democratic communication. This is particularly the case in Canada, as we have shown in this book. We have described freedom of expression as a two-tiered right, in that it applies unequally to Canadians, depending on their social position, access to the means of communication, and relationship to the various structures of power. All Canadians may have the right to freedom of expression, but some Canadians have more freedom of expression than others.

The first limitation on freedom of expression as the defining principle of law and policy for communication in Canada concerns its scope. Section

2(b) of the *Canadian Charter of Rights and Freedoms*, even in its broadest interpretations, is limited in terms of the communicative functions that it addresses.[1] The *Adbusters* case (described in Chapter 3) reveals that the *Charter* offers no detail on how the freedoms that it declares are to be preserved or enforced in the context of a media system that is understood by the courts to be in private hands and thus outside the reach of the *Charter*.[2]

Because section 2(b) of the *Charter* is explicit with regard to only certain elements of communication and applies to only certain actors, a further limitation on freedom of expression as the defining principle of law and policy for communication in Canada is that its realization is contingent upon the provision of other associated or flanking communication rights. Inadequate or nonexistent policy in neighbouring areas creates a chilling effect on freedom of expression in Canada. Our Communication Rights Assessment Framework and Toolkit (CRAFT) assessment suggests the following:

- Although all Canadians can expect the untrammelled ability to exercise the right to *express* themselves, only a very minimal segment of the population can, at present, claim to have any sort of direct access to the mainstream media and thus can reasonably expect to have their viewpoints *heard*.

- Untrammelled freedom of expression means that Canadians can and do freely generate and communicate ideas. The practical utility of what is expressed is too readily limited, however, by existing policies concerning knowledge dissemination and use. The effect is that the opportunities are diminished for Canadians to *learn, enhance,* and *create* on the basis of knowledge that is expressed.

- Copyright, public domain, and other such knowledge dissemination policies also restrict the ability of Canadians to *share* that which is freely expressed. The absence of effective privacy protection creates a situation in which communicating in Canada inherently involves an element of personal risk to the safety and property of any individual seeking to express thoughts and opinions. This means that, in practice, informed citizens need to think twice about exercising their freedom of expression.

- The ability to *respond* to the thoughts and opinions of others is a key element of freedom of expression. The great distance that exists between the largely corporate media in Canada and the daily lives of Canadians means that, in practice, few can respond to media content in any meaningful way. This is particularly problematic where the thoughts and opinions of someone (or some institution) who has more direct access to the media than you do results in a denial, in practice, of your right to honour and reputation.

• While Canadians are free to express their ideas and opinions, in practice their freedom to *seek and receive* the information that contributes to the *generation* of such ideas is more restricted. Highly concentrated media ownership functions, a priori, to undermine the diversity of views on offer. Key voices in the media are routinely placed in situations where they are given incentive to practise self-censorship. Freedom of information requests can be prohibitively complicated, time consuming, and costly for individuals, and there are many loopholes that government officials can use to avoid their obligation to release information. These factors constitute practical limits on the information that Canadians have access to in generating their thoughts and opinions, thereby restricting the scope and content of the thoughts and opinions that they are so free to express.

• Canada is an officially bilingual country with an increasingly multicultural population. No matter the freedom of the speaker to express ideas and the freedom of the receiver to seek them – such ideas are of diminished utility if they cannot be *understood*. With regard to the media at least, linguistic diversity is limited to official French/English bilingualism in Canada, which does nothing to ensure services and programming accessible to other language groups; this creates communication barriers for Aboriginal people, recent immigrants, and other cultural communities.

Seeking and receiving information, generating thoughts and opinions, having others hear, understand, learn from, and create on the basis of your freely expressed ideas and then *share and respond* to them. When viewed as part of the social cycle of communication, freedom of expression can occur in a given society only when the associated *flanking* communication rights are also present.

In short, in Canada anyone can stand on a soapbox and say whatever he or she pleases (with some notable exceptions, such as criminally sanctioned hate speech), but mass communication is highly restricted and this situation should not be viewed as a viable stand-in for true freedom of expression in a modern, media-driven society. Thus, our assessment of freedom of expression in Canada involves not only the declarative strength of section 2(b) of the *Charter* but also a horizontal view of the state of the art of communication rights.

Expression as Two-Tiered Freedom: The Growing Distance between People and Media in Canada

Overall, our assessment is that a great distance separates the Canadian communication system from the everyday lives of most Canadians. At present, Canadians have drastically different communication means at their disposal, and the realization of freedom of expression is stratified. An analogy from another sphere of social life illustrates what we mean.

The idea that some Canadians might have greater access than others to the realization of the right to health care is oft-discussed and overwhelmingly opposed within Canadian society. In his 2002 report *Canadians' Thoughts on Their Health Care System*, Matthew Mendelsohn draws on over a decade of public opinion research about health care to conclude that despite intense media coverage over this period on challenges to the system, support for a framework in which those who can afford to pay for it are able to receive better, faster health care has never inched beyond one-third of the Canadian population. This view, he argues, goes beyond fickle public reaction to current events and demonstrates more reflective and sustained thinking about the topic.[3] Opposition to so-called two-tiered health care is so vehement in Canada that, by one account, the 2004 federal election was in large part won when "the Liberals accused the newly united Conservatives of plotting to turn Medicare into a two-tiered system" (CBC News 2006b).[4]

It should be cause for grave concern, then, that freedom of expression in Canada is essentially a two-tiered freedom. Canadian communication law is structured around the right to freedom of expression and specification of its legitimate limits. Freedom of expression is what can be described as "constitutional communications policy" in Canada in the sense that enunciations of policy made in lesser Canadian statutes, including broadcasting and telecommunications laws, are subject to it.[5]

As our assessment shows, many of the problems and tensions in the realization of communication rights in Canada transcend specific government departments, industrial arrangements, and technical platforms. This is a poor reflection on both the realization of freedom of expression in Canada and, in turn, on the appropriateness of freedom of expression as the constitutional principle around which communication law and policy are structured in Canada.

This framework fails to effectively support democratic communication. Thus, the task of identifying possible policy remedies to communication rights problems cannot be completed without considering what supplementary principles and legal instruments might be necessary to strengthen the links between human rights and processes of communication in Canadian society.

In this sense, recognition of a right to communicate in Canadian law would establish a defining principle for communication governance in Canada. This would be a complex and controversial process. Indeed, the establishment of a Canadian right to communicate is not imminent; it is perhaps not even realistic.

That said, the communication rights of Canadians can be secured by virtue of the policy reform and practical interventions outlined in the previous chapters. This must remain the primary focus of an activist agenda. In parallel, however, the ideal of reorienting law and policy around a right to communicate would legitimate proposed solutions to most of the problems that we have underlined: a formal right to communicate would pave the way for greater policy coordination between different areas of government and across various platforms of communication, while providing the basis for a clear statement of fundamental roles and obligations for all with regard to communication. This would in turn raise awareness and contribute to greater enforcement of existing rules. Above all, a right to communicate would demand that communication law and policy reflect the entire social cycle of communication. How can this be done? In the next section, we make the case that the right to communicate can be a conceptually and politically viable policy alternative in the Canadian context.

Toward a Right to Communicate in Canada

As arguably the most influential contemporary discourse on communication rights and the right to communicate, the Communication Rights in the Information Society (CRIS) model represents one approach to positing the R2C as a constitutional principle for communication policy in Canada. Is this approach applicable in the Canadian national context?

As we discuss in Chapters 1 and 2, the CRIS approach to the political and conceptual controversies that surround the R2C embraces the lack of precision in the term and uses "the right to communicate" and "communication rights" somewhat interchangeably as umbrella terms. Under this normative banner, the CRIS campaign succeeded in mobilizing extensive civil society participation and catalyzing civil society actors, who were then able to exert some direct influence on the outcomes of the World Summit on the Information Society (WSIS) (see Kleinwächter 2004). This is obviously not the same thing as establishing a universal right to communicate. Mueller and colleagues (2007, 278), for example, argue that "a purely tactical appropriation of communication rights language comes at a price, however. It downplays the issue of how communication rights are translated into real institutions and processes, which in turn blunts the [CRIS] campaign's ability to develop and propose concrete policies and reforms. Advocacy remains at the normative level."

To the extent that this observation can be generalized to all efforts to apply the CRIS approach in real institutions and processes (and hence to the present discussion), the implication is that a balance is required between fluidity in deploying the language of rights and the level of specificity that would be required in order to institutionalize a right to communicate in a specific legal jurisdiction such as Canada.

Appropriating the idea of a right to communicate from the international context must not only be grounded in the conceptual and juridical tensions associated with it but also refer consistently to a singular function in a formal legal sense, in which a right to communicate should take its place alongside other fundamental human rights enshrined in law. This creates, in turn, two derivative questions: What would the right to communicate in Canada look like? Is it even possible?

Is the Right to Communicate Definable for Canada?

In Chapter 1, we introduced a series of conceptual and political tensions that have undermined previous efforts to establish a right to communicate. To suggest an analytical framework for assessing the realization of communication rights in Canada, we have argued for an invocation of the discourse of communication rights that sidesteps this controversy.

The policy recommendations presented in Chapter 9 as a result of our CRAFT assessment attest to the utility of the notion of communication rights as a basis for concerted policy intervention and development. It is clear, however, that a right to communicate – when pursued as a formal, legal construct – cannot be conceptually fluid, unproblematically invoked, or inconsistently applied. Even if we do not intend to develop it ourselves, we need to make the case that it is possible to formulate a workable singular definition of the right to communicate that is conceptually and politically viable for Canada.

As we saw in Chapter 1, the notion of the right to communicate was first developed in international organizations with regard to universal human rights frameworks. Generally speaking, however, it is entirely scalable to the national level. Although most efforts concerning communication rights and the right to communicate have tended to focus on their status in international affairs, interest in the national policies of specific countries has always been an important element of communication rights discourses. Even at the height of international activities surrounding the New World Information and Communication Order (NWICO), UN Educational, Scientific, and Cultural Organization (UNESCO) documents themselves pointed to the importance of the national level to the project.[6]

In the recent past, in parallel with its WSIS focus, the CRIS campaign established national chapters that were responsible for a series of evaluations of the provision of communication rights in various national and regional contexts (see CRIS 2005a). Among the premises that the CRIS campaign invokes to justify its focus on the global policy sphere are that the national level was never "fully equipped" to deal with the "governance of key aspects of communication rights," and that the rights provided by national states are increasingly being "on the one hand, sidestepped and rendered irrelevant by global corporations and, on the other weakened by global, regional and bilateral trade-related agreements." Nonetheless, Ó Siochrú continues that communication rights at the national level are largely being undermined by these global trends and activities (Ó Siochrú 2004c, 3). Thus, there is certainly a case to be made that while the global level is where the action is with regard to communication rights, the fight is still predominantly over shaping national policies.

Conceptual/Juridical Questions: Defining the Right to Communicate

During the UNESCO efforts (discussed in Chapters 1 and 2), a succession of studies and working groups were unable to arrive at an acceptable consensus on the basic definitional characteristics of the right to communicate.[7] Much of the controversy and uncertainty stemmed from what Fisher (1982, 24) described as "the conflict between the view of the state as the source and protector of fundamental freedoms and the view that individual human rights set a limit to the authority of the state." Communication is an inherently social process, after all: its value to the individual comes from connecting him or her to the collective, to relationships, communities, societies, and polities. To the last man on earth or a woman stranded on a desert island, the ability to communicate is of little value. Should the right to communicate, then, be interpreted as something to protect the individual's ability to participate in the collective, or the collective's obligation to facilitate communication, or both? This tension was, Fisher continued, "at the heart ... of the debate on the right to communicate." It was also largely viewed as an intractable conflict between mutually exclusive categories of human rights. The lack of agreement, even among its supporters, over what the right to communicate meant in practice certainly contributed to UNESCO's ultimate inability to establish a legal framework for it.[8] Does it remain an obstacle today?

As we describe in Chapters 1 and 2, there was a flurry of activity around the right to communicate in the 1970s. The evolution of the idea was largely driven by a core group of supporters. Some, like L.S. Harms, were communication scholars; others, like Desmond Fisher and Jean D'Arcy, were journalists or broadcasters. By the time the CRIS campaign revived interest in the right to communicate in the early 2000s, the issue had been for some time the preoccupation of a new generation of communication scholars, many of whom had been involved in UNESCO's NWICO debate.[9] Thus, the debate on the right to communicate largely picked up in 1999 where it had left off in 1982. As a result, the question of how to reconcile communication rights with freedom of expression and other concerns remained a trusted crutch for critics of a right to communicate as well as an obstacle to progress for its supporters.[10] It is not surprising that none of them were able to adequately move thinking about the right to communicate beyond the then conventional wisdom that the different approaches associated with first- and second-generation – that is, "positive" and "negative" – human rights constituted mutually exclusive frameworks. None were human rights specialists, after all, and it was not until the late 1980s that the inadequacies of this dichotomy began to receive serious attention within the human rights literature.

By the 1980s, human rights scholars were increasingly dissatisfied with the generational framework as a tool for categorizing human rights. The argument that rights could be categorized as positive or negative, and that this constituted a dichotomy, was repeatedly criticized as false; after all, civil and political rights – such as the right to a fair trial – include elements of positive obligations on states, while economic, social, and cultural rights – such as the right to organize – can similarly require that the state refrain from intervention. Generally, the generational approach is seen by contemporary human rights scholarship as an unhelpful oversimplification (Koch 2005).

This view was largely accepted as early as 1987, when Asbjøn Eide, the UN Special Rapporteur to the Subcommission on Human Rights, introduced a tripartite typology for assessing rights implementation on the basis of three mutually non-exclusive categories: *respect, protect,* and *fulfill* (Eide 1987, 1989; Shue 1996). The tripartite framework challenged and was widely accepted as a replacement for the generational framework for categorizing human rights. The tripartite typology is argued to bridge the conflicts that were traditionally perceived to separate individual rights from collective rights by illustrating that compliance with each and every human right – economic, social, cultural, civil, and political – may require various measures from passive non-interference to active ensuring of the satisfaction of individual needs, all depending on concrete circumstances (Koch 2005, 85). Various human rights scholars have since devised and applied still more multifaceted and complex typologies for analyzing the interactions between freedom and responsibility with regard to the implementation of different human rights. The specifics of these models, however, are far less important to the current discussion than the cautionary advice that Shue (1996, 160) imparts in his assessment of them: "Do not let any theorist tell you that the concrete reality of rights enforcement is so simple that all the implementation of any right can usefully be summed up either as positive or negative rights. The constructive point [of the effort within the literature to devise a more nuanced typology as an alternative to the positive/negative dichotomy] was: look at what it actually takes to enable people to be secure against the standard, predictable threats to their rights, focus on the duties required to implement the right." In other words, it may be time for the discussants in the debate over the right to communicate – supporters and critics alike – to follow Koch's suggestion (2005, 103) and "throw typologies overboard ... and focus on what it takes to provide proper human rights protection."

Cees Hamelink, author of some of the most important scholarly interventions in the debate on the right to communicate, co-authored (with Julia Hoffman) a 2008 reflection, "The State of the Right to Communicate," in which the authors make the case that communication's status as a collective process has been leveraged by collective actors – that is, by nation states that have appropriated the R2C agenda, looking on one hand to force open international information markets, and on the other to legitimize blocking of foreign media content and government control over domestic press (Hamelink and Hoffman 2008, 10). In contrast, the authors insist that "human rights law is concerned with human beings ... the emphasis on the implications of recognizing a right to communicate on collective actors such as states, however, may have muddied the waters ... even if the beginning of the debate may have been overshadowed by a concentration on state actors, the root of the right to communicate should be remembered to lie in arguments concerned with human dignity" (10-11).

A Normative Framework for the Right to Communicate in Canada
A Canadian right to communicate should acknowledge the following contextual realities:[11]

- A democratic society requires that all citizens be able to seek and receive ideas and information; generate their own ideas; express themselves; be heard and listen; be understood and understand; and learn from, enhance, respond to, and share ideas.
- Canada is a modern information society that values the communication rights of its citizens. The potential for individual Canadians to participate fully in the social cycle of communication is great, but some Canadians are less capable of doing so than others.
- Much of the mass communication system in Canada is regulated by public authorities, including sectors over which government agencies have a hands-on role in governance and others where government has made a policy decision to devolve its direct control to co-regulatory and industry self-regulatory bodies.[12]

The principles of a Canadian right to communicate could include affirmation:

- that freedom of expression and communication rights imply constraints on untrammelled activity of the press and broadcast media
- of basic principles regarding media ownership, and that these should form the basis of policy for an independent public authority (such as the Canadian Radio-television and Telecommunications Commission [CRTC]) to follow regarding media transactions
- of the public's right to know as a fundamental tenet of media ethics
- of the rights and responsibilities of journalists – defined as anyone who practises public communication – including protection for the

confidentiality of sources and from conflicts of interest that can arise
when journalists are pressed to cover other divisions of their parent
company
- that public communication in Canada requires a diverse set of dedicated
public institutions as well as adequate, stable sources of funding
- that information and media content produced with public subsidies
belong to Canadians and that Canadians have the right to open access
to this content for non-commercial purposes
- that all Canadians have a right to fair use of copyrighted material
- that Internet governance in Canada must be fair, transparent, and accountable to public interest concerns
- that privacy is essential to an individual's dignity, integrity, autonomy,
well-being, and freedom and to the full and meaningful exercise of human rights and freedoms; that every individual has a right to privacy,
including physical privacy, freedom from surveillance, freedom from
monitoring or interception of their private communications, and freedom
from the collection, use, and disclosure of their personal information
(adapted from Canada 2001b, sections 2 and 3); and that, to be lawful,
an infringement of the right to privacy must be justifiable (section 2 of
the *Charter*)
- that a component of the right to communicate is the right not to be
communicated with
- that all Canadians have the right to be protected from deliberate dissemination of misleading or distorted information
- that all Canadians have the right to access to our system of mass communication, to media literacy education, and to training in the use of
information and communication technologies
- that public communication in Canada should be open to a diversity of
voices, and should be a vehicle for discussing cultural differences and
protecting cultural and linguistic diversity.

What we are proposing, then, is a right to communicate that would give
Canadians the capabilities required in order to meaningfully participate in
the social cycle of communication. Where they do not possess such capabilities,
individual Canadians would be able to claim their right to communicate – in
some cases by demanding more of their government in the management of
Canada's communication resources, in others by insulating themselves from

government excesses. This right to communicate could increase government accountability, but it would also justify greater government involvement in the regulation of speech. Those inclined to see freedom of speech as sacrosanct tend to see this trade-off as unacceptable.

Cultural Questions: Accepting the Right to Communicate in Canada

In his seminal book on free speech, John Durham Peters (2005) reflects on the establishment and cultural cachet of the mythology surrounding the place of free speech in Western political philosophy and societies. In what he calls "the free speech story" (15), heroic revolutionists risked life, limb, and profit by defying censors and forming "a 'marketplace of ideas' where any notion, good, bad or ugly could be evaluated on its own merits." This marketplace of ideas is, according to Peters, "supposed to be the motor of democratic life and the place where the public blossoming of the logos so central to democracy can occur." According to Peters, those of us raised within the institutions of Western democracies are socialized within this ubiquitous narrative to such an extent that this understanding of free speech has become "as much a cultural commonplace as an explicit doctrine" (18).

To many, the very idea of a right to communicate, by implying that the government has not only licence to intervene but also a responsibility for intervening in the marketplace of ideas, is antithetical to the ideal of free speech. "Censorship is wicked" is, according to Peters (2005, 19), one of the defining claims of the free speech story. And, of course, censorship – the deliberate, self-serving suppression of the free speech of one party by another, more powerful party – is antithetical to the social cycle of communication, to communication rights, and to the aspirations of democratic societies. Censorship is indeed wicked. The challenge is to distinguish between the wickedness of censorship and the effort to push governments to reorganize the system of mass communication so that resources are allocated more justly. In Canada, as elsewhere, this is a formidable task.

In a text published just a few years after the coming into force of the *Charter*, legal scholar Harry Glasbeek (1986) predicted that section 2(b) could eventually be interpreted to "defend individuals generally and the media in particular from state controls, but not individuals or their defender, the state, from private interests" (102), and is, as such, "simply not designed to meet the structural problems created for democracy by a capitalist press which tends towards monopoly" (118). Hackett and Zhao (1998, 80) summarize Glasbeek's thesis as the fear that, with section 2(b) of the *Charter* at its core, free speech in Canada would be applied as "a property right of corporate entities, not as a human right of individual citizens." "Ordinary Canadians," Glasbeek continues, "ought to have a means to protect themselves from such influences" (101-2), but, in his view, we were always more likely to be seduced by the provocative language of section 2(b) into the mistaken belief that existing *Charter* protection of freedom of speech somehow advances our political freedom (118).

For those who have become accustomed to the reverential language that is typically used to cast the *Charter* as a fundamental part of what it means to be Canadian, Glasbeek's ominous predictions from over twenty years ago might seem extreme, particularly given the dystopian language and Marxist overtones used in his analysis. Yet, as Glasbeek predicted, Canadians seem to have accepted the right to free speech as a two-tiered freedom, and with it a level of inequality in their communication rights that is thought to be unacceptable with regard to other fundamental rights such as the right to health care. Any reform of Canada's explicit free speech doctrine would probably need to be preceded by a shift away from the view of free speech as an embargo on government-imposed restriction that is at present, as Glasbeek predicted, largely accepted as a cultural commonplace in Canada.

Free speech is not an absolute in Canada, however; democratically arrived at limits on what can and cannot be said have been established in areas such as hate speech. Invoking the right to communicate is a way of arguing that democratic conversations need to be had in order to establish where the limits of free speech should be most usefully drawn. As we discussed in the Introduction, the right to communicate is a way of enhancing freedom of expression rather than a substitute for it.

Establishing the Right to Communicate in Canada: An Activist Agenda

We have sought to make the case for a singular right to communicate in Canada, despite all of the controversy associated with the idea. A more practical question is where and how this right might be established in Canadian law and policy.

An obvious starting point is section 2(b) of the *Charter*, but amending the text of the *Charter* itself to include a right to communicate would be extremely difficult, if not politically impossible. Canadian law has been unequivocal that only governmental actions can be subjected to *Charter* scrutiny. While Canadian media are licensed and even in some cases funded by the government, the test for applying *Charter* scrutiny to such institutions involves making a judgment about whether or not they are acting as private entities or as governmental agencies in carrying out the capacity in which the alleged rights violation occurred.[13] In this respect, the application of the *Charter* to the Canadian media represents a classic invocation of the negative rights approach, in which rights claims are used exclusively in an effort to curb abuse of governmental power. The positive elements at the core of a Canadian right to communicate would therefore largely be excluded and diminished by the legal personality of the *Charter*, in the very unlikely event that the *Charter* were amended to include it. It is therefore not only more realistic but arguably more useful to explore other avenues for establishing a right to communicate elsewhere in Canadian law, to counterbalance the approach that the courts have taken thus far towards section 2(b) freedom of expression claims on the Canadian media.

An interesting and possibly more viable alternative has been suggested by a young legal scholar, Simon Grant, who proposes that communication rights activists focus on generating a precedent-setting court decision that explicitly refers to the right to communicate (see Appendix 3). In arguing that activists could intervene strategically in carefully selected *Charter* cases to have the idea of a right to communicate introduced into Canadian law, Grant writes:

> Canada's common-law tradition of public law means that previous court decisions serve as binding authorities for subsequent decisions. As a result, even if the court defines the "right to communicate" vaguely or imperfectly, communication rights activists could cite that decision when arguing in court or advocating in Parliament for a policy that engages the right to communicate. Ideally the decision would come from the Supreme Court of Canada, making it binding authority throughout Canada, but a favourable citation from a province's court of appeal would also be valuable because it would be binding authority in that province and would also have persuasive authority elsewhere in the country.

Grant points out that there are two ways in which activists and public interest organizations could participate in court cases involving *Charter* rights: as litigants or as interveners. Litigation – for example, "suing a branch of government for having infringed a *Charter* right" – is expensive, but the court has often recognized interested parties in a case as interveners, a more flexible and less costly path that allows parties to "submit (brief) arguments to the court which the judges may consider in reaching their decision" (Appendix 3). Feminist groups have used this strategy with some success, Grant notes.

This is only one potential approach. While we introduce it and, in Appendix 3, offer Grant's legal perspective in the hope that it might encourage subsequent activity in this area, we are also trying to make a broader point. We have argued that the establishment of a right to communicate in Canadian law could significantly contribute to improving the realization of communication rights on the ground, while conceding that it is an ideal that should be pursued only in parallel to dealing with more pragmatic policy reforms. Nonetheless, we are also arguing that the notion of a right to communicate is conceptually sustainable and that there are possibilities worth exploring in order to see it established in Canadian law. This is only a starting point. Clearly, further coordinated reflection on the conceptual foundations of a Canadian right to communicate as well as on the strategies that could be pursued for realizing it are required as follow-up.

Conclusion: Supporting Democratic Communication

In this book, a group of scholars committed to democratic communication have assessed the realization of communication rights in Canada and found the situation to be far from ideal. We have made the case that freedom of expression – the constitutional principle of communication law and policy in Canada – is a two-tiered freedom. While we have offered some policy recommendations aimed at facilitating the realization of communication rights in Canada, we have argued that, in parallel, the establishment of a Canadian right to communicate can and should be considered.

The call from the now-defunct Law Commission of Canada, which launched the study that resulted in this book, asked us to reflect on what "the legal and political implications of an established 'right to communicate' [would] be for democratic communication in Canada."[14]

Establishment of a right to communicate would reorient communication policy making in Canada toward supporting the social cycle of communication. This would be a drastic, even radical measure. But consider that, within the recent past, extensive reviews of both broadcasting and telecommunications in Canada have been premised on the need for fundamental changes in Canadian communication policy to adapt to a changing environment that is being shaped by technological convergence and globalization (see Canada 2003c and Sinclair et al. 2006). The groundbreaking study *Instant World* sounded the alarm about these developments from within the government of Canada as far back as 1971. As a result, the functions, institutions, and policies that shape communication in Canada are currently pulling in a variety of different directions and lack coordination as well as a clear statement about what exactly Canadians are entitled to from their system of communication. Overall, a lot is in flux at present, and it is not alarmist to say that drastic measures are the order of the day. Seen through the prism of communication rights, the social cycle of communication is being directly, sometimes negatively, affected by contemporary trends. The establishment of a right to communicate in Canada would go a long way toward ensuring that all the policies, institutions, actors, and issues that impact democratic communication in Canada can be addressed together, directly through a common public policy approach. The immediate challenge is to raise awareness among practitioners, policy makers, and particularly Canadian citizens about the interrelationships between issues involving media, access to ICTs, privacy rights, new technologies, and intellectual property. This challenge transcends the question of whether, where, and how a right to communicate could be codified in Canadian law.

A range of civil society participants, from nongovernmental organizations to academics, have been the key advocates for communication rights over the past twenty years. Progress demands that they remain so. At present, the determination and will, the range of skills and knowledge, and the uncompromised wider vision to pursue the communication rights agenda are found only in civil society.

How can civil society organizations leverage the wealth of material here to advance the issue of communication rights? Traditionally, civil society attempts to bring about change by influencing government and policy makers, often through the intermediary of public opinion. This is what "framing" the issues is all about.

Nevertheless, government could play a role, perhaps a critical one, in taking communication rights to the next stage both nationally and internationally.

Governments are particularly well placed to introduce the communication rights framework as a topic for discussion in the public sphere, since the state, and often only the state, has the legitimacy and capacity to become involved in and influence such a wide range of issues. Under appropriate conditions the incentive for government to proffer communication rights as a topic for debate is again the all-embracing nature of the concept, its capacity to relate together seemingly distinct issues under a general yet simple and comprehensible umbrella. As a topic for public exploration, the notion of achieving communication rights for everyone could spur debate on a range of issues and fire the public imagination over seemingly arcane or marginal issues. It would, however, take a courageous and far-seeing government to open such a debate.

The second phase of the international debate on communication rights, centred on UNESCO, developed a line of argument that communication rights should first be implemented at the national level and only later considered at the international level. Fisher (8-9) underlined this point in his status report in 1982. It is argued earlier in this book that the report of the 1971 Canadian Telecommission, *Instant World,* may have been "a crucial step in the evolution from abstract concept to global policy issue and basis for an activist movement" of the right to communicate. How much more effective would this have been if the Canadian government at the time had put more effort into implementing the concept at home?

Perhaps it is not too late for Canada to take the lead, both nationally and internationally.

Certainly, having put the case at the national level, a government would be in a strong position to develop and advocate for coherent, groundbreaking policies at the international level, straddling a number of institutions and arenas. Canada has already played this role in the area of cultural policy, building on its national experience in developing a powerful "cultural policy toolkit" to foster the adoption of the international *Convention on the Protection and Promotion of the Diversity of Cultural Expressions* (Grant and Wood 2004).[15] Serious policy consideration of communication rights and the right to communicate in Canada could serve a precedent for raising the issue in other international contexts, such as the follow-up activities related to the World Summit on the Information Society, the World Intellectual Property Organization, and the UN Internet Governance Forum, in which the government of Canada could collaborate with the civil society constituencies that have mobilized globally around these issues (see Raboy and Landry 2005).

It is not too late for Canada to take true global leadership in the area of communication rights and the right to communicate, but we must get our own house in order first. Scratch beneath the surface, as we have modestly tried to do in this book, and it is clear that the present linkages between rights, communication, policy, and practice are at best weak, where they are not misguided; that abstract and unenforceable claims to national sovereignty are favoured over the ability of citizens to use their media; that when it is convenient to do so, government appropriates public communication for the purpose of promoting an idealized notion of national identity; that rhetorical platitudes tend to take precedence over clear policies that are effectively monitored; and that the effort to cast this country as a champion of human and cultural rights is favoured over realizing communication rights at home and on the ground. It is not too late, but the starting point may need to be the recognition that the system needs a soul.

Relationships in Transition CFP 2005 – Communication Rights and the Right to Communicate

The Law Commission of Canada and the Social Sciences and Humanities Research Council of Canada

Communication is the core of democratic public life. In forms ranging from dialogue between citizens on a local, national or international scale, or between citizens and governments, to the various practices associated with the production, circulation and consumption of information, communication is central to the operation and legitimacy of democracy. In addition to these functions, communication also enables the social relationships and cultural practices that have been identified as foundational to the vibrant and diverse public cultures upon which democracy rests.

In recent years, several developments have combined to give communication renewed salience as a category of public and legal significance. These include: the proliferation of new information and communication technologies; the growing economic and strategic value of knowledge, information and communication; changes in the national and global political economy of media and communication; the emergence of new international institutions and regimes of media and communication governance; the increasing pace of Canada's development as a multicultural society, and the growing need to accommodate cultural pluralism in all aspects of social life; and the central role of information and communication technology in both the emergence of new categories of risk, and the development of strategies to meet them.

Traditionally, law concerning communication has been based on protection of the bedrock right to freedom of expression, and specification of its legitimate limits. The continuing importance of freedom of expression as a foundation for liberal democratic legal frameworks in relation to communication is unquestionable. However, as necessary as this principle is, it is no longer clear that a legal framework based primarily on freedom of expression is adequate to the diverse purposes we might imagine for law in supporting democratic communication under contemporary conditions. For example, while freedom of expression can be invoked to protect minority, weak or dissenting voices from suppression by state authorities, it cannot guarantee those voices a hearing on mass media channels whose ownership is increasingly concentrated and commercialized – a situation which itself is made possible by arguments derived from the principle of freedom of expression. In this scenario, the dissenter and the media corporation both enjoy the right to free expression, but only one party has the power to exercise that right, and can do so in a way that practically negates the right of the other.

Examples such as this point to the need to rethink the role law might play in facilitating and protecting the range of communication practices and relationships that are necessary for a robustly democratic public culture. The issue is not whether we can dispense with freedom of expression as a right but, rather, what other principles and legal instruments might be necessary to supplement this right, and to make it real in the complex political, economic and social context of contemporary Canada.

Exploration of this issue entails consideration of a broad range of other principles relevant to democratic communication. Some of these principles are already encoded in legal rights and protections, including: rights to assembly and association; religious freedom; access to information statutes; privacy rights; political rights, including rights to self-determination and electoral participation; intellectual property rights; and protection from slander and libel. Each of these principles faces new challenges and opportunities in the current technological and political-economic environment.

It is also possible that these "communication rights" need to be buttressed by a more expansive "right to communication." An umbrella-like right to communication could encompass a range of principles that are not reducible to either freedom of expression or the related communication rights listed above. These might include:

- equitable access to the means of mass communication and cultural production
- a right to practice, express and participate in one's own culture, in the language of one's choice
- availability of diverse, pluralistic media content that reflects the diverse, pluralistic culture of Canada
- equitable access to the benefits of scientific and technological innovation

- enhanced democratic representation and participation in national and international decision-making and governance in the areas of communication, technology and cultural policy
- enhanced access to privately-held information that bears on the public interest
- expanded individual privacy protections, including the right to communicate anonymously
- a right to adapt and reconfigure tools, media and content of communication to suit an individual or group's needs.

What would the legal and political implications of an established "right to communicate" be for democratic communication in Canada? Is it the best foundation for supporting democratic communication and cultural practices in the current context? How might law be used to elaborate, implement or support such a right and the practices and relationships it contemplates? What would be the legitimate limits of such a right, and what role should law play in establishing and enforcing these?

These and related questions can be pursued productively in relation to several issues prominent in contemporary discourse surrounding communication, media and new technology. These include: inequalities in access to media and information, including the "digital divide"; privacy, security and surveillance; communication technology and new forms of work and employment; concentration and transnationalization of media ownership; public and private censorship; intellectual property and piracy; media regulation in a "multi-channel" universe; communication technology and democratic education; emerging forms of electronically-mediated commerce and political participation; jurisdiction over transnational media enterprises; the relationship between state and market in the regulation of communication and media technology and content; the emergence of global institutions and regimes of media and communication governance; and the communication and media practices of civil society.

The Communication Rights Assessment Framework and Toolkit (CRAFT)

•••••• *Communication Rights in the Information Society (CRIS) Campaign*

As reproduced from *Assessing Communication Rights: A Handbook* (CRIS 2005a, 67-76)

Questions on Each Pillar and Attribute: Issues covered by the attributes of the Pillar can most easily be explained as a series of questions. These contain a normative aspect, and an affirmative answer to each represents a positive contribution to communication rights.

Each of the Pillars, and their attributes, are considered in turn.

Pillar A: Creating Spaces for Democratic Deliberation – The Public Sphere

COMMUNICATION RIGHTS AT HOME

Freedom of expression includes the right to hold and express dissenting views and to criticize those in power. It is a fundamental human right, and an absolute requirement for democracy.

A1: Is freedom of expression available to all people, in law and in practice?

A1.1 Is freedom of expression guaranteed in the constitution and in law, in line with international standards?

A1.2 Are guarantees of freedom of expression reflected in government policy and enforced effectively by government and judiciary?

A1.3 Is freedom of expression protected against corporate and business or other private interference?

A1.4 Is freedom of expression through leaflets, posters and other public means overly restricted?

A1.5 Are measures taken to ensure freedom from fear and an atmosphere of openness, including, for instance, how these are differently experienced by men and by women?

A1.6   Does the educational system provide critical media education?

A2:   Is there freedom of the press and media, including the electronic media?

A2.1   Is freedom of the press and media guaranteed constitutionally and in law, in line with international standards, and taking into account the public's right or reply, right to privacy etc.?

A2.2   Are press and media, in practice, free from government interference, from overt censorship to indirect financial or other pressures?

A2.3   Are press and media, in practice, free from commercial interference from their owners, shareholders, advertisers or others, direct or indirect?

A2.4   Are press and media, in practice, free from non-media commercial interference or censorship, such as from common carriers, cable operators, ISPs, search engines and wholesale bandwidth suppliers?

A2.5   Are there measures, including industry self-regulation, obliging media, publishing and dissemination companies (ISPs, search engines, bandwidth retailers, etc.) to act as "common carriers" in relation to all material that is legal under internationally accepted legal norms, including material critical of government, industry or other parties?

A2.6   Are human and civil rights of journalists adequately protected to enable them to carry out their work, especially in areas of conflict?

A2.7   Do journalists have editorial and material freedom to carry out their work, including reasonable job security, trade union membership, protection against gender discrimination, moral rights as authors, absence of employer coercion, etc.?

A3:   Is there access to, and ready availability, of public and government information?

A3.1   Is there robust freedom of information legislation, with minimum retention of government and public bodies, and maximum access by the public at large?

A3.2   Does the freedom of information legislation ensure that information is available in a timely and affordable manner to all?

A3.3   Does the public sector and government actively promote openness and transparency, through such means as: structures or offices to compile and release information in appropriate forms; publication of goals and plans for policies and public services; protection for public employees who disclose information in the public interest ("whistleblowers"); broadcasting of deliberations of elected representatives and public bodies; transparency of decision-making on matters of public interest?

A4:   Is there access to corporate information, where relevant to issues of public interest?

A4.1   Are there effective legal requirements for corporate disclosure legislation/regulation, beyond basic financial information, of all information available to corporations that may have a bearing on public policy and on the public interest?

A4.2   Is there access to corporate information in practice, including voluntary action?

A5:   Is there diversity of content in the media, and plurality of media sources?

A5.1   Are there effective means to regulate in the public interest by preventing concentration of media ownership, including concentration of ownership of a particular medium, cross-ownership between media, and cross-ownership of production, content dissemination, and/or infrastructure?

A5.2   Does the legislative framework support in practice the emergence of a plurality of media types at national and, as appropriate, regional and local levels: public service, commercial and community/independent media, including the transparent and equitable allocation of radio spectrum and other public goods?

A5.3   Does public service media have adequate resources available to them, especially in relation to news and current affairs?

A5.4   Are public service media fully independent of government, and free of arbitrary interference and unnecessarily cumbersome regulation?

A5.5   Do community and non-profit media have adequate resources, including public resources such as spectrum, especially for the media of disadvantaged and marginalized communities?

A5.6   Are community and non-profit media free from arbitrary interference from government and others?

A5.7   Are community and non-profit media transparent, democratic and participative?

A5.8   Are there enforceable regulatory obligations on commercial media, including broadcasters, as appropriate, to ensure they fulfil public service requirements?

A5.9   Are there mechanisms in place to deal with gross misrepresentation, stereotyping or other distortion within media content of women, ethnic groups, poorer and other marginalised groups?

A5.10 Are different social groups, including women, fairly represented among media employees, at every level, and are mechanisms in place to ensure that they are?

A5.11 Are there measures to prevent advertising from exerting undue influence on the public sphere, such as ensuring it is readily identifiable as advertising, limiting the volume of advertising, and regulation of content in the public interest?

A6: Is there universal access to relevant media by all communities?

A6.1 Are there effective measures to ensure affordability and accessibility of media content (including newspapers, radio and television) relevant to political discussion, especially for women and among poorer and marginalised groups, such as preferential tax regimes, free-to-air broadcasting or transport subsidy?

MEDIA AND COMMUNICATION INTERACTIONS EXTERNALLY

A7: Is the role of non-national media and communication a positive one for the public sphere?

A7.1 Are there effective measures nationally to ensure that foreign ownership of national media does not negatively affect the extent and quality of coverage of local issues, the quality of general media coverage, and the media environment generally?

A7.2 Are there effective measures nationally to ensure that cross-border media flows, such as direct broadcast satellite, do not negatively affect the extent and quality of coverage of local issues, the quality of general media coverage, and the media environment generally as it relates to the public sphere?

A7.3 Does Internet content from outside contribute to the availability of information relating to the public sphere?

A7.4 Does national civil society participate in transnational media, Internet or otherwise, that contributes to a transnational public sphere?

A8: Do international agreements and developments, and government positions in relation to them, support and enhance the role of media and communication in the public sphere?

A8.1 Do international agreements and multilateral institutions inside and outside the UN, in practice, support media and communication in relation to the public sphere, for instance, through the protection of, and support for free, diverse and open media nationally, and the right to discriminate in favour of such local media, and to regulate content originating outside in the interests of supporting the public sphere?

A8.2 Does the government advocate and support measures in relevant agreements and institutions that would support the role of media and communication in the public sphere?

A8.3 Is there consistency between government positions in relation to media and communication internationally and at home?

A8.4 Does the government maintain an independent position in relation to the actions of powerful governments, preventing undue external influence in relation to these issues?

DEMOCRACY AND PARTICIPATION IN COMMUNICATION GOVERNANCE

A9: Nationally, is there effective civil society participation in media and communication governance, as it relates to the public sphere?

A9.1 Are there adequate public consultations on, and opportunities to participation in, government media and communication national strategy and policy development that affect the public sphere?

A9.2 Are there effective ongoing means for public concerns and complaints to be heard and acted upon with regard to media policy and practice, including remedial actions, in this area?

A9.3 Are there adequate mechanisms for independent direct public participation in ongoing policy review and implementation, in a decentralised manner as appropriate, in this area?

A9.4 Has civil society and other actors developed and deployed governance mechanisms and instruments that support the role of media in the public sphere, recognised or not by government?

A9.5 Are there specific measures to ensure that women can actively participate in structures of consultation, representation and participation, and that gender-related issues are addressed?

A10: Internationally, is there effective civil society participation in media and communication governance as it relates to the public sphere?

A10.1 Are there mechanisms to ensure openness and transparency of government in international negotiations and institutions relating to media and the public sphere?

A10.2 Are there adequate opportunities for civil society, including women, to participate in international governance structures and environments in relation to the role of media and communication in the public sphere, in both a national and international context?

A10.3 Are civil society entities, such as NGOs and research centres, aware of transnational governance issues, nationally, regionally or internationally, and do they participate to any significant extent at these levels?

Pillar B: Knowledge Creation and Sharing for Equity and Creativeness – Enriching the Public Domain

Communication Rights at Home

B1: Do the governance and practice of knowledge generation, ownership and sharing strike an equitable and efficient balance between supporting widespread creativity and enabling widespread use of knowledge?

B1.1 Is there a national strategic and policy orientation to knowledge creation, dissemination and use (especially copyright, and including published and broadcast educational materials and software) with the explicit goal of enriching the public domain, satisfying the various needs for knowledge, and encouraging creativity from all sectors of society?

B.1.2 Are there public policies and actions to encourage and enable widespread generation and communication of knowledge, which might include: support for "fair use" of copyrighted material; constraints on digital rights management; recognition and protection for the "moral rights" of authors; or efforts to tailor IPRs to national conditions?

B1.3 Do government and public bodies actively interpret and implement national and international laws and agreements in copyright and relevant patents in favour of balanced knowledge sharing, such as: promoting new business and legal models reinforcing knowledge sharing; incentives for necessary research and knowledge creation; facilitating dissemination via the media; support for open source and free software, and for "development and community-friendly" approaches to knowledge sharing, or efforts to protect folklore from exploitation?

B2: Do knowledge and works supported by public funds automatically enter the public domain?

B2.1 Is there a public policy, supported by practical measures, to ensure that all knowledge generated through public funds immediately becomes part of the public domain?

B2.2   Is knowledge and information held by public bodies made available into the public domain?

B2.3   Do public service media, and other content funded by public funds, place their archives in the public domain?

B3:   Do all groups in society, including women and marginalized groups, have affordable and equitable access to the various means of sharing knowledge?

B3.1   Do different social groups (including gender, ethnic, linguistic, income) and geographical areas have access to knowledge in an equitable manner, carried by media, mass media and ICTs, in terms of availability, affordability and access?

B3.2   Is there affordable access to scientific and educational knowledge, disseminated by publishers by conventional and digital means?

B3.3   Are there effective measures to ensure affordability and accessibility of knowledge sharing media, especially among poorer and marginalised groups, such as preferential tax regimes, free-to-air broadcasting, must-carry obligations on cable operators etc.?

B3.4   Does the political and regulatory framework actively favour the extension of universal service/access as the priority for the media sector, including in ICTs, broadcast services and others?

B3.5   Are policy measures pursued in ICTs conventional and innovative, to ensure universal services and access to knowledge, for instance by providing subsidies?

B3.6   Is there active support for local industry development across ICT sectors, such as specific incentives, transition periods to build up local companies, and so forth?

B4:   Do all social groups have reasonable opportunities to produce and disseminate knowledge?

B4.1   Are there measures to ensure that all social groups, including women, have at least a minimum of society's knowledge available to them in appropriate form, via media and communication, including illiterate people?

B4.2   Are there measures to support knowledge production among all social groups, for dissemination via media?

B5: Are there widespread skills and capacities to enable people and communities to utilise media and communication to achieve individual and collective goals?

B5.1 Are opportunities for ICT skills and capacity development available to all communities, such as training, exchange programmes, or formal curriculum modules in public establishments such as schools, libraries or community centres?

B5.2 Are opportunities for media and communication training available to all communities, including formal, informal and community-based?

B5.3 Is media education a standard part of the educational curriculum?

MEDIA AND COMMUNICATION INTERACTIONS EXTERNALLY

B6: Is the role of non-national media and communication a positive one for knowledge sharing?

B6.1 Are there effective measures nationally to ensure that foreign ownership of national publishing companies, telecommunication and media, do not impact negatively on national knowledge generation and dissemination?

B6.2 Are there effective measures to counteract any negative effect of cross-border media-related knowledge flows, such as foreign-owned scientific and educational publishers, including in digital form?

B6.3 Is the Internet, or other media, used extensively as a means to support the availability and sharing of knowledge, and are there measures to support this from government or others?

B7: Do international agreements, and government positions in relation to them, support and enhance the role of media and communication in knowledge generation and sharing?

B7.1 Do international agreements, Treaties and conventions, and multilateral institutions inside and outside the UN, in practice, support media and communication in knowledge generation and sharing, for instance through ensuring a fair copyright regime, and the protection of "fair use" in the move to electronic publishing?

B7.2 Does the government advocate and support measures in these agreements and institutions in support of a balanced knowledge generation and dissemination regime?

B7.3 Is there consistency between government positions in these matters abroad and at home?

B7.4   Does the government maintain an independent position in relation to the actions of powerful governments, preventing undue external influence in relation to these issues?

DEMOCRACY AND PARTICIPATION IN COMMUNICATION GOVERNANCE

B8:   Nationally, is there effective civil society participation in media and communication governance, as it relates to knowledge generation and sharing?

B8.1   Are there adequate public consultations on, and opportunities for participation in, government knowledge production and dissemination of national strategy and policy development, including in copyright and knowledge ownership, telecommunication infrastructure (fixed, wireless) and services (telephony, mobile, data and Internet), and content?

B8.2   Are there effective ongoing means for public concerns and complaints to be heard and acted upon with regard to policy and practice, including remedial actions?

B8.3   Are there adequate mechanisms for direct public participation in ongoing policy review and implementation, in a decentralised manner as appropriate?

B8.4   Has civil society, and/or other actors, developed and deployed governance mechanisms and instruments in relation to knowledge generation and sharing, recognised or not by government?

B8.5   Are there specific measures to ensure that women can actively participate in structures of consultation, representation and participation, and that gender-related issues are addressed?

B9:   Internationally, is there effective civil society participation in the governance of knowledge generation, ownership and sharing?

B9.1   Are there mechanisms to ensure openness and transparency of government in international negotiations and institutions relating to knowledge generation, ownership and sharing?

B9.2   Are there adequate opportunities for civil society, including women, to participate in international governance structures and environments in relation to knowledge generation, ownership and sharing, in both a national and international context?

B9.3   Are civil society entities, such as NGOs and research centres, aware of transnational governance issues, nationally, regionally or internationally, and do they participate to any significant extent at these levels?

Pillar C: Civil Communication Rights

C1: Is there a right to equality before the law, and the protection of one's honour and reputation?

C.1.1 Is there explicit legal protection against incitement to discrimination, by media or other communication, in relation to all being equal before the law?

C.1.2 Is a right of reply available to the public, to protect against defamation, incitement to discrimination, and other related issues, in line with international standards?

C2: Is there a right to information privacy and data protection?

C2.1 Is there legislation to ensure that personal data are held for the minimum necessary period and used only for purposes authorised by the person to whom the data refers?

C2.2 Are such laws actively enforced, and can the public exercise this right in an affordable, transparent and proactive manner, including securing remedial action?

C2.3 Is there a strong culture of self-regulation and codes of practice in privacy and data protection, among civil society, government and private sector actors?

C3: Is there a right to privacy of communication?

C3.1 Are there laws and regulations to ensure a right to privacy of communication and the absence of surveillance, of Internet, telephony, postal or other means, with exceptions only in clearly defined and extreme circumstances, and covering access in private, public and commercial environments?

C3.2 Are such laws enforced in a transparent, non-partisan and proactive manner, including against government violations, with the possibility of redress where rights have been violated?

C3.3 Are there effective measures to control spam (unsolicited commercial e-mail), in order to prevent it hindering the general capacity for Internet interaction?

C4: In public and in workplaces, is there protection against excessive surveillance using communication technologies?

C4.1 Are there measures to protect against excessive video surveillance and the "chilling effect" it may have on freedom of association and movement?

MEDIA AND COMMUNICATION INTERACTIONS EXTERNALLY

C5:   Do non-national media and communication promote civil rights?

C5.1   Is there protection against external surveillance and interference in national Internet use?

C6:   Do international agreements, and government positions in relation to them, support and enhance the role of media and communication in civil rights?

C6.1   Do international agreements (regional, global) and multilateral institutions inside and outside the UN, in practice, support civil rights in media and communication?

C6.2   Does the government advocate and support measures in these agreements and institutions in support of civil rights in communication?

C6.3   Is there consistency between government positions in these matters abroad and at home?

C6.4   Does the government maintain an independent position in relation to the actions of powerful governments, preventing undue external influence in relation to these issues?

DEMOCRACY AND PARTICIPATION IN COMMUNICATION GOVERNANCE

C7:   Nationally, is there effective civil society participation in media and communication governance as it relates to civil rights and cultural production?

C7.1   Are there adequate public consultations on, and opportunities to participate in, government approach to civil rights in relation to communication?

C7.2   Are there effective ongoing means for public concerns and complaints to be heard and acted upon with regard to policy and practice, including remedial actions?

C7.3   Are there adequate mechanisms for independent direct public participation in ongoing policy review and implementation, in a decentralised manner as appropriate?

C7.4   Have civil society and other actors developed and deployed governance mechanisms and instruments in relation to securing civil rights, recognised or not by government?

C7.5   Are there specific measures to ensure that women can actively participate in structures of consultation, representation and participation, and that gender-related issues are addressed?

C8:   Internationally, is there effective civil society participation in the governance of civil rights?

C8.1   Are there mechanisms to ensure openness and transparency of government in international negotiations and institutions relating to civil rights relevant to communication?

C8.2   Does the government actively facilitate and support the participation of civil society in international governance arenas, including national to local level consultation to ensure that civil society views are taken into account when developing positions?

C8.3   Are there adequate opportunities for civil society, including women, to participate in international governance structures and environments in relation to communication-related civil rights, in both a national and international context?

Pillar D: Cultural Rights relating to Communication

D1:   Are the rights of all linguistic communities in relation to the use of their language recognised and enforced?

D1.1   Are all linguistic groups treated equally in terms of the right to use one's language in public and private communication?

D1.2   Are there adequate measures to enable the use of minority and endangered languages, including sign language and subtitling, in media and communication production and dissemination?

D1.3   Are there adequate measures to ensure that all linguistic communities have access to a minimum of society's knowledge available to them in appropriate language and form?

D1.4   Are there effective measures to ensure that minority linguistic groups can intervene and participate in media for a relevant to general political and social discussion?

D1.5   In relation to ICTs, are there technologies available to ensure that minority linguistic groups can use software and hardware?

D1.6   Is education available to all in junior, secondary and third level in native languages?

D2:   Is everyone enabled to freely participate in cultural life and practices of their communities, as they relate to media and communication?

D2.1   Is there specific recognition in public policy that cultural production is distinct from market-driven production of commodities?

D2.2　Are all cultural traditions adequately recognised in public funding and regulation of cultural practice in relation to the media?

D2.3　Are adequate measures in place to ensure that all cultures have affordable access to media-related cultural products and activities of their cultures, such as film and television, including their production as well as consumption?

D2.4　Are media-related cultural products available in the public domain for public use?

D2.5　Are media-related cultural products given sufficient long-term protection, in terms for instance of suitable archiving?

D3:　Is the media and communications environment supportive of individual, community and societal identity formation and evolution, enhancing diversity and mutual respect?

D3.1　Are positive measures taken to develop cultural diversity, for instance through recognition of the value of diverse national and immigrant cultures, of exchanges with external cultures etc.?

D3.2　Is there an awareness of, and action to prevent, an excessive influence of advertising and commercial pressures within the media in relation to culture and identity issues?

MEDIA AND COMMUNICATION INTERACTIONS EXTERNALLY

D4:　Does the influence of non-national media and communication promote cultural rights?

D4.1　Are there effective measures nationally to ensure the foreign ownership and participation in cultural production and dissemination do not have a negative impact on national and local cultural rights?

D4.2　Are there effective measures to counteract any negative effects of cross-border media-related cultural flows, such as foreign-owned/produced television, film, music and other cultural endeavours, especially where they are commercially motivated, while at the same time enhancing authentic cultural diversity and sharing?

D5:　Do international agreements and government positions in relation to them support and enhance the role of media and communication in cultural rights?

D5.1　Do international agreements (regional, global) and multilateral institutions inside and outside the UN, in practice, strengthen cultural rights in media and communication, for instance through recognition of the special nature of cultural products and support for cultural diversity?

D5.2 Do the government and public bodies advocate and support measures in these agreements and institutions in support of cultural rights in communication?

D5.3 Is there consistency between government positions in these matters abroad and at home?

D5.4 Does the government maintain an independent position in relation to the actions of powerful governments, preventing undue external influence in relation to these issues?

DEMOCRACY AND PARTICIPATION IN COMMUNICATION GOVERNANCE

D6:   Nationally, is there effective civil society participation in media and communication governance as it relates to cultural production?

D6.1 Are there adequate public consultations on, and opportunities for participation in, government cultural and linguistic strategy and policy development?

D6.2 Are there effective ongoing means for public concerns and complaints to be heard and acted upon with regard to policy and practice, including remedial actions?

D6.3 Are there adequate mechanisms for independent direct public participation in ongoing policy review and implementation, in a decentralised manner as appropriate?

D6.4 Have civil society and other actors developed and deployed governance mechanisms and instruments in relation to cultural rights, recognised or not by government?

D6.5 Are civil society entities, such as NGOs and research centres, aware of transnational governance issues, nationally, regionally or internationally, and do they participate to any significant extent at these levels?

D6.6 Are there specific measures to ensure that women can actively participate in structures of consultation, representation and participation, and that gender-related issues are addressed?

D7:   Internationally, is there effective civil society participation in the governance of cultural rights?

D7.1 Are there mechanisms to ensure openness and transparency of government in international negotiations and institutions relating to cultural rights relevant to communication?

D7.2   Are there adequate opportunities for civil society, including women, to participate in international governance structures and environments in relation to communication-related cultural rights, in both a national and international context?

D7.3   Are civil society entities, such as NGOs and research centres, aware of transnational governance issues, nationally, regionally or internationally, and do they participate to any significant extent at these levels?

Strategic *Charter* Litigation and the Right to Communicate in Canada

Simon Grant

In considering how the realization of law and policy for communication in Canada can be improved, the authors of this volume advocate greater enforcement of existing rules as well as a broadly based focus on what they call "communication rights" on the part of legislators and relevant administrative bodies such as the Canadian Radio-television and Telecommunications Commission (CRTC) in Canada. In parallel, they advocate the reframing of Canadian media and communication policy away from the current freedom of expression standard and toward a new approach that recognizes the "right to communicate." Chapter 10 of this volume asks whether the establishment of the right to communicate would contribute to improving law and policy for communication in Canada at present. This article addresses the closely related question of how a right to communicate might be introduced into Canadian law, and will look at ways in which Canada's pre-eminent rights instrument, the *Canadian Charter of Rights and Freedoms,* might be engaged in such a campaign.[1]

The focus of this discussion is on how the "right to communicate" could be entered into some form of Canadian law.[2] By "law" here I mean not only codified law (which would be difficult to amend to include a right to communicate) but also a decision of a court that could be used as a precedent in a future case, such as a favourable decision of a provincial Court of Appeal or the Supreme Court of Canada.

I propose a plan of strategic litigation through which communication rights activists could campaign to enshrine some form of a right to communicate in Canadian law, specifically in the context of the section 2(b) freedom of expression provision of the *Canadian Charter of Rights and Freedoms.* I argue that a high-level Canadian court decision that refers explicitly to a "right to communicate" (even without defining it in detail) would be both a valuable and a realistic goal of such strategic litigation. Communication rights activists could then invoke the precedent of this "right to communicate" court decision as an argument in subsequent campaigns.

In order to achieve this goal, I suggest that Canadian communication rights activists follow the example of feminist groups by submitting arguments to the court as interveners in cases that engage issues of concern to them. As strategic litigation also presents a risk of court decisions that are *unfavourable* to the right to communicate, however, I propose a two-part process of elimination to help communication rights activists concentrate their resources on cases with the greatest likelihood of a favourable result.

Why the *Charter*?

The *Canadian Charter of Rights and Freedoms* has been part of the Canadian Constitution since its enactment in 1982. The primary purpose of the *Charter* is to mediate the relationship between the state and the individual (Monahan 2002, especially 409). Unlike its quasi-constitutional predecessor, the *Canadian Bill of Rights*,[3] which has been used only once to override a federal statute,[4] the *Charter* is an entrenched part of the Constitution that applies to all federal and provincial acts (whether those be laws, decisions, or actions), is frequently applied by the courts, and can be amended only through the logistically difficult and politically fraught constitutional amending formula.

Judicial review of legislation or government action under the *Charter* is often seen as part of a "dialogue" between courts and legislatures, in which legislatures respond to the court's speech by enacting alternative statutes that modify or reverse judicial nullification (Hogg and Bushell Thornton 1997; Hogg et al. 2007). Since becoming popular, the "*Charter* dialogue" view has been criticized in particular for neglecting the privileged position occupied by courts in *Charter* dialogues (Petter 2007).

However lopsided the dialogue is in practice, one can certainly conceive of *Charter* litigation as an opportunity for actors such as communication rights activists to add their voices to the judicial side of that dialogue as interveners in the case, particularly if those activists find the legislative side of that dialogue closed off to them. Indeed, advocates of the right to communicate have themselves embraced a dialogic model of law. McIver and colleagues (2003) follow Dutch legal scholars Willem Witteveen and Bart van Klink (1999) in embracing a model of "communicative law" that "takes law as an invitation to dialogue between more or less equal parties: state officials ... intermediary organizations, and citizens." Although Witteveen and van Klink do not specifically discuss the *Charter*, their approach to the law fits well with how *Charter* review operates in practice.

The *Charter*'s greatest appeal is also a weakness. The text of the *Charter* (especially when read separately, without being read together with the limitation in section 1) seems to make bold, clear, even poetic promises on rights to which Canadians are entitled. Indeed, the *Charter* consistently enjoys far greater support in opinion polls than any political party or government in power: a pair of polls from early 2007 found that more than half of the respondents felt that the *Charter* was taking the country in the "right direction," while only 12 percent felt that the *Charter* was leading the country in the wrong direction (see Butler 2007). Interestingly, among supporters of the *Charter*, the most popular reason expressed for their support was that the *Charter* "works," an effective riposte to criticisms that many Canadians support the *Charter* without actually knowing what the text of the document says. Even to the extent that the *Charter* "works," however, it should be remembered that compared with the broad lawmaking powers of the legislatures or even international discussion forums, the *Charter* is a very blunt instrument indeed.

The *Charter* applies to all actions taken by government, including legislation, regulation, and actions taken under the common law. Even an omission that takes place in the context of a government action can be construed as a deliberate choice and therefore constitute an action subject to *Charter* review.[5] Public bodies under government control are subject to the *Charter* if there is an institutional and a structural link between the body and the government, although bodies performing a public service independently of government control, such as a university, hospital, or corporation, are generally not subject to the *Charter* except when they are implementing a specific government policy.[6]

The application provisions of the *Charter* thus present opportunities as well as challenges to an official recognition of a right to communicate. On the one hand, the *Charter* has actually enforced "teeth" lacked by international rights documents such as the *Universal Declaration of Human Rights* or UNESCO conventions.[7] The Supreme Court of Canada often invokes the *Charter* to nullify or "read down" legislation. Legislators and government officials in turn must bear in mind *Charter* provisions when drafting legislation or providing government services in order to avoid becoming exposed to a potential *Charter* challenge, which often costs hundreds of thousands of dollars to litigate (Petter 1989).

On the other hand, the form of the *Charter* severely limits contexts in which it can actually be invoked, particularly in the realm of freedom of expression. The *Charter* does not favour pre-emptive strikes. More typically, *Charter* claims require actual situations in which some government act or legislation has already violated the *Charter* rights of particular individuals. Unfortunately for the right to communicate, this means that the actions of media organizations (private or public) are not subject to the *Charter*, although government bodies that regulate those media organizations, such as the CRTC, would be subject to the *Charter*.

In light of the inherently limited applicability of the *Charter* (to laws and actions of public bodies, and not between private parties), Joel Bakan (1997, 4) argues that *Charter* rights are ultimately ineffective tools for effecting change because the causes and symptoms of social problems are typically too complex to fit within the juridically defined scope of a *Charter* rights claim, rendering court-imposed solutions crude and narrowly focused. Bakan's research offers important reasons to remain skeptical of the transformative potential of *Charter* rights, especially with respect to the inherent limitations of judges as would-be "solvers" of broader social problems. As a work of legal scholarship, however, Bakan's focus is primarily with actual laws and court decisions, rather than potential roles that could be played by activists and lawyers in *Charter* litigation.

A more behavioural approach to understanding *Charter* litigation would begin from the perspectives and interests of participants themselves, considering also the political environment of legal mobilization and specifically the ways in which the content and direction of legal change is shaped by the legal arguments as framed by legal actors. Adopting such an approach, political scientist Christopher Manfredi (2002, 47) conceives of *Charter* litigation as a "redistributive institution" and *Charter* rights as valuable resources for effecting policy outcomes that society-based actors such as activists and lawyers compete for and that state-based actors such as judges distribute. In this particular behaviouralist model, activists and lawyers can be recognized as sophisticated strategic actors who structure their claims – what Manfredi (2002) calls "legal mobilization" – with an eye to their own desired outcome as well as the limitations of the court and the proclivities of the law in being able to bring about an order that could effect some semblance of that outcome.

Manfredi's model is a better fit than Bakan's broad "social justice" perspective for a campaign for the right to communicate because it allows communication rights activists to begin with their own specific desired outcomes (such as some sort of judicial recognition of a right to communicate), and then to develop and deploy *Charter* arguments in an attempt to achieve those outcomes. In this model, the potential downsides of a campaign for a right to communicate could be assessed by communication rights activists themselves, rather than by the court.

Strategic *Charter* Litigation: Setting a Precedent

Communication rights activists may differ in how they define or assert the right to communicate. Such debates are chronicled in Chapters 1, 2, and 10 of this volume. When litigating before the courts, however, one goal in particular should be paramount: a precedent-setting court decision that explicitly refers to the "right to communicate."

Such a court decision would be tremendously valuable to communication rights activists. Canada's common-law tradition of public law means that previous court decisions serve as binding authorities for subsequent decisions. As a result, even if the court defines the "right to communicate" vaguely or imperfectly, communication rights activists could cite that decision when arguing in court or advocating in Parliament for a policy that engages the right to communicate. Ideally, the decision would come from the Supreme Court of Canada, making it binding authority throughout Canada, but a favourable citation from a province's court of appeal would also be valuable because it would be binding authority in that province and would also have persuasive authority elsewhere in the country.

Achieving such a court decision is also more realistic than it might at first appear. Amending the text of the *Charter* itself to include a right to communicate would be extremely difficult if not impossible. However, the Supreme Court of Canada alone decides dozens of *Charter* cases annually, some of which can extend to more than 100 pages of "reasons" for the decision. In addition to being precedent setting for future court cases, as a matter of English common-law tradition the reasons are based on arguments put to the court by the litigating parties. Therefore, it is not unrealistic to foresee a campaign of legal mobilization by communication rights activists leading to such a court decision, particularly if the court battles are carefully chosen and strategically argued.

Procedural Scenarios: Joining the *Charter* dialogue

There are two established ways in which activists and public interest organizations can participate in court cases involving *Charter* rights. The first and most direct way to enter the dialogue is as a litigant in a court action: for example, by suing a branch of government for having infringed a *Charter* right. Canadian courts have been more likely to grant standing to public interest litigants than have courts in other comparable jurisdictions such as the United States, the United Kingdom, and Australia.[8] Litigating before the Supreme Court of Canada is expensive, however, and many public interest groups are concerned primarily with a particular aspect of a case, such as how the decision could affect religious freedom or gender equality in Canada, or, in the case of communication rights activists, the right to communicate.

The second way to participate in a court action would be as an intervener. Being recognized as an intervener allows parties greater flexibility than they would have as litigants. An intervener is not on trial as a named party in the action, but the intervener may submit (brief) arguments to the court which the judges may consider in reaching their decision. As the Supreme Court held in *Canadian Council of Churches v. Canada (Minister of Employment and Immigration)*: "Public interests organizations are, as they should be, frequently granted intervener status. The views and submissions of interveners on issues of public importance frequently provide great assistance to the courts ... That assistance is given against a background of established facts and in a time frame and context that is controlled by the courts. A proper balance between providing for the submissions of public interest groups and preserving judicial resources is maintained."[9]

Special interest groups such as the feminist Women's Legal Education and Action Fund (LEAF) and the Canadian Civil Liberties Association have been particularly active interveners before the courts, submitting legal briefs to the court in cases dealing with constitutional law, criminal law, family law, and federal social policy. For example, feminist interveners in *Charter* cases have been particularly – and as at least one researcher argues, singularly – successful in persuading courts to adopt a contextual, effects-based analysis of discriminatory impact in equality cases (Langer 2005, n. 146).

The greatest hurdle to participating as an intervener may not be procedural at all but rather the cost of hiring lawyers to prepare the brief to the court. The procedure itself is fairly straightforward and conducive to a wide range of groups' being able to participate in court as interveners. The Ontario *Rules of Civil Procedure*, for example, allow that "any person may, with leave of a judge or at the invitation of the presiding judge or master, and without becoming a party to the proceeding, intervene as a friend of the court for the purpose of rendering assistance to the court by way of argument" (section 13.02).[10]

Activists interested in introducing a Canadian right to communicate might therefore take a page from the experience of feminist and civil libertarian activist groups and monitor Canada's appellate courts for cases that engage issues relevant to the right to communicate and then submit briefs as interveners in suitable cases.

Strategic Litigation and the *Charter*: Picking a Battle

Communication rights activists should be strategic when choosing cases in which to intervene. Obviously strategic litigation presents opportunities as well as risks: just as a well-chosen case and careful argumentation could lead to a valuable court decision recognizing a right to communicate, a dubious case or a sloppily presented argument could lead to a court decision explicitly *rejecting* such a right. The communication rights activist should therefore choose only cases involving freedom of expression, which is the nearest philosophical relative to the right to communicate.

Freedom of expression, the foundation of a right to communicate, is – as discussed in Chapters 3 and 10 – entrenched in section 2(b) of the *Charter*, which affirms that everyone has the "fundamental freedom ... of thought, belief, opinion and expression, including freedom of the press and other media of communication." All told, freedom of expression has probably seen the most case law of any *Charter* right, although for a variety of reasons it has generated less academic commentary than the section 15 right to equality. The scope of the guarantee of freedom of expression is said to include any conduct other than violence that is performed in order to convey meaning (see *Irwin Toy Ltd. v. Quebec (Attorney General)*).[11] The governing principle of the Supreme Court of Canada's definition of expression is therefore content neutrality. As the court held in *R. v. Keegstra*, "the content of a statement cannot deprive it of the protection accorded by s. 2(b), no matter how offensive it may be" (paragraph 828).[12]

Strategic Litigation and the *Charter*: Fighting the Battle

When choosing a particular freedom of expression case in which to intervene, communication rights activists should follow a process of elimination involving the following two questions:

- Does the case properly engage the *Charter*?
- Does the case come up against a legislative purpose that has already been recognized by the courts?

ENGAGING THE *CHARTER*

In any case selected for intervention by communication rights activists, it must be clearly established that the litigating parties and the relationships between them do indeed fall under the purview of *Charter* scrutiny. This is an important step; it is in this sense that a case can be said to engage the *Charter*. The great limitation of the *Charter*, as we have seen, is that it is only engaged in situations in which a public body is implementing a government policy. It would be extremely difficult, for example, to craft a *Charter*-based claim for a positive obligation on the part of the government to provide forums in which to exercise a right to communicate.[13] Only if the *Charter* is engaged should activists proceed as interveners. The risk of a decision with negative implications for the right to communicate would be slim, but intervening in such a case would waste resources.[14]

LEGISLATIVE PURPOSE

Second, the case should not come up against a legislative purpose that has already been recognized by the courts. Legal scholar June Ross (2003, 82) argues that, in *Charter* cases, free expression tends to receive a broad constitutional backing, but courts will show great deference to legislative efforts that infringe on free expression. An infringement of a *Charter* right can be allowed by the courts if its purpose can be justified under section 1 of the *Charter* as "a reasonable limit ... as can be demonstrably justified in a free and democratic society." Such a purpose need not doom the case for the purposes of the communication rights activist, but the claim itself would be less likely to succeed if it came up against government interest in restricting hate speech or child pornography, for example. Such a claim would offer the government too strong a line of reasoning against a right to communicate and would therefore risk creating conditions for a court to create a precedent of explicitly *rejecting* the existence of a right to communicate: the exact opposite of the goal of enshrining such a right. Even if only tangentially related to the core of a right to communicate, any such precedent could greatly compromise the ability of activists to litigate subsequently in favour of a right to communicate, and should therefore be avoided if possible.

It is therefore important for communication rights activists to be aware of the specific legislative purposes that courts have accepted and rejected as justifications for infringements of freedom of expression. Some of the most controversial court decisions around *Charter* section 2(b) have involved challenges to criminal prohibitions of hate propaganda *(R. v. Keegstra)*, obscenity

(R. v. Butler),[15] and child pornography *(R. v. Sharpe),*[16] with the court ruling that curbing each constitutes an infringement of freedom of expression that is justifiable under section 1 of the *Charter.* On the other hand, prohibitions against using public property for expressive purposes have been struck down.[17] Similarly, limits on third-party campaign-related election expenses and a ban against publishing polls in the days immediately before an election were also held to be invalid.[18] Communication rights activists should therefore avoid cases that engage any of these legislative purposes that courts have previously used or rejected as justifications for infringements on freedom of expression, as it is likely that judges in such cases will primarily defer to existing case law, leaving little scope for the introduction of original ideas, such as the right to communicate, into decisions.

Advancing the Right to Communicate in Canada

To enshrine an explicit right to communicate in a high-level Canadian court decision would be a valuable and realistic goal within a larger campaign by communication rights activists, both globally and in Canada.

Enshrining a right to communicate in such a way would require a careful campaign of strategic litigation. Strategic *Charter* litigation should complement rather than replace existing campaigns for a right to communicate, globally and in Canada. After all, as a tool for implementing policy, the *Charter* has great limitations compared with other policy instruments such as laws and international treaties: the *Charter* applies only to laws or government actors implementing public policy, and patent infringements of *Charter* rights can be justified if the court finds a valid legislative purpose under section 1. As a tool for strategic litigation, however, the *Charter* is peerless: one successful *Charter* claim can overturn laws and bind other courts to its reasoning. Whatever their position on the right to communicate as an intellectual concept, Canadian communication rights activists should consider the right to communicate and their position with respect to it in light of the very real opportunity to advance such a right in Canada through strategic *Charter* litigation.

Notes

PREFACE

1 See Appendix 1.

2 See ss. 5(1)c and 5(2) of the *Law Commission of Canada Act*, S.C. 1996, c. 9 (http://laws.justice.gc.ca/en/showtdm/cs/L-6.7).

3 Treasury Board President John Baird, as quoted in the *National Post* on 26 September 2006 (Gordon 2006). The status of an independent, government-funded agency that advises Parliament on how to modernize and improve legislation has always been something of a political football in Canada. The Law Reform Commission of Canada was similarly shut down by Brian Mulroney's Conservative government, only to have Jean Chrétien's Liberals recreate it as the Law Commission of Canada.

INTRODUCTION

1 Shea (1963) would later author a book called *Broadcasting the Canadian Way*.

2 For the sake of brevity, we will occasionally use the acronyms CR and R2C throughout this book to signify, respectively, the terms "communication rights" and "the right to communicate."

3 This committee was composed of officials from the Department of Communication and the Privy Council and the chairman of the Canadian Radio-television and Telecommunications Commission (CRTC).

4 Telecommission executive director Henry Hindley (1977, 10) professed that "those responsible for the Telecommission study had been much impressed by D'Arcy's paper." Enough so, he continued, that four of the telecommission studies were undertaken as a direct consequence of it.

5 For example, the famous 1980 report of the United Nations Educational, Scientific and Cultural Organization's (UNESCO) International Commission on the Study of Communication Problems, *Many Voices, One World* (also known as the MacBride Report), refers to *Instant World* by name in many different contexts (see UNESCO 2004, 113, 172-73, 178, 234, 265); and works on R2C-related issues as recent as Mueller et al. 2007 still situate their working definition of the concept relative to *Instant World*.

6   Community cable access was introduced in a CRTC policy report on cable tele-
    vision, *Canadian Broadcasting: A Single System*, published in 1971, the same year
    as *Instant World*. The CRTC's 1976 *Cable Television Regulations* imposed an obliga-
    tion on all cable television licensees to provide a community channel and, to
    ensure that it would be produced within the local community served, identified
    strict limits on the nature of the programming that could be aired and prohibited
    advertising on that channel (see CRTC 1971, 1976). The National Film Board's
    Challenge for Change program (known in French as Societé Nouvelle, or "New
    Society") was a well-funded project that lasted from the late 1960s until the early
    1980s and encouraged the use of film and video production as a catalyst for social
    change by giving voice to marginalized communities (see Baker et al. 2010).
7   Perhaps the best example of the prevalence of policy pragmatism over common
    sense is to be seen in the baffling array of legal and regulatory mechanisms that
    sometimes seem to take no account of one another. A good example of this is the
    two principal pieces of legislation in the field of communication in Canada, the
    Broadcasting Act, S.C. 1991, c. 11 (http://laws.justice.gc.ca/en/showtdm/cs/B-9.01)
    and the *Telecommunications Act*, S.C. 1993, c. 38 (http://laws.justice.gc.ca/en/
    showtdm/cs/T-3.4). A naïve reader of these texts cannot be blamed for failing to
    recognize that they refer to a common set of technologies, albeit to different func-
    tions of those technologies.
8   See, for example, Birdsall 1998, Birdsall et al. 2002, and Hicks 2007 for con-
    sideration of whether and how a right to communicate could be established in
    Canadian law; Dakroury 2005, 2006, 2009 for discussions of various issues re-
    lated to the violation of and compliance with the right to communicate in Canada;
    and Dakroury et al. 2009 for a survey of the historical controversies concerning
    the right to communicate internationally. A number of Canadian-based thinkers
    have also contributed to international discussions about establishing a universal
    right to communicate, including former civil servants such as William Birdsall and
    Henry Hindley; academics such as Leslie Regan Shade (Concordia University),
    Sheryl Hamilton (Carleton University), and Marc Raboy (McGill University); Wil-
    liam J. McIver Jr. of the National Research Council of Canada; and Montreal-based
    activist Alain Ambrosi (see Ambrosi and Abramson 1998; Ambrosi and Hamilton
    1998; Shade 2004; McIver and Birdsall 2004; Raboy 2003, 2006, etc.). There have
    also been important events in Canada associated with the international movement
    for the establishment of a universal right to communicate, including Dutch
    scholar Cees Hamelink's 2003 Graham Spry Lecture entitled "Toward a Human
    Right to Communicate" (Hamelink 2004).
9   Thus, for example, Canada's leading role in establishment of the 2005 UNESCO
    Convention on the Protection and Promotion of the Diversity of Cultural Expressions
    (http://unesdoc.unesco.org/images/0014/001429/142919e.pdf) and contributions
    to the 2003-05 World Summit on the Information Society (see, for examples, ITU
    2003a, 2005).

10   Unpublished letter of 21 February 1947, contained in the McGill University Ar-
      chives. Included in Glendon 2000 (252), with permission of Humphrey's literary
      executor, A.J. Hobbins, associate director of libraries at McGill. *Universal Declara-
      tion on Human Rights (UDHR)* (http://www.un.org/en/documents/udhr/).

11   The stated rationale for this position on the part of the government of Canada
      ostensibly had to do with uncertainty over how it would affect federal/provincial
      relations (Canada 1949); this dilemma was somehow resolved three days later,
      when Canada voted for the adoption of the *UDHR* in the UN General Assembly.
      Of the involvement of the government of Canada in the development of the *UDHR*,
      Humphrey (1984) wrote in his autobiography that he "knew that the internation-
      al promotion of human rights had no priority in Canada's foreign policy," but
      professed to being "shocked" and "unprepared" for Canada's abstention from the
      committee vote. "I had no doubt whatsoever," he continued, "that this quick change
      in position was dictated by the fact that the government did not relish the company
      in which it found itself ... It was therefore with bad grace that Canada joined the
      majority when the General Assembly adopted the Universal Declaration of Human
      Rights on the night of 10 December" (72). On his impressions of the plenary debate
      in which the *UDHR* was finally adopted, Humphrey wrote in his 11 December
      1948 diary entry that "one of the worst contributions was undoubtedly the Can-
      adian – a niggardly acceptance of the declaration" (Hobbins 1994, 90; see also
      Hobbins 1998). Humphrey's own words are hard to reconcile with the DFAIT
      website account of "our" heroic collaborative efforts in the drafting of the *UDHR*.

12   After his death in 1995, and in the lead-up to the fiftieth anniversary of the *UDHR*
      in 1998, official Canada moved quickly to associate itself with the accomplish-
      ments of John Humphrey. Humphrey had a street and memorial named after him
      in Côte Saint-Luc, Quebec; the National Arts Centre in Ottawa held a major ex-
      hibition on his life and achievements called "Citizen of the World"; Nelson
      Mandela dedicated a special Humphrey plaque on the Human Rights Monument
      in Ottawa; the government settled Humphrey's last case by agreeing to pay com-
      pensation to the Hong Kong veterans; and, on 7 October 1998, Canada Post
      launched a new 45-cent Humphrey stamp (Hobbins 2002).

13   The fall of the Berlin Wall and the resulting accession to single-superpower status
      of the United States instantly and dramatically reduced the strategic value of
      Canada's bilateral and NATO alliances with that country. In so doing, it raised the
      prospect that Canada's influence in international affairs – its celebrated tradition
      of "punching above its weight" – was about to decline to levels more in line with
      its size and relative power. Domestically, two referenda on the secession of Quebec
      from the Canadian federation meant that the status of the Canadian identity was
      both often debated and precarious during the 1980s and 1990s. Enforcing the
      narrative that to be Canadian means to champion human rights helped the fed-
      eral government to communicate a compelling notion of the Canadian identity

at home and to maintain a high standing in international affairs, and contributed to Canada's ability to compete in the global economic marketplace (Nimijean 2006; for a more general discussion of this theme, see van Ham 2001, which argues that in an era of globalization, national governments have become increasingly engaged in the transformation of national images and narratives in order to enhance their competitiveness in the global economy).

14   All of these issues are discussed in Part 2 of this volume.

15   Of course, we acknowledge that, in some areas, the US is not merely a convenient comparative context but an unavoidable interlocutor in Canadian communication policy making. For instance, much Canadian cultural policy aims to create and sustain a distinct market for Canadian creative production (see Chapter 4); interventions made by US companies and the US government itself present important challenges to Canadian policy debates on copyright (see Chapter 8); ICT access policy in Canada has intimate historical links with similar US policies (see Chapter 5); and, in an integrated marketplace for data storage, US post-9/11 security laws directly impact the privacy rights of Canadians (see Chapter 7).

16   We go into far greater detail on how freedom of expression is a two-tiered freedom in Canada in Chapter 10.

17   In particular, work derived from Habermas 1989.

18   For an alternative set of categorization concepts that follows a similar logic, see also James Carey's discussion (1985) of "ritual" versus "transmission" views of communication.

19   Free speech scholars and communication rights activists have long argued that the principle of freedom of expression tends to reflect and exacerbate rather than counterbalance the inequalities that exist within a given society. As early as the 1950s, the terms "one-way flow of information" and "communication imbalances" were developed to encapsulate what was just then beginning to emerge empirically in contemporary studies of communication flows such as the UNESCO study *One Week's News* (Kayser 1953) and the comprehensive analysis of the sources of international information conducted by the International Press Institute (1953).

20   These efforts produced a series of country reports (Gatheru and Mureithi 2004; Gagliardone et al. 2005; Somera and Alegre 2005; Intervozes 2005b; Planet Peace Project n.d.b) as well as internal process or implementation documents prepared for the CRIS campaign (Tuano and Alegre 2005; Intervozes 2005a; Planet Peace Project n.d.a; Gatheru and Mureithi n.d.).

21   The full list of questions included in the CRAFT can be found in Appendix 2 of this book. More details on the CRAFT can be found in CRIS 2005a and on the CRIS website (http://www.crisinfo.org/).

22   Besides the two authors of this chapter, contributors to the CRAFT assessment portion of this research included Leslie Regan Shade, William J. McIver Jr., Laura Murray, Gregory Taylor, Evan Light, Normand Landry, and Aysha Mawani.

23 As part of a McGill University colloquium series that brings together scholars in the faculties of arts and law, Professor Piper was asked to present and critique a paper based on an early draft of what would become Chapters 2-3 and 9-10 of this book (see Piper 2008). This book has benefited greatly from her legal perspective and constructive critical reading.

24 We recognize that this selection by no means covers the field of themes relevant to CR/R2C, and some might even consider our choices arbitrary.

25 *Broadcasting Act*, S.C. 1991, c. 11 (http://laws.justice.gc.ca/en/showtdm/cs/B-9.01).

CHAPTER 1: HISTORIES, CONTEXTS, AND CONTROVERSIES

1 See *Universal Declaration of Human Rights* (http://www.un.org/en/documents/udhr/) [*UDHR*]; *International Covenant on Civil and Political Rights* (http://www2.ohchr.org/english/law/ccpr.htm) [*ICCPR*]; *International Covenant on Economic, Social and Cultural Rights* (http://www2.ohchr.org/english/law/cescr.htm) [*ICESCR*]; as well as *Optional Protocol to the International Covenant on Civil and Political Rights* (http://www2.ohchr.org/english/law/ccpr-one.htm) and *Second Optional Protocol to the International Covenant on Civil and Political Rights, Aiming at the Abolition of the Death Penalty* (http://www2.ohchr.org/english/law/ccpr-death.htm).

2 The *ICCPR* version is slightly more elaborate. It reads:

    1 Everyone shall have the right to hold opinions without interference.
    2 Everyone shall have the right to freedom of expression; this right shall include freedom to seek, receive and impart information and ideas of all kinds, regardless of frontiers, either orally, in writing or in print, in the form of art, or through any other media of his choice.
    3 The exercise of the rights provided for in paragraph 2 of this article carries with it special duties and responsibilities. It may therefore be subject to certain restrictions, but these shall only be such as are provided by law and are necessary
       (a) For respect of the rights or reputations of others;
       (b) For the protection of national security or of public order *(ordre public)*, or of public health or morals.

3 This list, drawn from the CRIS handbook (CRIS 2005a, 24), is a distillation of selected portions of these three legal documents, including: *UDHR*, arts. 7, 12, 18, 19, 20, 21, 22, 26, and 27; *ICESCR*, arts. 13 and 15; *ICCPR*, arts. 1, 10, 17, 18, 19, 20, 21, 22, 25, and 27. The full text of all the above articles that are argued to be relevant to communication rights can be found in Annex 2 of the CRIS handbook.

4 Hamelink (2003), for instance, makes the case for the existence of a number of additional communication rights based on secondary texts, including:

    • the right to attention for the needs of disadvantaged groups
    • the right to diversity of creative work and media contents

- the right to protection against incitement to hatred and discrimination
- the right to development
- the right to corporate responsibility
- the right to presumption of innocence
- the right to protection of prisoners of war
- the right to information about matters of public interest
- the right to elimination of stereotyped contents
- the right to corporate ownership.

As before, each of these rights can be said to apply, under certain conditions, "in relation to media and communication." Hamelink bases this list of secondary communication rights on provisions found in fourteen official UN documents adopted between 1954 and 2007. Other sources, however, refer to an even larger number of legal documents "pertaining" to universal communication rights. Annex 1 of the 1985 UN Educational, Scientific, and Cultural Organization (UNESCO) director-general's report *The Right to Communicate* (UNESCO 1985) lists forty international documents linking human rights and communication, and Carlsson (2003, 36) suggests that forty-one international conventions and declarations "focused on the legal status of various elements in mass communication" were produced between the years 1948 and 1980 alone (see Padovani 2005 for more details).

5   Jean D'Arcy's status as a French media icon was recalled recently on the fiftieth anniversary of one of his most notable creations, the current affairs magazine *Cinq colonnes à la une*, which the newspaper *Le Figaro* described, in a full-page commemorative article, as the most famous program in the history of French television. At the time, France's nightly television news had to clear a government censor before broadcast and, according to *Le Figaro*, D'Arcy created *Cinq colonnes* in an attempt to loosen the government's leash (Héliot 2009).

6   At a Speech Communication Association conference in 1972, a Communication Rights Commission was created and a proposal was passed stating that the establishment of a universal right to communicate was a long-term goal for the organization. Graduate seminars on the right to communicate were established at the University of Hawaii as early as 1973, and over the next few years the university played host to a variety of meetings and visitors connected with the right to communicate. In 1974, with encouragement from UNESCO officials, the first Draft Resolution on the Right to Communicate was written for UNESCO by Harms and his colleagues Richstad and Kie at the East-West Communication Institute at the University of Hawaii. These scholars also edited and published two important collections of papers on the right to communicate: *The Right to Communicate: Collected Papers* (Harms et al. 1977) and *Evolving Perspectives on the Right to Communicate* (Richstad and Harms 1977). Both Harms and Richstad also contributed articles to the third major edited collection published on the subject

during this period: *The Right to Communicate: A New Human Right?* (Fisher and Harris 1983).

7   Since renamed the International Institute for Communications (IIC), the International Broadcast Institute (IBI) was "founded in 1968 with the support of the Ford Foundation by a group of senior US, Canadian, European and Japanese broadcasters, later to include telecommunications." The IIC's purpose is "to explore and research leading-edge issues such as the effects of convergence, the evolving regulatory framework, the production and distribution of content and their commercial, policy and cultural impacts" (http://www.iicom.org/index.htm). The right to communicate was put on the IBI agenda after a follow-up paper delivered by D'Arcy to the organization's annual meeting in 1973 (see D'Arcy 1977). The work was pushed forward at the IBI annual conference of 1975 by a working group under the chairmanship of Reuters manager Gerald Long. While the majority of contemporary activities concerning the right to communicate focused on the notion of a universal right to communicate based on an international legal instrument, the work done at the 1975 IBI conference also underlined the importance of national domestic frameworks to the provision of the right to communicate. The new description of the right to communicate produced by the conference working group, although clearly also focused on the notion of the right to communicate as "a basic human right," was accompanied by a recommendation for the "study of the application of the various forms of the right to communicate in countries where they [sic] have a long history of implementation" (Richstad and Harms 1977, 130).

8   This critical view of global communication struck a chord outside the Non-Aligned Movement (NAM) as well, and in the debates that followed, "doubts about trends in cultural and media 'imperialism,' and its long-term implications, were voiced not only by less developed countries but in many others, including France, Canada and Finland" (CRIS 2005a, 16).

9   This was the same General Conference of UNESCO at which the informal working group charged with defining the right to communicate presented the report that Harms and others had drafted in response to the Swedish resolution of 1974.

10   This was particularly significant because the US had been the largest contributor to UNESCO's operating budget. Between 1981 and 1983, the US contributed close to US$50 million annually. The United Kingdom's annual contribution was a more modest but still not insignificant US$8.8 million, while Singapore's was US$159,328. Collectively, the withdrawal of these three member states took with it almost 30 percent of UNESCO's total funding (UNESCO 1983).

11   The Canadian Commission for UNESCO facilitated the participation of various high-level Canadian specialists in the New World Information and Communication Order (NWICO) discussions: Marshall McLuhan was an original member of the MacBride Commission but became ill and was replaced by Betty Zimmerman, director of Radio-Canada International (Zimmerman thus became the only woman

member of the commission); and academics such as John Meisel, Bill Melody, and Thomas McPhail participated in various NWICO-themed or related symposia, as did prominent Toronto-based communication lawyer Peter Grant. While the 1981-82 *Report of the Secretary General* lauds the commission's efforts to "print hundreds of copies in xerox form" of the MacBride Commission report and "distribute them to groups and individuals free of charge," little seems to have come of the "expected ad-hoc working group" that was to be charged with following up on the MacBride Commission report and on coordinating Canadian responses to its conclusions and recommendations (Canadian Commission for UNESCO 1982, 7). No books or papers related to the NWICO debate were published by the Canadian Commission for UNESCO, and a 1982 seminar on the theme of "Towards a Canadian Perspective on International Communication Issues" appears to have been the only event organized regarding the implications of the NWICO debate on Canada (Canadian Commission for UNESCO 1981, 1985). Mary Vipond (2000) argues that instead of being a mass movement, the NWICO was largely driven by elites of the NAM countries, and there is little in the archives of the Canadian Commission for UNESCO to suggest that the case was any different in Canada (Canadian Commission for UNESCO 1980a, 1980b, 1980c, 1981, 1982, 1983, 1984, 1985).

12   A notable exception was a co-sponsored International Telecommunication Union (ITU)/UNESCO 1995 report, *The Right to Communicate: At What Price?* This rare interagency study wondered to what extent societal goals could be reconciled with commercial objectives in communication policy. It noted, among other things, the detrimental effects of economic barriers to access to telecommunication services; the lack of infrastructures in some countries; and the lack of an international universal telecommunication infrastructure – placing all of these issues under the umbrella of a communication rights framework (see ITU and UNESCO 1995).

13   The People's Communication Charter (n.d.) was a declarative statement circulated among non-governmental organizations (NGOs) and civil society organizations in the mid-1990s; its credo was that "people should be active and critical participants in their social reality and should be able to communicate their ideas and opinions." The Cultural Environment Movement was launched by media scholar and critic George Gerbner in 1996, "to raise awareness of why media 'ecologies of mind' matter" (Burns 2001). The Platform for the Democratization of Communication was "a group of NGOs formed in London in November 1996, whose adherents included groups such as the World Association of Community Radio Broadcasters (AMARC), the Association for Progressive Communication (APC), and the World Association for Christian Communication (WACC)" (Raboy 2004b, 95).

14   See Shade 2004 for an overview of various communication rights platforms.

15   Letter from Rev. Carlos A. Valle, secretary general of the WACC, quoted in Raboy 2004b. A copy of the letter is contained in the author's personal archives.

16   In the interest of transparency, it should be pointed out that Marc Raboy was a founding member of the CRIS campaign and Jeremy Shtern has been involved with various CRIS discussions through in-person meetings and online listservs and the like since 2003.

17   This perspective is developed substantially in Chapter 2.

CHAPTER 2: IMPLEMENTING COMMUNICATION RIGHTS

1   The International Institute for Communications was at this time called the International Broadcast Institute. See chapter 2, n. 6.

2   Later in this chapter, I outline exactly why I describe the World Summit on the Information Society (WSIS) as "compromised."

3   For a more complete discussion of the differences, see Fisher 1982 at s. 8, "The Individual in Society" (23-25).

4   The first International Telecommunication Union (ITU) brochure introducing the WSIS was typical: "The modern world is undergoing a fundamental transformation as the industrial society that marked the 20th century rapidly gives way to the information society of the 21st century. This dynamic promises a fundamental change in all aspects of our lives, including knowledge dissemination, social interaction, economic and business practices, political engagement, media, education, health, leisure and entertainment. We are indeed in the midst of a revolution, perhaps the greatest that humanity has ever experienced" (UNESCO 2002).

5   In its final position, ARTICLE 19 (2003) describes the right to communicate as "an umbrella term, encompassing within it a group of related, existing rights. This means that any elaboration of the right to communicate must take place within the framework of existing rights." ARTICLE 19's Law Programme director, Toby Mendel, notes why it is important to retain the right to communicate as a distinct concept. First, the rights it brings together "cumulatively, are more than the sum of their parts." And second, it is a "powerful organising theme for aspects of existing rights ... which ... are often given little priority" (5-6).

6   It is worth noting, however, that the European Commission and the former secretary-general of the ITU both drew attention of the right to communicate during this period. In a statement issued on the eve of the WSIS, UN Secretary-General Kofi Annan stated that "millions of people in the poorest countries are still excluded from the 'right to communicate,' increasingly seen as a fundamental human right" (United Nations 2003). And the European Commission noted: "The Summit should reinforce the right to communicate and to access information and knowledge" (17).

7   This process is documented in Ó Siochrú 2004a.

8   Paragraph 4 of the WSIS declaration (ITU 2003b) as quoted earlier is remarkably similar to the following statement of the UNESCO Right to Communicate Working Group taken from a meeting held in Ottawa in September 1980: "Communi-

cation is a fundamental social process which enables individuals and communities to exchange information and opinions. It is a basic human need and the foundation of all social organization" (quoted in Fisher 1982, 38).

9   Personal communication between the author and the chair of the committee.

10 See CRIS 2005a, 8-10.

11 For example, Jürgen Habermas, it might be argued, bases much of his philosophy on just such an underlying need, and his work would be broadly coherent with the notion of a right to communicate. Even as D'Arcy was developing his ideas, Habermas was working on the notion of "communicative competence" as a central part of his philosophy (Habermas 1970) that culminated with his theory of communicative action a decade later. And the transformational grammar of Noam Chomsky, which he first devised in the 1950s and which brought him fame long before his political writings, offered evidence of an innate capacity to generate language, at the very least underlining the central and critical impulse that communication represents for humans.

12 *Universal Declaration of Human Rights* (http://www.un.org/en/documents/udhr/); *International Covenant on Civil and Political Rights* (http://www2.ohchr.org/english/law/ccpr.htm); *International Covenant on Economic, Social and Cultural Rights* (http://www2.ohchr.org/english/law/cescr.htm); as well as *Optional Protocol to the International Covenant on Civil and Political Rights* (http://www2.ohchr.org/english/law/ccpr-one.htm) and *Second Optional Protocol to the International Covenant on Civil and Political Rights, Aiming at the Abolition of the Death Penalty* (http://www2.ohchr.org/english/law/ccpr-death.htm).

13 The CRIS campaign's final two-page WSIS statement, pointing to its future direction, mentioned "social justice" no less than six times, and "human rights" five times, usually in the same sentence. For example, "a creative cycle of democratic, participative, inclusive communication in society, between people and across all media, underpins all human rights and invigorates the struggle for social justice"; "CRIS thus aspires to work in close collaboration with, and as part of, the wider movement struggling for social justice and human rights globally" (CRIS 2005b).

14 See Buckley et al. 2008, especially ch. 1, where the right to communicate is raised several times. It should be noted that the author of this chapter is one of the co-authors of that book.

15 See http://www.communicationforsocialchange.org/.

16 Keck and Sikkink (1998) offer a useful analysis of such factors, focusing on "framing" as the central concept, and it has been applied to communication rights in Ó Siochrú 2005a.

17 Although when it does, it can be devastating. A well-documented case of the direct implication of media in a huge death toll is that of Radio Mille Collines, which, during the 1994 Rwanda massacres, broadcast not just hate messages but also specific information to abet ongoing genocide (cf. Dallaire 2005). But the

prowar positions adopted by most US mainstream print and television media leading up to the invasion of Iraq in 2003, which helped create an environment where invasion became acceptable and even inevitable, can in some respects be seen as equally culpable in the death of innocent people. Apart from the fact that the blood was spilled on foreign soil, a main difference in perception is that the connection between media activities and the killing was not nearly as direct. In addition to this distance, the mediation of the messages through US foreign policy as well as through contrasting motivations – the media were acting to maximize revenues, not stir up hatred – effectively allows them to evade responsibility.

18 A strong case can be made that many threats to the social communication cycle and communication rights today derive from an interrelated set of global dynamics focusing on the commercialization of communication and media at a global level, and that any solution must also be similarly interconnected and comprehensive (see Ó Siochrú 2005b).

19 Ó Siochrú (2005a) uses the terms "unifying frame" and "sub-frames" or "thematic frames" for the relationship between communication rights and more specific communication issues.

CHAPTER 3: THE HORIZONTAL VIEW

1 *Charter* rights in Canada are enforced through an additional track which will not substantively be addressed in this volume. The Canadian Human Rights Commission is empowered by the *Human Rights Act* "to investigate and try to settle complaints of discrimination in employment and in the provision of services within federal jurisdiction" (see http://www.chrc-ccdp.ca/about/default-en.asp). The Commission refers cases to the Canadian Human Rights Tribunal, which investigates and adjudicates accusations of discrimination. Given its relatively narrow mandate, the work of this Act-Commission-Tribunal nexus does not, for the most part, address communication rights issues. The notable exception is Article 13 of the *Human Rights Act*, which forbids the communication through telecommunication or Internet undertakings of "any matter that is likely to expose a person or persons to hatred or contempt by reason of the fact that person or those persons are identifiable on the basis of a prohibited ground of discrimination" (at 13 (1)). Enforcement of these particular restrictions on mediated hate speech falls under the jurisdiction of the *Human Rights Act* because such services are argued to fall "within the legislative authority of Parliament" (at 13 (1)) and comprise "services within the federal jurisdiction." Yet, the tenuous nature of this interpretation is evident through the subsequent clarification that the *Human Rights Act* "does not apply in respect of a matter that is communicated in whole or in part by means of the facilities of a broadcasting undertaking" (at 13 (2)). Furthermore, while a series of cases nominally relevant to communication rights have appeared before the Human Rights Tribunal, in particular around issues of Internet hate speech, a

recent report commissioned by the Human Rights Commission itself and written by prominent Canadian free speech scholar Richard Moon (2008) recommended that section 13 be repealed so that enforcement of hate speech law can be left to more suitable institutional frameworks. In addition, in considering the most recent section 13 case referred to it, the Canadian Human Rights Tribunal determined that section 13 violates *Charter* right 2(b) and simply refused to apply it (see *Warman v. Lemire*). Thus, whatever role the Canadian Human Rights Act/Commission/ Tribunal has played in regard to regulating communication in Canada is presently in retreat and reflection on its future at this point would be entirely speculative.

2   *Canadian Charter of Rights and Freedoms*, Part I of the *Constitution Act, 1982*, being Schedule B to the *Canada Act 1982* (U.K.), 1982, c. 11 (http://laws.justice.gc.ca/ en/charter/).

3   *R. v. Zundel*, [1992] 2 S.C.R. 731 (http://scc.lexum.umontreal.ca/en/1992/1992rcs2- 731/1992rcs2-731.html); *Ross v. New Brunswick School District No. 15*, [1996] 1 S.C.R. 825 (http://scc.lexum.umontreal.ca/en/1996/1996rcs1-825/1996rcs1-825. html).

4   *R.W.D.S.U., Local 558 v. Pepsi-Cola Canada Beverages (West) Ltd.*, [2002] 1 S.C.R. 156, 2002 SCC 8 (http://scc.lexum.umontreal.ca/en/2002/2002scc8/2002scc8. html).

5   This discussion of the *Adbusters* case, *infra* note 7, draws on research by Normand Landry (see also Landry 2006).

6   *Canada Elections Act*, S.C. 2000, c. 9 (http://laws.justice.gc.ca/en/ShowTdm/cs/ E-2.01//20090629/en).

7   *Adbusters Media Foundation v. Canadian Broadcasting Corporation*, 2008 BCSC 71 (http://www.courts.gov.bc.ca/jdb-txt/sc/08/00/2008bcsc0071.htm).

8   *Adbusters Media Foundation v. Canadian Broadcasting Corp.*, 1995 B.C.J. No. 2325 (S.C.) (http://www.courts.gov.bc.ca/jdb-txt/sc/95/15/s95-1528.htm).

9   *McKinney v. University of Guelph*, [1990] 3 S.C.R. 229 (http://scc.lexum.umontreal. ca/en/1990/1990rcs3-229/1990rcs3-229.html).

10 The *Adbusters* case is not over, however. In a decision released on 3 April 2009, the Court of Appeal for British Columbia determined that the judge in the 2008 case erred in assuming that he was bound by the 1995 ruling to dismiss the case based on the "government policy theory." Justice Donald determined that "buried in the submissions below is the argument, now articulated with clarity, that the broadcasters have been given the power to control expression in a public space and, regardless whether the broadcasters are public or private, the fact that they can decide who can exercise freedom of expression in a public space makes the *Charter* applicable to them" (paragraph 21). In concluding that "such questions can be addressed in due course" (paragraph 24) and that "it cannot be considered to be plain and obvious that ... the [Adbusters] action is bound to fail" (paragraph

25), Justice Donald granted Adbusters' appeal of the 2008 ruling (*Adbusters Media Foundation v. Canadian Broadcasting Corporation*, 2009 BCCA 148 [http://adbusters. org/files/pdf/adbusters_courtappeal_20090403.pdf]).

11 Adbusters' inability to advertise in the Canadian media can be contrasted with media entrepreneur Jim Shaw's ability to do the same. As part of a very public attempt to get out from under regulatory obligations that forced his highly profitable cable empire (Shaw Communications) to pay into the Canadian Television Fund (CTF), Shaw's personal statements were covered throughout the mainstream Canadian media as news (cf. Zerbisias 2007). In addition, Shaw Communications was able to run a series of ads in newspapers around the country attacking the CTF and proactively mitigating any public relations hit that Shaw might take by refusing to pay for Canadian television production by framing the issue in the language of corporate governance (see Shaw Communications n.d.). While the message of Adbusters' issue advertising might be detrimental to the interests of media ownership in Canada, Jim Shaw's issue advertising *is* the message of media ownership in Canada. The fact that the latter is disseminated through the Canadian media and the former is not is highly problematic for democratic communication in this country.

12 For the portions of the amendment discussed here, see Canada 2007a (at Section 120). These amendments refer to the *Canada Income Tax Act*, R.S. 1985, c. 1 (5th Supp.) (http://laws.justice.gc.ca/en/I-3.3/).

13 Director David Cronenberg told the Senate Standing Committee on Banking, Trade and Commerce on 14 May 2008 how Bill C-10 would induce self-censorship among funding-dependent Canadian filmmakers: "You cannot put a bank in the position of judging a project in terms of the Criminal Code, morality, ethics or public policy. That is not their business. It is much easier and safer for them, and it makes sense for them, to simply gracefully withdraw from the entire process ... what happens is that censorship becomes internalized, and artists begin to censor themselves out of fear" (Canada 2008d).

14 When the October 2008 Canadian federal election was called, Bill C-10 had been passed by the House of Commons but was still awaiting third and final reading and approval in the Senate. The Senate Standing Committee on Banking, Trade and Commerce hearings on the bill concluded in June 2008 but the committee had yet to produce its report by the time the election was called. Although the Harper Conservatives were re-elected to another minority government in the fall of 2008, they lost some ground during the campaign, in part due to backlash against the dismissive attitude that they exhibited in announcing a slate of proposed cuts to funding for arts and culture (see Hébert 2008). As of summer 2009, the committee had not yet produced its report on Bill C-10, and no other planned parliamentary activity on the bill was imminent. What remains to be seen is whether changing governmental priorities will mean that Bill C-10 has effectively

died or whether the Harper government is merely waiting until it has accumulated the necessary political capital to proceed with this sort of measure.

15 *CKOY Ltd. v. R.*, [1979] 1 S.C.R. 2 (http://scc.lexum.umontreal.ca/en/1978/1979rcs1-2/1979rcs1-2.html).

16 *Security of Information Act*, R.S.C. 1985, c. O-5 (http://laws.justice.gc.ca/en/showtdm/cs/O-5).

17 Paragraph 4 of the *Access to Information Act*, R.S.C., 1985, c. A-1 (http://laws.justice.gc.ca/en/showtdm/cs/A-1) reads: "(1) Subject to this Act, but notwithstanding any other Act of Parliament, every person who is (a) a Canadian citizen, or (b) a permanent resident within the meaning of subsection 2(1) of the Immigration and Refugee Protection Act, has a right to and shall, on request, be given access to any record under the control of a government institution."

18 *Federal Accountability Act*, S.C. 2006, c. 9 (http://laws.justice.gc.ca/en/showtdm/cs/F-5.5).

19 Bloc Québécois MP Carole Lavallée called the registry "a precious tool for democracy." New Democratic Party leader Jack Layton's perspective was that "if you boil it down, it's because the Conservatives don't trust Canadians" (quoted in CBC News 2008e).

20 Section 3(1)(b) of the *Broadcasting Act*, S.C. 1991, c. 11 (http://laws.justice.gc.ca/en/showtdm/cs/B-9.01), declares: "The Canadian broadcasting system, operating primarily in the English and French languages and comprising public, private and community elements, makes use of radio frequencies that are public property and provides, through its programming, a public service."

21 Section 3(1)(m) of the *Broadcasting Act* declares that CBC programming should:

  (ii) reflect Canada and its regions to national and regional audiences, while serving the special needs of those regions,

  (iii) actively contribute to the flow and exchange of cultural expression.

22 Section 3(1)(r) of the *Broadcasting Act* declares that alternative programming services should:

  (i) be innovative and be complementary to the programming provided for mass audiences,

  (ii) cater to tastes and interests not adequately provided for by the programming provided for mass audiences, and include programming devoted to culture and the arts.

23 *Canadian Multiculturalism Act*, R.S.C. 1985, c. 24 (4th Supp.) (http://laws.justice.gc.ca/en/showtdm/cs/C-18.7).

24 Section 3(1)(d)(iii) of the *Broadcasting Act* declares that the Canadian broadcasting system should, "through its programming and the employment opportunities arising out of its operations, serve the needs and interests, and reflect the circumstances

and aspirations, of Canadian men, women and children, including equal rights, the linguistic duality and multicultural and multiracial nature of Canadian society and the special place of aboriginal peoples within that society." Section 3(1)(i) states that the programming should:

    (i)   be varied and comprehensive, providing a balance of information, enlightenment and entertainment for men, women and children of all ages, interests and tastes,

    (ii) be drawn from local, regional, national and international sources.

25   Section 3(1)(o) of the *Broadcasting Act* states that "programming that reflects the Aboriginal cultures of Canada should be provided within the Canadian broadcasting system as resources become available for the purpose."

26   CanWest Global Communications owns the *National Post* newspaper and the Global Television Network, and CTVglobemedia owns the *Globe and Mail* and the Canadian Television Network (CTV).

27   Although the Canadian Radio-television and Telecommunications Commission (CRTC) created "developmental" licences in recent years to help community broadcasters begin operating at low power with limited resources, these stations have not been granted "protected status." This means that a commercial broadcaster can effectively be granted a licence that would knock the community station off the air before the community station could fully develop its operations and raise the funds required for the power increase necessary to stake a claim to its dial position and gain protected status. Such is the situation faced today by CJAI on Amherst Island, BC.

28   For the purposes of the Canadian Internet Usage Survey, Statistics Canada defines an "Internet user" as "someone who used the Internet from any location for personal non-business reasons in the 12 months preceding the survey" (Statistics Canada 2008).

29   The CBC archive does exist and is expanding, but it is by no means complete. There is no other television archive in Canada. For years, the only archive of the nightly news was published by the conservative think tank the Fraser Institute, in its publication *On Balance*. Much of this record was used to criticize the work of the CBC, in line with the guiding philosophy of the Fraser Institute that broadcasting should be primarily the domain of the private sector. *On Balance* has ceased publication. While the National Film Board has recently started putting up animated shorts on its website for free non-commercial access (http://www.nfb.ca/animation/objanim/en/films/), and has created an iPhone application that streams NFB films free of charge (http://www.nfb.ca/free-downloads/nfb-iphone-app/), in general it charges very high fees for use of its footage, as does the CBC.

30   Or, in the Creative Commons terminology, "open content" (see http://www.creativecommons.org or http://www.creativecommons.ca).

31 *Digital Millennium Copyright Act,* Pub. L. No. 105-304, 112 Stat. 2860 (1998) (http://www.copyright.gov/legislation/dmca.pdf).

32 *Charter,* s. 15(1) declares: "Every individual is equal before and under the law and has the right to the equal protection and equal benefit of the law without discrimination and, in particular, without discrimination based on race, national or ethnic origin, colour, religion, sex, age or mental or physical disability."

33 *Universal Declaration of Human Rights* (http://www.un.org/en/documents/udhr/); *International Covenant on Civil and Political Rights* (http://www2.ohchr.org/english/law/ccpr.htm), art. 17 declares: "No one shall be subjected to arbitrary ... attacks upon his honour and reputation. Everyone has the right to the protection of the law against such interference or attacks." Although not treated by the federal *Charter,* s. 4 of the Quebec *Charter of Human Rights and Freedoms,* R.S.Q. c. C-12 (http://www.cdpdj.qc.ca/en/commun/docs/charter.pdf) declares: "Every person has a right to the safeguard of his dignity, honour and reputation."

34 Various communication rights implications of the Arar case are discussed in greater detail in Chapters 4 and 7.

35 *Chiasson v. Fillion,* [2005] R.J.Q. 1066 (S.C.) (http://www.jugements.qc.ca/php/).

36 "Everyone has the right to life, liberty and security of the person and the right not to be deprived thereof except in accordance with the principles of fundamental justice."

37 "Everyone has the right to be secure against unreasonable search or seizure."

38 *R. v. Duarte,* [1990] 1 S.C.R. 30 (http://scc.lexum.umontreal.ca/en/1990/1990rcs1-30/1990rcs1-30.html).

39 *Privacy Act,* R.S. 1985, c. P-21 (http://laws.justice.gc.ca/en/showtdm/cs/P-21).

40 *Personal Information Protection and Electronic Documents Act,* S.C. 2000, c. 5 (http://laws.justice.gc.ca/en/showtdm/cs/P-8.6).

41 *Telecommunications Act,* S.C. 1993, c. 38 (http://laws.justice.gc.ca/en/showtdm/cs/T-3.4).

42 Section 16(1) of the *Charter* states: "English and French are the official languages of Canada and have equality of status and equal rights and privileges as to their use in all institutions of the Parliament and government of Canada." This is further elaborated through the right to translation of legal proceedings and to use either official language in legal proceedings (ss. 14 and 19(1)); the right to use either official language in proceedings of Parliament (s. 17(1)) as well as to communicate with and receive information from federal institutions in the official language of your choice (ss. 18(1) and 20(1)), and a series of qualified guarantees about the right to receive public education in both languages (s. 23). There are also a series of sections related specifically to New Brunswick, Canada's only officially bilingual province (ss. 16.1.1, 16.1.2, 16.2, 17.2, 18.2, 19.2, 20.2).

43 As this book was going to press, the CRTC had approved an application for distribution in Canada of the English-language service of Al Jazeera, Al Jazeera English (see Dixon 2009).

44   Section 18(1) of the *Broadcasting Act* states:

Except where otherwise provided, the Commission shall hold a public hearing in connection with:

(a)   the issue of a licence, other than a licence to carry on a temporary network
operation;

(b)   the suspension or revocation of a licence;

(c)   the establishing of any performance objectives for the purposes of paragraph 11(2)(b); and

(d)   the making of an order under subsection 12(2).

45   For example, frustration with the lack of real influence that they were able to
exert through the Telecommunications Policy Review Panel consultation process
led a coalition of community groups, non-governmental organizations, and civil
society organizations to hold an "alternative telecommunications policy forum"
in Ottawa in 2006 under the aegis of the Canadian Research Alliance for Community Innovation and Networking (http://www3.fis.utoronto.ca/research /iprp/
cracin/alttelecompolicyforum.ca/). Similarly, the Canadian Internet Policy and
Public Interest Clinic conducted an unofficial public consultation on the issue of
lawful access by compiling civil society responses and critiques on its website
(http://www.cippic.ca/en/projects-cases/lawful-access/).

46   Clement et al. (2001) wrote about this in the context of early ICT policy, and
Barney (2004 and 2005) argues that there is a "democratic deficit in Canadian ICT
policy and regulation."

CHAPTER 4: MEDIA

The author acknowledges contributions to this chapter from Geneviève Bonin,
Normand Landry, Evan Light, Aysha Mawani, and Gregory Taylor.

1   "Congress shall make no law respecting an establishment of religion, or prohibiting
the free exercise thereof; or abridging the freedom of speech, or of the press; or
the right of the people peaceably to assemble, and to petition the government for
a redress of grievances" ("Bill of Rights," http://www.archives.gov/exhibits/charters/
bill_of_rights.html). The US Supreme Court has consistently upheld the First
Amendment rights of the US press (Goodale 1997).

2   *War Measures Act*, S.C. 1914, c. 2 (http://www.cefresearch.com/matrix/Utilities/
Legal%20Documents/Acts/wma.htm).

3   *Emergencies Act*, R.S.C. 1985, c. 22 (4th Supp.) (http://laws.justice.gc.ca/en/
showtdm/cs/E-4.5).

4   *Canadian Charter of Rights and Freedoms,* Part I of the *Constitution Act, 1982,* being
Schedule B to the *Canada Act 1982* (U.K.), 1982, c. 11 (http://laws.justice.gc.ca/en/
charter/).

5   This discussion draws on research conducted for Raboy and Abramson 2005.
6   Bill 9, *An Act to Ensure the Publication of Accurate News and Information*, Legislature
    of Alberta, 1937 (3rd Session) (http://en.wikisource.org/wiki/Accurate_News_
    and_Information_Act). *Reference Re Alberta Statutes – The Bank Taxation Act; The
    Credit of Alberta Regulation Act; and the Accurate News and Information Act*, [1938]
    S.C.R. 100 (http://csc.lexum.umontreal.ca/en/1938/1938rcs0-100/1938rcs0-100.
    html).
7   See, for example, the so-called padlock case of *Switzman v. Elbing and A.G. of
    Quebec*, [1957] S.C.R. 285 (http://scc.lexum.umontreal.ca/en/1957/1957rcs0-285/
    1957rcs0-285.html), particularly Justice Rand's linkage of freedom of expression
    with "government by the free public opinion of an open society."
8   *Canadian Bill of Rights*, S.C. 1960, c. 44 (http://laws.justice.gc.ca/en/showtdm/
    cs/C-12.3).
9   For instance, the Quebec *Charter of Human Rights and Freedoms*, R.S.Q. c. C-12
    (http://www.cdpdj.qc.ca/en/commun/docs/charter.pdf) was first adopted by
    Quebec's National Assembly (provincial parliament) in 1975.
10 *O'Neill v. Canada (Attorney General)*, 2006 CanLII 35004 (ON S.C.) (http://www.
    canlii.org/en/on/onsc/doc/2006/2006canlii35004/2006canlii35004.html).
11 *Security of Information Act*, R.S.C. 1985, c. O-5 (http://laws.justice.gc.ca/en/
    showtdm/cs/O-5).
12 See *St. Elizabeth Home Society v. Hamilton (City)*, 2008 ONCA 182 (CanLII) (http://
    www.canlii.org/en/on/onca/doc/2008/2008onca182/2008onca182.html).
13 As this book went to press, a private member's bill presented by Bloc Québécois
    MP Serge Ménard was before the House of Commons. Bill C-426 would amend
    the *Canada Evidence Act* to restrict when a court can order a journalist to name a
    source and to require judges to impose strict conditions on any search warrant
    issued to seize a journalist's notes or other documents. The bill passed second
    reading on 28 November 2007, and the Committee Report of the Justice and Hu-
    man Rights Committee was delivered on 30 April 2008. The progress of the bill
    seems to have stalled, but if adopted, it would become Canada's first law to protect
    journalistic sources (see Canada 2007c).
14 *Universal Declaration of Human Rights* (http://www.un.org/en/documents/udhr/).
15 With one exception: in 1982, the Canadian Radio-television and Communica-
    tions Commission (CRTC) was instructed by a directive from the federal govern-
    ment to refuse applications for broadcast licences from daily newspaper owners
    in the same market. This measure was instituted by the Trudeau government
    because of concerns about the extent of the Irving media monopoly in New
    Brunswick. It was rescinded by the Mulroney government two years later.
16 TVA is the largest private, French-language television network in Canada. The
    name TVA is not an acronym. It refers to studio "A" of the network's production
    facilities.

17   Including the takeover by CTVglobemedia of CHUM (with the exception of CHUM CityTV stations, which were sold to Rogers) and Astral Media's takeover of Standard Broadcasting to make it Canada's largest radio station owner.

18   *Broadcasting Act*, S.C. 1991, c. 11 (http://laws.justice.gc.ca/en/showtdm/cs/B-9.01).

19   This section draws on research conducted for a report to the Canadian Department of Justice in the appeal of Genex Communications Inc. regarding the CRTC decision not to renew the licence of radio station CHOI-FM (see Raboy 2004a).

20   Obviously, this analysis does not take into account the hierarchical differentiation of broadcasting services that comes with subscriber-based delivery systems. These present a separate set of issues.

21   Put another way, *why* should we regulate broadcasting? Salter and Anderson (1985, 10) provided a simple answer to this question when they wrote that "the social fabric of Canada is indeed affected by the content of programs."

22   *Genex Communications v. Canada (Attorney General)*, 2005 FCA 283 (CanLII) (http://www.canlii.org/en/ca/fca/doc/2005/2005fca283/2005fca283.html).

23   See Raboy 1995a, 1995b.

24   I hope readers will agree that the risk of revisiting "old" data here is far outweighed by the freshness of the rich insights that these data still provide. Furthermore, I know of no more recent research that has approached the issues in this way (see Proulx and Raboy 2003). This research was part of a larger project funded by the Social Sciences and Humanities Research Council of Canada (SSHRC, 1995-98) and Quebec's Fonds pour la formation des chercheurs et l'aide à la recherche (FCAR, 1998-2001).

25   The sample of participants in this study consisted of a retired feminist organizer; a former political aide to a provincial government minister; an activist Catholic theologian; an information officer for a trade union federation; a social worker in an inner-city community centre; a biomedical engineer and supporter of Amnesty International; the head of a lobby group on race relations; an opposition city councillor; the director of communications for a large metropolitan hospital; a community organizer working with tenants' groups; a student member of a government committee on constitutional reform; a Mohawk elder; an active member of several ethnocultural organizations; an organizer with a federation of regional community groups; and a student active in local economic development.

26   As this book was going to press, the precarious link between stable funding for public broadcasting and regional programming was receiving a great deal of attention. The CBC had recently announced plans to scale back regional and original programming and eliminate more than 800 jobs in response to a collapse in the media advertising market linked to the "global economic crisis" of 2008-09 and the Harper government had refused to provide bridge funding (see Bradshaw 2009).

27   The lack of local programming, in particular the "Montrealisation" of French-language content on Radio-Canada, was discussed at length in the Standing

Committee on Canadian Heritage's most recent report on the CBC, submitted in early 2008. Two of its recommendations dealt specifically with this subject: "Recommendation 1.5: The Committee considers that CBC/Radio-Canada should increase the number of programmes that reflect all regions of Canada, including prime-time programming"; and "Recommendation 1.6: The Committee recommends an increase in the variety, drama, news, public affairs and documentary programming produced by the regional CBC/Radio-Canada stations and independent producers" (see Canada 2008c).

28 The problems of performance measurement and reporting within the CBC have been noted by the Auditor General of Canada (see Canada 2005c).

29 This section is based on research by Aysha Mawani.

30 *Canadian Multiculturalism Act*, R.S.C. 1985, c. 24 (4th Supp.) (http://laws.justice. gc.ca/en/showtdm/cs/C-18.7).

31 This section is based on the contribution of Evan Light.

32 In a situation similar to that faced by CJAI, multiple companies applied for a commercial licence that would mortally interfere with the low-power signal of CFMH. CFMH negotiated for one of these companies to finance its power upgrade (and complementary licence upgrade to protected status) and opposed all other applications.

CHAPTER 5: ACCESS

1 The blog is called "Community ICT" and describes itself as being "about Community Information and Communication Technologies FOR communities." The quotes that follow are all taken from a discussion that can be found at http://ict-cap.blogspot.com/search/label/CUTS%20to%20CAP.

2 *Communications Act of 1934*, Pub. L. No. 416, 48 Stat. 1064 (1934) (http://www. fcc.gov/Reports/1934new.pdf).

3 *Telecommunications Act of 1996*, Pub. L. No. 104-104, 110 Stat. 56 (1996) (http:// www.fcc.gov/Reports/tcom1996.pdf).

4 Vanda Rideout (2003, 5) further argues that the neoliberal telecommunications policy model "occurred in the context of a more inclusive process of continentalism. Aspects of this process include a competitive market in telecommunication services; the privatization of federal and provincial publicly owned telecommunications utilities, satellite operations, and international networks; and neo-regulation, which allows for very little public oversight of telecommunications service activity, relying instead on market regulations"; and William Birdsall (2000) contends that the current liberal public philosophy in North America prohibits the adoption of socially responsible policy that will curb disparities in access to Information and Communication Technologies (ICTs) in Canada.

5 *Telecommunications Act*, S.C. 1993, c. 38 (http://laws.justice.gc.ca/en/showtdm/ cs/T-3.4).

6   *Vancouver Regional FreeNet Assn. v. Canada (Minister of National Revenue – M.N.R.)*, [1996] F.C.J. No. 914 (http://www2.vcn.bc.ca/fullText).

7   Examples include: critical perspectives on the Internet and schools (see Moll and Robertson 2001; Looker and Thiessen 2003; and Shade and Dechief 2004) and Internet policy for postsecondary education (see Lewis et al. 2001; Abrami et al. 2006); assessments of e-learning initiatives and the impact of the Internet on professors' quality of teaching and research (see Menzies and Newson 2007); gendered perspectives on access and the Internet (see Crow and Longford 2000; Fritz 2004; Kennedy et al. 2003; Shade and Crow 2004); and overviews of youth-related digital divide issues (see Media Awareness Network 2004; for a survey of Canadian research, see Shade et al. 2005).

8   *General Agreement on Trade in Services* (http://www.wto.org/english/docs_e/legal_e/26-gats_01_e.htm).

9   Ministry of Foreign Affairs of Japan (http://www.mofa.go.jp/policy/economy/summit/2000/documents/charter.html).

10   See, for example: conceptual/philosophical treatments (Barney 2005; Dahlgren 2005); critiques from the perspective of grassroots and civil society groups (Mc-Caughey and Ayers 2003; Atton 2004; Castells 2004, especially pt. 2; Kahn and Kellner 2004); critical issues related to e-government (Longford 2004; Roy 2006); Canadian community networking (Moll and Shade 2001b; Rideout 2003; Clement et al. 2004; Cordell and Romanow 2005; Rideout and Reddick 2005); discussion of attempts to reinvigorate rural and urban centres through ICTs (Ramírez et al. 2005; Viseu et al. 2006); consideration of the particular issues facing Aboriginal communities (Alexander 2001; Beaton 2004).

11   See Surman and Reilly 2003 and Crow and Longford 2004 on ICT tools for civil society; Smeltzer and Shade 2003 on online activities leading up to the 2001 Summit of the Americas in Quebec City; and Ron Deibert's Citizen Lab at the University of Toronto (http://www.citizenlab.org).

12   See the Canadian Research Alliance for Community Innovation and Networking (http://www.cracin.ca) and the Alberta SuperNet Research Alliance (http://www.ucalgary.ca/comcul/), both funded by a Social Sciences and Humanities Research Council Initiative on the New Economy Research Alliance.

13   See Communautique (http://www.communautique.qc.ca/projets/archives-projets/plateforme-internet-citoyen.html); and K-Net (http://myknet.org/).

14   For an overview of the survey and biannual summarized reports of its findings, see Statistics Canada 2004, 2006, 2008.

15   To find out more about these initiatives, go to http://www.fred-ezone.com/ for Fred eZone and http://www.ilesansfil.org/tiki-index.php for the bilingual home page of Île sans fil. See also Powell and Shade 2006, Powell's 2008 PhD thesis (Powell 2008), and the Community Wireless Infrastructure Research Project (http://www.cwirp.ca).

16 The Bush administration's 2003 budget plan to eliminate two critical digital opportunity programs (the US Department of Education's Community Technology Centers program and the US Department of Commerce's Technology Opportunities Program) ran contrary to the conclusions of research from the public interest Benton Foundation, which made the case that the digital divide was larger than ever and that community technology investments were successful in lessening these various divides (see Dickard 2002).

17 See BB4US.net (http://www.bb4us.net/id10.html).

18 Denmark leads among all countries. The other leading countries are the Netherlands, Norway, Switzerland, Iceland, South Korea, Sweden, Finland, and Luxembourg. See the Organisation for Economic Co-operation and Development's Broadband Portal (http://www.oecd.org/document/54/0,3343,en_2649_34225_38690102_1_1_1_1,00.html).

19 See "Stop the Throttler" campaign (http://democraticmedia.ca/throttler). CDM changed its name to OpenMedia.ca in October 2009.

20 Save Our Net (http://saveournet.ca).

21 Internet for Everyone campaign (http://www.internetforeveryone.ca).

CHAPTER 6: INTERNET

An early discussion with Bill St. Arnaud of CANARIE helped the author to further the development of an analysis of trends in Internet architectures and applications. Research support and conceptual discussions with Mary Milliken were invaluable.

1 This does not address the issue of whether such expectations are actually held by the public. Evidence suggests they might not be. For example, a Zogby survey in 2007 found divergent expectations of privacy on the Internet between young and older respondents (Advisory Committee to the Congressional Internet Caucus 2007).

2 This was the same year that *Instant World* was published (see Introduction).

3 *Telecommunications Act*, S.C. 1993, c. 38 (http://laws.justice.gc.ca/en/showtdm/cs/T-3.4).

4 *Communications Act of 1934*, Pub. L. No. 416, 48 Stat. 1064 (1934) (http://www.fcc.gov/Reports/1934new.pdf).

5 The Canadian Radio-television and Telecommunications Commission (CRTC) has required wireless telephony companies to implement 9-1-1 on their networks by 1 February 2010.

6 This move by Google is not entirely unexpected. Cringely (2005) has pointed to Google's acquisition of "dark fibre" (i.e., unused fibreoptic cable networks) and its development of mobile data centres as a means of implementing its own Internet – the "Google Internet."

7 *Canadian Charter of Rights and Freedoms*, Part I of the *Constitution Act, 1982*, being Schedule B to the *Canada Act 1982* (U.K.), 1982, c. 11 (http://laws.justice.gc.ca/en/charter/).

8   *Universal Declaration of Human Rights* (http://www.un.org/en/documents/udhr/); *International Covenant on Civil and Political Rights* (http://www2.ohchr.org/english/law/ccpr.htm). On art. 19, see Chapter 1. Article 27 reads:

> (1) Everyone has the right freely to participate in the cultural life of the community, to enjoy the arts and to share in scientific advancement and its benefits.
> (2) Everyone has the right to the protection of the moral and material interests resulting from any scientific, literary or artistic production of which he is the author.

9   http://indiscover.net.

10 http://www.juga.com.

11 Some notable examples of Web 2.0 being used in Canadian communities include:

- *Pep Talk Community Health Resource Mapping Tool.* The University of Toronto Medical School has created a Google Maps mash-up that helps people locate health care facilities by type, medical condition, and postal code (2007) (http://icarus.med.utoronto.ca/mapping/ver0.6/default.asp).
- *Toronto Public Library Finder.* This mash-up site by Greg Smith (2006) shows the geographic locations of libraries as a set of icons on a Google map and provides the street address when the user clicks an icon. Alternatively, a user may select a library by name, in which case its geographic location and street address are shown (http://www.tplfinder.com).
- *Psychiatric Survivors of Ottawa Blog.* This web log sponsored by the Psychiatric Survivors of Ottawa (2007) enables people involved in the mental health system to share knowledge and opinions concerning their health and the care that they are receiving. One can search for blog entries based on key words or the name of a blogger (http://www.psychiatricsurvivors.org/weblog/index.php).

12 Crossing Boundaries National Council (http://www.crossingboundaries.ca).

13 Independent Media Center (http://canada.indymedia.org).

14 Technorati.com (http://www.technorati.com/about).

15 The CRTC defines a Category 4, which is not seen as highly relevant to this chapter. It involves business services provided using Internet Protocol suite-based technologies that operate within private domains, such as a corporate switchboard, or PBX, system.

16 Skype (http://skype.com).

17 Vonage (http://vonage.ca); Primus (http://primus.ca).

18 Just how precarious but crucial the links between VoIP and emergency services can be was tragically illustrated to Canadians in the spring of 2008. The Luck family called 9-1-1 from their home in Calgary after eighteen-month-old Elijah began

having trouble breathing. As subscribers to a category 2 VoIP service, the Lucks were connected not to 9-1-1 emergency services directly but to their VoIP company's contracted call centre in Ontario, whose job it is to relay the message via landline phone to local emergency services. When the Lucks were disconnected in the middle of this call, the call centre staff quickly moved to call 9-1-1 and, not having confirmed the details of the emergency with the Lucks, gave emergency services a billing address in Mississauga, Ontario, that had not been recently updated. The address had not been the Lucks' address or the residence at which they received telephone service for more than two years. Precious minutes were lost while paramedics searched the wrong part of the country in vain. The Lucks eventually gave up waiting and placed a second call to Calgary 9-1-1 from a neighbour's landline, but Elijah Luck died at some point during the thirty excruciating minutes that passed between the initial call and his arrival at the hospital (see Richards 2008).

19 Some of these are articulated in the Telecommunication Policy Review Panel's final report (see Sinclair et al. 2006).

CHAPTER 7: PRIVACY

An earlier version of this chapter was published in *Bulletin of Science, Technology and Society* 28 (2008): 80-91. My thanks to Jennifer Parisi of Concordia University's MA in Media Studies program for her immaculate research support.

1 See Chapter 4.

2 *USA PATRIOT Act (Uniting and Strengthening America by Providing Appropriate Tools Required to Intercept and Obstruct Terrorism Act of 2001)*, Pub. L. No. 107-56, 115 Stat. 272 (2001) (http://thomas.loc.gov/cgi-bin/bdquery/z?d107:HR03162:]).

3 *Universal Declaration of Human Rights* (http://www.un.org/en/documents/udhr/).

4 *International Covenant on Civil and Political Rights* (http://www2.ohchr.org/english/law/ccpr.htm).

5 *Canadian Charter of Rights and Freedoms*, Part I of the *Constitution Act, 1982*, being Schedule B to the *Canada Act 1982* (U.K.), 1982, c. 11 (http://laws.justice.gc.ca/en/charter/).

6 *R. v. Duarte*, [1990] 1 S.C.R. 30 (http://scc.lexum.umontreal.ca/en/1990/1990rcs1-30/1990rcs1-30.html).

7 *Privacy Act*, R.S. 1985, c. P-21 (http://laws.justice.gc.ca/en/showtdm/cs/P-21).

8 *Personal Information Protection and Electronic Documents Act*, S.C. 2000, c. 5 (http://laws.justice.gc.ca/en/showtdm/cs/P-8.6).

9 *Hunter et al. v. Southam Inc.*, [1984] 2 S.C.R. 145 (http://csc.lexum.umontreal.ca/en/1984/1984rcs2-145/1984rcs2-145.html).

10 *Anti-terrorism Act*, S.C. 2001, c. 41 (http://laws.justice.gc.ca/en/showtdm/cs/A-11.7).

11 *Criminal Code*, R.S. 1985, c. C-46 (http://laws.justice.gc.ca/en/showtdm/cs/C-46).

12 *Children's Online Privacy Protection Act of 1998*, Pub. L. No. 105-227, 112 Stat. 2581-728 (http://www.ftc.gov/ogc/coppa1.htm).

13 This refers to "second-generation" web applications, also dubbed the "participative Web." According to the Organisation for Economic Co-operation and Development (OECD 2007c), these are "intelligent web services and new Internet-based software applications that enable users to collaborate and contribute to developing, extending, rating, commenting on and distributing digital content and developing and customising Internet applications." Web 2.0 is defined and discussed in greater detail in Chapter 6.

14 See International Campaign against Mass Surveillance (https://id306.securedata. net/i-cams/Declaration_Eng.html).

15 *Security of Information Act*, R.S.C. 1985, c. O-5 (http://laws.justice.gc.ca/en/ showtdm/cs/O-5).

16 *Canada Evidence Act*, R.S. 1985, c. C-5 (http://laws.justice.gc.ca/en/showtdm/cs/ C-5).

17 *Proceeds of Crime (Money Laundering) and Terrorist Financing Act*, S.C. 2000, c. 17 (http://laws.justice.gc.ca/en/showtdm/cs/P-24.501).

18 *Charities Registration (Security Information) Act*, S.C. 2001, c. 41, s. 113 (http://laws. justice.gc.ca/en/showtdm/cs/C-27.55).

19 *Access to Information Act*, R.S.C. 1985, c. A-1 (http://laws.justice.gc.ca/en/showtdm/ cs/A-1).

20 *Aeronautics Act*, R.S. 1985, c. A-2 (http://laws.justice.gc.ca/en/showtdm/cs/A-2).

21 *Public Safety Act 2002*, S.C. 2004, c. 15 (http://laws.justice.gc.ca/en/showtdm/cs/ P-31.5).

22 *Convention on Cybercrime* (http://conventions.coe.int/Treaty/EN/Treaties/ HTML/185.htm).

23 See http://www.maherarar.ca and Chapter 4 for a discussion of media issues related to the violation of Arar's communication rights during this episode.

CHAPTER 8: COPYRIGHT

Kirsty Roberston provided valuable research assistance, including conducting interviews for this study.

1 For a wide array of such arguments, see *In the Public Interest: The Future of Canadian Copyright Law*, a collection of articles on the subject edited by Geist (2005b).

2 *Théberge v. Galerie d'Art du Petit Champlain inc.*, 2002 SCC 34, S.C.R. 336 (http:// www.canlii.org/en/ca/scc/doc/2002/2002scc34/2002scc34.html).

3 This is a truism of much literary theory; a famous statement is Mikhail Bakhtin's "The word in language is half someone else's" (Bakhtin and Holquist 1981, 293).

4 *Copyright Act*, R.S. 1985, c. C-42 (http://laws.justice.gc.ca/en/showtdm/cs/C-42).

5 See *Hager v. ECW Press Ltd. (T.D.)* (1998), [1999] 2 F.C. 287 (http://www.canlii. org/en/ca/fct/doc/1998/1998canlii9115/1998canlii9115.html). The Copyright Board has also made several recent pronouncements on substantiality (see Canada 2004e, 2006f).

6   Craig Walker, interview with Laura Murray, Kingston, 7 November 2006.

7   Craig Walker, e-mail to Laura Murray, 24 March 2008.

8   *Compagnie Générale des Établissements Michelin-Michelin & Cie v. National Automobile, Aerospace, Transportation and General Workers Union of Canada (CAW-Canada) (T.D.)*, 1996 CanLII 3920 (F.C.) (http://www.canlii.org/en/ca/fct/doc/1996/1996canlii 3920/1996canlii3920.html) [*Michelin*].

9   *Canadian Charter of Rights and Freedoms*, Part I of the *Constitution Act, 1982*, being Schedule B to the *Canada Act 1982* (U.K.), 1982, c. 11 (http://laws.justice.gc.ca/ en/charter/).

10 For a thorough critique of the *Michelin* case, see Bailey 2005; the quotation is from d'Agostino 2008.

11 *CCH Canadian Ltd. v. Law Society of Upper Canada*, [2004] 1 S.C.R. 339 (http://scc. lexum.umontreal.ca/en/2004/2004scc13/2004scc13.html) [*CCH Canadian*].

12 *Society of Composers, Authors and Music Publishers of Canada v. Canadian Assn. of Internet Providers*, [2004] 2 S.C.R. 427 (http://scc.lexum.umontreal.ca/en/2004/ 2004scc45/2004scc45.html).

13 *Copyright Act of 1976*, Pub. L. No. 94-553, 90 Stat. 2541 (1976) (http://www. copyright.gov/title17/).

14 A recent scholarly endorsement of expanded fair dealing is found in de Beer 2009. For voices from organizations and individual citizens, see CAUT 2008, submissions to the government copyright consultation process of summer 2009, documented at http://copyright.econsultation.ca/, and "Tracking the Copyright Consultation Roundtables: Fair Dealing Emerges as Top Issue," http://www.michaelgeist.ca/ content/view/4271/125/.

15 These exceptions are found in ss. 29, 30, 32, and 80 of the *Copyright Act*.

16 See Howard Knopf's testimony before the Standing Committee on Canadian Heritage (Canada 2004b). For one irate consumer response to the levy, see Jade 2007. Another controversial proposed exception is the "educational exception" for Internet use; see Murray 2004 and Trosow 2008 for discussion.

17 Distilled from the *Copyright Act*, ss. 14.1 and 28.2.

18 *Snow v. Eaton Centre Ltd.* (1982), 70 C.P.R. (2d) 105 (Ontario High Court of Justice).

19 *Prise de Parole Inc. v. Guérin éditeur Ltée*, [1996] F.C.J. No. 1427104 FTR 104, 66 C.P.R. (3d) 257, affd. (1996) 206 N.R. 311 (F.C.A.).

20 *World Intellectual Property Organization Copyright Treaty*, 20 December 1996, S. Treaty Doc. No. 105-17 (1997); 36 ILM 65 (1997) (http://www.wipo.int/treaties/en/ip/ wct/trtdocs_wo033.html).

21 *World Intellectual Property Organization Performances and Phonograms Treaty*, 20 December 1996 (http://www.wipo.int/treaties/en/ip/wppt/trtdocs_wo034.html).

22 These included: *Consultation Paper on Digital Copyright Issues* (Canada 2001c); *Supporting Culture and Innovation: Report on the Provisions and Operation of the Copyright Act* (often referred to as the "Section 92 Report") (Canada 2002b); *Status Report*

on *Copyright Reform Submitted to the Standing Committee on Canadian Heritage by the Minister of Canadian Heritage and the Minister of Industry* (Canada 2004g); *Interim Report on Copyright Reform* (often referred to as the "Bulte Report") (Canada 2004d).

23   See, for example, the Canadian Internet Policy and Public Interest Clinic/Public Interest Advocacy Centre (2004) response and the Canadian Federation of Students (2004) membership advisory on the subject.

24   *Digital Millennium Copyright Act*, Pub. L. No. 105-304, 112 Stat. 2860 (1998) (http://www.copyright.gov/legislation/dmca.pdf).

25   The Fair Copyright for Canada Facebook site can be viewed at http://www.facebook.com/group.php?gid=6315846683 (Facebook login required). In addition, and prior to the Facebook site, which dates to December 2007, Canadian websites and blogs centrally dedicated to discussion of copyright issues at present include http://www.digital-copyright.ca, http://www.cippic.ca, http://www.michaelgeist.ca, http://www.faircopyright.ca, http://excesscopyright.blogspot.com/, http://www.xanga.com/publicdomain, and http://www.onlinerights.ca/. The role of the Facebook site in delaying legislation was the second sign that grassroots activism has effects on Parliament: public interest activism played a role in the defeat of MP Sarmite Bulte in 2006 (O'Malley 2007).

26   In the summer of 2009, the Harper government conducted a multifaceted public consultation on copyright, including townhalls and online consultations (see http://copyright.econsultation.ca/).

27   For a study of trends in international negotiations over intellectual property more generally, see Ryan 1998.

28   *Berne Convention for the Protection of Literary and Artistic Works*, 9 September 1886 (1971 Paris revision) (http://www.wipo.int/treaties/en/ip/berne/trtdocs_wo001.html).

29   In addition, World Intellectual Property Organization (WIPO) and these treaties have come under increasing international criticism: the non-governmental organization (NGO) IP Justice has embarked on a WIPO campaign (see http://www.ipjustice.org), and a coalition of NGOs and activists drafted the 2004 *Geneva Declaration on the Future of the World Intellectual Property Organization* (Consumers International et al. 2004) to protest the agenda (see also Boyle 2004).

30   *Agreement on Trade-Related Aspects of Intellectual Property Rights*, Annex 1C of the *Marrakesh Agreement Establishing the World Trade Organization* (http://www.wto.org/english/docs_e/legal_e/27-trips_01_e.htm).

31   *General Agreement on Tariffs and Trade, 1994* (http://www.wto.org/english/docs_e/legal_e/06-gatt_e.htm).

32   *General Agreement on Trade in Services*, 15 April 1994, 1869 UNTS 183 (http://www.wto.org/english/docs_e/legal_e/26-gats_01_e.htm).

33   An example of the effects of US pressure is Bill C-59, an amendment to the *Criminal Code*, R.S. 1985, c. C-46, regarding camcording in movie theatres that was

rushed through Parliament in 2007 (see Canada 2007b). In the face of a massive public relations campaign condemning Canadian piracy (see MacDonald 2007) and a response from Michael Geist (2007d), Justice Minister Rob Nicholson drily noted in February 2007 that Canada's *Copyright Act* already features enforcement provisions for criminal infringement: "I do point out to people that the country is not completely bereft of laws in this area" (as quoted in Tibbetts 2007). Nonetheless, after a visit to Ottawa by California Governor Arnold Schwarzenegger and further relentless pressure, Canada complied with American demands in Bill C-59 (an episode discussed in Michael Geist's YouTube video *The Power of Lobbying*, http://www.youtube.com/watch?v=K3IpXAbi5Dw).

34 Note that the interviews were conducted long before Bill C-61 was introduced.

35 This point came out in numerous interviews conducted for this study, including: Norman Nawrocki, interview with Kirsty Robertson, Montreal, 22 September 2006; Karl Beveridge, interview with Kirsty Robertson, Toronto, 30 September 2006.

36 Susan Belyea, interview with Laura Murray, Kingston, ON, 1 December 2006.

37 Lateef Martin, interview with Kirsty Robertson, Montreal, 10 December 2006.

38 B.H. Yael and Johanna Householder, interview with Kirsty Robertson, 24 November 2006; Victoria Stanton, interview with Kirsty Robertson, Montreal, 13 September 2006.

39 Richard Fung, interview with Kirsty Robertson, Toronto, 27 November 2006.

40 Lateef Martin, interview with Kirsty Robertson, Montreal, 10 December 2006.

41 Norman Nawrocki, interview with Kirsty Robertson, Montreal, 22 September 2006.

42 Jan Allen, interview with Kirsty Robertson, 29 August 2006; Greg Young-Ing, interview with Laura Murray, by phone from Vancouver, 2 November 2006.

43 The website of the Professional Writers Association of Canada contains a great deal of information on these issues; see http://www.pwac.ca. Heather Robertson successfully took the *Globe and Mail* to court to assert her rights; see *Robertson v. Thomson Corp.*, [2006] 2 S.C.R. 363, 2006 SCC 43 (http://scc.lexum.umontreal.ca/en/2006/2006scc43/2006scc43.html).

44 Karl Beveridge, interview with Kirsty Robertson, Toronto, 30 September 2006; Greg Young-Ing, interview with Laura Murray, by phone from Vancouver, 2 November 2006.

45 Matthew Rankin, interview with Kirsty Robertson, by phone from Winnipeg, 18 September 2006.

46 Ibid.

47 B.H. Yael, interview with Kirsty Robertson, Toronto, 24 November 2006.

48 Gordon Huggan and Sarah Joyce, interview with Kirsty Robertson, Toronto, 26 September 2007.

49 Richard Fung, interview with Kirsty Robertson, Toronto, 27 November 2006.

50 Matthew Rankin, interview with Kirsty Robertson, by phone from Winnipeg, 18 September 2006.

51 Kevin McMahon, interview with Laura Murray, Toronto, 16 November 2006.

52 Karl Beveridge, interview with Kirsty Robertson, Toronto, 30 September 2006.

53 Jan Allen, interview with Kirsty Robertson, Kingston, ON, 29 August 2006.

54 Richard Fung, interview with Kirsty Robertson, Toronto, 27 November 2006.

55 Lateef Martin, interview with Kirsty Robertson, Montreal, 10 December 2006.

56 Diana Thorneycroft, interview with Kirsty Robertson, Toronto, 23 September 2006.

57 Susan Belyea, interview with Laura Murray, Kingston, ON, 1 December 2006.

58 Matthew Rankin, interview with Kirsty Robertson, by phone from Winnipeg, 18 September 2006.

59 Johanna Householder, interview with Kirsty Robertson, Toronto, 24 November 2006.

60 Victoria Stanton, interview with Kirsty Robertson, Montreal, 13 September 2006.

61 Kevin McMahon, interview with Laura Murray, Toronto, 16 November 2006.

62 Natasha Geerts, interview with Kirsty Robertson, Montreal, 8 September 2006.

CHAPTER 9: FIXING COMMUNICATION RIGHTS IN CANADA

1 *Broadcasting Act*, S.C. 1991, c. 11 (http://laws.justice.gc.ca/en/showtdm/cs/B-9.01).

2 *Federal Accountability Act*, S.C. 2006, c. 9 (http://laws.justice.gc.ca/en/showtdm/cs/F-5.5).

3 The *Broadcasting Act* (s. 3(1)(d)(iii)) states that the Canadian broadcasting system should, "through its programming and the employment opportunities arising out of its operations, serve the needs and interests, and reflect the circumstances and aspirations, of Canadian men, women and children, including equal rights, the linguistic duality and multicultural and multiracial nature of Canadian society and the special place of aboriginal peoples within that society."

4 The Canadian Radio-television and Telecommunications Commission's (CRTC) approval (2006a) of the sale of Bell Globemedia (including Canada's largest commercial television network, CTV, and one of Canada's two national newspapers, the *Globe and Mail*) to a consortium of other media conglomerates, including Torstar (the parent company of Canada's largest daily newspaper, the *Toronto Star*) was, for instance, contingent (see para. 10) on CTV's maintaining "separate and independent news management and presentation structures that are distinct from those of any newspaper operations" of the new owners. Media mergers are typically approved based on an explicit promise by the parties involved to maintain what the CRTC likes to call "separate newsrooms" within different wings of the same media conglomerates (cf. TQS/SRC conditions in CRTC 2001). It is not clear, beyond cursory glances at organizational hierarchy charts at the time of approval, what, if any, ongoing monitoring is done to ensure that these commitments are met. Nor is it obvious what the test is for ensuring that the editorial position of one property is not influencing that of another or, for that matter, what the threshold of too much influence would have to be in order to result in a finding that the transaction should be voided because the commitments on which its approval was made conditional are not being met.

5   This was the fate, for example, of a recommendation in the 2003 report *Our Cultural Sovereignty* to create a Canadian "broadcasting monitor" within the office of the Auditor General (see Canada 2003b, recommendation 97).

6   For instance, in a series of blog entries from the CRTC Diversity of Voices hearings in 2007, Geneviève Bonin (2007) pointed out that the mainstream media devoted far more coverage to their own interventions than to anyone else's, and Normand Landry (2007) reported that the previously cramped press gallery was entirely empty during the session devoted to the highly critical interventions from community groups and alternative media practitioners. Thus, while mainstream coverage might have reflected a range of viewpoints, that range was considerably narrower than the spectrum of voices that actually appeared at the hearing.

7   For instance, the Canadian Commission for the UN Educational, Scientific, and Cultural Organization was able to bring together numerous communication and media activist groups as well as other civil society organizations with more broadly based social justice concerns for a productive series of discussions leading up to the 2003-05 World Summit on the Information Society (Dugré 2004).

8   *Digital Millennium Copyright Act,* Pub. L. No. 105-304, 112 Stat. 2860 (1998) (http://www.copyright.gov/legislation/dmca.pdf).

9   For instance, the "Documentary Filmmakers' Statement of Best Practices in Fair Use" (Association of Independent Video and Filmmakers et al. n.d.) produced by a coalition of artists and academics to help inform documentary filmmakers working in the United States about copyright issues.

10 Howard Knopf's study (2006) of the legal situation of documentary filmmaking, sponsored by the Documentary Organization of Canada, is exemplary in this regard.

11 The recent publication of *Canadian Copyright: A Citizen's Guide* (Murray and Trosow 2007) is an effort toward this end.

12 With regard to the Internet and online services, the issue is doubly problematic for the realization of communication rights. Consolidated cross-media ownership has the potential not only to reduce content diversity but also, as we discuss in Chapter 5, to diminish competition in service provision.

13 For instance, in response to being asked, during the Diversity of Voices hearing, by CRTC chairman Konrad von Finckenstein whether there was a problem when the same company owned radio stations, television stations, and newspapers in the same local market, the president of the Canadian Association of Broadcasters replied: "No, we frankly see no diversity deficit in the Canadian broadcasting system first and foremost. We see a diversity surplus" (CRTC 2007, 448).

14 The National Film Board (NFB) called for a Canadian national digital strategy in its submission to the CRTC proceeding on the scope of new media broadcasting (NFB 2008), and again in its submission to the Canadian Broadcasting in New Media proceeding itself (NFB 2009). Echoing the call of the NFB, the CRTC (2009, section 74) points to initiatives such as the Digital Britain Review, Digital France 2012, New Zealand's Digital Strategy 2.0, Germany's iD2010, and Australia's

Digital Economy Future Directions to suggest that "several countries have already recognized the value and the importance of a national digital strategy and, as a result, have developed plans for their citizens' and economies' futures that ... send a clear message of the importance of a holistic approach to this environment."

15   Launched in 2006, the Internet Governance Forum (IGF) meets annually under the aegis of the secretary-general of the United Nations. At time of writing, it has met four times, in Athens (2006), Rio de Janeiro (2007), Hyderabad, India (2008), and Sharm el Sheikh, Egypt (2009). The IGF is intended to be a forum for multi-stakeholder dialogue, an institution endowed with the potential for influence and "soft power," not an agent in its own right in the international arena. For more on the IGF, including background information and reports on its proceedings, see http://www.intgovforum.org/cms/.

16   The United Kingdom was one of the first countries to hold a domestic IGF. Held at the Houses of Parliament, sponsored by Nominet UK, the UK IGF aims to "support delivery and communication of Internet Governance best practice and to showcase what could be done by addressing key Internet challenges at a national level" (the Right Honourable Alun Michael, MP, quoted in Holland 2008). Other countries and regional bodies have since convened their own IGFs.

17   The government of France, for example, has created a similar position of special envoy for the information society within its Ministry for Foreign and European Affairs.

18   *Telecommunications Act*, S.C. 1993, c. 38 (http://laws.justice.gc.ca/en/showtdm/cs/T-3.4).

19   *Children's Online Privacy Protection Act of 1998*, Pub. L. No. 105-227, 112 Stat. 2581-728 (http://www.ftc.gov/ogc/coppa1.htm).

20   *USA PATRIOT Act (Uniting and Strengthening America by Providing Appropriate Tools Required to Intercept and Obstruct Terrorism Act of 2001)*, Pub. L. No. 107-56, 115 Stat. 272 (2001) (http://thomas.loc.gov/cgi-bin/bdquery/z?d107:HR03162:]).

21   *Convention on the Protection and Promotion of the Diversity of Cultural Expressions* (http://unesdoc.unesco.org/images/0014/001429/142919e.pdf).

22   The Science Council of Canada's efforts (1971) to control data communication networks (some intra-Canadian traffic was being routed through the US) are an early example of this concern. Even the *Instant World* notion of a Canadian right to communicate was arguably an expression of sovereignty concerns.

23   *Bell ExpressVu Limited Partnership v. Rex*, [2002] 2 S.C.R. 559 case, which was decided by the Supreme Court of Canada exposed mainly domestic and interdependency sovereignty issues concerning the authority of the state to prevent individuals from receiving international satellite communications. Bell ExpressVu applied for an injunction against Richard Rex and his company Can-Am Satellites under s. 9(1)(c) of the *Radiocommunication Act*, R.S. 1985, c. R-2 (http://laws.justice.gc.ca/en/showtdm/cs/R-2), which states: "No person shall: ... (c) decode an encrypted subscription programming signal or encrypted network feed otherwise than under

and in accordance with an authorization from the lawful distributor of the signal or feed." Can-Am Satellites was in the business of providing Canadian customers with the ability to subscribe to US-based satellite services that had not been authorized to enter the Canadian market. Its business model delved into many shades of gray. Can-Am Satellites sold systems to Canadian customers that would enable them to receive and watch programming from US satellite services, and then provided US mailing addresses to Canadian customers to use as fronts because US broadcasters may not knowingly authorize their signals to be decoded by persons located outside the United States. Can-Am argued that only signals originating in Canada are subject to this law and, furthermore, that as there was no lawful distributor of the US signal in Canada, since there was no one actually licensed in Canada for Can-Am to approach about authorizing the decoding of the satellite signal in question, decoding them should not be prohibited. Both the Supreme Court of British Columbia and the majority in the British Columbia Court of Appeal supported this view. The Supreme Court of Canada disagreed, however, and maintained that the prohibition was clear and unambiguous: decoding an encrypted signal is contrary to the act. Thus, eventually the principle of Canadian sovereignty over the satellite signals that are decoded in its territory was maintained. In the process, however, a clear expression of demand for more and different options in programming on the part of Canadian citizens was quashed; an opportunistic entrepreneur was able to bend the rules and exploit gaps in existing policy for its own financial gain; and little progress was made on eradicating the gray zone in which international broadcast signals that are available and in demand in Canada can be legally accessed only after a public gatekeeper sees fit to authorize them.

24 *Privacy Act*, R.S. 1985, c. P-21 (http://laws.justice.gc.ca/en/showtdm/cs/P-21).

25 More generally, the suite of "war on terror" laws enacted in Canada and elsewhere after 9/11 are eroding established rights and undermining efforts to apply human rights to the digital communication environment. The *Arar* case (discussed in Chapters 4 and 7) and the *O'Neill* case (discussed in Chapter 4), for example, raise red flags about the links between issues like freedom of the press and privacy and Canada's security services. Canada's *Anti-terrorism Act*, S.C. 2001, c. 41 (http://laws.justice.gc.ca/en/showtdm/cs/A-11.7) and Lawful Access proposals (Canada 2005b) also need to be more widely debated and considered in terms of their threats to the public interest and the privacy rights of citizens and communities.

26 *Canadian Charter of Rights and Freedoms*, Part I of the *Constitution Act, 1982*, being Schedule B to the *Canada Act 1982* (U.K.), 1982, c. 11 (http://laws.justice.gc.ca/en/charter/).

CHAPTER 10: TOWARD A CANADIAN RIGHT TO COMMUNICATE

1 *Canadian Charter of Rights and Freedoms*, Part I of the *Constitution Act, 1982*, being Schedule B to the *Canada Act 1982* (U.K.), 1982, c. 11 (http://laws.justice.gc.ca/en/charter/).

2 *Adbusters Media Foundation v. Canadian Broadcasting Corp.*, 1995 B.C.J. No. 2325
   (S.C.) (http://www.courts.gov.bc.ca/jdb-txt/sc/95/15/s95-1528.htm); *Adbusters
   Media Foundation v. Canadian Broadcasting Corporation*, 2008 BCSC 71 (http://www.
   courts.gov.bc.ca/jdb-txt/sc/08/00/2008bcsc0071.htm).

3 Mendelsohn cites Yankelovich 1991 in defining this idea of public judgment.

4 The threat of two-tiered health care was also a key issue in the 2000 federal election (see CBC News 2000).

5 Thanks to Bram Dov Abramson for coming up with this concise and straightforward
   formulation for articulating the relationship between *Charter* s. 2(b) and communication policy in Canada (Abramson and Shtern n.d.).

6 In his UNESCO status report, for instance, Desmond Fisher (1982, 28) recognized
   that one precondition for evolving the right to communicate from concept to
   action is for "the state to embody in national law the freedoms embodied in the
   right to communicate."

7 For example: the eighteenth session of the UNESCO General Conference, held in
   1974, passed a resolution that authorized the director-general of UNESCO to
   "study and define the right to communicate" (UNESCO 1974); at the nineteenth
   General Conference of UNESCO in 1976, the final report of the UNESCO director-
   general's working group was submitted with the conclusion that "additional study
   and research on various aspects of the Right to Communicate" was required
   (Richstad and Harms 1977, 126); the MacBride Commission report wrote that
   "in developing what might be called a new era of social rights, we suggest all the
   implications of the right to communicate be further explored" (UNESCO 2004,
   265); the second medium-term plan of UNESCO, outlining activities planned for
   the years 1984-89, called for examining the "possibility of including communication both as a right of the individual and as a collective right, guaranteed to all
   communities and all nations" (UNESCO 1985, 3); at the twenty-second UNESCO
   General Conference in 1983, the director-general of UNESCO himself was "in-
   vited" to study how this could be achieved (see UNESCO 1985, 3); at the twenty-
   third UNESCO General Conference in 1985, *The Right to Communicate: Report of
   the Director-General* was presented; it described the right to communicate as a legal
   construct that was controversial even among its supporters and that would be
   complex to establish in international law. UNESCO never followed up on recommendations for even more study over the years 1986-87 (UNESCO 1985).

8 Jean D'Arcy (1981, 2) himself, for example, stated unproblematically that "for
   society, as for the individual, there is undoubtedly a right to communicate."

9 See, for example, the writing of Hamelink (2003, 2004) and Nordenstreng (1986;
   Traber and Nordenstreng 1992; Padovani and Nordenstreng 2005). Many of the
   scholars and activists involved in the New World Information and Communication
   Order coalesced around the International Association for Media and Communication Research, where issues related to the right to communicate continue to be
   discussed.

10   The fact that the intellectual framework of the communication rights movement has been set primarily by communication scholars and not by human rights thinkers would explain why the individual/collective dichotomy, despite the fact that its impact has been minimized in the human rights literature, remains a focus and obstacle to thinking about communication rights. The effect is that new and younger thinkers – supporters and critics alike – who came to the idea of a right to communicate through the CRIS campaign are uncovering a literature preoccupied with exactly this question.

11   This section draws, in part, on the "Draft Declaration on the Right to Communicate" prepared by Cees Hamelink during the WSIS (see Hamelink 2002).

12   The fact that the governmental decision to deregulate is itself most certainly an act of regulation and tends to precipitate a large-scale government intervention in the market contributes to what Horowitz (1989), in his study of the deregulation of American telecommunications, refers to as "the irony of regulatory reform."

13   The still-unresolved *Adbusters* case, discussed in Chapter 3, could yet result in a significant change to this practice.

14   See Appendix 1.

15   *Convention on the Protection and Promotion of the Diversity of Cultural Expressions* (http://unesdoc.unesco.org/images/0014/001429/142919e.pdf).

APPENDIX 3: STRATEGIC *CHARTER* LITIGATION AND THE RIGHT TO COMMUNICATE IN CANADA

1   *Canadian Charter of Rights and Freedoms*, Part I of the *Constitution Act, 1982*, being Schedule B to the *Canada Act 1982* (U.K.), 1982, c. 11 (http://laws.justice.gc.ca/en/charter/).

2   How exactly this right might be defined, as well as the strategic advisability of framing diverse positions on complex issues together as a right, are matters of some robust debate that has been chronicled and negotiated elsewhere in this book (see Chapters 1, 2, and 10) . This appendix is intended only to give an opinion about the best strategy for achieving the objectives of communication rights activism. As such, I deliberately take no position on either of these questions.

3   *Canadian Bill of Rights*, S.C. 1960, c. 44 (http://laws.justice.gc.ca/en/showtdm/cs/C-12.3).

4   The sole exception was *The Queen v. Drybones*, [1970] S.C.R. 282 (http://scc.lexum.umontreal.ca/en/1969/1970rcs0-282/1970rcs0-282.html), in which the court declared s. 94(b) of the *Indian Act*, R.S. 1985, c. I-5 (http://laws.justice.gc.ca/en/showtdm/cs/I-5) (prohibiting Indians from being intoxicated off a reserve) inoperative for violating the equality guarantee of the *Canadian Bill of Rights.*

5   As was established in the case of *Vriend v. Alberta*, [1998] 1 S.C.R. 493 (http://scc.lexum.umontreal.ca/en/1998/1998rcs1-493/1998rcs1-493.html).

6   The precedent-setting case of *McKinney v. University of Guelph*, [1990] 3 S.C.R. 229 (http://scc.lexum.umontreal.ca/en/1990/1990rcs3-229/1990rcs3-229.html), and

its application to the Canadian media was discussed in Chapters 3 and 10 of this volume. See also *Stoffman v. Vancouver General Hospital*, [1990] 3 S.C.R. 483 (http://scc.lexum.umontreal.ca/en/1990/1990rcs3-483/1990rcs3-483.html).

7 *Universal Declaration of Human Rights* (http://www.un.org/en/documents/udhr/).

8 See, for example, *Canadian Council of Churches v. Canada (Minister of Employment and Immigration)*, [1992] 1 S.C.R. 236 (http://scc.lexum.umontreal.ca/en/1992/1992rcs1-236/1992rcs1-236.html).

9 Ibid.

10 *Rules of Civil Procedure*, R.R.O. 1990, Reg. 194 (http://www.canlii.org/en/on/laws/regu/rro-1990-reg-194/latest/rro-1990-reg-194.html).

11 *Irwin Toy Ltd. v. Quebec (Attorney General)*, [1989] 1 S.C.R. 927 (http://scc.lexum.umontreal.ca/en/1989/1989rcs1-927/1989rcs1-927.html).

12 *R. v. Keegstra*, [1990] 3 S.C.R. 697 (http://scc.lexum.umontreal.ca/en/1990/1990rcs3-697/1990rcs3-697.html).

13 Such a claim could theoretically be possible: in certain circumstances, it might be possible, following *Vriend v. Alberta*, that a government omission was implicated in denying a forum that the government had provided to others. Such a claim would seem more likely to succeed within the context of an equality-based claim, as in *Vriend*, rather than a claim based on freedom of expression.

14 The case of *Adbusters Media Foundation v. Canadian Broadcasting Corporation*, 2008 BCSC 71 (http://www.courts.gov.bc.ca/jdb-txt/sc/08/00/2008bcsc0071.htm), discussed in Chapters 3 and 10 for instance, would clearly have been a poor choice in venue shopping the right to communicate, despite the obvious appeal of its underlying facts to communication rights activists. It was questionable from the start whether the case engaged the *Charter* as described earlier, if not outright clear that it did not.

15 *R. v. Butler*, [1992] 1 S.C.R. 452 (http://scc.lexum.umontreal.ca/en/1992/1992rcs1-452/1992rcs1-452.html).

16 *R. v. Sharpe*, [2001] 1 S.C.R. 45, 2001 SCC 2 (http://scc.lexum.umontreal.ca/en/2001/2001scc2/2001scc2.html).

17 See *Committee for the Commonwealth of Canada v. Canada*, [1991] 1 S.C.R. 139 (http://scc.lexum.umontreal.ca/en/1991/1991rcs1-139/1991rcs1-139.html); *Ramsden v. Peterborough (City)*, [1993] 2 S.C.R. 1084 (http://scc.lexum.umontreal.ca/en/1993/1993rcs2-1084/1993rcs2-1084.html).

18 See *Libman v. Quebec (Attorney General)*, [1997] 3 S.C.R. 569 (http://scc.lexum.umontreal.ca/en/1997/1997rcs3-569/1997rcs3-569.html); *Thomson Newspapers Co. v. Canada (Attorney General)*, [1998] 1 S.C.R. 877 (http://scc.lexum.umontreal.ca/en/1998/1998rcs1-877/1998rcs1-877.html). See also *Harper v. Canada (Attorney General)*, [2004] 1 S.C.R. 827, 2004 SCC 33 (http://scc.lexum.umontreal.ca/en/2004/2004scc33/2004scc33.html), which upheld restrictions on third-party election expenditures (s. 1).

Works Cited

LEGISLATION (CANADA)

Access to Information Act, R.S.C. 1985, c. A-1. Department of Justice Canada, http://laws.justice.gc.ca/en/showtdm/cs/A-1.

Aeronautics Act, R.S. 1985, c. A-2. Department of Justice Canada, http://laws.justice.gc.ca/en/showtdm/cs/A-2.

Anti-terrorism Act, S.C. 2001, c. 41. Department of Justice Canada, http://laws.justice.gc.ca/en/showtdm/cs/A-11.7.

Broadcasting Act, S.C. 1991, c. 11. Department of Justice Canada, http://laws.justice.gc.ca/en/showtdm/cs/B-9.01.

Canada Elections Act, S.C. 2000, c. 9. Department of Justice Canada, http://laws.justice.gc.ca/en/ShowTdm/cs/E-2.01//20090629/en.

Canada Evidence Act, R.S. 1985, c. C-5. Department of Justice Canada, http://laws.justice.gc.ca/en/showtdm/cs/C-5.

Canada Income Tax Act, R.S. 1985, c. 1 (5th Supp.). Department of Justice Canada, http://laws.justice.gc.ca/en/I-3.3/.

Canadian Bill of Rights, S.C. 1960, c. 44. Department of Justice Canada, http://laws.justice.gc.ca/en/showtdm/cs/C-12.3.

Canadian Charter of Rights and Freedoms, Part I of the *Constitution Act, 1982*, being Schedule B to the *Canada Act 1982* (U.K.), 1982, c. 11. Department of Justice Canada, http://laws.justice.gc.ca/en/charter/.

Canadian Human Rights Act, R.S. 1985, c. H-6. Department of Justice Canada, http://laws.justice.gc.ca/en/h-6/index.html.

Canadian Multiculturalism Act, R.S.C. 1985, c. 24 (4th Supp.). Department of Justice Canada, http://laws.justice.gc.ca/en/showtdm/cs/C-18.7.

Charities Registration (Security Information) Act, S.C. 2001, c. 41, s. 113. Department of Justice Canada, http://laws.justice.gc.ca/en/showtdm/cs/C-27.55.

Charter of Human Rights and Freedoms, R.S.Q. c. C-12. La Commission des droits de la personne et des droits de la jeunesse, http://www.cdpdj.qc.ca/en/commun/docs/charter.pdf.

Copyright Act, R.S. 1985, c. C-42. Department of Justice Canada, http://laws.justice.gc.ca/en/showtdm/cs/C-42.

Criminal Code, R.S. 1985, c. C-46. Department of Justice Canada, http://laws.justice. gc.ca/en/showtdm/cs/C-46.

Emergencies Act, R.S.C. 1985, c. 22 (4th Supp.). Department of Justice Canada, http:// laws.justice.gc.ca/en/showtdm/cs/E-4.5.

Federal Accountability Act, S.C. 2006, c. 9. Department of Justice Canada, http://laws. justice.gc.ca/en/showtdm/cs/F-5.5.

Law Commission of Canada Act, S.C. 1996, c. 9. Department of Justice Canada, http:// laws.justice.gc.ca/en/showtdm/cs/L-6.7.

Personal Information Protection and Electronic Documents Act, S.C. 2000, c. 5. Department of Justice Canada, http://laws.justice.gc.ca/en/showtdm/cs/P-8.6.

Privacy Act, R.S. 1985, c. P-21. Department of Justice Canada, http://laws.justice.gc.ca/ en/showtdm/cs/P-21.

Proceeds of Crime (Money Laundering) and Terrorist Financing Act, S.C. 2000, c. 17. Department of Justice Canada, http://laws.justice.gc.ca/en/showtdm/cs/P-24.501.

Public Safety Act 2002, S.C. 2004, c. 15. Department of Justice Canada, http://laws.justice. gc.ca/en/showtdm/cs/P-31.5.

Radiocommunication Act, R.S. 1985, c. R-2. Department of Justice Canada, http://laws. justice.gc.ca/en/showtdm/cs/R-2.

Rules of Civil Procedure, R.R.O. 1990, Reg. 194. Canadian Legal Information Institute, http://www.canlii.org/en/on/laws/regu/rro-1990-reg-194/latest/rro-1990-reg-194. html.

Security of Information Act, R.S.C. 1985, c. O-5. Department of Justice Canada, http:// laws.justice.gc.ca/en/showtdm/cs/O-5.

Telecommunications Act, S.C. 1993, c. 38. Department of Justice Canada, http://laws. justice.gc.ca/en/showtdm/cs/T-3.4.

War Measures Act, S.C. 1914, c. 2. Canadian Expeditionary Force Study Group, http:// www.cefresearch.com/matrix/Utilities/Legal%20Documents/Acts/wma.htm.

LEGISLATION (UNITED STATES)

Children's Online Privacy Protection Act of 1998, Pub. L. No. 105-227, 112 Stat. 2581-728 (1998). Federal Trade Commission, http://www.ftc.gov/ogc/coppa1.htm.

Communications Act of 1934, Pub. L. No. 416, 48 Stat. 1064 (1934). Federal Communications Commission, http://www.fcc.gov/Reports/1934new.pdf.

Copyright Act of 1976, Pub. L. No. 94-553, 90 Stat. 2541 (1976). US Copyright Office, http://www.copyright.gov/title17/.

Digital Millennium Copyright Act, Pub. L. No. 105-304, 112 Stat. 2860 (1998). US Copyright Office, http://www.copyright.gov/legislation/dmca.pdf.

Telecommunications Act of 1996, Pub. L. No. 104-104, 110 Stat. 56 (1996). Federal Communications Commission, http://www.fcc.gov/Reports/tcom1996.pdf.

USA PATRIOT Act (Uniting and Strengthening America by Providing Appropriate Tools Required to Intercept and Obstruct Terrorism Act of 2001), Pub. L. No. 107-56, 115 Stat. 272

(2001). Library of Congress, http://thomas.loc.gov/cgi-bin/bdquery/z?d107: HR03162:].

INTERNATIONAL DOCUMENTS

Agreement on Trade-Related Aspects of Intellectual Property Rights, 15 April 1994, Annex IC to the *Marrakesh Agreement Establishing the World Trade Organization,* Legal Instruments – Results of the Uruguay Round, 33 ILM 1125, 1197 (1994). World Trade Organization, http://www.wto.org/english/docs_e/legal_e/27-trips_01_e.htm.

Berne Convention for the Protection of Literary and Artistic Works, 9 September 1886 (1971 Paris revision), 1161 UNTS 30. World Intellectual Property Organization, http://www.wipo.int/treaties/en/ip/berne/trtdocs_wo001.html.

Convention on Cybercrime, 23 November 2001, CETS No. 185. Council of Europe, http://conventions.coe.int/Treaty/EN/Treaties/HTML/185.htm.

Convention on the Protection and Promotion of the Diversity of Cultural Expressions, 20 October 2005, 33rd session of the General Conference. UNESCO, http://unesdoc.unesco.org/images/0014/001429/142919e.pdf.

General Agreement on Tariffs and Trade, 15 April 1994, Annex IA to the *Marrakesh Agreement Establishing the World Trade Organization,* 1867 UNTS 187; 33 ILM 1153. World Trade Organization, http://www.wto.org/english/docs_e/legal_e/06-gatt_e.htm.

General Agreement on Trade in Services, 15 April 1994, 1869 UNTS 183. World Trade Organization, http://www.wto.org/english/docs_e/legal_e/26-gats_01_e.htm.

International Covenant on Civil and Political Rights, 19 December 1966, 999 UNTS 171. United Nations, http://www2.ohchr.org/english/law/ccpr.htm.

International Covenant on Economic, Social and Cultural Rights, 16 December 1966, 993 UNTS 3. United Nations, http://www2.ohchr.org/english/law/cescr.htm.

Optional Protocol to the International Covenant on Civil and Political Rights, 16 December 1966, G.A. res. 2200A (XXI), 21 U.N. GAOR Supp. (No. 16) at 59, U.N. Doc. A/6316 (1966), 999 UNTS 302. United Nations, http://www2.ohchr.org/english/law/ccpr-one.htm.

Second Optional Protocol to the International Covenant on Civil and Political Rights, Aiming at the Abolition of the Death Penalty, 15 December 1989, 1642 UNTS 414. United Nations, http://www2.ohchr.org/english/law/ccpr-death.htm.

Universal Declaration of Human Rights, GA Res. 217(III), UN GAOR, 3d Sess., Supp. No. 13, UN Doc. A/810 (1948). United Nations, http://www.un.org/en/documents/udhr/.

World Intellectual Property Organization Copyright Treaty, 20 December 1996, S. Treaty Doc. No. 105-17 (1997); 36 ILM 65 (1997). World Intellectual Property Organization, http://www.wipo.int/treaties/en/ip/wct/trtdocs_wo033.html.

World Intellectual Property Organization Performances and Phonograms Treaty, 20 December 1996, S. Treaty Doc. No. 105-17, 36 ILM 76 (1997). World Intellectual Property Organization, http://www.wipo.int/treaties/en/ip/wppt/trtdocs_wo034.html.

JURISPRUDENCE

Adbusters Media Foundation v. Canadian Broadcasting Corp., 1995 B.C.J. No. 2325 (S.C.). Courts of British Columbia, http://www.courts.gov.bc.ca/jdb-txt/sc/95/15/s95-1528.htm.

Adbusters Media Foundation v. Canadian Broadcasting Corporation, 2008 BCSC 71. Courts of British Columbia, http://www.courts.gov.bc.ca/jdb-txt/sc/08/00/2008bcsc0071.htm.

Adbusters Media Foundation v. Canadian Broadcasting Corporation, 2009 BCCA 148. Court of Appeal for British Columbia, http://adbusters.org/files/pdf/adbusters_courtappeal_20090403.pdf.

Bell ExpressVu Limited Partnership v. Rex, [2002] 2 S.C.R. 559. Judgments of the Supreme Court of Canada, http://scc.lexum.umontreal.ca/en/2002/2002scc42/2002scc42.html.

Canadian Council of Churches v. Canada (Minister of Employment and Immigration), [1992] 1 S.C.R. 236. Judgments of the Supreme Court of Canada, http://scc.lexum.umontreal.ca/en/1992/1992rcs1-236/1992rcs1-236.html.

CCH Canadian Ltd. v. Law Society of Upper Canada, [2004] 1 S.C.R. 339. Judgments of the Supreme Court of Canada, http://scc.lexum.umontreal.ca/en/2004/2004scc13/2004scc13.html.

Chiasson v. Fillion, [2005] R.J.Q. 1066 (S.C.). Société québécoise d'information juridique, http://www.jugements.qc.ca/php/.

CKOY Ltd. v. R., [1979] 1 S.C.R. 2. Judgments of the Supreme Court of Canada, http://scc.lexum.umontreal.ca/en/1978/1979rcs1-2/1979rcs1-2.html.

Committee for the Commonwealth of Canada v. Canada, [1991] 1 S.C.R. 139. Judgments of the Supreme Court of Canada, http://scc.lexum.umontreal.ca/en/1991/1991rcs1-139/1991rcs1-139.html.

Compagnie Générale des Établissements Michelin-Michelin & Cie v. National Automobile, Aerospace, Transportation and General Workers Union of Canada (CAW-Canada) (T.D.), 1996 CanLII 3920 (F.C.). Canadian Legal Information Institute, http://www.canlii.org/en/ca/fct/doc/1996/1996canlii3920/1996canlii3920.html.

Genex Communications v. Canada (Attorney General), 2005 FCA 283 (CanLII). Canadian Legal Information Institute, http://www.canlii.org/en/ca/fca/doc/2005/2005fca283/2005fca283.html.

Hager v. ECW Press Ltd. (T.D.) (1998), [1999] 2 F.C. 287. Canadian Legal Information Institute, http://www.canlii.org/en/ca/fct/doc/1998/1998canlii9115/1998canlii9115.html.

Harper v. Canada (Attorney General), [2004] 1 S.C.R. 827, 2004 SCC 33. Judgments of the Supreme Court of Canada, http://scc.lexum.umontreal.ca/en/2004/2004scc33/2004scc33.html.

Hunter et al. v. Southam Inc., [1984] 2 S.C.R. 145. Judgments of the Supreme Court of Canada, http://csc.lexum.umontreal.ca/en/1984/1984rcs2-145/1984rcs2-145.html.

Irwin Toy Ltd. v. Quebec (Attorney General), [1989] 1 S.C.R. 927. Judgments of the Supreme Court of Canada, http://scc.lexum.umontreal.ca/en/1989/1989rcs1-927/1989rcs 1-927.html.

Libman v. Quebec (Attorney General), [1997] 3 S.C.R. 569. Judgments of the Supreme Court of Canada, http://scc.lexum.umontreal.ca/en/1997/1997rcs3-569/1997 rcs3-569.html.

McKinney v. University of Guelph, [1990] 3 S.C.R. 229. Judgments of the Supreme Court of Canada, http://scc.lexum.umontreal.ca/en/1990/1990rcs3-229/1990rcs 3-229.html.

O'Neill v. Canada (Attorney General), 2006 CanLII 35004 (ON S.C.). Canadian Legal Information Institute, http://www.canlii.org/en/on/onsc/doc/2006/2006canlii 35004/2006canlii35004.html.

Prise de Parole Inc. v. Guérin éditeur Ltée, [1996] F.C.J. No. 1427104 FTR 104, 66 C.P.R. (3d) 257, affd. (1996) 206 N.R. 311 (F.C.A.).

R. v. Butler, [1992] 1 S.C.R. 452. Judgments of the Supreme Court of Canada, http://scc. lexum.umontreal.ca/en/1992/1992rcs1-452/1992rcs1-452.html.

R. v. Duarte, [1990] 1 S.C.R. 30. Judgments of the Supreme Court of Canada, http://scc. lexum.umontreal.ca/en/1990/1990rcs1-30/1990rcs1-30.html.

R. v. Keegstra, [1990] 3 S.C.R. 697. Judgments of the Supreme Court of Canada, http:// scc.lexum.umontreal.ca/en/1990/1990rcs3-697/1990rcs3-697.html.

R. v. Sharpe, [2001] 1 S.C.R. 45, 2001 SCC 2. Judgments of the Supreme Court of Canada, http://scc.lexum.umontreal.ca/en/2001/2001scc2/2001scc2.html.

R. v. Zundel, [1992] 2 S.C.R. 731. Judgments of the Supreme Court of Canada, http:// scc.lexum.umontreal.ca/en/1992/1992rcs2-731/1992rcs2-731.html.

Ramsden v. Peterborough (City), [1993] 2 S.C.R. 1084. Judgments of the Supreme Court of Canada, http://scc.lexum.umontreal.ca/en/1993/1993rcs2-1084/1993rcs 2-1084.html.

Reference Re Alberta Statutes – The Bank Taxation Act; The Credit of Alberta Regulation Act; and the Accurate News and Information Act, [1938] S.C.R. 100. Judgments of the Supreme Court of Canada, http://csc.lexum.umontreal.ca/en/1938/1938rcs 0-100/1938rcs0-100.html.

Robertson v. Thomson Corp., [2006] 2 S.C.R. 363, 2006 SCC 43. Judgments of the Supreme Court of Canada, http://scc.lexum.umontreal.ca/en/2006/2006scc43/2006scc43. html.

Ross v. New Brunswick School District No. 15, [1996] 1 S.C.R. 825. Judgments of the Supreme Court of Canada, http://scc.lexum.umontreal.ca/en/1996/1996rcs 1-825/1996rcs1-825.html.

R.W.D.S.U., Local 558 v. Pepsi-Cola Canada Beverages (West) Ltd., [2002] 1 S.C.R. 156, 2002 SCC 8. Judgments of the Supreme Court of Canada, http://scc.lexum.umont-real.ca/en/2002/2002scc8/2002scc8.html.

Snow v. The Eaton Centre Ltd. (1982), 70 C.P.R. (2d) 105 (Ontario High Court of Justice).

Society of Composers, Authors and Music Publishers of Canada v. Canadian Assn. of Internet Providers, [2004] 2 S.C.R. 427. Judgments of the Supreme Court of Canada, http://scc.lexum.umontreal.ca/en/2004/2004scc45/2004scc45.html.

St. Elizabeth Home Society v. Hamilton (City), 2008 ONCA 182 (CanLII). Canadian Legal Information Institute, http://www.canlii.org/en/on/onca/doc/2008/2008onca182/2008onca182.html.

Stoffman v. Vancouver General Hospital, [1990] 3 S.C.R. 483. Judgments of the Supreme Court of Canada, http://scc.lexum.umontreal.ca/en/1990/1990rcs3-483/1990rcs3-483.html.

Switzman v. Elbing and A.G. of Quebec, [1957] S.C.R. 285. Judgments of the Supreme Court of Canada, http://scc.lexum.umontreal.ca/en/1957/1957rcs0-285/1957rcs0-285.html.

The Queen v. Drybones, [1970] S.C.R. 282. Judgments of the Supreme Court of Canada, http://scc.lexum.umontreal.ca/en/1969/1970rcs0-282/1970rcs0-282.html.

Théberge v. Galerie d'Art du Petit Champlain inc., 2002 SCC 34, S.C.R. 336. Canadian Legal Information Institute, http://www.canlii.org/en/ca/scc/doc/2002/2002scc34/2002scc34.html.

Thomson Newspapers Co. v. Canada (Attorney General), [1998] 1 S.C.R. 877. Judgments of the Supreme Court of Canada, http://scc.lexum.umontreal.ca/en/1998/1998rc1-877/1998rcs1-877.html.

Vancouver Regional FreeNet Assn. v. Canada (Minister of National Revenue – M.N.R.), [1996] F.C.J. No. 914. Vancouver Community Network, http://www2.vcn.bc.ca/fullText.

Vriend v. Alberta, [1998] 1 S.C.R. 493. Judgments of the Supreme Court of Canada, http://scc.lexum.umontreal.ca/en/1998/1998rcs1-493/1998rcs1-493.html.

Warman v. Lemire, [2009] C.H.R.T. 262009/09/02. Canadian Human Rights Tribunal, http://chrt-tcdp.gc.ca/search/files/t1073_5405chrt26.pdf.

BOOKS, ARTICLES, AND ONLINE MATERIALS

Abrami, P., R. Bernard, A. Wade, R.F. Schmid, E. Borokhovski, R. Tamin, M. Surkes, et al. 2006. A review of e-learning in Canada: A rough sketch of the evidence, gaps and promising directions. *Canadian Journal of Learning and Technology* 32 (3). http://www.cjlt.ca/index.php/cjlt/issue/view/5.

Abramson, B., and G. Buchanan. 2009. CRTC new media policy released. McCarthy-Tétrault, http://www.mccarthy.ca/article_detail.aspx?id=4554.

Abramson, B., G. Buchanan, and H. Intven. (2009). CRTC shapes Canadian "net neutrality" rules. McCarthy Tétrault, http://www.mccarthy.ca/article_detail.aspx?id=4720.

Abramson, B., and J. Shtern. n.d. Responding to network neutrality: Market definition for post-convergence communications services. Unpublished draft.

Abramson, B., J. Shtern, and G. Taylor. 2008. "More and better" research? Critical communication studies and the problem of policy relevance. *Canadian Journal of Communication* 33 (2): 303-17.

Adams, R. 2001. Beyond numbers and demographics: "Experience-near" explorations of the digital divide. *Computers and Society* 33 (3): 5-8.

Advisory Committee to the Congressional Internet Caucus. 2007. What is privacy? Poll exposes generational divide on expectations of privacy, according to Zogby/Congressional Internet Caucus Advisory Committee survey. http://www.netcaucus.org/press/privacypoll.shtml.

Alexander, C. 2001. Wiring the nation! Including First Nations? Aboriginal Canadians and federal e-government initiatives. *Journal of Canadian Studies* 35 (4): 277-96.

Ambrosi, A. 2001. Initiatives et propositions citoyennes pour une appropriation sociale des TIC en Amérique du Nord. In *Réseaux citoyens, réseaux numériques, et nouveaux espaces pour l'action collective*, ed. V. Peugeot, 133-80. Paris: Charles Léopold Mayer et Vecam.

Ambrosi, A., and B. Abramson. 1998. Imaging the right to communicate. Paper written to close the Virtual Conference on the Right to Communicate and the Communication of Rights. http://www.nettime.org/Lists-Archives/nettime-l-9807/msg00018.html.

Ambrosi, A., and S. Hamilton. 1998. The right to communicate and the communication of rights: Creating enabling conditions. *Javnost* 5 (4): 94-100.

Amnesty International. 2007. *Canada and the international protection of human rights: An erosion of leadership?* Amnesty International Canada, http://www.amnesty.ca/amnestynews/upload/Human_Rights_Agenda_2007.pdf.

Anderson, N. 2009. Canadian ISPs stand up for content blocking, throttling. Ars Technica, http://arstechnica.com.

Appleby, T., and J. Freeman. 2009. Police find trusty partner in CCTV. *Globe and Mail*, 23 January. http://www.theglobeandmail.com/servlet/story/RTGAM.20090123.wvideo24/BNStory/Technology/home.

Appropriation Art Coalition. 2008. Canadian bill made in the USA. Appropriation Art, http://www.appropriationart.ca/212.htm.

ARTICLE 19. 2003. Statement on the right to communicate by ARTICLE 19 Global Campaign for Free Expression. ARTICLE 19, http://www.article19.org/pdfs/publications/right-to-communicate.pdf.

Association of Independent Video and Filmmakers, Independent Feature Project, International Documentary Association, National Alliance for Media Arts and Culture, and Women in Film and Video (Washington, DC, chapter). n.d. *Documentary filmmakers' statement of best practices in fair use*. American University Center for Social Media, http://www.centerforsocialmedia.org/resources/publications/statement_of_best_practices_in_fair_use/.

Atton, C. 2004. *An alternative Internet: Radical media, politics and creativity*. Edinburgh: Edinburgh University Press.

Aufderheide, P. 1999. *Communications policy and the public interest: The Telecommunications Act of 1996*. New York: Guilford Press.

Austen, I. 2006. A blogger who's a court-approved journalist. *New York Times,* 27 November. http://www.nytimes.com/2006/11/27/business/media/27blog.html?ex=1322283600&en=18bfd70c0ed20a88&ei=5088&partner=rssnyt&emc=rss.

Austin, L. 2003. Privacy and the question of technology. *Law and Philosophy* 22: 119-66.

Babe, R. 1998. Convergence and divergence: Telecommunications old and new. In *Understanding telecommunications and public policy,* ed. K. Adams and W. Birdsall, 15-34. Ottawa: Canadian Library Association.

Bailey, J. 2005. Deflating the Michelin man: Protecting users' rights in the Canadian copyright reform process. In *In the public interest: The future of Canadian copyright law,* ed. M. Geist, 125-66. Toronto: Irwin Law.

Bakan, J. 1997. *Just words: Constitutional rights and social wrongs.* Toronto: University of Toronto Press.

Baker, M., T. Waugh, and E. Winton, eds. 2010. *Challenge for change/société nouvelle: The collection.* Montreal and Kingston: McGill-Queen's University Press.

Baker, S. 2007. Google and the wisdom of clouds. *BusinessWeek,* 13 December 2007. http://www.businessweek.com/magazine/content/07_52/b4064048925836.htm?chan=magazine+channel_top+stories.

Bakhtin, M., and M. Holquist. 1981. *The dialogic imagination: Four essays.* Austin: University of Texas Press.

Barlow, M. 2005. *Too close for comfort: Canada's future within fortress North America.* Toronto: McClelland and Stewart.

Barney, D. 2004. The democratic deficit in Canadian ICT policy and regulation. In *Seeking convergence in policy and practice: Communications in the public interest,* vol. 2, ed. M. Moll and L. Shade, 93-110. Ottawa: Canadian Centre for Policy Alternatives.

–. 2005. *Communication technology.* Vancouver: UBC Press.

Bassett, C. 2007. Forms of reconciliation: On contemporary surveillance. *Cultural Studies* 21 (1): 82-94.

Beaton, B. 2004. The K-Net story: Community ICT development work. *Journal of Community Informatics* 1 (1): 5-6.

Beeby, D. 2009. Ottawa recalls sensitive database in BC border project. *Globe and Mail,* 15 February. http://www.theglobeandmail.com/servlet/story/RTGAM.20090215.wborderprivacy0215/BNStory/National/home?cid=al_gam_mostemail.

Bennett, C., and C. Raab. 2006. *The governance of privacy: Policy instruments in global perspective.* Cambridge, MA: MIT Press.

Bennett, C., and M. French. 2003. The state of privacy in the Canadian state: The fallout from 9/11. *Journal of Contingencies and Crisis Management* 11 (1): 2-11.

Berners-Lee, T., J. Hendler, and O. Lassila. 2001. The Semantic Web: A new form of web content that is meaningful to computers will unleash a revolution of new possibilities. *Scientific American,* May 2001. http://www.sciam.com/article.cfm?articleID=00048144-10D2-1C70-84A9809EC588EF21.

Binder, C. 1952. Freedom of information and the United Nations. *International Organization* 6 (2): 210-26.

Birdsall, W. 1998. A Canadian right to communicate? *Government Information in Canada/ Information gouvernementale au Canada*, no. 15 (September). http://library2.usask. ca/gic/15/birdsall.html.

–. 2000. The digital divide in the liberal state: The Canadian perspective. *First Monday* 5 (12). http://www.firstmonday.dk/issues/issue5_12/birdsall/index.html.

Birdsall, W., W. McIver, and M. Rasmussen. 2002. Translating a right to communicate into policy. Right to Communicate Group, http://www.righttocommunicate.org/ viewReference.atm?id=26.

Blogger.com. n.d. How do I create a backup of my entire blog? http://help.blogger.com/ bin/answer.py?answer=130&query=backup&topic=0&type=f.

Bonin, G. 2007. The bigger you are, the more coverage you get: CRTC "Diversity of Voices" hearings, day 2. Media@McGill, http://media.mcgill.ca/en/node/861.

–. 2008. "Protecting" the diversity of voices: The CRTC announces its policy. Media@ McGill, http://media.mcgill.ca/en/node/1020.

Bouchard, G., and C. Taylor. 2008. *Building the future: A time for reconciliation (abridged report)*. Quebec: La Commission de consultation sur les pratiques d'accommodement reliées aux différences culturelles.

Boyle, J. 2003. The second enclosure movement and the construction of the public domain. *Law and Contemporary Problems* 66: 33-74.

–. 2004. A manifesto on WIPO and the future of intellectual property. *Duke Law and Technology Review*, no. 9. http://www.law.duke.edu/journals/dltr/articles/2004dltr 0009.html.

Bradshaw, J. 2009. CBC cuts 800 jobs to save $171-million. *Globe and Mail*, 25 March. http://www.theglobeandmail.com/servlet/story/RTGAM.20090325.wcbc0325/ BNStory/National/home.

British Columbia Freedom of Information and Privacy Association (BCFIPA). 2005. Canada's Anti-terrorism Act: An unjustified limitation of freedom of information and privacy rights (submission to the House of Commons Subcommittee on Public Safety and National Security). BCFIPA, http://fipa.bc.ca/home/hot_ topics/13.

Buchwald, C. 1997. Canadian universality policy and the information infrastructure: Past lessons, future directions. *Canadian Journal of Communication* 22 (2): 161-93.

Buckley, S., K. Duer, T. Mendel, S. Ó Siochrú, M.E. Price, and M. Raboy. 2008. *Broadcasting, voice and accountability: A public interest approach to policy, law, and regulation*. Ann Arbor: University of Michigan Press.

Bullock, K., and G. Jafri. 2001. Media (mis)representations: Muslim women in the Canadian nation. *Canadian Woman Studies* 20 (2): 35-40.

Burns, A. 2001. George Gerbner and the cultural environment movement. Disinformation, http://www.disinfo.com/archive/pages/dossier/id349/pg1/.

Butler, D. 2007. Charting the impact of the Charter. *Ottawa Citizen*, 15 April 2007. http:// osgoode.yorku.ca/media2.nsf/83303ffe5af03ed585256ae6005379c9/64ce7416ea ae3dae852572ba00658f3a!OpenDocument.

Campbell, D. 2001. Can the digital divide be contained? *International Labour Review* 140 (2): 119-41.

Canada. 1949. Department of External Affairs. *Canada and the United Nations 1948.* Department of External Affairs Conference Series 1948, no. 1. Ottawa: King's Printer.

–. 1970. Special Senate Committee on Mass Media. *Report.* Ottawa: Information Canada.

–. 1971. Department of Communication. Telecommission Directing Committee. *Instant world: A report on telecommunications in Canada.* Ottawa: Information Canada.

–. 1981. Royal Commission on Newspapers. *Report.* Ottawa: Supply and Services Canada.

–. 1995. Department of Foreign Affairs and International Trade. *Canada in the world: Canadian foreign policy review 1995.* DFAIT, http://www.international.gc.ca/foreign_policy/cnd-world/menu-en.asp.

–. 1996. Information Highway Advisory Council. *Building the information society: Moving Canada into the 21st century.* Ottawa: Minister of Supply and Services.

–. 1997a. Information Highway Advisory Council. *Preparing Canada for a digital world.* Ottawa: Industry Canada.

–. 1997b. House of Commons. Standing Committee on Human Rights and the Status of Persons with Disabilities. *Privacy: Where do we draw the line?* Office of the Privacy Commissioner of Canada, http://www.privcom.gc.ca/information/02_06_03d_e.pdf.

–. 2001a. Senate of Canada. Bill S-7, *An act to amend the Broadcasting Act.* Parliament of Canada, http://www.parl.gc.ca/legisinfo/index.asp?Language=E&query=2712&Session=9&List=toc.

–. 2001b. Senate of Canada. Bill S-21, *An act to guarantee the human right to privacy. First reading.* Parliament of Canada, http://www2.parl.gc.ca/Sites/LOP/LEGISINFO/index.asp?Language=E&Session=9&query=2828&List=toc.

–. 2001c. Intellectual Property Policy Directorate. Industry Canada and Copyright Policy Branch. Canadian Heritage. *Consultation paper on digital copyright issues.* Industry Canada, http://www.ic.gc.ca/eic/site/crp-prda.nsf/vwapj/digital.pdf/.../digital.pdf.

–. 2001d. *Debates of the Senate. Hansard* 139 (16), 1700. Parliament of Canada, http://www.parl.gc.ca/37/1/parlbus/chambus/senate/deb-e/pdf/016db_2001-03-15-E.pdf.

–. 2001e. Intellectual Property Policy Directorate. Industry Canada and Copyright Policy Branch. Canadian Heritage. *A framework for copyright reform.* Industry Canada, http://strategis.ic.gc.ca/epic/site/crp-prda.nsf/en/rp01101e.html.

–. 2001f. Senate of Canada. Standing Committee on Social Affairs, Science, and Technology. *Thirteenth report.* Parliament of Canada, http://www.parl.gc.ca/37/1/parlbus/commbus/senate/com-e/soci-e/rep-e/rep13dec01-e.htm.

–. 2002a. Department of Justice. *Lawful access – consultation document.* Department of Justice Canada, http://www.canada.justice.gc.ca/en/cons/la_al/law_access.pdf.

–. 2002b. Industry Canada. *Supporting culture and innovation: Report on the provisions and operation of the Copyright Act.* Industry Canada, http://strategis.ic.gc.ca/epic/site/crp-prda.nsf/en/rp00863e.html.

–. 2003a. Department of Foreign Affairs and International Trade. *A dialogue on foreign policy.* Government of Canada Depository Service Program, http://dsp-psd.pwgsc.gc.ca/Collection/E2-481-2003E.pdf.

–. 2003b. House of Commons. Standing Committee on Canadian Heritage. *Our cultural sovereignty: The second century of Canadian broadcasting.* Ottawa: Communication Canada.

–. 2003c. Department of Canadian Heritage. *The Government of Canada's response to the report of the Standing Committee on Canadian Heritage, Our cultural sovereignty: The second century of Canadian broadcasting.* Canadian Heritage, http://www2.parl.gc.ca/Content/HOC/Committee/381/CHPC/GovResponse/RP1726418/CHPC_Rpt02_GvtRsp/GvtRsp_Part1-e.pdf.

–. 2004a. Industry Canada. Office of Consumer Affairs. *Canadian code of practice for consumer protection in electronic commerce.* Consumer Measures Committee, http://cmcweb.ca.

–. 2004b. House of Commons. Standing Committee on Canadian Heritage. *Evidence: Tuesday, April 20, 2004.* Parliament of Canada, http://cmte.parl.gc.ca/Content/HOC/committee/373/heri/evidence/ev1304938/heriev07-e.htm#Int-886519.

–. 2004c. Department of Canadian Heritage. *Integration and cultural diversity – report of the panel on access to third-language public television services.* Ottawa: Canadian Heritage.

–. 2004d. House of Commons. Standing Committee on Canadian Heritage. *Interim report on copyright reform.* Parliament of Canada, http://cmte.parl.gc.ca/Content/HOC/committee/373/heri/reports/rp1350628/herirp01/herirp01-e.pdf.

–. 2004e. Copyright Board of Canada. *Licence application by Pointe-a-Callière, Montreal Museum of Archeology and History for the reproduction of quotations.* Copyright Board of Canada, http://www.cb-cda.gc.ca/unlocatable/other/1-b.pdf.

–. 2004f. Commission of Inquiry into the Actions of Canadian Officials in Relation to Maher Arar. *Opening statement of Maher Arar and his counsel to the Commission of Inquiry.* Maherarar.ca, http://www.maherarar.ca/cms/images/uploads/Arar_opening_statementfinal.pdf.

–. 2004g. Minister of Canadian Heritage and Minister of Industry. *Status report on copyright reform submitted to the Standing Committee on Canadian Heritage by the Minister of Canadian Heritage and the Minister of Industry.* Industry Canada, http://strategis.ic.gc.ca/epic/site/crp-prda.nsf/en/rp01134e.html.

–. 2005a. House of Commons. Bill C-60, *An act to amend the Copyright Act.* Parliament of Canada, http://www.parl.gc.ca/LEGISINFO/index.asp?List=ls&Query=4527&Session=13&Language=e.

–. 2005b. House of Commons. Bill C-74, *The Modernization of Investigative Techniques Act.* Parliament of Canada, http://www2.parl.gc.ca/HousePublications/Publication. aspx?pub=bill&doc=C-74&parl=38&ses=1&language=E.

–. 2005c. Office of the Auditor General of Canada. *Canadian Broadcasting Corporation, November 30, 2005: Special examination report presented to the board of directors.* CBC, http://www.cbc.radio-canada.ca/docs/auditor/pdf/oag2005_e.pdf.

–. 2005d. Department of Justice. *Lawful access FAQ.* Department of Justice Canada, http://www.justice.gc.ca/en/cons/la_al/summary/faq.html.

–. 2006a. Office of the Privacy Commissioner of Canada. *Fact sheet: RFID technology.* Office of the Privacy Commissioner of Canada, http://www.privcom.gc.ca/fs-fi/02_05_d_28_e.asp.

–. 2006b. Senate of Canada. Standing Committee on Transport and Communications. *Final report on the Canadian news media.* Parliament of Canada, http://www.parl. gc.ca/39/1/parlbus/commbus/senate/Com-e/tran-e/rep-e/repfinjun06vol1-e.htm.

–. 2006c. Commission of Inquiry into the Actions of Canadian Officials in Relation to Maher Arar. *A new review mechanism for the RCMP's national security activities.* Security Intelligence Review Committee, http://www.sirc-csars.gc.ca/pdfs/cm_arar_rcmpgrc-eng.pdf.

–. 2006d. Commission of Inquiry into the Actions of Canadian Officials in Relation to Maher Arar. *Press release: Arar Commission releases its findings on the handling of the Maher Arar case.* Library and Archives Canada, http://epe.lac-bac.gc.ca/100/206/301/pco-bcp/commissions/maher_arar/07-09-13/www.ararcommission.ca/eng/ReleaseFinal_Sept18.pdf.

–. 2006e. Treasury Board of Canada Secretariat. *Privacy matters: The federal strategy to address concerns about the USA PATRIOT Act and transborder data flows.* Treasury Board of Canada Secretariat, http://www.tbs-sct.gc.ca/pubs_pol/gospubs/tbm_128/pm-prp/pm-prp01-eng.asp.

–. 2006f. Copyright Board of Canada. *Re breakthough films.* Copyright Board of Canada, http://cb-cda.gc.ca/unlocatable/156r-b.pdf.

–. 2006g. Commission of Inquiry into the Actions of Canadian Officials in Relation to Maher Arar. *Report of the events relating to Maher Arar: Analysis and recommendations.* Security Intelligence Review Committee, http://www.sirc-csars.gc.ca/pdfs/cm_arar_rec-eng.pdf.

–. 2007a. House of Commons. Bill C-10, *Income Tax Amendments Act, 2006.* 2nd Session, 39th Parliament, 56 Elizabeth II. Parliament of Canada, http://www2.parl.gc.ca/HousePublications/Publication.aspx?Language=E&Parl=39&Ses=2&Mode=1&Pub=Bill&Doc=C-10_3.

–. 2007b. House of Commons. Bill C-59, *An act to amend the Criminal Code (unauthorized recording of a movie).* 1st Session, 39th Parliament, 55-56 Elizabeth II. Parliament of Canada, http://www2.parl.gc.ca/HousePublications/Publication.aspx?Docid=2993072&file=4.

–. 2007c. House of Commons. Bill C-426, *An act to amend the Canada Evidence Act (protection of journalistic sources and search warrants)*. 1st Session, 39th Parliament, 55-56 Elizabeth II. Parliament of Canada, http://www2.parl.gc.ca/HousePublications/Publication.aspx?Language=E&Parl=39&Ses=2&Mode=1&Pub=Bill&Doc=C-426_1&File=24#1.

–. 2007d. Office of the Privacy Commissioner of Canada. *Identity theft: Submission presented to the Standing Committee on Access to Information, Privacy and Ethics*. Office of the Privacy Commissioner of Canada, http://www.privcom.gc.ca/parl/2007/sub_070508_e.asp.

–. 2008a. House of Commons. Bill C-61, *An act to amend the Copyright Act*. 2nd Session, 39th Parliament, 56-57 Elizabeth II. Parliament of Canada, http://www2.parl.gc.ca/HousePublications/Publication.aspx?Language=E&Parl=39&Ses=2&Mode=1&Pub=Bill&Doc=C-61_1.

–. 2008b. House of Commons. Bill C-552, *An act to amend the Telecommunications Act (Internet neutrality)*. 2nd Session, 39th Parliament, 56-57 Elizabeth II. Parliament of Canada, http://www2.parl.gc.ca/HousePublications/Publication.aspx?Language=E&Parl=39&Ses=2&Mode=1&Pub=Bill&Doc=C-552_1&File=24.

–. 2008c. House of Commons. Standing Committee on Canadian Heritage. *CBC/Radio Canada: Defining distinctiveness in the changing media landscape*. Parliament of Canada, http://cmte.parl.gc.ca/Content/HOC/committee/392/chpc/reports/rp3297009/chpcrp06-e.html.

–. 2008d. Senate of Canada. Standing Committee on Banking, Trade and Commerce. *Evidence. Ottawa, Wednesday, May 14, 2008*. Parliament of Canada, http://www.parl.gc.ca/39/2/parlbus/commbus/senate/Com-e/bank-e/45416-e.htm?Language=E&Parl=39&Ses=2&comm_id=3.

–. 2009a. Office of the Prime Minister. Backgrounder: PM announces major improvement to broadband Internet access in rural Canada. Office of the Prime Minister, http://www.pm.gc.ca/eng/media.asp?id=2703.

–. 2009b. House of Commons. Bill C-46, *The Investigative Powers for the 21st Century (IP21C) Act*. Parliament of Canada, http://www2.parl.gc.ca/Sites/LOP/LEGISINFO/index.asp?Language=E&query=5886&List=toc.

–. 2009c. House of Commons. Bill C-47, *The Technical Assistance for Law Enforcement in the 21st Century Act*. Parliament of Canada, http://www2.parl.gc.ca/HousePublications/Publication.aspx?DocId=4007628&Language=e&Mode=1&File=47.

–. 2009d. Department of Finance. *Federal budget 2009 – Highlights*. Department of Finance Canada, http://www.budget.gc.ca/2009/plan/bpc3d-eng.asp.

–. 2009e. Office of the Privacy Commissioner of Canada. Facebook agrees to address Privacy Commissioner's concerns. Office of the Privacy Commissioner of Canada, http://www.priv.gc.ca/media/nr-c/2009/nr-c_090827_e.cfm.

–. n.d. Department of Foreign Affairs and International Trade (DFAIT). *Canada's international human rights policy*. DFAIT, http://www.international.gc.ca/foreign_policy/human-rights/hr1-rights-en.asp.

Canadian Association of Broadcasters. 2002. *Canadian Association of Broadcasters' code of ethics administered by the Canadian Broadcast Standards Council*. Canadian Association of Broadcasters, http://www.cab-acr.ca/english/social/codes/ethics.shtm.

Canadian Association of Journalists. 2008. CAJ urges Ottawa to reverse decision on information database. Canadian Association of Journalists, http://micro.newswire.ca/release.cgi?rkey=1605054901&view=42015-0&Start=0.

Canadian Commission for the UN Educational, Scientific, and Cultural Organization (UNESCO). 1980a. *Canadians and UNESCO*. Canadian Commission for UNESCO occasional paper no. 36. Ottawa: Canadian Commission for UNESCO.

–. 1980b. *Report of the secretary general 1979-1980*. Canadian Commission for UNESCO occasional paper no. 37. Ottawa: Canadian Commission for UNESCO.

–. 1980c. *Twenty-second annual meeting*. Ottawa: Canadian Commission for UNESCO.

–. 1981. *Report of the secretary general 1980-1981*. Canadian Commission for UNESCO occasional paper no. 38. Ottawa: Canadian Commission for UNESCO.

–. 1982. *Report of the secretary general 1981-1982*. Canadian Commission for UNESCO occasional paper no. 40. Ottawa: Canadian Commission for UNESCO.

–. 1983. *Report of the secretary general 1982-1983*. Canadian Commission for UNESCO occasional paper no. 43. Ottawa: Canadian Commission for UNESCO.

–. 1984. *Report of the secretary general 1983-1984*. Canadian Commission for UNESCO occasional paper no. 47. Ottawa: Canadian Commission for UNESCO.

–. 1985. *Canada and UNESCO – A working partnership*. Ottawa: Canadian Commission for UNESCO.

Canadian Federation of Students. 2004. November 2004 membership advisory: Renewal of the Copyright Act. Canadian Federation of Students, http://www.cfs-fcee.ca/html/english/research/factsheets/MemAdv-2004Copyright-e.pdf.

Canadian Journalists for Free Expression. 2008. CJFE calls decision in source protection case an important step forward. Canadian Journalists for Free Expression, http://www.cjfe.org/releases/2008/ebulletin0408.pdf.

Canadian Press. 2009. Journalist's contempt conviction overturned. *Toronto Star*, 13 February. http://www.thestar.com/News/Canada/article/346911.

Carey, J. 1985. *Communication as culture: Essays on media and society*. Boston: Unwin Hyman.

CARL (Canadian Association of Research Libraries). 2008. Key considerations of the Canadian Association of Research Libraries for a new copyright bill with reference to the 2008 Bill C-61: An act to amend the Copyright Act. CARL, http://www.carl-abrc.ca/projects/copyright/copyright-e.html.

Carlsson, U. 2003. The rise and fall of NWICO: From a vision of international regulation to a reality of multilevel governance. *Nordicom Review* 24 (2): 31-67.

Castells, M. 2004. *The information age: Economy, society, and culture.* London: Blackwell Publishing.

Cauchon, P. 2005. Médias: Problèmes de convergence. *Le Devoir,* 28 November. http://www.ledevoir.com/2005/11/28/96282.html?350.

CAUT (Canadian Association of University Teachers). 2008. Intellectual property advisory no. 3: Fair dealing. CAUT, http://www.caut.ca/uploads/IP-Advisory3-en.pdf.

CBC News. 2000. Health care tops federal campaign agenda. *Cbcnews.ca,* 1 November. http://www.cbc.ca/canada/story/2000/10/31/elexn001031.html.

–. 2004a. Hamilton reporter fined $31,600 for contempt. *Cbcnews.ca,* 8 December. http://www.cbc.ca/canada/story/2004/12/07/peters041207.html.

–. 2004b. Text of throne speech: Oct. 5, 2004. *CBCNews.ca,* 5 October. http://www.cbc.ca/news/background/cdngovernment/thronespeechtext0410.html.

–. 2006a. Blogger arrested at Atlantica conference. *Cbcnews.ca,* 12 June. http://www.cbc.ca/canada/new-brunswick/story/2006/06/12/nb_protest20060609.html.

–. 2006b. In depth: Health care. *Cbcnews.ca,* 22 August. http://www.cbc.ca/news/background/healthcare/.

–. 2007. 2 Canadian boys with same name land on "no fly" list. *Cbcnews.ca,* 30 June. http://www.cbc.ca/canada/story/2007/06/29/nofly-kids.html.

–. 2008a. $500M for rural broadband, Harper says. *Cbcnews.ca,* 11 October. http://www.cbc.ca/news/canadavotes/story/2008/10/11/broadband-conservative.html.

–. 2008b. Artists call Tory plan to vet films "censorship." *Cbcnews.ca,* 28 February. http://www.cbc.ca/canada/story/2008/02/28/film-tax-credits.html.

–. 2008c. Bell crimps P2P file-sharing during peak hours. *Cbcnews.ca,* 25 March. http://www.cbc.ca/consumer/story/2008/03/25/bell-throttling.html?ref=rss.

–. 2008d. CRTC opens net neutrality debate to public. *Cbcnews.ca,* 15 May. http://www.cbc.ca/technology/story/2008/05/15/tech-internet.html.

–. 2008e. MPs urge Tories to reinstate access to information database. *Cbcnews.ca,* 5 May. http://www.cbc.ca/canada/story/2008/05/05/information-registry.html?ref=rss.

–. 2009. Privacy advocates concerned about potential Internet wiretapping law. *Cbcnews.ca,* 13 February. http://www.cbc.ca/technology/story/2009/02/12/privacy-wiretap.html.

CBC/Radio-Canada. 2006. Final written comments of CBC/Radio-Canada: Notice of public hearing CRTC 2006-5: TV policy review. CBC, http://www.cbc.radio-canada.ca/submissions/2006.shtml.

CBNC (Crossing Boundaries National Council). 2007. *Elected officials in the information age: The Crossing Boundaries National Council "wired elected official" pilot project.* Crossing Boundaries National Council, http://www.crossingboundaries.ca/files/weo_pilot_report_final_feb07__2_.pdf.

CCPA (Canadian Centre for Policy Alternatives). 2009. Alternative federal budget 2009. CCPA, http://policyalternatives.ca/.

Center for Constitutional Rights. 2008. Extraordinary rendition: The story of Maher Arar. Center for Constitutional Rights, http://ccrjustice.org/files/12.12.08%20 FINAL%20arar%20factsheet_0.pdf.

Centre d'études sur les médias. 2008. Portrait de la propriété dans le secteur des quotidiens au Québec et au Canada. Centre d'études sur les médias, http://www.cem.ulaval.ca/concentration_medias/.

Chester, J. 2007. Digital destiny: New media and the future of democracy. New York: New Press.

CFHSS (Canadian Federation for the Humanities and Social Sciences). 2007. Canadian Federation for the Humanities and Social Sciences (CFHSS) position on copyright policy November 2007. CFHSS, http://www.fedcan.ca/english/advocacy/copyright/position2007.cfm.

CIPPIC (Canadian Internet and Public Interest Clinic). 2006. Compliance with Canadian data protection laws: Are retailers measuring up? CIPPIC, http://www.cippic.ca/en/bulletin/compliance_report_06-07-06_(color)_(cover-english).pdf.

–. 2007. Lawful access: Police surveillance. CIPPIC, http://www.cippic.ca/en/projects-cases/lawful-access/.

–. 2008. News release: CIPPIC files privacy complaint against Facebook. CIPPIC, http://www.cippic.ca/uploads/NewsRelease_30May08.pdf.

CIPPIC/PIAC. 2004. The Canadian Internet Policy and Public Interest Clinic (CIPPIC) and the Public Interest Advocacy Centre (PIAC) response to the May 2004 Standing Committee on Canadian Heritage interim report on copyright reform. CIPPIC, http://www.cippic.ca/en/news/documents/Response_to_Bulte_Report_FINAL.pdf.

Clark, D. 2005. Contemplating a new Internet: An upcoming NSF initiative. Global Environment for Network Innovations, http://groups.geni.net/geni/attachment/wiki/OldGPGReferencesLinks/NGN_FIND_ddc.pdf?format=raw.

Clark, D., K. Sollins, J. Wroclawski, D. Katabi, J. Kulik, X. Yang, R. Braden, et al. 2003. Final technical report. New Arch: Future Generation Internet Architecture. Rome, NY: Air Force Research Laboratory. University of Southern California, Information Sciences Institute, http://www.isi.edu/newarch/iDOCS/final.finalreport.pdf.

Clement, A., M. Gurstein, G. Longford, R. Luke, M. Moll, L. Shade, D. Dechief et al. 2004. The Canadian Research Alliance for Community Innovation and Networking (CRACIN): A research partnership and agenda for community networking in Canada. Journal of Community Informatics 1 (1): 7-20.

Clement, A., M. Moll, and L. Shade. 2001. Debating universal access in the Canadian context: The role of public interest organizations. In E-commerce vs. e-commons: Communications in the public interest, ed. M. Moll and L. Shade, 23-48. Ottawa: Canadian Centre for Policy Alternatives.

Clement, A., and L. Shade. 2000. The access rainbow: Conceptualizing universal access to the information/communication infrastructure. In Community informatics: En-

abling communities with information and communications technologies, ed. M. Gurstein, 32-51. Hershey, PA: Idea Group Publishing.

CMCC (Canadian Music Creators Coalition). 2007. Musicians to industry groups: "Not in our names": Recent American judgment a preview of the worst case scenario for Canadian music fans. CMCC, http://www.musiccreators.ca/wp/?p=231.

Comcast Corporation. 2008. Comcast and BitTorrent form collaboration to address network management, network architecture and content distribution (press release). Comcast, http://www.comcast.com/About/PressRelease/PressReleaseDetail. ashx?PRID=740.

Conseil de presse du Québec. 2005. Les décisions rendues par le Conseil: numéro D2004-10-029. Conseil de presse du Québec, http://www.conseildepresse.qc.ca/ index.php?option=com_content&task=blogcategory&id=33&Itemid=155&did=1 470&limitstart=0&lang=fr.

Consumers International, Médecins Sans Frontières, International Federation of Library Associations and Institutions, Third World Network, Electronic Frontier Foundation, J. Sulston, et al. 2004 Geneva declaration on the future of the World Intellectual Property Organization. Consumer Project on Technology, http://www.cptech. org/ip/wipo/genevadeclaration.html.

Cooper, M., and G. Kimmelman. 2001. The digital divide confronts the Telecommunications Act of 1996: Economic reality versus public policy. In *The digital divide: Facing a crisis or creating a myth?* ed. B. Compaine, 199-221. Cambridge, MA: MIT Press.

Cordell, A., and P. Romanow. 2005. Community networking and public benefits. *Journal of Community Informatics* 2 (1): 6-20.

Cringely, R. 2005. Google-Mart: Sam Walton taught Google more about how to dominate the Internet than Microsoft ever did. The Pulpit, http://www.pbs.org/cringely/ pulpit/2005/pulpit_20051117_000873.html.

CRIS (Communication Rights in the Information Society). 2005a. Assessing communication rights: A handbook. CRIS, http://www.crisinfo.org/pdf/ggpen.pdf.

–. 2005b. *CRIS commitment.* Tunis: Campaign for Communication Rights in the Information Society.

Crow, B., and G. Longford. 2000. Digital restructuring: Gender, class and citizenship in the information society in Canada. *Citizenship Studies* 4 (2): 207-30.

Crow, B., and M. Longford. 2004. Digital activism in Canada. In *Seeking convergence in policy and practice: Communications in the public interest*, vol. 2, ed. M. Moll and L. Shade, 347-60. Ottawa: Canadian Centre for Policy Alternatives.

CRTC (Canadian Radio-television and Telecommunications Commission). 1971. *Canadian broadcasting: "A single system."* Policy statement on cable television, 16 July. Ottawa: CRTC.

–. 1976. *Cable television regulations.* Ottawa: CRTC.

–. 1986. *Radio regulations.* CRTC, http://www.crtc.gc.ca/eng/LEGAL/Radioreg.htm.

–. 1995. *Competition and culture on Canada's information highway: Managing the realities of transition*. CRTC, http://www.crtc.gc.ca/ENG/HIGHWAY/HWY9505.HTM.

–. 1999. Broadcasting Public Notice CRTC 1999-84, Telecom Public Notice CRTC 99-14: New media. CRTC, http://www.crtc.gc.ca/archive/eng/notices/1999/pb99-84.htm.

–. 2001. Decision CRTC 2001-746: Transfer of effective control of TQS – transfer of the assets of Cogeco Radio Television Inc. stations at Trois-Rivières, Sherbrooke and Chicoutimi/Jonquière, affiliated with TQS and SRC – amendment to TQS licenses – applications approved. CRTC, http://www.crtc.gc.ca/archive/ENG/Decisions/2001/db2001-746.htm.

–. 2004a. Broadcasting Decision CRTC 2004-271: CHOI-FM – non-renewal of licence. CRTC, http://www.crtc.gc.ca/eng/archive/2004/db2004-271.htm.

–. 2004b. News release: The CRTC decides not to renew the licence of CHOI-FM Québec. CRTC, http://crtc.gc.ca/eng/NEWS/RELEASES/2004/r040713.htm.

–. 2004c. Public consultation: Voice over Internet Protocol. 21 September. CRTC, http://www.crtc.gc.ca/ENG/transcripts/2004/tt0921.htm.

–. 2004d. Public consultation: Voice over Internet Protocol. 22 September. CRTC, http://www.crtc.gc.ca/ENG/transcripts/2004/tt0922.htm.

–. 2004e. Telecom Public Notices 2004-2, 2004-2-1: Regulatory framework for voice communication services using Internet Protocol. 21 September. CRTC, http://www.crtc.gc.ca/eng/process/2004/sep21_t.htm.

–. 2005a. Broadcasting Public Notice CRTC 2005-61: Introduction to broadcasting decisions CRTC 2005-246 to 2005-248: Licensing of new satellite and terrestrial subscription radio undertakings. CRTC, http://www.crtc.gc.ca/eng/archive/2005/pb2005-61.htm.

–. 2005b. Canadian telecommunications policy review: Discussion paper. CRTC, http://www.crtc.gc.ca/Eng/publications/reports/t_review05.htm#n61.

–. 2005c. Telecom Decision CRTC 2005-21: Emergency service obligations for local VoIP service providers. CRTC, http://www.crtc.gc.ca/archive/ENG/decisions/2005/dt2005-21.htm.

–. 2005d. Telecom Decision CRTC 2005-28: Regulatory framework for voice communication services using Internet Protocol. CRTC, http://www.crtc.gc.ca/archive/eng/Decisions/1997/DT97-8.htm.

–. 2006a. Broadcasting Decision CRTC 2006-309: Bell Globemedia Inc., on behalf of its licensed subsidiaries – change in effective control. CRTC, http://www.crtc.gc.ca/archive/eng/Decisions/2006/db2006-309.htm.

–. 2006b. Broadcasting Notice of Public Hearing CRTC 2006-5: Review of certain aspects of the regulatory framework for over-the-air television. CRTC, http://www.crtc.gc.ca/archive/eng/hearings/2006/n2006-5.htm.

–. 2006c. *Broadcasting policy monitoring report 2006*. CRTC, www.crtc.gc.ca/eng/publications/reports/PolicyMonitoring/2006/bpmr2006.pdf.

–. 2006d. Telecom Decision CRTC 2006-61: Access to the quality of service enhancement service of Shaw Cablesystems G.P. (Shaw) and packet cable functionality of Rogers

Communications Inc., Shaw, and Vidéotron ltée. CRTC, http://www.crtc.gc.ca/archive/ENG/Decisions/2006/dt2006-61.htm.

–. 2007. Transcript of proceedings before the CRTC. Subject: Diversity of Voices. CRTC, http://www.crtc.gc.ca/eng/transcripts/2007/tb0917.htm.

–. 2008a. Broadcasting Notice of Public Hearing CRTC 2008-11 (Canadian broadcasting in new media). CRTC, http://www.crtc.gc.ca/eng/archive/2008/n2008-11.htm.

–. 2008b. Broadcasting Public Notice CRTC 2008-4: Regulatory policy – Diversity of Voices. CRTC, http://www.crtc.gc.ca/archive/ENG/Notices/2008/pb2008-4.htm.

–. 2008c. Broadcasting Public Notice CRTC 2008-44: Call for comments on the scope of a future proceeding on Canadian broadcasting in new media. CRTC, http://www.crtc.gc.ca/archive/ENG/Notices/2008/pb2008-44.htm.

–. 2008d. CRTC report to the Minister of Canadian Heritage on the Canadian Television Fund. CRTC, http://www.crtc.gc.ca/eng/publications/reports/ctf080605.htm.

–. 2008e. Letter re: Application requesting certain orders directing Bell Canada to cease and desist from "throttling" its wholesale ADSL access services. CRTC, http://www.crtc.gc.ca/archive/ENG/Letters/2008/lt080515.htm.

–. 2008f. Press release: CRTC establishes a new approach to media ownership. CRTC, http://www.crtc.gc.ca/ENG/NEWS/RELEASES/2008/r080115.htm?Print=True.

–. 2008g. Public hearing: Review of the regulatory frameworks for broadcasting distribution undertakings and discretionary programming services. CRTC, http://www.crtc.gc.ca/Broadcast/eng/HEARINGS/2008/04_08ag.htm.

–. 2008h. Telecom Public Notice CRTC 2008-19 (Review of the Internet traffic management practices of Internet service providers). CRTC, http://www.crtc.gc.ca/eng/archive/2008/pt2008-19.htm.

–. 2008i. Telecom Decision CRTC 2008-39: Canadian Association of Internet Providers' request for interim relief regarding Bell Canada's practice of "throttling" its wholesale ADSL access services. CRTC, http://www.crtc.gc.ca/archive/ENG/Decisions/2008/dt2008-39.htm.

–. 2008j. Telecom Decision CRTC 2008-108: The Canadian Association of Internet Providers' application regarding Bell Canada's traffic shaping of its wholesale Gateway Access Service. CRTC, http://www.crtc.gc.ca/eng/archive/2008/dt2008-108.htm.

–. 2009a. Broadcasting Regulatory Policy CRTC 2009-329: Review of broadcasting in new media. CRTC, http://www.crtc.gc.ca/eng/archive/2009/2009-329.htm.

–. 2009b. Broadcasting Regulatory Policy CRTC 2009-725: Addition of Al Jazeera English to the lists of eligible satellite services for distribution on a digital basis. CRTC, http://www.crtc.gc.ca/eng/archive/2009/2009-725.htm.

–. 2009c. Telecom Regulatory Policy CRTC 2009-657: Review of the Internet traffic management practices of Internet service providers. CRTC, http://www.crtc.gc.ca/eng/archive/2009/2009-657.htm.

CTV. 2008. CTV acquires rights to hockey theme song. CTV News, 8 June. http://www.ctv.ca/servlet/ArticleNews/story/CTVNews/20080609/hnic_theme_080609/20080609?hub=TopStories.

D'Agostino, G. 2008. Healing fair dealing? A comparative copyright analysis of Canada's fair dealing to UK fair dealing and US fair use. *McGill Law Journal* 53: 309-63.

Dahlgren, P. 2005. The Internet, public spheres, and political communication: Dispersion and deliberation. *Political Communication* 22 (2): 147-62.

Dakroury, A. 2005. Whose right to communicate: Al-Jazeera or CRTC? *Global Media Journal: American Edition* 4 (7). http://lass.calumet.purdue.edu/cca/gmj/fa05/graduatefa05/gmj-fa05gradinv-dakroury.htm.

–. 2006. Pluralism and the right to communicate in Canada. *Media Development: Journal of the World Association for Christian Communication* 2006 (1): 36-40.

–. 2009. *Communication and human rights.* Dubuque, IA: Kendall Hunt.

Dakroury, A., M. Eid, and Y. Kamalipour, eds. 2009. *The right to communicate: Historical hopes, global debates and future premises.* Dubuque, IA: Kendall Hunt.

Dallaire, R. (with B. Beardsley). 2005. *Shake hands with the devil: The failure of humanity in Rwanda.* New York: Carroll and Graf.

D'Arcy, J. 1969. Direct broadcast satellites and the right to communicate. *EBU Review* 118: 14-18. Republished in L. Harms, J. Richstad, and K. Kie, eds., *Right to communicate: Collected papers,* 1-9 (Honolulu: University of Hawaii Press, 1977).

–. 1977. The right of man to communicate. In *Right to communicate: Collected papers,* ed. L. Harms, J. Richstad, and K. Kie, 45-52. Honolulu: University of Hawaii Press.

–. 1981. *The right to communicate.* Document no. 36 of the International Commission for the Study of Communication Problems. Paris: UNESCO.

de Beer, J. Copyright and innovation in the networked information economy. Working Paper, Social Science Research Network, http://ssrn.com/abstract=1410158.

Deibert, R. 2002. Civil society activism on the World Wide Web: The case of the anti-MAI lobby. In *Street protests and fantasy parks: Globalization, culture, and the state,* ed. D. Cameron and J. Stein, 88-108. Vancouver: UBC Press.

Deibert, R., J. Palfrey, G. Rohozinski, and J. Zittrain, eds. 2008. *Access denied: The practice and policy of global Internet filtering.* Cambridge, MA: MIT Press.

Denham, E. 2009. Report of findings into the complaint filed by the Canadian Internet Policy and Public Interest Clinic against Facebook Inc. under the *Personal Information Protection and Documents Act.* Office of the Privacy Commissioner of Canada, http://www.priv.gc.ca/cf-dc/2009/2009_008_0716_e.cfm.

Dewey, J. 1927. *The public and its problems.* New York: H. Holt.

Dickard, N. 2002. *Federal retrenchment on the digital divide: Potential national impact.* Policy brief no. 1. Washington, DC: Benton Foundation. Benton Foundation, http://www.benton.org/publibrary/policybriefs/brief01.pdf.

Dickinson, P., and J. Ellison. 1999. Getting connected or staying unplugged: The growing use of computer communications services. Statistics Canada, http://www.statcan.ca/cgi-bin/downpub/listpub.cgi?catno=63F0002XIB1999027.

Dickinson, P., and G. Sciadas. 1999. Canadians connected. Science and technology redesign project. *Canadian Economic Observer* (Catalogue 11-010-XPB) 3: 1-22.

Dixon, G. 2009. Al Jazeera applies for Canadian licence. *Globe and Mail,* 17 February. http://www.theglobeandmail.com/news/arts/article972310.ece.

DOC (Documentary Organization of Canada). 2006. Canada's documentary film heritage and its future in jeopardy: Copyright reform urgently needed to protect our documentary films. DOC, http://www.docorg.ca/pdf/Dec4-06-FINAL%20 PRESS%20RELEASE.pdf.

Dowding, M. 2001. *National information infrastructure development in Canada and the U.S.: (Re)defining universal service and universal access in the age of techo-economic convergence.* PhD dissertation, Faculty of Information Studies, University of Toronto.

–. 2002. Universal access in IHAC and NIIAC: Transformed narrative and meaning in information policy. In *Citizenship and participation in the information age,* ed. by M. Pendakur and R. Harris, 211-18. Aurora, ON: Garamond Press.

Drake, W., and R. Jørgensen. 2006. Introduction. In *Human rights in the global information society,* ed. R. Jørgensen, 1-50. Cambridge, MA: MIT Press.

Dugré, P., ed. 2004. *Paving the road to Tunis/WSIS II.* Ottawa: Canadian Commission for UNESCO.

Dunbar, L., and C. Leblanc. 2007. *Review of the regulatory framework for broadcasting services in Canada: Final report.* CRTC, http://www.crtc.gc.ca/ENG/publications/reports/ dunbarleblanc.htm.

Eide, A. 1987. *Report on the right to adequate food as a human right.* Doc. EICN.4/Sub. 211987123. New York: United Nations Commission on Human Rights.

–. 1989. Realization of social and economic rights and the minimum threshold approach. *Human Rights Law Journal* 10 (1-2): 35-51.

EKOS Research Associates. 2006. *Revisiting the privacy landscape a year later.* Office of the Privacy Commissioner of Canada, http://www.privcom.gc.ca/information/survey/ 2006/ekos_2006_e.asp.

Electronic Frontier Foundation. 2007. Unintended consequences: Seven years under the DMCA. Electronic Frontier Foundation, http://www.eff.org/wp/unintended-consequences-seven-years-under-dmca.

EPIC (Electronic Privacy Information Center). 2009. In the matter of Facebook, Inc.: Complaint and request for injunction (draft), request for investigation and for other relief. Before the Federal Trade Commission, Washington, DC. EPIC, http:// epic.org/privacy/facebook/default.html.

European Commission. 1998. High Level Group on Audiovisual Policy. *The digital age: European audiovisual policy.* Brussels: European Commission. European Commission, http://ec.europa.eu/avpolicy/info_centre/library/studies/index_en.htm.

–. 2003. Towards a global partnership in the information society: EU perspective in the context of the United Nations World Summit on the Information Society. European Commission, http://ec.europa.eu/information_society/activities/ internationalrel/docs/wsis/acte_en.pdf.

Facebook. 2008. Terms of use. Facebook, http://www.facebook.com/terms.php.

Feldmann, A. 2007. Internet clean-slate design: What and why? *ACM SIGCOMM Computer Communication Review* 37 (3): 59-64.

Fisher, D. 1982. *The right to communicate: A status report*. Paris: UNESCO.

–. 2002. *The right to communicate: A new beginning*. Right to Communicate, http://www.righttocommunicate.org/viewReference.atm?id=10.

Fisher, D., and L. Harris, eds. 1983. *The right to communicate: A new human right?* Dublin: Boole.

Fleras, A., and J. Kunz. 2001. *Media and minorities, representing diversity in a multicultural Canada*. Toronto: Thompson Educational Publishing.

Foley, J. 2005. The weblog question: People are starting weblogs in growing numbers, but the owner of the content isn't always clear. *InformationWeek*, 31 January. http://www.informationweek.com/story/showArticle.jhtml?articleID=59100462&tid=5979.

Franklin, U. 1996. Stormy weather: Conflicting forces in the information society. Closing address at the 18th International Privacy and Data Protection Conference, Ottawa (excerpted in Canada 1997b, 33-34).

Fremeth, H. 2006. What role can researchers play in connecting the public discussion on communication policy with the communication policy process? Paper presented at the Converging in Parallel conference, Montreal. http://bazu.org/parallel/panel2.html#fremeth.

Fritz, M. 2004. *The gender divide and Internet access in Canada: A critical analysis of concepts, policies, and measurements*. MA thesis, Carleton University.

Gagliardone I., J. Nardi, C. Padovani, G. Nesti, A. Toffalin, and A. Luciano. 2005. *Global Governance Project: European report*. Unpublished research report prepared for the CRIS Campaign and Ford Foundation. Bologna, Italy: Global Governance Project, Italian Team.

Garnham, N. 1997. Amartya Sen's "capabilities" approach to the evaluation of welfare: Its application to communications. *Javnost* 4: 25-34.

Gatheru, W., and M. Mureithi. n.d. *Report on the implementation process of the CRIS communication rights and global governance framework in Kenya*. Unpublished report prepared for the CRIS Campaign and Ford Foundation. Nairobi, Kenya: Research Team and the Association for Progressive Communication.

–. 2004. *Global governance and communication rights: A status review for Kenya (final report)*. Nairobi, Kenya: Association for Progressive Communication and the CRIS Campaign.

Geist, M. 2004. A tale of two sectors (and one disruptive technology). Politech, http://seclists.org/politech/2004/Sep/0023.html.

–. 2005a. Beware big brother disguised as "lawful access." *Toronto Star*, 22 August, C3.

–, ed. 2005b. *In the public interest: The future of Canadian copyright law*. Toronto: Irwin Law.

–. 2005c. The wrong analogy: More on the CRTC VoIP decision. Michael Geist, http://www.michaelgeist.ca/content/view/851/135/.

–. 2007a. Facebook more than just a cool tool for kids. *Toronto Star*, 17 December. http://www.thestar.com/printArticle/286164.

–. 2007b. The policy response to the user-generated content boom. Michael Geist, http://www.michaelgeist.ca/content/view/1599/159/.

–. 2007c. Rogers experimenting with content substitution. Michael Geist, http://www.michaelgeist.ca/content/view/2460/125/.

–. 2007d. U.S. movie piracy claims mostly fiction. *Toronto Star*, 5 February. http://www.thestar.com/Business/article/178181.

–. 2008a. Canadian Heritage committee report raises net neutrality. Michael Geist, http://www.michaelgeist.ca/content/view/2723/125/.

–. 2008b. Facebook helps digital advocates hook up on Parliament Hill. *Ottawa Citizen*, 3 June. http://www.canada.com/ottawacitizen/news/bustech/story.html?id=a6392626-a802-4ca9-a6c8-c015e3196fb4.

Glasbeek, H. 1986. Comment: Entrenchment of freedom of speech for the press – fettering freedom of speech from the people. In *The media, the courts and the Charter*, ed. P. Anisman and A. Linden, 101-18. Toronto: Carswell.

Glendon, M.A. 2000. John P. Humphrey and the drafting of the Universal Declaration of Human Rights. *Journal of the History of International Law* 2 (2): 250-60.

–. 2001. *A world made new: Eleanor Roosevelt and the Universal Declaration of Human Rights*. New York: Random House.

Goodale, J. 1997. The First Amendment and freedom of the press. *Issues of Democracy* 2 (1): 9-14.

Google. 2007. Net neutrality. Google, http://www.google.com/help/netneutrality.html.

Gordon, J. 2006. Tories' program cuts see $1B savings. *National Post*, 26 September. http://www.nationalpost.com/news/story.html?id=6e2fd91b-b20d-4b4d-9b58-55fa090d2af6&k=834&p=1.

Gorham, B. 2006. US shows off new border ID card: RFID technology, Canada debates whether to follow suit. *Montreal Gazette*, 18 October, A14.

Grant, P., and C. Wood. 2004. *Blockbusters and trade wars: Popular culture in a globalized world*. Vancouver: Douglas and McIntyre.

Grieshaber-Otto, J., and S. Sinclair. 2004. *Return to sender: The impact of GATS "pro-competitive regulations" on postal and other public services*. Ottawa: Canadian Centre for Policy Alternatives.

Grimes, S., and L. Shade. 2005. Neopian economics of play: Children's cyberpets and online communities as immersive advertising in NeoPets.com. *International Journal of Media and Cultural Politics* 1 (2): 181-98.

Gunkel, D. 2003. Second thoughts: Toward a critique of the digital divide. *New Media and Society* 5 (4): 499-522.

Gurstein, M. 2003. Effective use: A community informatics strategy beyond the digital divide. *First Monday* 8 (12). http://firstmonday.org/issues/issue8_12/gurstein/index.html.

Habermas, J. 1970. Towards a theory of communicative competence. *Inquiry* 13 (4): 360-75.

–. 1989. *The structural transformation of the public sphere: An inquiry into a category of bourgeois society.* Cambridge, MA: MIT Press.

Hackett, R., and Y. Zhao. 1998. *Sustaining democracy? Journalism and the politics of objectivity.* Toronto: Garamond Press.

Hamelink, C. 2002. Draft declaration on the right to communicate. Geneva: World Summit on the Information Society.

–. 2003. Human rights for the information society. In *Communicating in the information society,* ed. B. Girard and S. Ó Siochrú, 121-63. Geneva: United Nations Research Institute for Social Development.

–. 2004. 2003 Graham Spry Lecture: Toward a human right to communicate. *Canadian Journal of Communication* 29 (2): 205-12.

Hamelink, C., and J. Hoffman. 2008. The state of the right to communicate. *Global Media Journal – American Edition* 7 (13). http://lass.calumet.purdue.edu/cca/gmj/fa08/gmj-fa08-hamelink-hoffman.htm.

Harms, L., J. Richstad, and K. Kie ed. 1977. *The right to communicate: Collected papers.* Honolulu: University of Hawaii Press.

Hébert, C. 2008. Tories' arts cuts spark ire in Quebec. *Toronto Star,* 29 August. http://www.thestar.com/comment/columnists/article/487496.

Heinrich, J., and V. Dufour. 2008. *Circus Quebecus: Sous le chapiteau de la commission Bouchard-Taylor.* Montreal: Les Éditions du Boréal.

Héliot, A. 2009. Cinq colonnes à la une. La part humaine. *Le Figaro,* 13 July 2009, 18.

Henry, F., and C. Tator. 2000. The role and practice of racialized discourse in culture and cultural production. *Journal of Canadian Studies* 35 (3): 120-37.

Hicks, D. 2007. The right to communicate, past mistakes and future possibilities. *Dalhousie Journal of Information and Management* 3 (1). http://djim.management.dal.ca/issues/issue3_1/hicks/index.htm.

Hier, S., J. Greenberg, K. Walby, and D. Lett. 2007. Media, communication and the establishment of public camera surveillance programmes in Canada. *Media, Culture and Society* 29 (5): 727-51.

Higham, R. 1998. The politics of culture in Canada: Creating an environment for maximising human development. Paper presented to the 4 June 1998 meeting of the Canadian Cultural Research Network, Ottawa.

Hindley, H. 1977. Communication rights in an instant world. In *Right to communicate: Collected papers,* ed. L. Harms, J. Richstad, and K. Kie, 10-28. Honolulu: University of Hawaii Press.

Hobbins, A.J., ed. 1994. *On the edge of greatness: The diaries of John Humphrey, first director of the United Nations Division of Human Rights. Volume 1, 1948-1949.* Montreal: McGill University Libraries – Fontanus Monograph Series.

–. 1998. Eleanor Roosevelt, John Humphrey and Canadian opposition to the Universal Declaration of Human Rights: Looking back on the 50th anniversary of the UDHR. *International Journal* 53 (1): 326-41.

–. 2002. John Humphrey's schooldays: The influence of school experience on the Canadian who drafted the Universal Declaration of Human Rights. *McGill Journal of Education* (Spring): 141-58.

Hoffmann-Riem, W. 1996. *Regulating media: The licensing and supervision of broadcasting in six countries.* New York: Guilford Press.

Hogg, P., and A. Bushell Thornton. 1997. The Charter dialogue between courts and legislatures. *Osgoode Hall Law Journal* 35: 75-124.

Hogg, P., A. Bushell Thornton, and W. Wright. 2007. Charter dialogue revisited – Or "much ado about metaphors." *Osgoode Hall Law Journal* 45: 1-50.

Holland, M. 2008. The UK IGF is officially launched, against the backdrop of Nominet's Web best practice challenge. ITPro Internet News, http://www.itpro.co.uk/175698/uk-internet-governance-forum-opens-its-doors.

Horowitz, R. 1989 The irony of regulatory reform: The deregulation of American telecommunications. New York: Oxford University Press.

Hosein, G. 2006. Privacy as freedom. In *Human rights in the global information society,* ed. R. Jørgensen, 121-48. Cambridge, MA: MIT Press.

Hossain, F., A. Cox, J. McGrath, and S. Weitberg. 2009. The stimulus plan: How to spend $787 billion. *New York Times,* 13 February. http://projects.nytimes.com/44th_president/stimulus.

Hudson, H. 2004. Universal access: What have we learned from the e-rate? *Telecommunications Policy* 28: 309-21.

Huffington Post. 2007. Obama promises to reinstate net neutrality during first year in office. *Huffington Post,* 29 October. http://www.huffingtonpost.com/2007/10/29/obama-promises-to-reinsta_n_70317.html.

Human Rights Watch. 2006. Race to the bottom: Corporate complicity in Chinese Internet censorship. Human Rights Watch, http://www.hrw.org/en/reports/2006/08/09/race-bottom.

Humphrey, J. 1984. *Human rights and the United Nations: A great adventure.* New York: Transnational Publishers.

ICAMS. n.d. Campaign declaration. The International Campaign against Mass Surveillance, https://id306.securedata.net/i-cams/Declaration_Eng.html.

International Press Institute. 1953. *The flow of news.* Zurich: International Press Institute.

Intervozes. 2005a. *Global Governance Project Brazilian process report.* Unpublished report prepared for the CRIS Campaign and Ford Foundation. São Paolo, Brazil: Intervozes – Coletivo Brasil de Comunicação Social.

–. 2005b. *Research report: Communication rights in Brazil.* Unpublished report prepared for the CRIS Campaign and Ford Foundation. São Paolo, Brazil: Intervozes – Coletivo Brasil de Comunicação Social.

IPRP (Information Policy Research Program). 1998. Key elements of a national access strategy: A public interest proposal. University of Toronto, Faculty of Information Studies, http://www.fis.utoronto.ca/research/iprp/ua/nacstrat.htm.

ITU (International Telecommunication Union). 2003a. The World Summit on the Information Society: A plan of action. ITU, http://www.itu.int/wsis/docs/geneva/official/poa.html.

–. 2003b. The World Summit on the Information Society: Declaration of principles building the information society: A global challenge in the new millennium. ITU, http://www.itu.int/wsis/docs/geneva/official/dop.html.

–. 2005. The World Summit on the Information Society: The Tunis agenda for the information society. ITU, http://www.itu.int/wsis/docs2/tunis/off/6rev1.html.

ITU and UNESCO. 1995. *The right to communicate: At what price?* UNESCO, http://unesdoc.unesco.org/images/0010/001008/100803e.pdf.

Jade, C. 2007. Canadian music industry wants to re-impose "iPod tax." *Infinite Loop: Ars Technica's Apple Centric Journal*, 10 February. http://arstechnica.com/journals/apple.ars/2007/2/10/6992.

Jiwani, Y. 2005. War talk – engendering terror: Race, gender and representation in Canadian print media. *International Journal of Media and Cultural Politics* 1 (1): 15-21.

John, R. 1999. Theodore N. Vail and the civic origins of universal service. *Business and Economic History* 28 (2): 71-81.

Kahin, B., and J. Keller, eds. 1995. *Public access to the Internet*. Cambridge, MA: MIT Press.

Kahn, R., and D. Kellner. 2004. New media and Internet activism: From the "battle of Seattle" to blogging. *New Media and Society* 6 (1): 87-95.

Karim, H.K. 2006. Nation and diaspora: Rethinking multiculturalism in a transnational context. *International Journal of Media and Cultural Politics* 2 (3): 267-82.

Kayser, J. 1953. One week's news: A comparative study of 17 major dailies for a seven day period. UNESCO, http://unesdoc.unesco.org/images/0006/000628/062870eo.pdf.

Keck, M., and K. Sikkink. 1998. *Activists beyond borders*. Ithaca, NY: Cornell University Press.

Kennedy, T., B. Wellman, and K. Klement. 2003. Gendering the digital divide. *IT and Society* 1 (5): 72-96.

Kenny, C. 2006. *Overselling the Web: Development and the Internet*. Boulder, CO: Lynn Rienner.

Kesterton, W. 1969. A short history of the press in Canada. *International Communication Gazette* 15 (2): 85-92.

Kleinwächter, W. 2004. WSIS: A new diplomacy? Multistakeholder approach and bottom up policy global ICT governance. Berkman Center for Internet and Society at Harvard Law School, http://cyber.law.harvard.edu/wsis/Kleinwachter.html.

Knopf, H. 2006. The copyright clearance culture and Canadian documentaries: A white paper on behalf of the Documentary Organization of Canada. Documentary Organization of Canada, http://docorg.ca/files/White%20Paper_HPK_Copyright&Documentaries.pdf.

Koch, I.E. 2005. Dichotomies, trichotomies or waves of duties? *Human Rights Law Review* 5 (1): 81-103.

Kortteinen, J., K. Myntti, and L. Hannikainen. 1999. Article 19. In *The Universal Declaration of Human Rights: A common standard of achievement*, ed. G. Alfredsoson and A. Eide, 393-416. The Hague: Kluwer Law International.

Krasner, S. 1999. *Sovereignty: Organized hypocrisy.* Princeton, NJ: Princeton University Press.

Kuhlen, R. 2004. Why are communication rights so controversial? World Association for Christian Communication, http://archive.waccglobal.org/wacc/programmes/ recognising_and_building_communication_rights/why_are_communication_ rights_so_controversial.

Kumar, V., and C. Rhoads. 2008. Google wants its own fast track on the Web. *Wall Street Journal*, 15 December. http://online.wsj.com/article/SB122929270127905065.html.

Landry, N. 2006. *Le front social de la communication:* Adbusters *et la contestation de l'économie politique de la communication canadienne.* MA thesis, Université de Montréal.

–. 2007. Le CRTC entend le secteur communautaire et associatif: Dernière journée d'audiences publiques. Media@McGill, http://media.mcgill.ca/en/node/873.

Langer, R. 2005. Five years of Canadian feminist advocacy: Is it still possible to make a difference? *Windsor Year Book of Access to Justice* 23 (1): 115-43.

Lawson, P. 2005. The PIPEDA five-year review: An opportunity to be grasped. *Canadian Privacy Law Review* 2 (10): 109-15.

Lemay-Yates Associates, Inc. 2005. A discussion of the evolution of VoIP regulation worldwide. Report presented to the Canadian Cable Telecommunications Association.

Lewis, B., C. Massey, and R. Smith. 2001. *A tower under siege: Education and technology policy in Canada.* Montreal and Kingston: McGill-Queen's University Press.

Livingstone, S., and P. Lunt. 2007. Representing citizens and consumers in media and communication regulation. *Annals of the American Academy of Political and Social Science* 611 (1): 51-65.

Loader, B., and L. Keeble. 2004. *Challenging the digital divide? A literature review of community informatics initiatives.* York, UK: Joseph Rowntree Foundation.

Longford, G. 2004. Rethinking the virtual state: A critical perspective on e-government. In *Seeking convergence in policy and practice: Communications in the public interest*, vol. 2, ed. M. Moll and L. Shade, 107-38. Ottawa: Canadian Centre for Policy Alternatives.

Longford, G., M. Moll, and L. Shade. 2008. From the "right to communicate" to "consumer right of access": Telecom policy visions from 1970-2007. In *For sale to the highest bidder: Telecom policy in Canada*, ed. M. Moll and L. Shade, 3-16. Ottawa: Canadian Centre for Policy Alternatives.

Looker, D., and V. Thiessen. 2003. The digital divide in Canadian schools: Factors affecting student access to and use of information technology. Statistics Canada, http://www.statcan.gc.ca/bsolc/olc-cel/olc-cel?catno=81-597-X&lang=eng.

Lyon, D. 2003. Introduction. In *Surveillance as social sorting: Privacy, risk and digital discrimination*, ed. D. Lyon, 1-9. London: Routledge.

MacCharles, T. 2009. Obama won't ease restrictions at border. *Toronto Star,* 17 April, A10.

MacDonald, G. 2007. Pirates of the Canadians. *Globe and Mail,* 13 January. http://www.theglobeandmail.com/servlet/story/RTGAM.20070112.wpirates13/BNStory/Entertainment/.

Macdonald, R. 2002. *Lessons of everyday law.* Published for the Law Commission of Canada and the School of Policy Studies, Queen's University. Kingston and Montreal: McGill-Queen's University Press.

MacLeod, I. 2004. A question of balance. *Ottawa Citizen,* 11 December, A1.

Mahtani, M. 2001. Representing minorities: Canadian media and minority identities. *Canadian Ethnic Studies* 33 (3): 99-134.

Manfredi, C. 2002. Strategic behaviour and the Canadian Charter of Rights and Freedoms. In *The Myth of the Sacred: The Charter, the Courts, and the Politics of the Constitution in Canada,* ed. P. James, D. Abelson, and M. Lusztig, 147-70. Montreal and Kingston: McGill-Queen's University Press.

Manley, J. 1998. Speaking notes to Yale University's Distinguished Lecture, New Haven, CT, 26 March. Yale University, http://www.eng.yale.edu/news/web_tracks/manley/default.htm.

Mansell, R. 2001. The deep structure of knowledge societies. In *Vital links for a knowledge culture: Public access to new information and communication technologies,* ed. L. Jeffrey, 55-73. Strasbourg: Council of Europe Publishing.

McCaughey, M., and M. Ayers. 2003. *Cyberactivism: Online activism in theory and practice.* New York: Routledge.

McIver, W., W. Birdsall, and M. Rasmussen. 2003. The Internet and the right to communicate. *First Monday* 8 (12). http://www.firstmonday.org/issues/issue8_12/mciver/.

McIver, W., and W. Birdsall. 2004. Technological evolution and the right to communicate: The implications for electronic democracy. *Electronic Journal of Communication* 14 (3-4). http://www.cios.org/EJCPUBLIC/014/3/01433.html.

McPhail, T., and B. McPhail. 1990. *Communication: The Canadian experience.* Mississauga, ON: Copp Clark Pitman.

McTaggart, C. 2006. Was the Internet ever neutral? Prepared for the 34th Research Conference on Communication, Information and Internet Policy, George Mason University School of Law, Arlington, VA, 30 September. University of Michigan School of Information, http://web.si.umich.edu/tprc/papers/2006/593/mctaggart-tprc06rev.pdf.

Media Awareness Network. 2004. Young Canadians in a wired world – Phase II – focus groups. Mediaawareness.ca, http://www.media-awareness.ca/english/research/YCWW/phaseII/focus_groups.cfm.

Mendel, T. 2003. *The right to communicate: An overview.* London: ARTICLE 19.

Mendelsohn, M. 2002. *Canadians' thoughts on their health care system: Preserving the Canadian model through innovation.* Report prepared for the Commission on the Future of Healthcare. Queen's University, http://www.queensu.ca/cora/_files/Mendelsohn English.pdf.

Menzies, H., and J. Newson. 2007. No time to think. *Time and Society* 16 (1): 83-98.

Mertl, S. 2008. BC gives CCTV the green light. *Toronto Star*, 27 October. http://www.thestar.com/News/Canada/article/525504.

Middleton, C., and J. Ellison. 2008. *Understanding Internet usage among broadband households: A study of household Internet use survey data.* Science, Innovation and Electronic Information Division Working Papers. Ottawa: Statistics Canada.

Middleton, C., and C. Sorensen. 2005. How connected are Canadians? Inequities in Canadian households' Internet access. *Canadian Journal of Communication* 30 (4): 463-83.

Mitrovica, A. 2007. Hear no evil, write no lies. *The Walrus* (December./January): 37-42.

Moll, M. 2007. The good news about CAP. *Making Waves* 18 (2): 10-13.

Moll, M., and H. Robertson. 2001. A "high-wired" balancing act: Technological change and public education in Canada. *Canadian Journal of Educational Communication* 27 (3): 157-74.

Moll, M., and L. Shade. 2001a. *E-commerce vs. e-commons: Communications in the public interest.* Ottawa: Canadian Centre for Policy Alternatives.

–. 2001b. Community networking in Canada: Do you believe in magic? In *E-commerce vs. e-commons: Communications in the public interest,* ed. M. Moll and L. Shade, 165-81. Ottawa: Canadian Centre for Policy Alternatives.

–. 2008. *For sale to the highest bidder: Telecom policy in Canada.* Ottawa: Canadian Centre for Policy Alternatives.

Monahan, P. 2002. *Constitutional law.* Toronto: Irwin Law.

Moon, R. 2000. *The constitutional protection of freedom of expression.* Toronto: University of Toronto Press.

–. 2008. *Report to the Canadian Human Rights Commission concerning section 13 of the Canadian Human Rights Act and the regulation of hate speech on the Internet.* Ottawa: Canadian Human Rights Commission.

Mueller, M. 2007. Net neutrality as global principle for Internet governance. Internet Governance Project, http://internetgovernance.org.

Mueller, M., B. Kuerbis, and C. Pagé. 2007. Democratizing global communication? Global civil society and the Campaign for Communication Rights in the Information Society. *International Journal of Communication* 1: 267-96.

Muhlberger, P. (forthcoming). Online communication and democratic citizenship. In *Democracy in a network society,* ed. J. van Dijk and K. Hacker. London: Sage.

Murray, L. 2004. Protecting ourselves to death: Canada, copyright, and the Internet. *First Monday* 9 (10). http://www.uic.edu/htbin/cgiwrap/bin/ojs/index.php/fm/issue/view/176.

Murray, L., and C. Berggold. 2009. See you in court: Can Canadians practice parody? *Fuse Magazine* 32 (2): 12-17.

Murray L., and S. Trosow. 2007. *Canadian copyright: A citizen's guide.* Toronto: Between the Lines.

MySpace. 2006. MySpace.com terms of use agreement, 15 June. MySpace, http://www1. myspace.com/index.cfm?fuseaction=misc.terms.

NFB (National Film Board). 2008. National Film Board of Canada: Broadcasting Notice CRTC 2008-44 comments on the scope of a future proceeding on Canadian broadcasting in new media. CRTC, http://www.crtc.gc.ca/eng/archive/2009/2009-329. htm.

–. 2009. National Film Board of Canada: Broadcasting Notice of Public Hearing CRTC 2008-11 comments on Canadian broadcasting in new media. NFB, http://www. onf-nfb.gc.ca/.../medias/.../publications/broadcasting-notice-public-hearing-CRTC-2008-11-08-12-05.pdf.

Nimijean, R. 2006.The politics of branding Canada: The international-domestic nexus and the rethinking of Canada's place in the world. *Revista Mexicana de Estudios Canadienses* 11 (6). http://revista.amec.com.mx/num_11_2006.html.

Nissenbaum, H. 2004. Privacy as contextual integrity. *Washington Law Review* 79: 101-39.

Noakes, S. 2008. In depth: Bill C-10 and Canada's film industry. *Cbcnews.ca,* 10 April. http://www.cbc.ca/arts/film/billc-10.html.

Noam, E. 1994. Beyond liberalization II: The impending doom of common carriage. *Telecommunications Policy* 18 (6): 435-52.

Nordenstreng, K., ed. 1986. *New international information and communication order: Sourcebook.* Prague: International Organization of Journalists.

Norman, D. 2002. *The design of everyday things.* New York: Basic Books (Perseus).

Norris, P. 2001. *Digital divide: Civic engagement, information poverty and the Internet worldwide.* Cambridge, UK: Cambridge University Press.

Nowak, Peter. 2008. Government urged to spend spectrum proceeds on broadband. *Cbcnews.ca,* 14 July. http://www.cbc.ca/technology/story/2008/07/14/tech-spectrum. html.

O'Connell, P., ed. 2005. At SBC, it's all about "scale and scope." *BusinessWeek Online,* http://www.businessweek.com/@@n34h*IUQu7KtOwgA/magazine/content/ 05_45/b3958092.htm.

O'Donnell, S., S. Perley, B. Walmark, K. Burton, B. Beaton, and A. Sark. 2007. Community-based broadband organizations and video communications for remote and rural First Nations in Canada. In *Proceedings of the Community Informatics Research Network (CIRN) 2007 conference,* Prato, Italy, 5-7 November.

OECD (Organisation for Economic Co-operation and Development). 2001. *Understanding the digital divide.* OECD, http://www.oecd.org/dsti/sti/prod/Digital_divide.pdf.

–. 2005. OECD broadband statistics, June 2005. OECD, http://www.oecd.org/document/ 16/0,2340,en_2649_34225_35526608_1_1_1_1,00.html.

–. 2007a. Working Party on Telecommunication and Information Services Policies. *Internet traffic prioritization: An overview.* Paris: OECD.

–. 2007b. OECD broadband subscribers per 100 inhabitants, by technology, December 2007. OECD, http://www.oecd.org/document/54/0,3343,en_2649_33703_38690102_1_1_1_1,00.html.

–. 2007c. *Participative Web and user-created content: Web 2.0, wikis, and social networking.* Paris: OECD.

–. 2008. OECD key indicators, broadband subscribers per 100 inhabitants in OECD countries, December 2008. OECD, http://www.oecd.org/document/23/0,3343, en_2649_34449_33987543_1_1_1_37441,00.html.

Ohio University. 2007. Ohio University announces changes in file-sharing policies. Press release. Ohio University, http://www.ohio.edu/students/filesharing.cfm.

OIPCBC (Office of the Information and Privacy Commissioner of British Columbia). 2004. *Privacy and the USA Patriot Act: Implications for British Columbia public sector outsourcing.* OIPCBC, http://www.oipc.bc.ca/sector_public/archives/usa_patriot_act/pdfs/report/privacy-final.pdf.

Ojo, T. 2006. Ethnic print media in the multicultural nation of Canada: A case study of the black newspaper in Montreal. *Journalism* 7 (3): 343-61.

O'Malley, K. 2007. A copycat campaign. *Macleans.ca,* Kady O'Malley's blog: 17 January. Reprinted MekTek forums: 19 January 2007, http://www.mektek.net/forums/index.php?showtopic=79802.

O'Neill, J. 2003. Canada's dossier on Maher Arar. *Ottawa Citizen,* 8 November, A.1.

OPC (Office of the Privacy Commissioner of Canada). 2002. *Annual report to Parliament, 2001-02.* Office of the Privacy Commissioner of Canada, http://www.privcom.gc.ca/information/02_05_e.asp#002.

–. 2005. *Response to the government of Canada's "lawful access" consultations.* Office of the Privacy Commissioner of Canada, http://www.privcom.gc.ca/information/pub/sub_la_050505_e.asp.

–. 2006a. *Annual report to Parliament 2005: Report on the Personal Information Protection and Electronic Documents Act.* Office of the Privacy Commissioner of Canada, http://www.privcom.gc.ca/information/ar/200506/2005_pipeda_e.pdf.

–. 2006b. *Annual report to Parliament 2005-2006.* Office of the Privacy Commissioner of Canada, http://www.privcom.gc.ca/information/ar/200506/200506_pa_e.pdf.

–. 2006c. *PIPEDA review discussion document: Protecting privacy in an intrusive world.* Office of the Privacy Commissioner of Canada, http://www.privcom.gc.ca/information/pub/pipeda_review_060718_e.asp.

O'Reilly, T. 2005. What is Web 2.0? Design patterns and business models for the next generation of software. O'Reilly, http://www.oreillynet.com/pub/a/oreilly/tim/news/2005/09/30/what-is-web-20.html.

Organizing for America. n.d. Barack Obama: Connecting and empowering all Americans through technology and innovation. Barackobama.com, http://www.barackobama.com/issues/technology/.

Oscapella, E. 2000. Canada's Privacy Rights Charter: A report. *Privacy Laws and Business International Newsletter 31*. World Legal Information Institute, http://www.worldlii.org/int/journals/PLBIN/2000/31.html.

Ó Siochrú, S. 2004a. A tale of paragraph 4: Stating the obvious at the WSIS. *Information Technologies and International Development* 1 (3-4): 49-50.

–. 2004b. Will the real WSIS please stand up? The historic encounter of the "information society" and the "communication society." *Gazette: The International Journal for Communication Studies* 66 (3-4): 203-24.

–. 2004c. Communication rights defend, expand and create spaces for democratic discussion. World Association for Christian Communication, http://www.wacc.org.uk/wacc/publications/media_development/2004_3/communication_rights_defend_expand_and_create_spaces_for_democratic_discussion.

–. 2005a. Finding a frame: Towards a transnational advocacy campaign to democratize communication. In *Democratizing global media: One world, many struggles*, ed. R. Hackett and Y. Zhao, 289-311. New York and Oxford: Roman and Littlefield.

–. 2005b. Global media governance as a potential site of civil society intervention. In *Democratizing global media: One world, many struggles*, ed. R. Hackett and Y. Zhao, 205-21. New York and Oxford: Roman and Littlefield.

Ó Siochrú, S., and B. Girard. 2002. *Global media governance: A beginner's guide.* Boulder, CO, and London: Rowman and Littlefield.

Padovani, C. 2005. Debating communication imbalances from the MacBride Report to the World Summit on the Information Society: An analysis of a changing discourse. *Global Media and Communication* 1 (3): 316-38.

Padovani, C., and K. Nordenstreng. 2005. From NWICO to WSIS: Another world information and communication order? *Global Media and Communication* 1 (3): 264-72.

Panetta, A., and J. Bronskill. 2006. Tories backing away from key plank in proposed Accountability Act. Free Dominion, http://www.freedominion.com.pa/phpBB2/viewtopic.php?p=715286.

Paré, D. 2004. The digital divide: Why the "the" is misleading. In *Human rights in the digital age*, ed. A. Murray and M. Klang, 85-98. London: Cavendish Publishing.

Peissl, W. 2003. Surveillance and security: A dodgy relationship. *Journal of Contingencies and Crisis Management* 11 (1): 19-24.

People's Communication Charter. n.d. People's communication charter text. People's Communication Charter, http://www.pccharter.net/charteren.html.

Perkins, T. 2006. Privacy chief eyes US border – Federal court asked to overturn commissioner's ruling. *Toronto Star*, 17 July. http://www.thestar.com/NASApp/cs/ContentServer?pagename=thestar/Layout/Article_Type1&call_pageid=971358637177&c=Article&cid=1153087815066.

Peslak, A. 2005. An ethical exploration of privacy and radio frequency identification. *Journal of Business Ethics* 59 (4): 327-45.

Peters, J. 2005. *Courting the abyss: Free speech and the liberal tradition.* Chicago: University of Chicago Press.

Peters, K. 1995. Police join St. Elizabeth probe: Investigators join regional coroner in looking into "high mortality rate" after deaths of 42 seniors at home. *Hamilton Spectator,* 23 June, C.1.

Petter, A. 1989. Canada's Charter flight: Soaring backwards into the future. *Journal of Law and Society* 16 (2): 151-65.

–. 2007. Taking dialogue theory much too seriously (or perhaps Charter dialogue isn't such a good thing after all). *Osgoode Hall Law Journal* 45: 147-67.

Pickard, V. 2007. Neoliberal visions and revisions in global communications policy from NWICO to WSIS. *Journal of Communication Inquiry* 32 (2): 118-39.

Piper, T. 2008. Two tiers of freedom: Communication rights and the right to communicate in Canada by Marc Raboy and Jeremy Shtern. Presentation given at the 2nd session of the McGill University Arts/Law Colloquium, Montreal, 8 February.

Planet Peace Project. n.d.a. Global governance and communication rights – a report on the implementation of the project: Colombia. Unpublished report prepared for the CRIS Campaign and the Ford Foundation. Bogotá, Colombia: Planet Peace Project in collaboration with COLNODO – APC and ORION project.

–. n.d.b. Global governance and communication rights main report: Colombia. Unpublished report prepared for the CRIS Campaign and the Ford Foundation. Bogotá, Colombia: Planet Peace Project in collaboration with COLNODO – APC and ORION project.

Powell, A. 2008. *Co-productions of technology, culture and policy in North America's community wireless networking movement.* PhD dissertation, Department of Communication Studies, Concordia University.

Powell, A., and L. Shade. 2006. Going Wi-Fi in Canada: Municipal and community initiatives. *Government Information Quarterly* 23 (3-4): 381-403.

Proulx, S., and N. Lecomte. 2005. *Une monographie de Communautique.* CRACIN working paper no. 7, September 2005. Toronto: Canadian Research Alliance for Community Innovation and Networking.

Proulx, S., and M. Raboy. 2003. Viewers on television: Between policy and uses. *Gazette* 65 (4-5): 331-46.

PWAC (Professional Writers Association of Canada). 2007. Professional Writers Association of Canada calls, again, for respect for copyright in contracts. News release. PWAC, http://www.pwac.ca/files/PDF/Press.Oct07.Contracts.pdf.

Raboy, M. 1990. *Missed opportunities: The story of Canada's broadcasting policy.* Montreal and Kingston: McGill-Queen's University Press.

–. 1995a. Influencing public policy on Canadian broadcasting. *Canadian Public Administration* 38 (3): 411-32.

–. 1995b. The role of public consultation in shaping the Canadian broadcasting system. *Canadian Journal of Political Science* 28 (3): 455-77.

–. 2003. Media and democratization in the information society. In *Communicating in the information society*, ed. S. Ó Siochrú and B. Girard, 103-21. Geneva: United Nations Research Institute for Social Development.

–. 2004a. CRTC is doing its job. *Montreal Gazette*, 16 July. Friends of Canadian Broadcasting, http://www.friends.ca/News/Friends_News/archives/articles07160406.asp.

–. 2004b. The origins of civil society involvement in the WSIS. *Information Technologies and International Development* 1 (3-4): 95-96.

–. 2004c. The World Summit on the Information Society and its legacy for global governance. *Gazette: The International Journal for Communication Studies* 66: 225-32.

–. 2006. The 2005 Graham Spry Memorial Lecture: Making media – creating the conditions for communication in the public good. *Canadian Journal of Communication* 31 (2): 289-306.

Raboy, M., and B. Abramson. 2005. *Media regulation in Canada*. A report prepared for the Institute of European Media Law, Saarbrücken, and the Hans-Bredow-Institute, Hamburg, study on co-regulatory measures in the media sector.

Raboy, M., and G. Bonin. 2008. From culture to business to culture: Shifting winds at the CRTC. In *For sale to the highest bidder: Telecom policy in Canada*, ed. L. Shade and M. Moll, 61-72. Ottawa: Canadian Centre for Policy Alternatives.

Raboy, M., and N. Landry. 2005. *Civil society, communication and global governance: Issues from the World Summit on the Information Society*. New York: Peter Lang.

Raboy, M., and J. Shtern. 2005. The Internet as a global public good: Towards a Canadian position on Internet governance for WSIS phase II. In *Paving the Road to Tunis/WSIS II*, ed. P. Dugré, 126-32. Ottawa: Canadian Commission for UNESCO.

Ramírez, R., H. Aitkin, G. Kora, and D. Richardson. 2005. Community engagement, performance measurement and sustainability: Experiences from Canadian community-based networks. *Canadian Journal of Communication* 30 (2): 259-79.

Reddick, A. 2000. *The dual digital divide: The information highway in Canada*. Ottawa: Public Interest Advocacy Centre.

Reddick, A., and C. Boucher. 2002. Tracking the dual digital divide. Human Resources and Skills Development Canada, http://www.hrsdc.gc.ca/en/hip/lld/olt/Skills_Development/OLTResearch/tracking_dual_digital_divide.shtml.

Reddick, A., C. Boucher, and M. Groseilliers. 2001. *Rethinking the information highway: Rethinking the dual digital divide*. Ottawa: Human Resources and Skills Development Canada, http://olt-bta.hrdc-drhc.gc.ca/resources/information_highway(2001)_e.pdf.

Regan, P. 2004. Old issues, new context: Privacy, information collection, and homeland security. *Government Information Quarterly* 21: 481-97.

Reporters Without Borders. 2006. "World press freedom index 2006." Reporters Without Borders, http://www.rsf.org/en-classement70-2006.html.

–. 2009. "World press freedom index 2009." Reporters Without Borders, http://www.rsf.org/en-classement1003-2009.html.

Reporters Without Borders Canada. 2004. Dangerous precedent as journalist sentenced for protecting his sources. Reporters Without Borders Canada, http://www. rsfcanada.org/article.php3?id_article=97.

Richards, G. 2008. Ambulance in toddler death sent to wrong city. *Canwest News Services*, 1 May. http://www.canada.com/topics/news/national/story.html?id=34cc49 f4-d0a5-4377-8139-bc66253b8764&k=46053.

Richstad, J., and L. Harms, eds. 1977. *Evolving perspectives on the right to communicate.* Honolulu: East-West Center, East-West Communication Institute.

Richstad, J., L. Harms, and K. Kie. 1977. The emergence of the right to communicate, 1970-1975. In *The right to communicate: Collected papers*, ed. L. Harms, J. Richstad, and K. Kie, 112-36. Honolulu: University of Hawaii Press.

Rideout, V. 2003. *Continentalizing Canadian telecommunications: The politics of regulatory reform.* Montreal and Kingston: McGill-Queen's University Press.

Rideout, V., and A. Reddick. 2005. Sustaining community access to technology: Who should pay and why! *Journal of Community Informatics* 1 (2): 45-62.

Risen, J. 2005. Bush lets US spy on callers without courts. *New York Times*, 15 December. http://www.nytimes.com/2005/12/16/politics/16program.html?ei=5090&en= e32072d786623ac1&ex=1292389200.

Ross, J. 2003. The protection of freedom of expression by the Supreme Court of Canada. In *The Canadian Charter of Rights and Freedoms: Reflections on the Charter after twenty years*, ed. J.E. Magnet, G.A. Beaudoin, G. Gall, and C. Manfredi, 81-109. Toronto: LexisNexis Butterworths.

Rotenberg, M. 2007. Remarks made at Internet privacy symposium: Research findings from the Office of the Privacy Commissioner of Canada Contributions Program. University of Ottawa, Law and Technology Group, 23 February.

Roth, K. 2004. Defending economic, social and cultural rights: Practical issues faced by an international human rights organization. *Human Rights Quarterly* 26: 63-73.

Roth, L. 2005. *Something new in the air: The story of First People's broadcasting in Canada.* Montreal and Kingston: McGill-Queen's University Press.

Roy, J. 2006. *E-government in Canada: Transformation for the digital age.* Ottawa: University of Ottawa Press.

Ryan, M. 1998. *Knowledge diplomacy: Global competition and the politics of intellectual property.* Washington, DC: Brookings Institution.

Saint-Amour, P. 2003. *The copyrights: Intellectual property and the literary imagination.* Ithaca, NY: Cornell University Press.

Saint-Jean, A. 2003a. Rapport final tome 1 : Les effets de la concentration des médias au Québec: Analyse et recommendations. Québec: Comité conseil sur la qualité et la diversité de l'information.

–. 2003b. Rapport final tome 2: Les effets de la concentration des médias au Québec: Problématique, recherche et consultations. Québec: Comité conseil sur la qualité et la diversité de l'information.

Sallot, J. 2007. Terror vote fails as Dion reins in liberals. *Globe and Mail*, 28 February, A1.

Salter, L., and P. Anderson. 1985. Responsive broadcasting: Mechanisms for handling complaints about broadcast program content. Report prepared for the Canadian government, Department of Communications.

Saltzer, J., D. Reed, and D. Clark. 1984. End-to-end arguments in system design. Massachusetts Institute of Technology, http://web.mit.edu/Saltzer/www/publications/endtoend/endtoend.pdf.

Schement, J. 2001. Of gaps by which democracy we measure. In *The digital divide: Facing a crisis or creating a myth?* ed. B. Compaine, 303-7. Cambridge, MA: MIT Press.

Schement, J., and S. Forbes. 2000. Identifying temporary and permanent gaps in universal service. *Information Society* 16 (2): 117-26.

Schneiderman, D. 2004. Canadian constitutionalism, the rule of law, and economic globalization. In *Participatory justice in a global economy: The new rule of law,* ed. P. Hughes and P. Molinari, 65-85. Montreal: Thémis. Canadian Institute for the Administration of Justice, http://www.ciaj-icaj.ca/francais/publications/2003/schneiderman.pdf.

Schultz, R. 2005. Mandates and operations of the CRTC and Competition Bureau in media mergers and acquisitions. Unpublished research report prepared for the Senate Standing Committee on Transportation and Communications review of the state of Canadian media.

Sciadas, G. 2002. The digital divide in Canada. *Innovation Analysis Bulletin* 4 (3). Statistics Canada, http://www.statcan.ca/english/IPS/Data/88-003-XPE20020036378.htm.

Science Council of Canada. 1971. *A trans-Canada computer communications network: Phase I of a major program on computers.* Ottawa: Information Canada.

Selwyn, N. 2004. Reconsidering political and popular understandings of the digital divide. *New Media and Society* 6 (3): 341-62.

Shade, L. 2003. Here comes the Dot Force! The new cavalry for equity? *Gazette: The International Journal for Communication Studies* 65 (2): 107-20.

–. 2004. Situating communication rights historically. In *Seeking convergence in policy and practice: Communications in the public interest,* vol. 2, ed. M. Moll and L. Shade, 83-92. Ottawa: Canadian Centre for Policy Alternatives.

–. 2008. Public interest activism in Canadian ICT policy: Blowin' in the policy winds. *Global Media Journal (Canadian Edition)* 1 (1): 107-21. http://www.gmj.uottawa.ca/current-issue_e.html#.

Shade, L., and B. Crow. 2004. Canadian feminist perspectives on digital technology. *Topia: Canadian Journal of Cultural Studies* 11 (Spring): 161-76.

Shade, L., and D. Dechief. 2004. Canada's SchoolNet: Wiring up schools? in *Global Perspectives on e-learning: Rhetoric and reality,* ed. A. Carr-Chellman, 131-44. Thousand Oaks, CA: Sage Publications.

Shade, L., N. Porter, and W. Sanchez. 2005. "You can see anything on the Internet," "you can do anything on the Internet!": Young Canadians talk about the Internet. *Canadian Journal of Communication* 30 (4): 503-26.

Shannon, C., and W. Weaver. 1949. *A mathematical model of communication*. Urbana, IL: University of Illinois Press.

Shaw Communications. n.d. What do you call a $250 million boondoggle? Shaw Communications, https://secure.shaw.ca/apps/Secure/CRTCForms/CTF.aspx.

Shea, A. 1949. Book review of Canada and the United Nations 1948. *Canadian Journal of Economics and Political Science/Revue canadienne d'economique et de science politique* 15 (3): 439-40.

–. 1963. *Broadcasting the Canadian way*. Montreal: Harvest House.

Shtern, J. 2006. A civilization of many minds: The WSIS and the emergence of multiple, competing visions of the Internet. In *The IAMCR CAIRO 2006 Proceedings*, 87-92. Cairo: International Association for Media and Communication Research.

Shue, H. 1996. *Basic rights: Subsistence, affluence and US foreign policy*, 2nd ed. Princeton, NJ: Princeton University Press.

Sinclair, G., H. Intven, and A. Tremblay. 2006. *Telecommunications Policy Review Panel: Final report 2006*. Telecommunications Policy Review Panel, http://www.telecomreview.ca.

Slater, D., and T. Wu. 2008. Homes with tails: What if you could own your Internet connection? New America Foundation, Wireless Future Program, working paper no. 23. New America Foundation, http://www.newamerica.net/files/HomesWithTails_wu_slater.pdf.

Smeltzer, S., and L. Shade. 2003. Resisting the market model of the information highway in Canada. In *Public broadcasting and the public interest*, ed. Mike McCauley, 226-37. Armonk, NY: M.E. Sharpe.

Somera, N., and A. Alegre. 2005. Communication rights project: Philippines global governance project@PH process report ver. 4. Unpublished report prepared for the CRIS Campaign and the Ford Foundation. Manila, Philippines: Foundation for Media Alternatives.

Statistics Canada. 2004. Household Internet use survey (2003 data). *The Daily*, 8 July. http://www.statcan.ca/Daily/English/040708/d040708a.htm.

–. 2006. Canadian Internet use survey (2005 data). *The Daily*, 15 August. http://www.statcan.ca/Daily/English/060815/d060815b.htm.

–. 2007. Residential telephone service survey: December 2006. *The Daily*, 4 May. http://www.statcan.ca/Daily/English/070504/d070504a.htm.

–. 2008 Canadian Internet use survey (2007 data). *The Daily*, 12 June. http://www.statcan.gc.ca/daily-quotidien/080612/dq080612b-eng.htm.

Steeves, V. 2006. Privacy and new media. In *Mediascapes: New patterns in Canadian communication*, 2nd ed., ed. P. Attallah and L. Shade, 250-65. Toronto: Thomson Nelson.

Steinhardt, B. 2003. Does privacy have a future after 9/11? *Journal of Contingencies and Crisis Management* 11 (1): 32-36.

Steinstra, D., J. Watzke, and G. Birch. 2007. A three-way dance: The global public good and accessibility in information technologies. *Information Society* 23: 149-58.

Sun Microsystems. n.d. Sun guidelines on public discourse. Sun Microsystems, http://www.sun.com/communities/guidelines.jsp.

Surman, M., and K. Reilly. 2003. *Appropriating the Internet for social change: Towards the strategic use of networked technologies by transnational civil society organizations.* New York: Social Science Research Council.

Tambini, D., and J. Cowling. 2004. *From public service broadcasting to public service communication.* London: Institute for Public Policy Research.

Tambini, D., and S. Verhulst. 2000. The transition to digital and content regulation. In *Communications revolution and reform,* ed. D. Tambini, 5-20. London: Institute for Public Policy Research.

Tawfik, M. 2005. Is the WTO/TRIPS agreement user-friendly? Canadian Library Association, http://www.cla.ca/AM/TemplateRedirect.cfm?template=/CM/ContentDisplay.cfm&ContentID=4255.

Taylor, C. 1992. *Multiculturalism and the politics of recognition.* Princeton, NJ: Princeton University Press.

–. 1993. *Reconciling the solitudes: Essays on Canadian federalism and nationalism.* Montreal and Kingston: McGill-Queen's University Press.

Thussu, D. 2006. *International communication: Continuity and change,* 2nd ed. London: Hodder Education.

Tibbetts, J. 2007. Tories will not act to curb movie piracy. *National Post,* 13 February, A7.

Tomuschat, C. 2003. *Human rights: Between idealism and realism.* Oxford: Oxford University Press.

Toronto Police Service. n.d. Toronto Police Service closed circuit television. Toronto Police Service, http://www.torontopolice.on.ca/media/text/20061214-tps_cctv_project.pdf.

Traber, M., and K. Nordenstreng. 1992. *Few voices, many worlds: Towards a media reform movement.* London: World Association for Christian Communication.

Trosow, S. 2008. Educational use of the Internet amendment: Is it necessary? Sam Trosow, http://samtrosow.ca/content/view/27/1/.

Trudel, P. 1984. *Droit de l'information et de la communication.* Montreal: Thémis.

–. 2008. Projet de loi C-10 – une violation injustifiée de la liberté d'expression. *Le Devoir,* 7 April. http://www.ledevoir.com/2008/04/07/183930.html.

Tuano, P., and A. Alegre. 2005. Communication rights in Philippines, national report summary. Unpublished report prepared for the CRIS Campaign and the Ford Foundation. Manila, Philippines: Foundation for Media Alternatives.

Turner, S.D. 2007. "Shooting the messenger": Myth vs. reality – U.S. broadband policy and international broadband rankings. Free Press, http://freepress.net/files/shooting_the_messenger.pdf.

United Nations. 2003. Statement on World Telecommunication Day, UN Secretary-General, 17 May, New York.

UNESCO (United Nations Educational, Scientific and Cultural Organization). 1974. The Eighteenth Session of the General Conference. UNESCO Resolution 4.121, *Right to communicate*. Right to Communicate, http://www.righttocommunicate.org/viewDocument.atm?sectionName=rights&id=2.

–. 1980. International Commission for the Study of Communication Problems. *Many voices, one world*. Paris: UNESCO. Reissued as *Many voices one world: Towards a new, more just, and more efficient world information and communication order*. Lanham, MD: Rowman and Littlefield, 2004.

–. 1983. The Twenty-second Session of the General Conference. *Contribution des états membres: Point 38.2 de l'ordre de jour provisoire*. Paris: UNESCO.

–. 1985. The Twenty-third Session of the General Conference. *The right to communicate: Report of the Director-General*. Paris: UNESCO.

–. 2002. *Briefing session with permanent delegations on the World Summit on the Information Society: Background documents*. UNESCO, http://portal.unesco.org/ci/en/file_download.php/b974ea024adf047d58a02366f1eae77bWSIS_Perm_Delg_2002_3_background.doc.

–. n.d. International Commission for the Study of Communication Problems. *From the free flow of information to the free and balanced flow of information*. Commission document no. 8. Paris: UNESCO.

US. 2006. Office of the US Trade Representative. *2006 special 301 report*. Office of the US Trade Representative, http://www.ustr.gov/Document_Library/Reports_Publications/2006/2006_Special_301_Review/Section_Index.html.

Van Ham, P. 2001. The rise of the brand state: The postmodern politics of image and reputation. *Foreign Affairs* 80 (5): 2-6.

Van Schewick, B., and D. Farber. 2009. Point/counterpoint: Network neutrality nuances. *Communications of the ACM* 52 (2): 31-37. Association for Computing Machinery, http://doi.acm.org/10.1145/1461928.1461942.

Vaver, D. 2000. *Copyright law*. Toronto: Irwin Law.

Veenhof, B., B. Wellman, C. Quell, and B. Hogan. 2008. *How Canadians' use of the Internet affects social life and civic participation*. Ottawa: Statistics Canada.

Vipond, M. 2000. *The mass media in Canada*, 3rd ed. Toronto: James Lorimer.

Viseu, A., A. Clement, J. Aspinall, and T. Kennedy. 2006. The interplay of public and private spaces in Internet access. *Information, Communication and Society* 9 (5): 633-56.

Voices 21. 1999. A global movement for people's voices in media and communication in the 21st century: Full statement. Voices 21, http://comunica.org/v21/statement.htm.

W3C. 2006. My data, your data, the Web's data: Challenges of data ownership. Discussion panel held at W3C Technical Plenary and WG Meeting Week, Mandelieu, France, 1 March. W3C, http://www.w3.org/2006/03/01-TechPlenAgenda.html.

Walters, G. 2001. *Human rights in an information age: A philosophical analysis.* Toronto: University of Toronto Press.

Warschauer, M. 2003. *Technology and social inclusion: Rethinking the digital divide.* Cambridge, MA: MIT Press.

Webb, M. 2007. *Illusions of security: Global surveillance and democracy in the post-9/11 world.* San Francisco: City Lights.

Weil, D. 2005. Microsoft's employee guidelines for successful blogging. DebbieWeil, http://blogwrite.blogs.com/blogwrite/2005/01/microsofts_empl.html.

White, P. 2009. Unmanned drone prowls over the lonely prairie. *Globe and Mail,* 18 February. http://www.theglobeandmail.com/servlet/story/LAC.20090218. DRONES18/TPStory/TPInternational/America/.

Whitton, J. 1949. The United Nations conference on freedom of information and the movement against international propaganda. *American Journal of International Law* 43 (1): 73-87.

Williams, R. 1976. *Keywords: A vocabulary of culture and society.* New York: Oxford University Press.

Winnipeg Police Service. n.d. Closed circuit television pilot project. City of Winnipeg, http://www.winnipeg.ca/police/CCTV/default.stm.

Witteveen, W., and B. van Klink. 1999. Why is soft law really law? *RegelMaat: Journal for Legislative Studies* (3): 126-40.

Worboy, M. 2008. No censorship threat in Bill C-10: Verner. *Canwest News Service,* 4 March. http://www.canada.com/topics/news/story.html?id=bb3a9a5e-e1f9-4b03-a0f7-2fe42794982a&k=80275.

World Commission on Culture and Development. 1995. *Our creative diversity: Report of the World Commission on Culture and Development.* Paris: UNESCO.

Yahoo! n.d. Yahoo! personal blog guidelines: 1.0. Jeremy D. Zawodny, http://jeremy.zawodny.com/yahoo/yahoo-blog-guidelines.pdf.

Yankelovich, D. 1991. Coming to public judgment: Making democracy work in a complex world. Syracuse, NY: Syracuse University Press.

Zerbisias, A. 2007. Shaw could kill TV fund. *Toronto Star,* 23 January. http://www.thestar.com/article/173774.

... About the Authors

WILLIAM J. MCIVER JR. is a computer scientist who is interested in understanding the social impacts of information and communication technologies and in designing technologies to address life-critical issues in communities. He is based in Fredericton, New Brunswick, where he is a Senior Research Officer in the People-Centred Technologies Group within the National Research Council of Canada's Institute for Information Technology.

LAURA J. MURRAY is Associate Professor in the Department of English at Queen's University in Kingston, Ontario. She is the co-author, with Samuel E. Trosow, of *Canadian Copyright: A Citizen's Guide* (Between the Lines, 2007), and she writes the blog www.faircopyright.ca. Her current research concerns relations between intellectual property and alternative economies of creativity, such as those operating in academic research, indigenous communities, open source software design, journalism, and the culinary arts.

SEÁN Ó SIOCHRÚ is a researcher, writer, and advocate on communication rights issues and the international spokesperson of the Communication Rights in the Information Society (CRIS) Campaign. Working mainly for international organizations and NGOs on media and communication policy, programs, and evaluation, he is the author of several books and serves as chair of Dublin Community Television in his native Ireland.

MARC RABOY is Professor and Beaverbrook Chair in Ethics, Media and Communications in the Department of Art History and Communication Studies at McGill University in Montreal. He is a former journalist in a wide variety of media, the author or editor of numerous books and journal articles on media and communication policy, and a frequent consultant to governments, NGOs, and international organizations. He is the director of Media@McGill, a hub of research, scholarship, and public outreach on issues and controversies in media, technology, and culture.

LESLIE REGAN SHADE is Associate Professor in the Department of Communication Studies at Concordia University in Montreal. Her teaching and research focus primarily on the social, ethical, and policy aspects of information and communication technologies, particularly on gender and youth. Her research contributions straddle the line between academic and non-academic audiences, including policy makers and not-for-profit groups.

JEREMY SHTERN is a Fonds québécois de la recherche sur la société et la culture postdoctoral fellow in the Faculty of Communication and Design at Ryerson University in Toronto and is affiliated with the Media@McGill unit for critical communication studies at McGill University in Montreal. His research focuses on the intersection of media and communication policy, globalization, and digital technologies.

Index

9-1-1 emergency services, 156, 157, 173, 240, 315*n*5, 316*n*18

9/11 terrorist attacks: impact on human rights, 42-43, 187-88; impact on journalistic freedom, 70; impact on right to privacy, 82, 175-77, 185-92; and reduced funding for access to ICTs, 133; and representation of minorities in media, 74, 114. *See also* anti-terrorism laws

Aboriginal peoples: and *Broadcasting Act*, 104, 109-10, 308*n*25; customary laws (artists), 208; and diversity in media content and language, 72, 74, 251; Internet access for youth education, 129; media services for, 85, 87-88, 111; and network neutrality in remote communities, 157-58; SchoolNet, 132

Aboriginal Peoples Television Network (APTN), 87-88, 111

access to ICTs: as CR, 122, 125-26, 130-31, 143; citizen activism for, 143-44; consumer right vs citizen right, 136-37; digital divides, 127-29; factors affecting, 75-76, 79, 129-32; government funding, 76-77, 122, 132-34;

in developing countries, 127, 128-29; measuring, 135-36; and network neutrality, 155-58; policy over-simplification, 134-35; rural and remote communities, 75, 88, 120-23, 127, 130-34, 140(t), 142(t), 144, 147, 156-57, 169-70, 239-40; socio-technical model, 137-38, 138(f), 139-42(t); universality as policy goal, 122-25

access to information: about copyright law, 211-14; as human right, 30; assessing, 17; current status in Canada, 71-72, 220; indispensable to democracy, 3; public right to, 259; recommendations, 259

Access to Information Act, 71, 188

access to knowledge: assessing, 17; current status in Canada, 12, 77-79; curtailed by copyright, 43, 78; recommendations, 233; and VoIP, 171; and Web 2.0, 163, 165

access to means of communication: assessing, 17; current status in Canada, 12, 74-77, 250; and governmental powers of censorship, 69

Adbusters Media Foundation, 65-67, 305*n*10, 306*n*11

Advanced Research Projects Agency Network (ARPANET), 75, 146
advertising: by media owners vs media criticizers, 306n11; during elections, 66; and freedom of expression vs R2C, 65-67; and marketers use of web information, 185
Aeronautics Act, 189
affordances, 145-46, 162, 165, 174
age, and access to ICTs, 127, 129
Al Jazeera, 87, 309n43
Al Jazeera English, 309n43
Alberta, 92-93, 172
Alliance Atlantis, 99
Alliance canadienne des radiodiffuseurs communautaires du Canada (ARC), 116
Alliance of Canadian Cinema, Television and Radio Artists, 208
al-Qaeda, 94
alternative broadcasting, 35, 72, 248, 307n22
Ambrosi, Alain, 295n8
American Civil Liberties Union (ACLU), 186, 187
American Telephone and Telegraph Company, 123
Amnesty International, 9, 49
Annan, Kofi, 302n6
anti-terrorism laws and policies: *Anti-terrorism Act*, 188-89, 194; and Arar case, 80, 93-94; *Canada Evidence Act*, 188; *Charities Registration (Security Information) Act*, 188; *Criminal Code*, 188; in United States, 186-87; *Lawful Access*, 189-90, 194; and loss of privacy rights, 175, 181, 186, 188-92, 325n25; *Official Secrets Act*, 188; *Proceeds of Crime (Money Laundering) and Terrorist Financing Act*, 188-89; *Public Safety Act*, 189; *Security of*

Information Act, 93, 96, 188. *See also* 9/11 terrorist attacks
Appropriation Art Coalition, 205, 209
Arab countries, 28
Arabic-language satellite television services, 87, 309n43
Arabs, depictions in media, 74, 114
Arar, Maher: arrest, deportation, and torture, 80, 176; cleared of all charges, 194; O'Neill's article about, 93; privacy issues, 177, 194, 325n25; and right to protection against damage to honour and reputation, 80, 177; role of media and communication in case, 10, 94, 95
Arbour, Louise, 9
artists: access to copyright law and information about it, 211-14; experiences with copyright, as owners, 207-8; experiences with copyright, as users of work of others, 209-11
Asians, depictions in media, 74, 114
Association des radiodiffuseurs communautaires du Québec (ARCQ), 116
Astral Media, 116, 312n17
authorship rights, 30

Bakhtin, Mikhail, 318n3
bandwidth, 76, 148, 155-56, 236
Barlow, Maude, 192
BB4US.net, 133
Bell Canada, 143, 153-54, 235
Bell ExpressVu, 243, 324n23
Bell Globemedia, 322n4
BellAliant, 170
Berne Convention for the Protection of Literary and Artistic Works, 206
Bernier, Maxime, 124
bilingualism: being replaced by recognition of other languages, 86-87; and *Broadcasting Act*, 110, 111-13;

foundational principle in Canada, 84-85, 111, 309n42; on CBC/Radio-Canada, 112, 312n27; undermines other minority languages, 85, 251

Bill C-10, 68-69, 306n13

Bill C-46, 191-92

Bill C-47, 191-92

Bill C-60, 204

Bill C-61, 78, 198, 204-5

Bill C-426, 311n13

Bill S-21, 181

biometric encryption, 181, 188

Birdsall, William, 295n8

BlackBerrys, 126

Blogger.com, 166, 168

blogs, 143, 163-68, 198, 234

Bonin, Geneviève, 323n6

Bouchard-Taylor Commission, 85-86

Brazil, 16, 56-58

British Columbia, 66-67, 193, 202

broadband services: access to, 131, 143-44; cost and access issues, 76; funding cuts, 133; in Canada, 134; in United States, 133-34; and network neutrality, 156; predicted by *Instant World*, 6. *See also* Internet

broadcasting: alternative, 35, 72, 248, 307n22; changing definition, 119; commercial, 66-67, 72-73, 104, 115; community, 6, 24, 53, 72-73, 88, 104, 115-17, 220, 231-32, 308n27; definition, 104; difference from press, 99-100; diversity regulations, 72-74, 307n20, 307n21, 307n24; invasiveness, 101; languages available, 84-88; ownership regulations, 96, 98-99; pervasiveness, 100-1; public service, 10, 66-67, 72, 74, 104, 115; publicness, 101; regulation of, vs non-regulation of press, 99-104; simultaneous substitution, 118; why

regulate?, 312n21. *See also* cable; Internet; radio; satellite communications; television

Broadcasting Act: as instrument of CR, 104-9; definition of Canadian national broadcasting system, 115; effect on Canadians' individual and collective rights, 109-19; gaps and lapses, 219-20, 295n7; recommendations for, 222, 232, 238, 245-47; requires cultural diversity, 113-14, 322n3; requires linguistic diversity, 84-85, 322n3; requires plurality of sources and diverse content, 72-74, 307n20, 307n21, 307n24; requires public consultation in policy, 88, 104-5, 113

Brockville (ON), 83

Butt, Alistair, 176-77

cable, 6, 75, 88, 111, 115, 295n6

Calgary, 130

Campaign for Democratic Media (CDM), 143

Campbell, Gordon, 193

campus radio, 115

Canada: abandonment of R2C concept, 6; broadband use, 131; contributions to debates on CR/R2C, 3-7, 242, 300n11, 323n7; contributions to discourse on IT4D, 7; cultural sovereignty and broadcasting, 100, 243, 245-47; deep integration of security systems and economies with US, 192-93; early political controversies over R2C, 300n8; international obligations, 11, 203-4, 206-7, 241-42, 320n33; Internet use, 130; press history, 91-92; rhetoric vs action in promoting CR, 10, 18-19; rhetoric vs action in promoting human rights, 8-10, 296n13; use of RFID for border crossings, 83-84; Wi-Fi initiatives, 131. *See also* Department of Communication (DOC); government

Canada Evidence Act, 188, 311n13

Canadian Artists' Representation/Le Front des artistes canadiens, 208

Canadian Association of Broadcasters, 103, 323n13

Canadian Association of Internet Providers (CAIP), 153-54, 201, 235

Canadian Auto Workers, 200

Canadian Broadcast Standards Council, 223

Canadian Broadcasting Corporation (CBC): access, 220; *Adbusters* case, 66-67; and black market satellite services, 246; budget cuts, 74, 112, 312n26; and copyright, 210; English and French programming, 84-85; funding, compared to community media, 116; incomplete archives, 308n29; recommendations for, 232, 233; requests relief from over-the-air television delivery obligations, 77, 113; requirement for geographical and linguistic diversity, 72, 74, 77, 111-13, 307n21

Canadian Centre for Policy Alternatives (CCPA), 134

Canadian Charter of Rights and Freedoms: and equality of individuals, 309n32; and freedom of expression, 64-67, 96, 201, 250, 261; and freedom of the press and media, 69-70, 92-93; juridical limits on rights and freedoms, 64-65, 67, 103-4; and network neutrality, 159; restricted to governmental actions, 66-67, 261-62; and right to equality before the law, 79;

and right to honour and dignity, 81; and right to privacy, 81-82, 180, 181; using to advance R2C, 262-63, 285-93

Canadian Content Online, 132

Canadian content requirements, 117-19, 233, 235, 240, 245-47

Canadian Human Rights Act, 304n1

Canadian Human Rights Commission, 247, 304n1

Canadian Human Rights Tribunal, 304n1

Canadian Institutes of Health Research, 78

Canadian Internet Governance Forum (CIGF), 237-38

Canadian Internet Policy and Public Interest Clinic (CIPPIC), 84, 166-67, 190-92, 224, 310n45

Canadian Multiculturalism Act, 72, 113-14

Canadian Music Creators' Coalition, 205

Canadian Radio League, 117

Canadian Radio-television and Telecommunications Commission (CRTC): allows economic considerations to trump policy objectives, 110, 124; asked by CBC to be relieved of over-the-air television delivery requirements, 77, 113; changing role, 117-19; CHOI-FM case, 80-81, 103, 220; and community broadcasters, 73, 116-17, 308n27; community cable access requirement, 6, 295n6; and community radio, 115-17; enforcer of *Broadcasting Act*, 104; ethnic licences, 114; media ownership regulations, 96, 98-99; and network 9-1-1 emergency services, 156, 315n5; on new media broadcasting, 235; on traffic shaping and network neutrality, 153-55, 161, 174, 234-36;

on universal access to ICTs, 124; principle of technology neutrality, 76; public consultations, 88-89, 117-18, 161, 310n44; recommendations for, 222, 230, 232, 238; regulation of VoIP, 76, 170-71, 234, 315n5; requirement for provision of APTN, 111; third-language approvals, 87

Canadian Research Alliance for Community Innovation and Networking (CRACIN), 310n45

Canadian Security Intelligence Service (CSIS), 94, 189

Canadian Television Fund (CTF), 68, 118, 306n11

Canadian Television Network (CTV), 97-98, 308n26, 322n4

Can-Am Satellites, 324n23

CanWest Global Communications, 73, 97, 99, 202, 308n26

CanWest Global Television, 66-67

capitalism, 46

Carr, Jody, 165

CCH Canadian Ltd., 201-2

censorship: and collective CR, 38; distinguishing from more just allocation of resources, 260-61; government powers, over film and television, 68, 69-70, 306n13; media powers, over advertising, 66; through non-neutral network policies, 158

Centre d'études sur les médias, 73

CFMH radio, 116, 313n32

Challenge for Change, 6

Charities Registration (Security Information) Act, 188

Charter of Privacy Rights, 82, 179, 182, 195

chat services, 163, 166

Chiasson, Sophie, 81

children, vulnerability to privacy threats, 185, 239

China, 49

Chinese satellite TV, 87

CHOI-FM, 80-81, 103, 220

Chomsky, Noam, 303n11

Chrétien government, 9

CHUM, 312n17

civil society sector: efforts toward public consultations in policy, 89; lobbying at WSIS, 53; recommendations to develop, 223-27; take up third stage of CR debates, 42, 46

CJAI radio, 116, 308n27

CKOY Ltd., 69

closed circuit TV (CCTV) surveillance, 83

cloud computing, 164

Cold War, 27, 42, 45

Colombia, 16, 57

Comcast Corporation, 153

Commission on Accommodation Practices Related to Cultural Differences, 85-86

common carriage principles, 150-51, 240

Communautique, 129

communication: indispensable to democracy, 12, 53; lack of obvious link to negative media trends, 54; lawful search and seizure of, 189-92; role in empowerment, identity, and culture, 53; role in human rights, 10, 14; role of copyright, 196-97; social cycle of (*see* social cycle of communication); technological evolution predicted by *Instant World*, 5-6; transmission vs sharing, 13

communication activists, 10, 35, 46

communication rights (CR): access to ICTs, 122, 125-26, 130-31, 143; arise out of social cycle of communication, 14-15; as cognitive frame for activists and wider publics, 47, 53-56; as part of human rights, 25, 29-30, 49-51; assessing through CRAFT, 16-19, 63-64, 270-84; Canadian contributions, 3-7, 9, 26, 295*n*9; Canadian lapses, 8-10, 18-19; and civil society participation, 39, 47-48; compared to freedom of expression, 13(f), 14-15, 249; complexity of, 54-55; and copyright law, 198-99, 204-5, 214-15; defined, 10-11, 14; "flanking" rights needed, 14-15, 30, 39, 69, 250-51, 298*n*4; gaps between policy/principles and practice, 219-21; gaps in international agreements, 26; and global development, 52-53; global vs Canadian, 11-12, 26; impacts of Semantic Web, 164-65; impacts of VoIP, 172-73; impacts of Web 2.0, 164-68; implementing through CRAFT, 56-59; importance of public hearings, 117-18; in broader context of rights in general, 109-19; indispensable to democracy, 3-4, 263-66; international debates, 41-48; and legal principles about media and communication, 29; list of, 30; need for ongoing investment in infrastructure, 77; and network neutrality, 155, 158-61; privacy as fundamental, 174-75, 180; recommendations (*see* policy and law recommendations); and regulatory challenges related to Internet, 173-74; and social justice, 41, 51-52; under *Broadcasting Act*, 104-9; and Western dominance in technology, 33. *See also* right to communicate (R2C)

Communication Rights Assessment Framework and Toolkit (CRAFT): bias toward negative evaluations, 17-19; development of, 16; full copy of, 270-84; implementation in four countries, 16, 48, 53, 56-58; use of, in this study, 16-19, 58-59, 63-64

Communication Rights in the Information Society (CRIS): CRAFT approach, 16-18, 270-84; focus on global policy, 255; founded, 10, 36; impact on discussion of CR, 39, 46, 47-48, 253-55, 256; involvement of Raboy and Shtern, 302*n*16; on CR and social cycle of communication, 15, 39; on CR's enabling rights, 30; on social cycle of communication, 197; use of human rights arguments, 49-50; use of social justice arguments, 52, 303*n*13

communities: capacity to use technologies, 75, 79; FreeNets, 126; Internet access sites, 76, 79, 120-22, 131-32, 143; no longer strictly face-to-face, 12; Wi-Fi initiatives, 131

Community Access Program (CAP), 76, 79, 120-22, 132, 143

community broadcasting: cable television, 6, 115; campus radio, 115; carriage rights, 115-16; equality with other types of broadcasting?, 115; in *Broadcasting Act*, 72-73, 104; in Northern Canada, 88; offers "voice" to excluded communities, 53, 73; potential for diversity undermined by lack of governmental support, 24, 73, 220, 308*n*27; radio, 115-17; recommendations for, 231-32

Community Radio Fund of Canada (CRFC), 116, 117

Competition Bureau, 96, 189, 222

computers, 5

confidentiality of journalistic sources, 70,
94-96, 311n13
Convention on Cybercrime, 189
Co-ordination of Access to Information
Requests System (CAIRS), 71,
307n17
copyright: ability to both enable and
hamper CR, 198-99, 208, 214-15;
artists' access to information about
the law, 211-13; artists' access to the
law, 213-14; artists' experiences
with, as copyright owners, 207-8;
artists' experiences with, as users of
work of others, 209-11; and blogs,
167; fair dealing, 200-2; and government information, 77; international obligations, 203-4, 206-7,
320n33; legislation and legislative
reform, 203-7; moral rights, 202-3;
of journalists, 70, 208; overly cautious approach to, 74, 78; purposes,
43, 78, 196-97; recommendations
for, 226, 232-34, 242, 259; reform
pressures, 78; and social cycle of
communication, 197-98; substantiality requirement, 199-200; term,
200
Copyright Act: provisions, 199-203;
reforms, 203-6
corporate sector: as advertisers, 67; as
copyright owners, 209-10; as medi-
ators of artists' access to audiences
and markets, 208; increasing influence, 44
Cotler, Irwin, 188
Council of Canadians, 192
Council of Europe, *Convention on Cybercrime*, 189
Creative Commons licence, 198
Criminal Code, 183, 188
Cronenberg, David, 68, 306n13

Cross, James, 92
Crossing Boundaries National Council
(CBNC), 164
Crown corporations, 224
CTVglobemedia, 73, 97, 99, 308n26,
312n17, 322n4
cultural diversity: as fundamental characteristic of Canada, 72, 113-14;
Bouchard-Taylor Commission, 85;
in media, 7, 17, 72, 74, 86, 113-15,
307n24; recommendations for, 229,
231, 241, 246-47; under *Broadcasting
Act*, 104-5, 112; undermined by official bilingualism?, 85, 251; vulnerable value in Canada, 110-11
Cultural Environment Movement, 35,
301n13
culture: and access to ICTs, 125; Canadian identity/sovereignty and broadcasting, 100, 104, 241; importance
in Canadian rhetoric, 9; minority
rights, 17, 30, 246; right to participate in one's own, 30; role in governance, 110-11; role of media, 46,
53, 85; and Web 2.0, 164
Cyber Yugoslavia, 164

D'Arcy, Jean: French media icon, 299n5;
influence on Telecommission,
294n4; introduces notion of R2C,
4-5, 31, 41, 44, 145, 256, 326n8;
limitations of his concept of R2C,
45-46; on communication and
social structure, 44-45; participation
in MacBride Commission, 34
data mining, 184-85, 187, 245
data ownership, 166-67, 240
data storage, 82, 244, 245
Davey, Keith, 97
decolonization, 33
deep integration, 192-93

democracy: and broadcasting regulations, 100; Canadian belief in, 8; and digital divide, 129; importance of CR/R2C, 3-4, 12, 34, 93, 252, 258, 263-66; public sphere as central tenet, 53
democratization of communication, 33-36
de-monopolization, 33
Denmark, 315n18
Department of Canadian Heritage, 68, 77, 116-17, 124
Department of Communication (DOC), 3-7, 31
Department of Foreign Affairs and International Trade (DFAIT), 8, 296n11
Department of Justice, 68
deregulation of national telecommunication policy, 10
developing countries: access to ICTs, 127, 128-29; gain voice through media, 53; NAM, 32-34; technological mediation of communication, 43
development, international, 33, 52-53
digital divide: defined, 127; demographic divide, 127, 129; and digital capabilities, 136-37; factors affecting, 130; global divide, 127, 128; policy shifts, 133-36; social divide, 127-28, 130
digital materials, 114, 204-5
disabled persons, 110, 126, 240
diversity: as fundamental characteristic of Canada, 72; cultural (see cultural diversity); of media content, 10, 17, 66, 72-74; recommendations for, 228-32, 259
DNA databases, 185
documentary filmmakers, 212-13
Documentary Organization of Canada, 205
Domain Name System (DNS), 148

Donald, Ian, 305n10
Duarte, Mario, 180
Dunbar, Laurence, 118

East Asia, 35
East-West Communication Institute, University of Hawaii, 31-32, 299n6
Eaton Centre, Toronto, 203
education: and access to ICTs, 127, 129, 130; as human right, 30; and copyright law, 202, 204, 205, 233; on media, 227-28, 259
Ehrcke, William, 66
Eide, Asbjøn, 257
election advertising, 66
e-mail: access under Lawful Access, 190; junk, 165; ownership, 166; predicted by Instant World, 6; privacy issues, 84; RIAs, 163
employers, 84, 167
end-to-end principle, 151-52
Europe, 200
European Commission, 102, 302n6
European Union, 16, 186-87
Extensible Markup Language (XML), 168

Facebook, 84, 143, 166-67, 224-25
Fair Copyright for Canada, 205
FAST program, 83-84
Federal Accountability Act, 71, 220
Federal Communications Commission (FCC, US), 123, 139(t), 166
Fillion, Jeff, 80, 81, 103
films, 68-69, 212-13
Finestone, Sheila, 89, 179, 181-82, 184
Finland, 300n8
First Nations SchoolNet, 132
Fisher, Desmond, 38, 45, 255, 256
Focus on the Global South, 187
Foreign Intelligence Surveillance Court (FISC, US), 186

foreign ownership, 10, 96, 231
France, 27, 31, 300n8, 324n17
Fredericton, 6, 131
free speech. *See* freedom of expression
freedom of assembly, 4, 30
freedom of expression: as human right, 29-30, 298n2; as way to engage public in CR, 50-51; assessing, 16-17; balancing with societal values, 102-4; and communication imbalances, 14, 31, 50-51, 249, 252-53, 261, 297n19; compared to CR, 13(f), 14-15; and confidentiality of journalistic sources, 70, 94-96, 311n13; and copyright, 197, 201; current status in Canada, 64-69, 220, 250-51; importance of dissemination, 197; importance to democracy, 3, 12; in constitutional law, 12; in United States, 11; and individual vs collective rights, 45, 49; limitations of, 249-51; recommendations, 247-48; restricted by concentration of media ownership, 96-99; and social cycle of communication, 198; and technology, 4
freedom of information, 27-28, 258
freedom of opinion, 30, 298n2
freedom of the press and media: assessing, 17; current status in Canada, 69-70; difficulty of ensuring, 3; meaning, in Canada, 92-96; and network neutrality, 159
FreeNets, 126
Friends' Committee on National Legislation, 187
Front de Libération du Québec (FLQ), 92

Galerie d'Art du Petit Champlain case, 201
Gatineau, Quebec, 130
Geist, Michael, 205, 321n33

gender, and access to ICTs, 127, 129
General Agreement on Tariffs and Trade, 206
General Agreement on Trade in Services (GATS), 206
genetic testing, 181
Genex Communications, 103
Gerbner, George, 301n13
Glendon, Mary Ann, 7-8
Global Television Network, 97-98, 308n26
globalization of communication: rapid expansion beginning in late 1960s, 44; recommendations, 241-43, 245-47; transborder data flow, 192-94; Western dominance, 33
Globe and Mail, 99, 222, 308n26, 322n4
Google, 152-53, 157, 162, 315n6
government: access to governmental information, 71, 77; access to ICTs, 79, 125; *Charter's* restriction to, 66-67, 261-62; civil servants' failure to create information, 71; and enforcement of CR, 37-39, 45, 255-56; funding for community broadcasters, 24, 73, 116-17, 220, 308n27; funding for Internet access in public spaces, 131-32; funding for public communication, 259; intentional release of false information, 80; and negative vs positive human rights, 37; power to judge morality of production content, 68; privacy issues, 175-77, 179; recommendations for, 223, 225-26, 238, 245-47. *See also* Canada; right to participate in government
Government Online, 132
Grant, Peter, 301n11
Graydon, Cliff, 177
Green Party, 143

GroundWire, 117
Guérin éditeur Ltée case, 203

Habermas, Jürgen, 303*n*11
Halifax Gazette, 91
Hamelink, Cees, 13, 257, 295*n*8, 298*n*4
Hamilton, Doreen, 165
Hamilton, Sheryl, 295*n*8
Hamilton (ON), 94
Hamilton Spectator, 94
Harms, L.S., 32, 34, 256, 299*n*6
Harper government: 2006 mandate to
    amend Access to Information Act, 71;
    and copyright law, 78; funding cuts
    to arts and culture, 306*n*13, 312*n*26;
    investment in broadband, 134, 144;
    market-led approaches to telecom-
    munications, 123-24
hate speech, 66, 304*n*1
Hewlett-Packard, 167
Hindley, Henry, 294*n*4, 295*n*8
Hoffmann-Riem, Wolfgang, 101-2
Holmes (Justice), 66, 67
HomelessnessNation.org, 79
House of Commons Standing Commit-
    tee on Canadian Heritage (Lincoln
    Committee): copyright studies, 204;
    on Aboriginal cultural programming
    under Broadcasting Act, 74, 110; on
    media ownership, 98, 231; public
    consultations, 89; and public dis-
    satisfaction with CBC's lack of
    regional programming, 112; region-
    al diversity recommendations to
    CBC/Radio-Canada, 232, 312*n*27
Huggan, Gordon, 209
human rights: application and enforce-
    ment of, 37, 49; based on linear
    communication process, 13; Can-
    ada's questionable role in promot-
    ing, 8-9; compared to social justice,
51-52; and drafting of UDHR, 8,
    27-29, 180; "first-generation" vs
    "second-generation," 37-39, 256;
    impacts of 9/11 terrorist attacks, 42-
    43, 187-88; in relation to CR, 14,
    29-30, 49-51; in relation to R2C, 36-
    39, 255-56; individual vs collective,
    37, 45, 49, 256-58; international
    agreements, 11, 26, 29-30; and net-
    work neutrality, 150; role of media
    and communication, 10; tripartite
    framework for assessing, 257
human rights activists, 10, 158
Humphrey, John, 7-8, 296*n*11, 296*n*12
Hypertext Transfer Protocol (HTTP),
    152, 168

Iceland, 315*n*18
immigrants, 85, 86, 246, 251
income, and access to ICTs, 75-76, 127,
    130
Independent Media Centre, 165
Industry Canada: CAP, 76, 79, 120-22,
    132, 143; community radio, 73;
    Connecting Canadians agenda, 76,
    120, 124, 132-34; and early Internet
    development and access, 124
information and communication tech-
    nology (ICT): access (see access to
    ICTs); affordances, 145-46; anti-
    social by-products, 6; as enabler of
    communication, 43; as fundamental
    CR, 122; as mediator of communi-
    cation, 43; Canada's reputation as
    leader, 122; connectivity budget
    cuts, 76, 122; convergence predicted
    by Instant World, 5-6; defined, 122;
    focus of WSIS, 46; new, impacts on
    CR, 145; policy focus, 122, 131,
    133-36; and political need to ensure
    minimum services of R2C, 4; and

potential for more participatory user environment, 122, 138; privacy issues, 83, 176, 179, 184-85, 190-92; recommendations for, 234-41; and social structure, 44-45, 49; use by communication and other activists, 35; and "war on terror," 192; Western dominance, and global communication rights, 33

Information Highway Advisory Council (IHAC), 124

information technology for development (IT4D), 7, 128

Instant World: A Report on Telecommunications in Canada, 4-7, 24, 31, 178, 294n5

intellectual property, 7, 78

International Bill of Rights. *See International Covenant on Civil and Political Rights (ICCPR); International Covenant on Economic, Social and Cultural Rights (ICESCR); Universal Declaration of Human Rights (UDHR)*

International Broadcast Institute (IBI), 32, 300n7, 302n1

International Campaign Against Mass Surveillance (ICAMS), 187, 245

International Civil Liberties Monitoring Group, 187

International Covenant on Civil and Political Rights (ICCPR): core of international human rights, 26, 30, 298n2; includes right to freedom of expression, 29; represents "first-generation" human rights, 36-37; and right to equality before the law, 79

International Covenant on Economic, Social and Cultural Rights (ICESCR), 26, 30, 36-37

international development, 33, 52-53

International Institute for Communications (IIC), 41, 300n7

International Telecommunication Union (ITU), 44, 238, 301n12, 302n4

Internet: affordances, 145-46; as enabler of communication, 43; Canadian subscription rates, 75; communication with children, 185; Community Access Program (CAP), 76, 79, 120-22, 132, 143; copyright law, 205-6; cost of high-speed services, 76; CRTC's lack of regulation over, 118-19; early development, 124; and freedom of the press/media, 70; how it works, 147-48; in Northern communities, 88; increasing use by activists, 35, 143; interception of information, under Lawful Access, 189; meaning of being disconnected, 131; neutrality, 143, 149-52, 150(f), 155-61, 172-73; no requirement for diversity, 72; non-neutrality arguments, 152-55; ownership issues, 43; policies and CR, 173-74; policy objectives, 146-47; predicted by *Instant World*, 6; privacy issues, 84, 179, 185; recommendations for, 234-38, 259; regulatory challenges, 173-74; Semantic Web, 161, 162, 164, 165, 168; social networking, 84, 129, 143, 162, 164, 185, 240; traffic shaping, 143, 148-49, 153-54, 156, 158-61, 173, 235, 254-55; universality of access, as policy goal, 123; use by anti-globalization movement, 35; user definition, 308n28; VoIP, 76, 88, 159, 161, 168-73, 174, 234, 316n18; Web 2.0, 122, 161-68, 173, 185, 240, 318n13; website non-diversity, 72. *See also* access to ICTs; broadband services; information and communication technology (ICT)

Internet Cooperation for Assigned Names and Numbers (ICANN), 238

Internet for Everyone, 143

Internet Governance Forum (IGF), 44, 237-38, 324n15

Internet network neutrality, 10

Internet service providers (ISPs): attitudes toward network neutrality, 152-57, 174; commercial, 152-57, 174; and copyright law, 205; nonprofit, 126; privacy issues, 190-92; recommendations, 236, 240

investigative hearings, 189

iPhones, 126

Iraq, 304n17

Irving, 311n15

journalists: bloggers as, 167-68; confidentiality of sources, 70, 94-96, 311n13; copyright over work, 70, 208; right to know vs right to privacy, 179; rights and responsibilities, 258-59; subject to restraints because of concentrated ownership, 70, 229-30; undermined by post-9/11 security measures, 70

Joyce, Sarah, 209

Keewaytinook Okimakanak First Nations tribal council, 158, 169

Kent, Tom, 97

Kenya, 16, 57-58

Kies, K., 299n6

Kitchener (ON), 115

Klein, Kris, 191

K-Net. See Kuhkenah Network (K-Net)

Kuhkenah Network (K-Net), 129, 158

La Forest, Gérard, 67

Landry, Normand, 323n6

language: and access to ICTs, 127; as human right, 30; bilingualism in broadcasting, 110, 111-13, 312n27; bilingualism in Canada, 84-85, 111, 309n42; CBC's mandate for diversity, 72; and freedom of expression, 251; marginal, disappearance of, 43; multilingualism in Canada, 86-87; rights, assessing, 17; under *Broadcasting Act*, 104, 111

Laporte, Pierre, 92

laptop ownership, 131

Lasn, Kalle, 67

Latin American countries, 28, 35

Lavallée, Carole, 307n19

Law Commission of Canada (LCC), 10-12, 263, 267-69

Law Society of Upper Canada, 201-2

Lawful Access, 189-90

laws: anti-terrorism, 80, 93-94, 96, 186-89, 194; copyright, 199-206; and enforcement of human rights, 37-38, 49, 51, 298n2; and freedom of expression, 12, 68-69; and offensive media content, 68; privacy, 82, 89, 176-77, 180, 181-84, 188-89, 245; and right to equality, 17, 79-81. *See also Canadian Charter of Rights and Freedoms; specific acts*

Layton, Jack, 307n19

LeBel, Louis, 65

LeBlanc, Charles, 70, 167-68

Leblanc, Christian, 118

LeBreton, Marjory, 182-83

Letourneau, J.A., 103

libraries: copyright concerns, 201-2, 204, 205, 233; Internet access, 75, 120, 131-32, 138, 140(t)

LibraryNet, 132

Lincoln, Clifford, 231

Loukidelis, David, 193
Luck, Elijah, 316n18
Luxembourg, 315n18

MacBride, Sean, 34
MacBride Commission, 34, 46, 300n11
Manley, John, 125
Many Voices, One World, 34, 294n5, 300n11
marketplace: and neoliberal policies of deregulation and privatization, 123, 136-37, 313n4; and network neutrality, 155-56; and privacy concerns, 183
mash-ups, 162
mass media: access through Semantic Web and Web 2.0, 165; and broadcasting regulation, 101-2; content commodification, 43; discretionary censorship and self-interest, 66; dominance of, as argument for collective CR, 38. *See also* media
M'Bow, Amadou-Mahtar, 32, 34
McIver, William J., Jr., 295n8
McKinney, D.W., 67
McLachlin, Beverley, 65
McLuhan, Marshall, 300n11
McPhail, Thomas, 301n11
media: argue against collective CR, 38; community-based, 43, 53; delegates included at 1948 Conference on Freedom of Information, 27; difficulty of ensuring they are responsible and free, 3; diversity in content, 7, 10, 17, 72-74; and early political controversies over R2C, 28; freedom of expression vs R2C, 65-67; freedom under *Charter*, 69-70, 92-96; freedom undermined by media structures, new media platforms, and post-9/11 environment, 69-70; and

intellectual property rights, 7; lack of direct/obvious link to negative communication trends, 54, 303n17; monitoring and analyzing, 222-23; negative reaction to MacBride report, 34; new, anticipated by *Instant World*, 5-6; not "value-free containers" of information, 35; origins, in Canada, 91-92; ownership issues, 7, 10, 33, 43, 46, 70, 73, 96-99, 258, 322n4, 323n13; plurality of sources, 17, 33, 72-74; public funding of, 7, 116-17, 306n13, 312n26; recommendations on ownership, 229-31; recommendations to diversify, 228-32; regulation of broadcasting vs non-regulation of press, 99-104; and right to protection from damage to honour and reputation, 80-81; role in cultural diversity, 84-88; role in development, 52-53; role in human rights, 10. *See also* mass media; press; *specific types*
media activists, 10, 35
media literacy education, 227-28, 259
Meisel, John, 301n11
Melody, Bill, 301n11
Ménard, Serge, 311n13
Mendel, Toby, 302n5
Mesplet, Fleury, 91
Mexico, 200
Michelin, 200
Microsoft, 167
minorities: abuse by radio "shock jock," 80, 81, 103; broadcasting by and for, 114-15; cultural and linguistic rights, 17, 30, 84-88; religious, and human rights, 30; under- and misrepresentation in media, 74, 85-86, 113-15
mobile technologies: access to, 126; and freedom of the press/media, 70; lack

of CRTC regulation over, 118; usage in Canada, 172

Montreal: community radio, 115; homeless youth, 79; Internet use, 130; municipal Wi-Fi project, 6; newspaper history, 91; Wi-Fi initiative, 131

Montreal Gazette, 91

Moon, Richard, 247, 305n1

morality. *See* censorship; copyright; freedom of expression

Mulroney government, 311n15

multiculturalism. *See* cultural diversity

multilingualism, 85, 86-87, 251

multiracialism, 104-5, 112

museums, 204, 233

Muslims, depictions in media, 74, 114

MySpace.com, 166

National Campus and Community Radio Association (NCRA), 116-17

National Film Board (NFB): access, 220, 308n29; Challenge for Change initiative, 6, 79, 295n6; "Citizenshift," 77; and copyright, 210; overly cautious approach to copyright, 74; recommendations for, 233

National Post, 308n26

Netherlands, 315n18

network neutrality: arguments against, 152-53, 155; arguments for, 149-52, 159; defined, 149; emerging issue, 143; how it works, 150(f), 160(f); impacts on CR, 158-61, 172-73; in United States, 235; and international data transfer, 159-60; and process of social communication, 155-58; recommendations, 236

New Brunswick, 70, 98, 168, 311n15

New International Economic Order (NIEO), 32-33, 52

new media. *See* media; *specific types*

New World Information and Communication Order (NWICO), 33-35, 39, 41-42, 45, 52, 300n11

newspapers: daily, licence restrictions, 311n15; ethnic, 114; history in Canada, 91; lack of governmental regulation, 97; no requirement for diversity, 72; ownership concentration, 73, 97; ownership convergence with other media, 97-98

NEXUS program, 83-84

Nicholson, Rob, 321n33

Nissenbaum, Helen, 177, 194

Non-Aligned Movement (NAM), 32-34

nongovernmental organizations (NGOs): definition of R2C, 47, 302n5; human rights debates, 47, 50; implementation of CRAFT in four countries, 56-58; lobbying at WSIS and WSF, 53; on communications issues, global emergence in early 2000s, 35, 301n13; recommendations, 223-27; take up third stage of CR debates, 42, 46

Northern Canada, 79, 88

Norway, 315n18

O'Connor, Dennis, 94, 176, 177, 194

Office of the Privacy Commissioner (OPC): argues against Lawful Access provisions, 190; calls for anti-spam legislation, 83; counters US powers under anti-terrorism laws, 193; critical report on Facebook, 84, 166-67; lack of jurisdiction outside Canada, 193; role, 82, 183, 193, 222, 224-25

Official Secrets Act, 188

Okinawa Charter on Global Information Society, 128

O'Neill, Juliet, 10, 93, 95, 325n25

Ontario: cases on confidentiality of
    sources, 94-95; K-Net, 129, 157-58
Organisation for Economic Co-operation
    and Development (OECD), 128,
    160
Ottawa (ON), 115, 126, 130, 133
Ottawa Citizen, 93

Pacific Community Networks Association,
    120
Panel on Access to Third-Language Pub-
    lic Television Services, 86
parodies, 201-2
People's Communication Charter, 35,
    301n13
Pepsi-Cola Canada, 64-67
personal data: government collection of,
    188; international transfer, 187-88;
    and outsourcing to non-Canadian
    firms, 193, 241; recommendations,
    245; right to redress, 187; trans-
    border data flows, 192-94
*Personal Information Protection and Elec-
    tronic Documents Act (PIPEDA)*, 82,
    89, 181, 188-89
Peterborough (ON), 83
Peters, John Durham, 260
Peters, Ken, 94-95
Philippines, 16, 57
Piper, Tina, 17
Platform for Communication Rights, 36
Platform for the Democratization of
    Communication, 35, 36, 301n13
plurality of media sources, 17, 33, 72-74
police, 189-92
policies: balancing public, private, and
    community broadcasting, 117; for
    Internet, 146-47; impact of *Instant
    World*, 4-5; need to be based on so-
    cial cycle of communication, 13; on
    access to ICTs and capacity to use

them, 75, 79, 133-37; on access to
    knowledge creation, dissemination,
    and use, 77-79; public consultations
    and access to process, 88-90; rela-
    tionship with rights discourse and
    practice, 9, 12-14, 295n7; trade-offs
    and balances needed, 14; US influ-
    ence on, 297n15
policy and law recommendations: over-
    view, 221; to develop civil society
    sector, 223-27; to diversify, 228-32;
    to monitor, analyze, and enforce,
    221-23; to raise public awareness,
    227-28; to re-examine linkages be-
    tween cultural nationalism, global-
    ization, and multiculturalism, 241-
    47; to reduce copyright restrictions,
    232-34; to reframe freedom of ex-
    pression, 247-48; to reorient and
    widen ITC policy, 234-41
policy research, 222-23
poor people, 46
Power Corporation of Canada, 98
press: argues against collective CR, 38;
    confidentiality of sources, 70, 94-96,
    311n13; constraints needed, 258;
    democratization of, 33; difference
    from broadcasting, 99-100; freedom
    of, 3, 17, 28, 64, 69-70, 92-96; his-
    tory of, in Canada, 91-92; non-
    regulation of, vs regulation of
    broadcasting, 99-104; "shield" laws
    in US, 95; weakened by Web 2.0?,
    165; Western dominance, 33. *See
    also* media; newspapers
preventive detention, 189
Primus, 170
Prise de Parole Inc., 203
privacy: as fundamental CR, 178, 180,
    194-95; as human right, 30, 175,
    179-80; assessing status of, 17;

Canadian concern about, 176, 182; centrality to R2C, 178; current status in Canada, 81-84; effect of post-9/11 security measures, 82, 175-77, 185-92; and ICTs, 158, 176, 179, 184-85; informational model of, 177-78, 194-95; and Internet, 145, 315n1; and less powerful members of society, 178; and mass media, 179; reasonable expectation, 181; recommendations, 259; and surveillance technologies, 83, 176, 177-79, 181, 184-85, 259; and transborder data flow, 192-94; and use of ICTs by governments, 175; violations of, by government, 80, 93, 176; vs right to know, 178-79; ways to define, 179-80

Privacy Act, 82, 180, 182-83, 188, 245

privacy laws: called for by *Instant World*, 178; Canadian ignorance of, 176, 177; education about, 228; Finestone's proposal of *Privacy Rights Charter*, 181-84; linked to *UDHR*, 180; not specific in *Charter*, 81-82, 180; *PIPEDA*, 82, 89, 181, 182, 184, 188-89; *Privacy Act*, 82, 180, 182-83, 188, 245; recommendations, 239, 241, 245

Privacy Rights Charter, 181-84

privacy rights organizations, 186

Proceeds of Crime (Money Laundering) and Terrorist Financing Act, 188-89

programming, on-demand, 6

public broadcasting services: and Aboriginal programming, 85; *Adbusters* case, 66-67; bilingual services undermining provision in other minority languages, 85; and copyright, 210; difference from press, 99-100; equality with other types of broadcasting?, 115; funding, 116; lack of information archives, 77-78, 308n29; reduction of, 10, 73, 74; requirement for geographical and linguistic diversity, 72, 73, 111-13; through social networking sites, 143

public consultation: by CRTC, 88-89, 117-18, 161, 310n44; by Lincoln Committee, 89; importance to CR, 117-18; on *PIPEDA*, 89; recommendations on, 225, 232, 238; requirements under *Broadcasting Act*, 88, 104-5, 113

Public Safety Act, 189

Quebec: commission on media and cultural diversity, 85; digital divide, 129; funding for community media, 116; inquiry on quality and diversity of information, 97; media ownership concentration, 73, 98; October Crisis, 92; press history, 91-92; public enthusiasm for *auteur* material, 69; VoIP or cable telephone service usage, 172

Quebec City, 103

Quebecor, 73, 98, 118

quotations, 318n3

Raboy, Marc, 295n8, 302n16

race, and access to ICTs, 127

racism, 74, 85, 114, 194

radio: and *Broadcasting Act*, 307n20; community, 115-17; content ubiquity predicted by *Instant World*, 5; continuing expansion in poorer countries, 43; ethnic stations, 114; ownership and CR, 10, 43; regulation history, 100; scarcity of frequencies, 100; universality of access, 123

radio frequency identification (RFID), 83-84, 185, 193-94
Radio Mille Collines, 303n17
Radio-Canada, 112, 116, 246, 312n27
Radwanski, George, 175, 185-86
recommendations. *See* policy and law recommendations
Reid, John, 71
religion, 30, 309n1
Reporters Without Borders, 70, 95
Revenue Canada, 126
Rex, Richard, 243, 324n23
rich Internet applications (RIAs), 162, 164
Richstad, J., 299n6
right of association (copyright law), 202
right of attribution (copyright law), 202-3
right of integrity (copyright law), 202-3
right to assembly. *See* freedom of assembly
right to communicate (R2C): arises out of social cycle of communication, 14-15, 31-32; as fundamental to Canadian society, 4; attempts to define for UN adoption, 45; called for by MacBride report, 34; Canadian contributions to, 3-7, 26, 31, 295n8; conceptual/juridical tensions, 36-39; CRIS campaign, 35-36, 39-40; defined by NGOs, 47, 302n5; and freedom of expression, 65-67; horizontal view, 15-19; institutionalizing in Canada, defining, 255-57; institutionalizing in Canada, normative framework, 258-60; institutionalizing in Canada, strategies toward, 261-63, 285-93; institutionalizing in Canada, understanding and accepting, 260-61; institutionalizing in Canada, viability, 253-55; minor-ities, 114-15; not in government policy or legislation, 6; notion introduced by D'Arcy, 4-5, 31, 41, 44-45, 145, 256, 326n8; political controversies and movements, 26-29, 32-34; and privacy, 178; would provide clear guiding principles for communication policy, 249, 253. *See also* communication rights (CR)
right to education, 30
right to equality before the law, 17, 79-81
right to one's honour and reputation, and to protection against unwarranted damage to them: and Arar case, 94, 177; as human right, 30, 298n2; assessing, 17; and copyright, 203; current status in Canada, 79-81, 309n33
right to participate in government, 17, 30, 88-90, 164-66
right to privacy. *See* privacy
right to self-determination, 17, 30, 88-90
Rogers Communications, 87, 159, 172, 312n17
Royal Canadian Mounted Police (RCMP): Arar case, 80, 93-94, 95, 176, 194; Lawful Access provisions, 189; release of air passenger and crew information to, 189
Royal Commission on Newspapers, 97
rural and remote communities: access to ICTs in general, 127, 133-34, 140(t), 142(t), 144, 147, 156-57, 239-40; importance of VoIP, 169-70; Internet access, 75, 88, 120-23, 130-32, 134, 144
Rwanda, 303n17

satellite communications: access to, in Canada, 75; as leading to R2C, 44, 145; and globalization, 243;

interception of information, under Lawful Access, 189; predicted by *Instant World*, 6; radio, no right of carriage for community broadcasters, 115-16

Save Our Net, 143

SchoolNet, 76, 132

schools: First Nations, 129; Internet access, 75-76, 120, 123-24, 126, 129-32, 140(t)

Schwarzenegger, Arnold, 321*n*33

Science Council of Canada, 75, 146

Security of Information Act, 70, 93, 95-96, 188

Semantic Web, 161, 163, 164, 165, 168

Senate Standing Committee on Social Affairs, Science and Technology, 82, 182

Senate Standing Committee on Transport and Communication, 95-96, 98

Shade, Leslie Regan, 295*n*8

Shaw, Jim, 306*n*11

Shaw Communications, 118, 172, 306*n*11

Shtern, Jeremy, 302*n*16

Singapore, 34

Skype, 152, 160, 170, 171

smart cards, 181

Smart Communities, 132

Snow, Michael, 203

social cycle of communication: as basis for Canadian law and policy in supporting democratic communication, 13-15, 258-59; defined, 13; enshrining within human rights framework, 26-27, 39; illustration of, 13(f); impacts of global developments, 43; importance to cultural and intellectual invention, 197; in cultural production, 198; inadequately addressed by freedom of expression, 31, 249-51, 252-53

social justice: as Canadian value, 9; as way to engage public in CR, 41, 51-52; CRIS as player in international movement, 10; greater focus on, in 1990s, 9, 46; in communication law and policy, 12; and use of ICTs, 129

social networking, 84, 129, 143, 162, 164, 185, 240

Social Sciences and Humanities Research Council of Canada (SSHRCC), 10-11, 78, 267-69

social structure, 44-45, 49

society: as aggregation of individuals, 45-46; bringing CR arguments to, through development paradigm, 52-53; bringing CR arguments to, through human rights, 49-51; bringing CR arguments to, through social justice, 51-52; bringing CR arguments to, through use of CR as cognitive frame, 53-56; imbalances within and between countries, 46; recommendations for raising awareness, 227-28

Society of Composers, Authors and Music Publishers of Canada, 201, 208

socioeconomics, and access to ICTs, 125, 126, 129-30

South Asians, depictions in media, 74, 114

South Korea, 134, 315*n*18

Soviet Union, 8, 28, 33-34

spam, 83

Special Senate Committee on Mass Media, 97

Speech Communication Association (SCA), 31, 299*n*6

Spence, W.F., 69

Spry, Graham, 117, 243

Standard Broadcasting, 116, 312*n*17

state. *See* government

Statewatch, 187
Stoddart, Jennifer, 167, 184, 191
Sun Microsystems, 167
Supreme Court of Canada: copyright rulings, 201-2; and limits on *Charter* rights and freedoms, 64-65, 67; on Alberta's 1937 attempt to force newspapers to publish government comment, 92-93; on right to privacy, 81-82, 180
surveillance: powers under Lawful Access, 190-91; and right to privacy, 83, 176, 177-79, 181, 184-85, 259; through non-neutral network policies, 158
Sweden, 28, 32, 315n18
Switzerland, 315n18
Sympatico Internet Service, 153

tagging, in blogs, 162
technology. *See* information and communication technology (ICT)
Technorati.com, 166
Telecommission, 3-7, 178, 294nn3-4
telecommunication networks: common carriage principles, 150-51; increasing use predicted by *Instant World*, 5; network neutrality, 149-61. *See also* Internet
telecommunications: continuing expansion in poorer countries, 43; neoliberal policies of deregulation and privatization, 123-24, 313n4; policy goal of universality, 122-23; tracking of individuals, 190; transmission data monitoring, 190
Telecommunications Act: common carriage principles, 151; does not consider *Broadcasting Act*, 295n7; guarantee of reliable and affordable communication, 173; and Internet service,

153; issues of national interest, 159, 243-44; on universal service, 147; policy objectives, 147; privacy principles, 82; pro-market principles, 123-24; recommendations for, 245
Telecommunications Policy Review Panel (TPRP), 136-37, 147, 231, 310n45
Telefilm Canada, 68
telephony: access to, in Canada, 75; interception of information, under Lawful Access, 189; mobile, 172; policy objectives, 147; service in Northern Ontario, 157-58; universality of access, as policy goal, 123; VoIP, 76, 88, 159, 161, 168-73, 174, 234, 316n18
television: access to, in Canada, 75; community, 116; content ubiquity predicted by *Instant World*, 5; continuing expansion in poorer countries, 43; ethnic stations, 114; freedom of expression vs R2C, 65-67; government power to censor, 68; languages available in Canada, 86-87; over-the-air requirement for CBC, 77, 113; ownership and CR, 43; requirement for APTN provision, 111
Telus, 170
Théberge, Claude, 201, 203
Thorneycroft, Diana, 211
throttling, 143, 148
Tobin, Amon, 211
Toronto, 6, 79, 83
Toronto Star, 222, 322n4
traffic shaping: Bell Canada's use of, 143, 153-54, 235; CRTC consultations on, 154-55; defined, 148, 149; and international data transfers, 160; necessity for, 148-49; and network neutrality, 149, 156; and VoIP, 173

Transmission Control Protocol/Internet Protocol (TCP/IP), 148, 149-50, 150(f), 152, 159
Trudeau government, 310n15
TVA, 98, 311n16

United Kingdom: common carriage principles, 151; domestic IGF, 324n16; leaves UNESCO, 34, 300n10; and political controversies over R2C, 27-28, 34; public broadcasting online, 235; radio regulation history, 100
United Nations Economic and Social Council (ECOSOC), 27, 29
United Nations Educational, Scientific and Cultural Organization (UNESCO): as stage for second phase of CR debates, 41-42, 256; *Convention on the Protection and Promotion of the Diversity of Cultural Expressions*, 242, 295n9; International Commission on the Study of Communication Problems, 34, 294n5; on balancing freedom of expression with unacceptable licence, 102-3; R2C studies, 32, 255, 300n10, 326n7; statement on right to communicate, 255, 302n8, 326n6; weakening influence, 43-44
United Nations General Assembly (UNGA), 28-29
United Nations High Commissioner for Human Rights, 9, 50
United Nations Human Rights Commission (UNHRC), 3, 7-8, 28-29, 296n11
United Nations World Summit on the Information Society. *See* World Summit on the Information Society (WSIS)

United States: 9/11 terrorist attacks, 42-43, 70, 82, 93, 96, 133, 144, 177, 186-87; aerial surveillance, 177; and Arar case, 80, 93-94, 95; broadband use, 133; Canadian alliances with, 296n13; *Communication Act* (1934), 123; copyright law, 78, 200, 202, 204, 205, 206-7, 320n33; deep integration of security systems and economies with Canada, 192-93; freedom of speech in, 11, 92, 310n1; increasing use of Internet for social protest movements, 35; influence on Canadian policy making, 297n15; invasion of Iraq, 304n17; leaves UNESCO, 34, 300n10; media ownership limits, 73, 96; network neutrality issues, 235; and political controversies over R2C, 27-28, 34; press history, 91-92; press shield laws, 95; privacy laws, 176, 179, 185, 193; radio regulation history, 100; shift away from funding to improve access to ICTs, 133, 315n16; *Telecommunications Act* (1996), 123; telecommunications policy, 122-23; traffic shaping policies, 156; transborder data flows with Canada, 192-94; use of RFID for border crossings, 83-84, 193-94; wiretapping, post-9/11, 186
Universal Declaration of Human Rights (UDHR): and attempts to define R2C, 45; Canada's reluctant acceptance of, 296n11; core of international human rights, 26, 30; human rights divided into *ICCPR* and *ICESCR*, 36-37; includes right to freedom of expression, 29; and network neutrality, 161; planning and

drafting of, 7-8, 27-29; and right of access to information and to communicate, 96; and right to equality before the law, 79; and right to privacy, 180
universality: goal of ICT policy, 122-23; history in Canada, 124; intrinsic to Canadian identity, 74, 123
University of Guelph, 67
University of Hawaii, 32, 299n6
US-Canada border: aerial surveillance, 177; data flow, 192-94; Smart Border Action Plan, 187; use of RFID, 83-84, 193-94
USSR. *See* Soviet Union

Vail, Theodore, 123
Vancouver (BC): community radio, 115; homeless youth, 79; media ownership concentration, 98; newspaper ownership concentration, 7, 97; use of CCTV, 83
Vancouver Sun, 202
Verner, Josée, 68
Vidéotron, 98, 172
Virtual Museum of Canada, 77
Voice over Internet Protocol (VoIP): benefits, 160, 168-69, 171-72; categories, 169(f), 169-70, 316n15; CRTC's public consultations, 88, 161; disadvantages, 316n18; how it works, 168-69; impact on CR, 172-73; and network traffic shaping, 174; regulatory framework, 76, 170-71, 234
Voices 21, 35-36
VolNet, 132
Voluntary Sector Network Support Program, 132
von Finckenstein, Konrad, 323n13

Vonage, 152-53, 170

The Walrus, 94
War Measures Act, 92
Warman v. Lemire, 305n1
Web 2.0: Canadian inDiscover.net, 165; data ownership and control, 240; defined, 162, 318n13; impacts on CR, 164-68; inclusions, 162; privacy issues, 185; and process of social communication, 162-64
Western countries: dominance in global communication, 33; opposition to NWICO, 33-34
Whitacre, Edward, 153
Wi-Fi, 6, 126, 131
Williams, Raymond, 12
Winnipeg, 83
wireless technologies, 189
women, 46, 222
World Bank, 44, 52
World Forum on Communication Rights, 48
World Intellectual Property Organization (WIPO): copyright treaty, 78, 203, 204; Internet treaties, 206, 320n29; performances and phonograms treaty, 78, 203-4
World Press Freedom Committee, 34
World Press Freedom Index, 70
World Social Forum (WSF), 10, 48, 53
World Summit on the Information Society (WSIS): and attempt to bridge global digital divide, 128; breadth of discussion, 46-47, 302n3; and formation of IGF, 237; impact on discussion of CR in civil society, 47-48; initiates high-level international discussion of rights and processes of communications, 10, 42; Internet

Governance Forum, 44; lobbying by civil society organizations, 53; lobbying by communication activists, 10, 36, 39, 50, 52, 303*n*13; official declaration of R2C avoided, 47; participants, 47-48; planning for, 46-47, 302*n*6
World Trade Organization (WTO), 44, 55, 206

World Wide Web Consortium (W3C, 2006), 166

Yahoo!, 152-53, 167
youth, vulnerability to privacy threats, 185
YouTube, 143, 152

Zimmerman, Betty, 300*n*11